CHRIST THE KING

Meditations on Matthew's Gospel

G. Wright Doyle

lightmessages.com

Copyright © 2011, by G. Wright Doyle.

CHRIST THE KING
Meditations on Matthew's Gospel
G. Wright Doyle
civirginia@nexet.net
www.chinainst.org
Printed in the United States of America
Light Messages Publishers
Durham, North Carolina
ISBN: 978-1-61153-015-5

ALL RIGHTS RESERVED

No part of this publication may be reproduced, stored in a retrieval system, or transmitted in any form or by any means, electronic, mechanical, photocopying, recording, scanning or otherwise, except for brief quotations in printed reviews or as permitted under Section 107 or 108 of the 1976 International Copyright Act, without the prior permission of the publisher.

All Scripture quotations, unless otherwise noted are taken from the New King James Version®. Copyright © 1982 by Thomas Nelson, Inc. Used by permission. All rights reserved.

To Sarah and Brandon

Table of Contents

Introduction 1
Acknowledgments 5
1 A King is Born! 7
2 The Boy King 19
3 The Herald of the King 29
4 The Inauguration of the King 35
5 The King's New Law 47
6 The King Points Us to His Father 95
7 The King's Narrow Highway 121
8 The King's Authority over Evil 129
9 The King's Compassion 143
10 The King's Messengers 157
11 The King Vindicates His Herald 163
12 The King Counters His Critics 169
13 The King Explains His Kingdom 197
14 The King Cares for His People 217
15 The King Expands His Territory 227
16 The King Calls Us to Faith 241
17 The King's Glory and Suffering 249
18 Greatness in the Kingdom 257
19 The King on Family and Wealth 279
20 Servants of the Servant King 301
21 The King Enters His Capital 305
22 The King Confounds His Enemies 317
23 The King Exposes Hypocrites 331
24 The King Predicts His Return 343
25 The King Calls Us to Watch 355
26 The King's Departure 361
27 The Suffering King 377
28 The King's Commission 385
The Author 407

Introduction

Jesus Christ is King.

The entire Gospel of Matthew, from beginning to end, proclaims this fact.

Matthew begins his account of the life of Jesus with His human genealogy, which states at the outset that Jesus is "the Son of David," even before we learn that He is also "the Son of Abraham." David, mightiest of Israel's warriors, had received a promise from God: "I will set up your seed [i.e., descendant] after you, who will come from your body, and I will establish his kingdom.... I will establish the throne of his kingdom forever" (2 Samuel 7:12–13). Matthew means to show that Jesus of Nazareth is that King.

At the end of the Gospel, the risen Jesus declares that "all authority ... in heaven and earth" has been given to Him by God the Father (28:18). Between these clear declarations of His divine kingship, Matthew records many other events, sayings, and Scriptures to prove his case.

Jesus preached that the kingdom of heaven [that is, the kingdom of God] was at hand, meaning that when He, the King, had come, He had brought with Him, the first rays of kingdom light (4:17). He demonstrated His kingly authority over disease, demons, and even death. The roaring waves and mighty winds obeyed His commands, as did the lame, the blind, and the lepers.

He taught like one with authority, and not like the religious leaders of the day (7:29). He pardoned crimes against God's law, which only a divine King can do (9:5–7). He ordered men to leave all and follow Him, as if He possessed the right to tear them from family and work (4:19–22).

When questioned about His violation of current customs about keeping the Sabbath, He boldly declared Himself, as Son of Man, to be Lord of the Sabbath (12:8). This title—Son of Man—was His favorite way of describing Himself; it recalls the prophecy of Daniel, who in a vision saw "*One* like the Son of Man, coming with the clouds of heaven!" (Daniel 7:13)

> He came to the Ancient of Days,
> And they brought Him near before Him.

> Then to Him was given dominion and glory and a kingdom,
> That all peoples, nations, and languages should serve Him.
> His dominion is an everlasting dominion,
> Which shall not pass away,
> And His kingdom the one
> Which shall not be destroyed.
>
> Daniel 7:13–14

Manifestly, then, Jesus saw Himself to be that heavenly King, who had now come to earth to inaugurate His reign.

Like David before Him, however, Jesus spent years in powerless obscurity before emerging into public as God's anointed one. Also like David, whose kingdom came to him gradually, Jesus was first repudiated by the current rulers.

In fact, however, Jesus meant to establish His kingdom in two definite stages: First as the Man Jesus, who was born, lived, taught, healed, gathered a band of disciples, died, rose, and ascended to heaven.

Then, at the end of this age, He will return to judge the living and the dead, and to usher in His visible rule on earth (24:30, 44; 25:1–13). At that time, the mystery of His miraculous birth from the Virgin Mary by the Holy Spirit will be understood, as will the name given to Him by the angel, Immanuel, which is "God with us." Jesus is not only fully man, but also fully God. The baby born in Bethlehem was the incarnation of the eternal Word of God, the second Person of the Trinity, the Son who is equal with the Father and the Spirit.

The meditations which fill these pages attempt to focus our eyes, minds, and hearts upon King Jesus. I hope that you will catch glimpses of the King in all His beauty. At the same time, this book seeks to help people become faithful followers of the King, who alone is worthy of our love, our allegiance, and our very lives.

A few words about the nature of this volume:

These reflections on the Gospel of Matthew grew out of a year-long series of sermons which I preached on Matthew about a dozen years ago, and from which I then produced brief devotional messages which were sent out by email to hundreds of readers. Many encouraged me to publish them, so here they are.

Chapter headings usually only highlight a major theme of that chapter, and are not meant to be fully descriptive of its contents. This is not a verse-by-verse treatment of Matthew, but almost all the verses in the Gospel are treated or referenced in what follows, so the result is virtually a devotional commentary on the whole Gospel. Likewise, I have not tried to write an academic work, though the findings of scholars have informed my understanding and interpretation of Matthew at almost every point.

As much as possible, I have allowed Matthew to interpret himself. That is, most of my references to other parts of the Bible are to relevant passages in Matthew's Gospel. I have found this method of interpretation to yield very rich rewards for understanding.

Citations to Matthew within parentheses will usually consist simply of the verse reference "(7:11)," with "Matthew" being implied. Otherwise, I include the name of the book of the Bible also: "(John 3:16)." Scripture quotations are from the *New King James Version*. Words in italics in citations from the Bible reflect the usage of the *New King James Version*, in which words not in the original Greek or Hebrew are italicized in the English translation.

Freed from the restrictions of writing a formal commentary, I have not tried to give proportionate attention to each passage in Matthew. Some sections of the First Gospel are discussed quite briefly, or even only alluded to, while others receive extended attention. Though all are relatively short, the meditations vary in length. The style also ranges from what Augustine and other ancient rhetoricians would label "plain," to the "middle" and occasionally even "grand" manner of expression. That is, some passages are meant mainly to instruct, while others aim also to please and even to move the reader.

Acknowledgments

I am indebted to the writings of A.B. Bruce, Donald Guthrie, Matthew Henry, G.E. Ladd, J.C. Ryle, John Stott, R.V.G. Tasker, and a number of recent commentators.

I especially wish to acknowledge my reliance upon the commentary on Matthew by D.A. Carson, to which I have referred a few times as "Carson."[1] His marvelous exposition of the Gospel of John has also influenced my understanding of the Jesus portrayed in Matthew. (Neither he nor any other scholars are to be charged with any mistakes of fact or interpretation contained in my treatment of Matthew.)

Janet Dusan and Laura Mason spent many hours editing and formatting these pages. I owe a great debt to them. I wish also to thank Wally Turnbull for his help with layout, cover design, and publishing.

---

[1] D.A. Carson, Matthew, in Frank E. Gabelein, General Editor, *The Expositor's Bible Commentary*, Volume 8 (Grand Rapids: Zondervan Publishing House, 1984).

1 A King is Born!

Jesus Christ, the Son of David
Matthew 1:1 Part–1

The book of the genealogy of Jesus Christ, the son of David, the son of Abraham…

David overcame Goliath by the weakness of a sling;
Jesus defeated Satan through the weakness of the Cross.

David attracted men of the lowest sort;
Jesus consorted with sinners and chose men of humble station.

David would not take the life of wicked King Saul;
Jesus refused to lead the mob against evil rulers.

David took an innocent man's life to get another wife;
Jesus gave His own innocent life to gain His only Bride.

David was a man of war, his hands stained with the blood of the sword;
Jesus was a man of peace, from whose pierced hands flowed cleansing blood.

David was the "sweet singer of Israel";
Jesus is the subject of David's songs and countless others.

David wrote, "The LORD *is* my shepherd" (Psalm 23:1);
Jesus said, "I am the good shepherd" (John 10:11, 14).

David sang of the bridegroom-king;
Jesus is that kingly Bridegroom.

David heard the Lord say of his seed, "I will establish the throne of his kingdom forever" (2 Samuel 7:13);
Jesus is the one whose "throne … is forever and ever" (Hebrews 1:8).

David received the promise for his sons, "I will be his Father, and he shall be My son" (2 Samuel 7:14);
Jesus heard the Lord say of himself, "This is My beloved Son, in whom I am well pleased" (3:17).

David spoke of those who
   "are abundantly satisfied with the fullness of Your house,

Christ the King

>> And You give them drink from the river of Your pleasures.
>> For with You is the fountain of life;
>> In Your light we see light" (Psalm 36:8).

Jesus declared,
>> "I am the bread of life.
>> He who comes to Me shall never hunger,
>> and he who believes in Me shall never thirst" (John 6:35)
>> "I am the resurrection and the life" (John 11:25)
>> "I am the light of the world" (John 8:12).

O, come, let us adore the one of whom great David was only a shadow!

Jesus Christ, the Son of...Abraham
Matthew 1:1 Part–2

The book of the genealogy of Jesus Christ, the son of David, the son of Abraham...

Abraham left the wealth and power of Ur to go to Palestine;
Jesus left the palaces of heaven to descend to Bethlehem.

Abraham offered his son Isaac on the altar;
Jesus offered Himself on the Cross.

Abraham's son did not die; God substituted a ram instead;
Jesus was the Lamb of God who takes away the sin of the world.

Abraham received his son back from the dead, as it were;
Jesus Himself rose from the dead, in fact.

Abraham believed God, and it was accounted to him as righteousness;
Jesus has become righteousness itself to all who believe in him.

God promised Abraham that he would become a great nation;
In Christ, the Church is a holy nation, a people for God's possession.

God promised Abraham that his name would be great;
Jesus Christ has been given the name that is above every name.

God promised Abraham that he would be a blessing;
In Christ we are blessed with every spiritual blessing.

God promised Abraham that his people would inherit the land of Canaan;

A King is Born

In Christ all believers are heirs to the entire world.
God promised Abraham that in him all the families of the earth would
> be blessed;
In Christ all nations, tribes, peoples, and tongues, blessed by God,
> offer up constant blessing and praise to God and to the Lamb.

Burdened Past, Brilliant Prospects
Matthew 1:1d–16

The book of the genealogy of Jesus Christ, the Son of David, the Son of Abraham: Abraham begot Isaac, Isaac begot Jacob, and Jacob begot Judah and his brothers.... Salmon begot Boaz by Rahab... David the king begot Solomon by her who had been the wife of Uriah.... Ahaz ... Manasseh ... And Jacob begot Joseph the husband of Mary, of whom was born Jesus who is called Christ.

Ponder the weight of the past which Jesus brought into this world.

Abraham, who twice claimed that Sarah was his sister in order to save his own skin. Isaac, who followed his father's corrupt example out of the same craven fear.

Jacob, the cheat, whose sons committed all manner of offenses, including selling their brother Joseph into slavery out of their invidious hatred.

Rahab, a Gentile harlot. David, the murderous adulterer. Bathsheba—her tainted name does not even appear—who bathed naked in plain view while her husband fought the king's battles.

Wicked kings like Ahaz and Manasseh.

Could anything good come out of such a twisted family background?

But ponder also the grace and the glory of God.

"Joseph the husband of Mary, of whom was born Jesus who is called Christ."

Joseph, kind and just. Mary, humble and obedient.

And Jesus, the anointed Savior of the world.

Much can be said here, but at the least, we must affirm that God can turn a blighted past into a bright future, radiant with prospects of grace and glory.

"Conceived by the Holy Spirit"
Matthew 1:18

Now the birth of Jesus Christ was as follows: After His mother Mary was betrothed to Joseph, before they came together, she was found with child of the Holy Spirit.

The conception of Jesus Christ by the Holy Spirit in the womb of Mary was a stunning, spectacular, unique miracle, the greatest act of God since the creation of the world.

Consider:

God became a man.

A man became God.

The Creator became a creature.

Eternity entered into time.

The infinite became finite.

Spirit joined with matter.

Limitless power took on little strength.

The march of death was stopped by the coming of endless life.

The pervasive, inexorable stain of sin was stopped for one crucial birth, that it might be decisively defeated at the Cross and Resurrection.

For the first time since the Fall of Adam, a human being came into this world completely holy, totally consecrated to God, and equipped to reverse the effects of original sin.

The Spirit who hovered over the waters at Creation moved within Mary to perform something that only God could do.

Nothing less than a new creation took place in the body of a young Jewish woman.

That same Holy Spirit has been "poured out on [believers] abundantly through Jesus Christ our Savior" (Titus 3:6).

Is Jesus God?
Matthew 1:20–23

"...that which is conceived in her is of the Holy Spirit. And she will bring forth a Son, and you shall call His name JESUS, for He will save his people from their sins." So all this was done that it might be fulfilled which was spoken by the Lord through the prophet, saying: "Behold, the virgin shall be with child, and bear and Son, and they shall call His name Immanuel,' which is translated, "God with us."

Matthew had begun his gospel with the genealogy of Jesus, "the Son of David, the Son of Abraham" (1:1). That showed His human origin and nature.

Now, however, he relates the words of the angel to Joseph, Mary's fiancé, which highlight the rest of the story. Jesus is not just a man, but also God. We know this for several reasons:

> This unique child was conceived by the power and presence of the Holy Spirit. In addition to His human nature, He possessed from the beginning a divine nature, implanted in Mary by the Holy Spirit.

> His name, Jesus, means something like, "Yahweh saves" in the original Hebrew. Though Joshua had borne the same name, here, because of the presence of the Spirit in His conception, the "Yahweh" part of Jesus' name carries its full reference to the God of Israel.

> "He will save His people from their sins" shows that He must be fully divine, since only God can bring salvation.

> The prophecy of Isaiah includes the title, "Immanuel," which, as Matthew explains, means "God with us."

The rest of Matthew's Gospel offers ample proof of Jesus' deity, and calls us to worship and obey Him.

Jesus the Man
Matthew 1:20–21

"That which is conceived in her is of the Holy Spirit. And she will bring forth a Son..."

Although the angel's words to Joseph show that Jesus is God, they also point to His humanity. In every way, Jesus was a true man.

Physically, He was conceived in Mary's womb and born as an infant like the rest of us. He grew up, learned to be a carpenter, and lived among His people. When He fasted, He was hungry (4:2). He worked so hard that He could fall asleep in a storm-tossed boat (8:24). His body felt the sharp sting of the lash, the blows from mocking soldiers, the piercing crown of thorns. Nails pierced His hands and feet with horrible pain when they crucified Him. On the Cross, His parched tongue cried out, "I thirst" (26:67; 27:26, 29, 30, 35, 48; John 19:28). Finally, He died (Mark 15:37).

Mentally and emotionally, He thought and felt as we do, except without sin. He could be astonished at the presence of faith (8:10) or the lack of it (8:26; 17:17). He was moved with compassion (9:36; 15:32; 20:34), grief (John 11:35), and profound sorrow (26:38).

Spiritually, He related to God His Father in constant meditation upon the Word of God (4:4; John 8:40); prayer (11:25–26; John 11:41–42) and obedience (26:39, 42; John 5:30). He could be tempted as we are (4:1–11), though He did not sin (Hebrews 4:15).

"Therefore, in all things He had to be made like *His* brethren, that He might be a merciful and faithful High Priest ... to make propitiation for the sins of the people" (Hebrews 2:17).

"For we do not have a High Priest who cannot sympathize with our weaknesses, but was in all *points* tempted as *we are*... Let us therefore come boldly to the throne of grace, that we may obtain mercy and find grace to help in time of need" (Hebrews 4:15–16).

Salvation from What?
Matthew 1:21 Part–1

"He will save His people from their sins."

With these words, the angel announced to Joseph what Mary's child would come to do.

Jesus was not born primarily to deliver us from sickness, poverty, pain, confusion, and conflict. Followers of Christ are not exempt from the troubles of daily life. Indeed, Jesus promised that "In the world you will have tribulation [trouble]" (John 16:33).

It is true that Jesus did heal many who were ill; taught His followers the way of wisdom and life; on three occasions provided food for His disciples and hearers; and called people into a new manner of living that fostered more loving relationships.

But by no means did He fulfill the expectations of the Jewish people for an earthly savior, one who would rid them of the hated Romans and usher in an era of prosperity and peace.

Why? Because His mission centered not on the symptoms, but on the source, of all unhappiness: Sin. All of His works of mercy pointed to His coming victory over this ancient and primary enemy (9:6).

By sin, death entered the world (Romans 5:12), for sin separates us from God, the fountain of life (Isaiah 59:2; Psalm 36:9). Only by dealing with our guilt before a Holy Judge could Jesus open to us the gates of everlasting joy.

So, let us also concentrate upon the main cause of all our troubles: Our relationship with God and with others. And let us trust daily in Jesus, who came to "save His people from their sins."

Savior from What?
Matthew 1:21 Part–2

"And she shall bring forth a Son, and you shall call His name Jesus, for He will save His people from their sins."

These words to Joseph by the angel explain precisely what Jesus came to do: To save His people from their sins.

Notice that Jesus did not come primarily to save people from *sickness*, though He did heal all who came to him.

Nor did He protect them from other types of *suffering*. In fact, He promised that His followers would face persecution and affliction of all sorts.

Nor did He guarantee that believers in Him would have no *sorrow*. Otherwise, why would He say, "Blessed are those who mourn, for they shall be comforted" (5:4)?

No! The eternal Son of God became a man, the God-Man, Jesus, for a particular purpose: To save His people from their sins.

First, He delivered them from the *penalty* of sin by dying on the Cross that they might be forgiven.

Now, He frees them from the enslaving *power* of sin by the work of the Holy Spirit, who lives within all who trust in Christ.

Finally, at His return, He will bring freedom from the very *presence* of sin. The new heaven and new earth, in which His people will live with God, will know nothing but full delight in, and obedience to, our Maker and Lord.

What Is "Salvation"?
Matthew 1:21 Part–3

"You shall call His name Jesus, for He will save His people from their sins."

In what ways did Jesus save His people?

> He delivered them from bondage to self and to the world by calling them to follow Him (4:18–22).
>
> He freed them from all sorts of illness by healing them (4:23–24).

He liberated them from bondage to demons by expelling evil spirits (4:24).

He emancipated them from ignorance by teaching them about happiness (5:2–12), holiness (5:13–7:27), His kingdom (13), Himself (11:25–30), His cross and resurrection (16:21; 17:22–23; 20:17–19; 28), hypocrisy (23), His coming (24–25)—and much more.

He redeemed them from the guilt of sin by declaring pardon (9:2) and by suffering the penalty of God's holy wrath (27:46).

He rescued them from death by rising from the grave (28:1–17).

He released them from futile living by giving them the Great Commission (28:18–20).

He relieved them from the burden of the Law by inviting them to come and find rest for the soul (11:28–30).

This same Jesus is alive today, strong to save all who trust in Him!

Who Gets Saved?
Matthew 1:21 Part–4

"You shall call His name JESUS, for He will save His people from their sins."

As soon as we read this verse, we ask, Who are "His people"? In other words, Who can be saved? To put it another way, How can we be saved?

Throughout his Gospel, Matthew tells us what Jesus said about this:

"Repent, for the kingdom of heaven is at hand [has drawn near]" (4:17).

"Follow Me…" (4:19).

Blessed *are* the poor in spirit,… those who mourn,… the meek,…those who hunger and thirst for righteousness,…the merciful,… the pure in heart,…the peacemakers,… those who are persecuted…" (5:3–10).

"In this manner, therefore, pray: Our Father in heaven … forgive us our debts,…do not lead us into temptation, but deliver us from the evil one" (6:9, 12–13).

"Ask, and it will be given to you; seek, and you will find; knock and it will be opened to you" (7:7).

"Enter by the narrow gate...Not everyone who says to Me, 'Lord, Lord,' shall enter the kingdom of heaven, but he who does the will of My Father in heaven" (7:13, 21).

"Come to Me, all *you* who labor and are heavy laden, and I will give you rest. Take My yoke upon you and learn from Me..." (11:28–29)

"If anyone desires to come after Me, let him deny himself, and take up his cross, and follow Me" (16:24).

"Unless you are converted and become as little children, you will by no means enter the kingdom of heaven" (18:3).

"He who endures to the end will be saved....Therefore whoever confesses Me before men, him I will also confess before My Father who is in heaven" (10:22, 32).

How Does Jesus Save?
Matthew 1:21 Part–5

"He will save His people from their sins."

Now that He has died, risen, and ascended to the Father's right hand, just how does Jesus "save His people from their sins"? He has completed the work of redemption and made it possible for us to be reconciled with God. But how do people now come into the blessings Jesus has obtained for His followers?

The answer is as simple as it is startling: Through Christians! Even though believers in Christ are both finite and fallen, beset with all sorts of faults and failings, yet Christ uses them to "save" others.

From Matthew's Gospel, we can discern the ways in which Jesus works through His people to bring others to himself:

Performing good works. "Let your light so shine before men that they may see your good works and glorify your Father who is in heaven" (5:16). Believers in Christ should be distinguished by purity of life and passionate love for God and their neighbor (5:3–48; 6:19–34; 22:37–39), expressed by obedience to their Lord's commands (7:21, 24; 28:20).

Prayer: "In this manner, therefore, pray: Our Father in heaven, Hallowed be Your name. Your kingdom come. Your will be done on earth as *it is* in heaven" (6:9–10).

A King is Born

Preaching the Good News: "As you go, preach, saying, 'The kingdom of heaven is at hand'" (10:7). "And this Gospel of the kingdom will be preached in all the world as a witness to all the nations, and then the end will come" (24:14).

Practical help for people in need: "Heal the sick, cleanse the lepers, raise the dead, cast out demons" (10:8).

One last point: The order of these activities is important. Purity of life and persistent prayer must come first.

"God with Us"
Matthew 1:23 Part–1

"And they shall call His name Immanuel," which is translated, "God with us."

The rest of Matthew's Gospel documents the evidence for the full deity of Jesus.

From the very beginning of His ministry, He healed "all kinds of sickness and all kinds of disease among the people" (4:23).

Again and again, He demanded absolute obedience, starting with His call to the first disciples, "Follow Me" (4:19).

He claimed to be the final judge of the eternal destiny of everyone on earth (7:21–23; 25:31–46).

He manifested His authority over the created world by walking on water and stilling wind and wave (8:23–27; 14:25–26).

He pronounced forgiveness of sins, which the Pharisees rightly knew to be an implicit assertion of deity (9:2–3).

He said, "Heaven and earth will pass away, but My words will by no means pass away"—thus ascribing eternity both to Himself and to His words (24:35).

He declared that "All things have been delivered to Me by My Father…" and "All authority has been given to Me in heaven and on earth" (11:27; 28:18).

He asserted that He "will come in the glory of His Father with His angels, and then He will reward each according to his works"—thus associating to Himself not only the glory of God but God's right to reward and punish (16:27). He commanded His disciples to baptize "in the name of the Father, and of the Son, and of the Holy Spirit" (28:19).

Truly, Jesus deserves our worship, adoration, trust, and full obedience!

Alone No More
Matthew 1:23 Part–2

"Behold, the virgin shall be with child, and bear a Son, and they shall call His name Immanuel," which is translated, "God with us."

Even before His birth, the angel proclaims Jesus as the Great Companion.

At the end of his Gospel, Matthew records Jesus' final words: "…lo, I am with you always, *even* to the end of the age" (28:20).

"Immanuel"—"God with us"—in the person of Jesus Christ, banishes loneliness and replaces fear with faith, despair with hope, and sorrow with joy.

Jesus was with His disciples as *teacher*, instructing them in the ways of happiness and holiness (5–7); the paths of effective service (10); the nature and growth of the Kingdom of God (13); life with others (18–19); the perils of hypocrisy (23); and the end of the age (24–25).

Jesus was with them as *healer* of "all kinds of sickness and all kinds of disease" (4:23; 9:35; 14:34–36; 15:30–31).

Jesus was with them as *deliverer* from demons (4:24; 9:32–34; 12:22; 15:22, 28) and from danger (8:23–27).

Jesus was with them as *High Priest*, pronouncing forgiveness of sins (9:2).

Jesus was with them as *Shepherd*, providing for their physical needs (14:13–21; 15:32–38).

Jesus was with them as *Suffering Servant*, walking before them the way of the Cross (16:24; 17:22–23; 20:18–19; 26:47–27:50).

Jesus was with them as *Risen Lord*, to whom had been given all authority in heaven and on earth (28:9, 16–18).

That same Jesus is with us today.

2 The Boy King

Responding to Jesus
Matthew 2:2 Part–1

"Where is He who has been born King of the Jews? For we have seen His star in the East and have come to worship Him."

The wise men from the East traveled hundreds—perhaps thousands—of miles in order to worship Jesus, whom they knew only to be the King of the Jews.

"Worship" can take many forms:

> The wise men fell down before Him and offered precious gifts (2:11).
>
> When they heard Him say, "Follow Me," the first disciples left their family and financial security to obey (4:18–22).
>
> Jesus compared the one who "hears these sayings of Mine, and does them," to a man who built his house on a firm foundation (7:24–25).
>
> The crowds who heard Him "were astonished at His teaching, for He taught them as one having authority" (7:28–29).
>
> Multitudes "brought to Him all sick people who were afflicted with various diseases and torments" (4:24).
>
> The unruly wind and waves obeyed His voice and became calm (8:26). Seeing His power over the forces of nature, His disciples "worshiped Him, saying, 'Truly, You are the Son of God'" (14:33).
>
> The multitudes "marveled and glorified God" for His healing power and pardoning mercy (9:1–8).
>
> Those who had been healed "spread the news about Him" to all their friends (9:31).
>
> Jesus Himself gave this summons: "Come to Me, all *you* who labor and are heavy laden, and I will give you rest. Take My yoke upon you, and learn from Me…" (11:28–29). Later, He added, "If anyone desires to come after Me, let him deny himself, and take up his cross, and follow Me" (16:24).

To worship is to love, to adore, to trust, to follow, and to obey!

Why Worship?
Matthew 2:2 Part–2

"We have seen His star in the East and have come to worship Him."

The wise men from the East traveled many miles for one purpose: To worship the new King of the Jews.

But why?

Some people worship God for what He has done in the past. Others worship Him because of what He will do in the future. Both are legitimate.

But the Magi worshiped Jesus, not for what He had done or would do, but simply for who He was. Guided by a star and perhaps some knowledge of the Hebrew Scriptures, they presented costly gifts and sincere adoration to a little baby simply because He deserved it.

How much more should we adore Him, with our vastly superior knowledge of His identity!

He is the eternal Word of God who "became flesh and dwelt among us ... full of grace and truth" (John 1:14). Son of God and Son of Man, He is the Bread of life; the Light of the world; the Good Shepherd; the Way, the Truth, and the Life; the Lamb who took away the sin of the world.

King of kings and Lord of Lords, He is the crucified, risen, ascended ruler of the universe. Having offered Himself as a sacrifice for our sins, He is now a merciful and faithful High Priest for us before God in heaven.

He is the Alpha and the Omega, the Beginning and the End. The Bright Morning Star. The Head of the church. The heavenly Bridegroom. The holy and true Witness of God. The Lamb slain from before the foundation of the world.

"O come, let us adore Him."

Evil in High Places
Matthew 2:3

When Herod the king heard this, he was troubled, and all Jerusalem with him.

What news could upset such powerful people?

Wise men had come from the East, following a star which they considered to point to a new-born child, who was king of the Jews.

Herod knew the child was not his, and thus trembled with fear. What new rival had appeared on the scene? Why would scholars from the East—perhaps Persia, or even China—think that a certain star announced the birth of another king for the Jews?

Herod was not a Jew. He came from Idumea, formerly called Edom, and was a descendant of Esau, the brother of Jacob. He knew that he had no right to sit on the throne of David.

But why were the Jewish leaders also troubled? ("All Jerusalem" probably refers to chief priests and scribes whom Herod summoned for advice.)

The priests also knew that they had no real right to rule the Temple, for they had received their office wrongly, through political appointment by illegitimate rulers. Perhaps this new king would remove them.

The scribes were teachers of the Law of God. Did they fear that this king would repeal the mass of human traditions they had added to God's Word?

So, instead of praising God for fulfilling His promise to send a Messiah, and rejoicing that even foreigners were coming to worship Him, the powerful men trembled with fear.

That is one reason Jesus was born: To dethrone wicked rulers when He returns to judge the living and the dead. He came also to die for both them and us, since "there is none righteous, no, not one" (Romans 3:10). All who repent and believe will be saved.

God's Beloved Son
Matthew 2:14–15 Part–1

When [Joseph] arose, he took the young Child and His mother by night and departed for Egypt, and was there until the death of Herod, that it might be fulfilled which was spoken by the Lord through the prophet, saying, "Out of Egypt I called My Son."

The verse to which Matthew refers is found in the eleventh chapter of Hosea, one of the most moving passages in the entire Bible. Here God declares His undying love for Israel, His adopted son:

> When Israel *was* a child, I loved him,
> And out of Egypt I called My son...
> I taught Ephraim to walk...
> I drew them with gentle cords,
> With bands of love...
> I stooped *and* fed them.
>
> Hosea 11:1, 3–4

Despite this tender care, however, Israel turned his back upon Yahweh:

> They sacrificed to the Baals,
> And burned incense to carved images.
>
> Hosea 11:2

So, divine justice required harsh discipline, which fell time and again, until Israel was finally taken into exile in Babylon.

Even then, however, Yahweh's love was not withdrawn:

> How can I give you up, Ephraim? *How* can I hand you over,
>   Israel?...
> My heart churns within Me;
> My sympathy is stirred.
> I will not execute the fierceness of My anger;
> I will not again destroy Ephraim.
>
> Hosea 11:8–9

Matthew's reference to Jesus as God's Son, who was sent down to Egypt and then brought back, tells us why. It is He who would "save His people from their sins" by dying on the Cross for their redemption. Sinless, Jesus would be stricken for the crimes of God's people, so that the righteous anger of the Lord would not fall upon them. Or upon us.

The Boy King

Jesus, The True Israel
Matthew 2:15 Part–2

"Out of Egypt I have called My Son."

By applying this quotation from Hosea to Jesus, Matthew identifies Him as the true Israel, the fulfillment of all the types, shadows, and promises of the Old Testament.

In Abraham, God said, all nations will be blessed.
Jesus begins His preaching with the Beatitudes, and ends with the Great Commission.

Joseph was sold by his brothers and rose to the right hand of Pharaoh.
Jesus was sold by a follower, deserted by His disciples, and rejected by His brothers, but rose to the right hand of God.

Moses delivered the Israelites from slavery in Egypt.
Jesus set people free from the power of disease, demons, and death, as well as the dominion of sin.

Israel spent forty years in the wilderness, sinning repeatedly.
Jesus spent forty days in the desert, tempted but without sin.

Joshua led God's people into the Promised Land.
Jesus (the Greek form of the name "Joshua") leads his followers into the New Heaven and the New Earth.

Samson, chained between pillars in a pagan temple conquered by his self-sacrificing death.
Jesus, nailed upon a Roman cross, defeated Satan and his pagan servants.

To David was given the promise of an eternal kingdom for his descendants.
Jesus announced the coming of the Kingdom of God, received the acclamation, "Hosanna to the Son of David," and asserted that "All authority has been given to Me in heaven and on earth."

Solomon drew seekers from far away by his wisdom.
Jesus attracted huge crowds through His teaching, and identified Himself as Wisdom itself.

Sinful priests offered sacrifices in the Temple.
Sinless Jesus, true priest and temple of God, offered Himself once for all as a fully-perfect, and sufficient sacrifice for our sins.

Elijah raised from the dead the son of the widow of Zarephath.

Jesus raised from the dead the son of the widow of Nain.
Elisha parted the waters of Jordan in the power of his mentor Elijah.
Jesus walked on water by His own power.

Unlike barren Israel, Jesus is the True Vine, filled with life for all His branches. May we constantly abide in Him by faith, bearing fruit to His glory and that of the Father!

Son(s) of God
Matthew 2:15 Part–3

"Out of Egypt I called My Son."

Jesus was not only a man who lived in first-century Palestine, but also the eternal Son of God.

This unique God-Man was conceived by the Holy Spirit (1:20), so that He could rightly inherit the promised name, Immanuel, which means, "God with us" (1:23).

At His baptism, and again on the Mount of Transfiguration, He heard the voice of God the Father saying, "This is My beloved Son, in whom I am well pleased" (3:17; 17:5).

Satan assumed that Jesus was God's Son, saying, "If You are the Son of God…" (4:3, 6). Demons recognized His identity and cringed before His authority (8:29).

Jesus Himself called God His Father in a way that no one else had done (10:32; 11:25).

What does this mean for us? Many things, but at least this: the Son of God became also the Son of Man, a unique Person with two natures, so that He might "save His people from their sins" (1:21). On the Cross, when the Father temporarily deserted Him, pouring out righteous wrath upon His own Son, Jesus earned our reconciliation with God.

As a result, all who believe in Him, can become "sons" of God. That is, by faith we are joined to Jesus, the Son of God. To use the language of John and of Paul, we are "in Him" (John 17:21; Romans 8:1; 14–17).

So, like baby Jesus, who was taken down to Egypt and kept there until

The Boy King

the king who sought his life had died, we are secure in the love of God the Father. The very hairs of our head are numbered, and we are much more valuable than the little sparrows whose lives are preserved by the Father's will, so that we do not have to be afraid of anything that might happen to us (10:29–31).

So, being saved by the Son, we are also safe in the Son of God.

Mourning Loss Part–1
Matthew 2:18

"A voice is heard in Ramah
Lamentation, weeping, and great mourning,
Rachel weeping for her children,
Refusing to be comforted,
Because they are no more."

By quoting this passage from Jeremiah 31:15, Matthew injects hope into the otherwise dismal account of the brutal slaughter of innocent children by jealous King Herod.

As the prophet Jeremiah declared long ago, though God chastises His people severely, He does not abandon them. The land of Israel was bereft of her children by the exile to Babylon, but hear these words of promise:

> Then out of them shall proceed thanksgiving
> And the voice of those who make merry;
> I will multiply them, and they shall not diminish;…
> Their children also shall be as before,…
> Yes, I have loved you with an everlasting love;…
> Therefore they shall come and sing in the height of Zion,…
> And they shall sorrow no more at all.…
> For I will turn their mourning to joy,
> Will comfort them,
> And make them rejoice rather than sorrow.…
> There is hope in your future, says the LORD,
> That *your* children shall come back to their own border.
> Jeremiah 30:19, 20; 31:3, 12, 13, 17

True to His promise, God did bring the people of Israel back from Babylon into the Promised Land. Why would God not utterly forsake wayward Israel? Because God loves His erring child:

> *Is* Ephraim My dear Son?
> *Is he* a pleasant child?...
> Therefore My heart years for him;
> I will surely have mercy on him, says the LORD.
>
> Jeremiah 31:20

Mourning Loss Part–2
Matthew 2:18

"...Rachel weeping for her children,
Refusing to be comforted,
Because they are no more."

We have seen that Jeremiah 31, from which this quotation was taken by Matthew, brims with hope for Israel's future. The people would return from exile in Babylon and the land of Benjamin would again be filled with children. Mourning would turn to joy.

Moreover, God would "make a new covenant with the house of Israel."

> I will put My law in their minds, and write it on their hearts; and I will be their God, and they shall be My people. No more shall every man teach his neighbor, and every man his brother, saying, "Know the LORD," for they all shall know Me, from the least of them to the greatest of them, says the LORD. For I will forgive their iniquity, and their sin I will remember no more.
>
> Jeremiah 31:31, 33–34

The time would come when God's people would obey Him from the heart. They would know the Lord. And this would come about because God would forgive their sins.

The letter to the Hebrews tells us that Jesus Christ has ushered in this New Covenant by His sacrificial death on the Cross (Hebrews 10:16–23).

Now let us return to Bethlehem and the slaughter of those innocent young boys. We can see why Matthew recalled the words of God

The Boy King

recorded by Jeremiah, for they infuse hope into an otherwise dark and dismal story.

Jesus, who was called God's Son only three verses earlier in Matthew's Gospel (2:15), later heard the Father say at His baptism, "This is My beloved Son, in whom I am well pleased" (3:17). He is the true Israel, who alone pleased God by His flawless conduct.

This uniquely innocent Son of God suffered on the Cross that His people might be saved from their sins (1:21). The single guiltless boy in Bethlehem was saved from Herod's cruelty in order that guilty souls could be delivered from God's righteous wrath.

We were by nature "sons of disobedience" and therefore "children of wrath" (Ephesians 2:2–3). Now, in Christ Jesus, we are "sons of God", indwelt by His Spirit, Who enables us to call God "Abba, Father" (Romans 8:14–15). As a result, nothing—not even death—can "separate us from the love of God which is in Christ Jesus our Lord" (Romans 8:38–39).

Knowing God and His love, we can mourn earthly loss with everlasting hope.

Christ the King

3 The Herald of the King

Preparing for the King
Matthew 3:1–6

In those says John the Baptist came preaching in the wilderness of Judea, and saying, "Repent, for the kingdom of heaven is at hand!"

John was sent by God to "Prepare the way of the LORD," in fulfillment of the prophecy of Isaiah 40:3.

How did he seek to get people ready for the coming of Jesus, the long-promised Messiah and Savior of Israel?

By calling upon them to repent of their sins, and give proof of that change of heart by submitting to water baptism and bearing "fruits worthy of repentance" (3:8).

From this we learn that:

> If we want to know Jesus as our Savior and Lord, we must humble ourselves before His holiness. That gate is narrow that leads to life, and only those who admit their transgressions, mourn over them, and look to Christ alone for salvation from them, will enter the kingdom.

> If we truly hate our wrongdoing, we shall forsake the love of this world and join John and his eager listeners in the wilderness—that is, we shall consider the glitz, the glamour, and the "good things" of life less valuable than getting right with God.

> True contrition for evil thoughts and deeds will produce a changed life, by the power of faith in Christ and His indwelling Spirit (as we shall see when we look at verse 11).

> If we want to help others to prepare for the coming of Christ, then we must, like John, conduct ourselves in a way that differs from those around us. Not, probably, by dressing differently, as John did (3:4)—although our clothing should be simple and modest—but certainly by denying ourselves many legitimate pleasures and privileges.

The Peril of Pride
Matthew 3:7–8

But when he [John the Baptist] saw many of the Pharisees and Sadducees coming to his baptism, he said to them, 'Brood of vipers! Who warned you to flee from the wrath to come? Therefore bear fruits worthy of repentance...'

John the Baptist rebuked the Pharisees and Sadducees, not because they came to be baptized, but because they came with the wrong motives. They were still in the grip of pride, which prevented them from true repentance and thus receiving forgiveness of sins.

The Pharisees were proud of their performance, for they thought that they kept God's law as well as possible. The Sadducees were proud of the power and their position. As the rulers in Judea, they held the reins of political power and prestige in their hands. Thus, the Pharisees thought they did not need God's forgiveness, and the Sadducees imagined that they did not need God at all.

We fall into the same danger whenever we succumb to pride. Do you resist, and even resent, criticism? Do you defend yourself, or even attack others, when someone tries to point out a failing or a fault? Do you try, in ways subtle or blatant, to build your own reputation in the eyes of others? Are you more aware of the sins of others than you are of your own? Then you are a modern-day Pharisee.

On the other hand, when we neglect, or even disbelieve, God's power; when we seek worldly success and prominence; when we limit God by our own notions of what He can or cannot do—then we are like the Sadducees. To the degree that we are complacent about ourselves and happy to be in control; to the extent that we try to rule our lives rather than submitting to God's rule, we fall into the same net they did.

May we heed the warning of God through His servant John and seek true repentance, which will result in a changed life of humble dependence upon God's grace and providential power in our lives.

The Fire to Come
Matthew 3:10, 12

"And even now the ax is laid to the root of the trees. Therefore every tree which does not bear good fruit is cut down and thrown into the fire.... His winnowing fan is *in His hand, and He will thoroughly clean out His threshing floor, and gather His wheat into the barn; but He will burn up the chaff with unquenchable fire."*

John repeatedly warns his hearers of "the wrath to come" (3:7), which he describes as a fire—the most painful of torments.

This awful judgment will come from Jesus, who will either baptize people with the Holy Spirit, or with fire (3:11; Luke 3:16).

It will come upon all who do not "repent" and "bear fruits worthy of repentance" (3:2, 8).

The fire of judgment will never end; nothing can extinguish it; the flames will burn forever (3:12).

Jesus also spoke often of God's wrath which will come upon those who do not "Repent, and believe in the Gospel" (Mark 1:15). True repentance and sincere faith are demonstrated by changed conduct, so Jesus warns that "Every tree that does not bear good fruit is cut down and thrown into the fire" (7:19).

This "fire of hell" awaits those who carry grudges (5:22) and those who do not receive the Gospel of God and who therefore "practice lawlessness" (13:41). They will be "cast ... into the furnace of fire. There will be wailing and gnashing of teeth" (13:42, 50).

Like John, Jesus emphasized that this fiery judgment will never end; it will be "everlasting" (18:8).

What about you? Have you repented of your sins and put your faith in Jesus Christ as Savior? If so, then thank God every day that you have been saved from everlasting torment in the fires of hell.

If you have not yet turned from sin and sought salvation in Christ, then now—even today—is the time to ask God to save you from eternal misery in hell.

Holy Spirit Baptism
Matthew 3:11

I indeed baptize you with water unto repentance, but He who is coming after me is mightier than I, whose sandals I am not worthy to carry. He will baptize you with the Holy Spirit...

John not only announces judgment to come upon all who refuse to repent and believe the Gospel. He also proclaims the good news of Christ.

The Coming One will baptize repentant believers with the Holy Spirit (Mark 1:8; Luke 3:16; John 1:33; Acts 1:5; 1 Corinthians 12:13).

John, though he was the greatest of the prophets under the Old Covenant, could only point to Christ. Like the entire Old Testament, he brought people to the threshold of new life, but not into that life itself.

His baptism was with water only, signifying a hunger for freedom and forgiveness of sins. Like the regulations given through Moses, John's ministry dealt with the outer man only; it could not bring inner cleansing and release.

Jesus, on the other hand, was mightier than John; He was holier than this holy man; and He could effect inner transformation by giving His followers the Spirit of God.

From other passages of the Bible, we find that the Baptism with the Holy Spirit is another facet of that complex reality which we call "salvation." Some of the other terms used for this life-changing event include:

Being born again (John 3:3, 5; Titus 3:5–6).

Receiving the gift of the Holy Spirit (John 7:39; Acts 1:8; 2:38; 8:15, 17:10:47; Romans 8:15; Galatians 3:2).

Having the Holy Spirit poured out upon one (Joel 2:28; Acts 2:17, 18, 33: 10:45; Romans 5:5; Titus 3:16).

Receiving repentance unto life (Acts 11:18).

Believing on the Lord Jesus Christ (Acts 11:17).

Being saved (Acts 11:14; 1 Corinthians 1:18; Ephesians 2:8–9).

Receiving new life (John 3:16; 5:24; Ephesians 2:5; etc.).

Becoming children of God (John 1:12–13; 1 John 3:1).

If you have received this greatest of all blessings from God, praise Him daily with a grateful heart. If you have not, come to Him in humble prayer until you do receive the Spirit of God through faith in Jesus Christ.

The Path to Blessing
Matthew 3:17

"And suddenly a voice came from heaven, saying, 'This is My beloved Son, in whom I am well pleased.'"

When did Jesus hear these words of blessing? Only after He had come up from the Jordan River, where He had been baptized by John the Baptist. John had at first refused to baptize Jesus, saying, "I need to be baptized by You" (3:14). But Jesus had insisted: "Permit *it to be so now*, for thus it is fitting for us to fulfill all righteousness" (3:15).

Without going into all that Jesus' statement might mean, let us concentrate only upon the essential significance of His baptism: By submitting to John's baptism, which was "for the remission of sins" (Mark 1:4), Jesus clearly identified Himself with sinful humanity. In other words, though He was morally spotless, He was willing to be considered filthy and in need of cleansing. He knew this was the Father's will for Him, and that it would lead to the ultimate degradation, death upon a cross like a common criminal.

After He had thus humbled Himself, Jesus heard the Father's affirming words, "This is My beloved Son, in whom I am well pleased." In Jesus' experience, we discern clearly the path of blessing for all who trust in Him: If we will only admit that we are wrong and sinful, God will recognize us as His beloved children.

In other words, if we confess our sins, He will forgive us. Not only so, but if we come daily to Him with humble admission of our many faults and failings, the Father will send the Holy Spirit to us constantly to renew His blessing upon us. And if we follow this same pattern in our relationships with others, refusing to defend or justify ourselves but freely admitting our mistakes and offenses, we shall find favor, not only with God, but with man as well. This is truly the blessed life!

Christ the King

4 The Inauguration of the King

Victory over Temptation
Matthew 4:1–11

"It is written, 'Man shall not live by bread alone, but by every word that proceeds from the mouth of God.'"

These words by Jesus, and the two other quotations from the Hebrew Bible, He used to counter Satan's wiles and show us how to overcome temptation. Consider:

The nature of temptation: Jesus was hungry and alone in a barren wilderness. Satan—a real person—suggested that He use His divine powers to provide a meal for Himself. Jesus was unknown, and had come to save Israel. Satan suggested that He pull off a spectacular stunt to propel Himself into instant popularity. As God's Son, Jesus was heir to the kingdom of God. Satan promised full authority over the earth, if only Jesus would worship him. In each case, the Tempter played upon a privilege that Jesus as Son of God could have invoked for His own immediate benefit. His goal: To distract Jesus from the ministry of humble reliance on God, complete submission to the Father's will, and the death on the Cross which alone would accomplish the purposes of God in His life.

The way to victory over temptation: Just as Satan assailed the mind, so Jesus used God's written Word to fortify His thoughts against the devices of the devil. He would not allow circumstances, need, opportunity, or His own personal profit and prominence to divert Him from trust in God's promises and obedience to His commands. Victory over temptation comes to those whose minds are saturated with the Word of God in such a way that they can deflect sinful thoughts with Scriptures that apply to that particular situation.

The result of Jesus' victory: Adam and Eve fell in a lush garden. Jesus conquered in a trackless wasteland. They had each other. He was alone. They disbelieved God and trusted Satan's lies. Jesus took the Word of God as truth, and all else as deadly deception. They caused us all to be alienated from God. Jesus brought us near.

In His triumph, Jesus began to "save His people from their sins" (1:21). The baneful consequences of the Fall began to be reversed in the blessed conquest of Christ.

If we follow His example, we shall vanquish Satan as He did. If we trust in Him and the salvation which He brings, we shall know God's gracious favor and presence now, and someday see Him face to face in a new garden.

The Light of Life
Matthew 4:16

The people who sat in darkness have seen a great light, and upon those who sat in the region and shadow of death light has dawned.

Matthew quotes these words from Isaiah 9:2 to introduce the ministry of Jesus in Galilee. Though many devout Jews lived there, the area was called "Galilee of the Gentiles" (4:15) because of the heavy non-Jewish population.

Before Jesus began walking among them, preaching about the kingdom of God and working mighty miracles, the inhabitants lived in total darkness. They were lost in ignorance; deceived by false "gods"; captive to sin; estranged from God; without any hope in life; and headed for eternal doom.

But now the light has come! Jesus, who called Himself "the light of the world" (John 8:12), dispels darkness in all its forms.

He preached the good news of God's rule, and showed us how to live, thus banishing ignorance.

In His own person and through His teaching, He pointed men to the only true God, thereby delivering them from deception.

When He died on the Cross He redeemed believers from the penalty of sin; His gift of the Holy Spirit frees them from the power of sin.

His sacrificial death satisfied God's holy wrath, so that now we can have peace with the righteous Judge of the world.

The Inauguration of the King

His glorious resurrection ensures that all who follow Him will not suffer endless misery in hell, but will enter into everlasting life. This assurance gives us unshakable hope.

Shall we continue to sit in darkness, or shall we lay hold of the Light of life?

To Greet a King
Matthew 4:17

From that time Jesus began to preach and to say, "Repent, for the kingdom of heaven is at hand [has drawn near]."

To repent is to recognize the error of your ways; to regret having offended God; to renounce your sinful attitudes and actions; and to return to God in humble faith.

Why did Jesus command people to repent? Because "the kingdom of heaven is at hand."

God has always ruled the universe as King over all. Nothing escapes His sovereign control. His kingdom entered a new phase, however, when His son Jesus began His public ministry of preaching, teaching, and healing.

As eternal Son of God, Jesus also is King. His coming introduced a new dynamic into the world. Wherever He went, people saw the light; they felt His love; they experienced liberation from guilt, from the power of sin, from illness, and even from evil spirits. God's power became manifest in the lives of His people in a new way.

To enjoy the benefits of the kingdom of heaven, however, we must greet the King with humble hearts. Like the Hebrews of old we must recognize how wrong we have been in our beliefs and our behavior. As we see our costly errors, we shall feel regret for our iniquities. That will make us renounce and turn away from our destructive patterns of life. Then we shall turn towards the only one who can bring true happiness, Jesus, the righteous, holy, omnipotent, and loving King.

As John the Baptist proclaimed, the coming King will either baptize repentant people with the Holy Spirit or burn stubborn rebels with unquenchable fire. Which will it be for us?

"Follow Me" Part–1
Matthew 4:19–20

Then He said to them, "Follow Me, and I will make you fishers of men." They immediately left their nets and followed Him.

Jesus issues the same summons to us today. Why did those first disciples follow Him? Why should we follow Him? Matthew gives us several compelling reasons:

Jesus "will save His people from their sins" (1:21).

He is "Immanuel… God with us" (1:23).

He is the promised "Ruler Who will shepherd" God's people (2:6).

John the Baptist, the greatest man of his time, described Jesus as "mightier than I, whose sandals I am not worthy to carry" (3:11).

To those who follow Him, Jesus will give the baptism of the Holy Spirit (3:11).

Those who refuse Him will suffer another fate: "He will burn up the chaff with unquenchable fire" (3:12).

God the Father said of Him, "This is My beloved Son, in whom I am well pleased" (3:17).

He alone was able to withstand all the wiles and temptations of Satan (4:1–11).

He is the Light shining upon those who sat in the darkness of "the region and shadow of death" (4:16).

Because He is the Son of David, the promised King, with Him comes the Kingdom of God for all who repent (4:17).

He promises to transform His followers from being mere fishermen, engaged in work with only temporary results, to "fishers of men"—those whom He will use to bring others to God and thus to eternal life (4:19).

Is there any good reason NOT to follow Jesus?

The Inauguration of the King

"Follow Me" Part–2
Matthew 4:19

"Follow Me and I will make you fishers of men."

What does it mean to follow Jesus?

He summons us, first, to adhere to His words.

To be more specific, we are to follow His creed. Followers of Jesus will believe what He taught, about:

God: That He is a loving heavenly Father who gives good gifts (7:11). He is also a righteous and just judge, who will punish unrepentant sinners (5:29–30). Our Father will hear the prayers of all who come to Him in sincere faith (6:6), providing our daily needs, forgiving our sins, and protecting us from temptation and evil (6:11–13).

Jesus Christ: He is Lord (7:21), and thus equal with God the Father. In a unique way, He is the Son of God (7:21), as well as the unique Son of Man (9:6). Thus, He has power to issue commands (5:21–48), to heal (8:13), to forgive sins (9:6), to condemn unrepentant sinners (7:23), to enable men to know God the Father (11:27), to grant real rest (11:28), and to give His life as a ransom for sinners (20:28).

Jesus' disciples will also follow His commands. Matthew's Gospel is filled with His instructions, which are not optional guidelines but authoritative orders. They include:

"Repent, for the kingdom of heaven is at hand" (4:17).

"Love your enemies" (5:44).

"Seek first the kingdom of God and His righteousness" (6:33).

"Ask, and it will be given you" (7:7).

"Go therefore and make disciples of all the nations, baptizing them in the name of the Father and of the Son and of the Holy Spirit, teaching them to observe all things that I have commanded you" (28:18–20).

Jesus said, "If you abide in My word, you are My disciples indeed. And you shall know the truth, and the truth shall make you free" (John 8:31–32).

To follow Jesus' words is to walk the path of truth and freedom. Shall we?

Follow Me Part–3
Matthew 4:19

"Follow Me, and I will make you fishers of men."

We have seen that to follow Jesus is to adhere to His words. But that is not all. Disciples of Christ will also follow in His ways. Like Him, they will walk the path of:

Testimony to God's truth: "And Jesus went about all Galilee, teaching in their synagogues" (4:23).

Meeting people's physical needs: "… Jesus went about … healing all kinds of sickness and all kinds of disease among the people" (4:23).

Living a simple life: "Foxes have holes and birds of the air *have* nests, but the Son of Man has nowhere to lay *His* head" (8:20).

Gentleness and humility: "Take My yoke upon you and learn from Me, for I am gentle and lowly in heart" (11:29).

Rejection: "A prophet is not without honor except in his own country and in his own house" (13:57).

Sacrificial service: "… just as the Son of Man did not come to be served, but to serve, and to give His life a ransom for many" (20:28).

Self-denial: "And he who does not take his cross and follow Me is not worthy of Me" (10:38).

Suffering for the sake of the Gospel: "A disciple is not above *his* teacher, nor a servant above his master" (10:24).

Everlasting life: "… he who loses his life for My sake will find it" (10:39). "Blessed are you when they revile and persecute you …. Rejoice and be exceedingly glad, for great *is* your reward in heaven" (5:11–12).

Follow Me Part–4
Matthew 4:19

"Follow Me, and I will make you fishers of men."

If Jesus' disciples obey His teachings, how will that make them "fishers of men"? Think for a moment what it would be like if Christians actually lived, to a substantial degree, as Jesus told them to live. They would be:

Poor in spirit—aware of their spiritual poverty and reliant upon God alone.

Sorry for their sins and sensitive to the suffering of those around them.

Meek and gentle in all their dealings with others.

Consumed with passion, but for righteousness, not for position, or power, or possessions, or pleasure.

Merciful to others, for they themselves have been forgiven by God.

Intent on one purpose—knowing and serving God—and thus not distracted by the idols of this world, especially materialism.

Peacemakers, who strive to avoid unnecessary conflicts and to resolve those which inevitably arise. They would not be contentious.

Willing to suffer for what is right and true, and unafraid of bearing testimony to Christ, no matter what the cost (5:3–12).

Free from resentment, devoted to sexual purity, faithful to marriage vows, and filled with love even for their enemies (5:21–48).

Free from worry about money and things, fully trusting that God would take care of them (6:25–34).

Committed to personal growth in holiness, but non-judgmental of others (7:1–14).

In short, so full of good works, that people could not help but praise the God whom they know as Father (5:16).

Follow Me Part–5
Matthew 4:19

"Follow Me, and I will make you fishers of men."

Notice the *promise*: Jesus will make His followers fishers of men.

He does not promise to make them wealthy, or healthy. He does not offer them fame, or comfort, or popularity, or pleasure. He only promises that they will attract men to God through faith in Christ.

What does this promise tell us about the *purpose* of Christ in calling people to follow Him?

It seems that Jesus intends to make His disciples into disciple-makers. We see this also from His last words to these same men: "Go therefore and make disciples of all the nations" (28:19).

In other words, Jesus' goal in calling people to follow Him—aside from the primary aim of drawing them into intimacy with God through fellowship with Christ—is to use them to bring others to Him.

If that is the case, should those who believe in Christ not align themselves with the will of God, and orient their entire lives towards one main objective—to attract others into that same communion with God that they enjoy through faith in Jesus?

What a difference that would make! Instead of striving for success, or a good reputation, or material comfort, or even human love, Christians would seek first to draw others with them into the Kingdom of God.

With that aim dominating all others, how our lives would change! We would gladly give up anything dear to us if that would help others come to know Christ. To make Jesus seem more attractive to others, we would ask God to transform us into better representatives of His Son in this world.

Our greatest pleasures would come, not from getting, but from giving; not from self-indulgence, but from self-denial; not from success, but from sacrifice. The joy of seeing someone else enter God's gracious kingdom would surpass all other pleasures—except our own delight in being with our Lord.

If to "catch" others for Christ forms the center of God's *purpose* for Christians, then to become better "fishers of men" should hold first place in our *prayers*.

"O Lord Jesus, draw me closer to Yourself, that I might help others draw near to You. Amen."

Why Jesus Heals
Matthew 4:23 Part–1

And Jesus went about all Galilee, teaching in their synagogues, preaching the gospel of the kingdom, and healing all kinds of sickness and all kinds of disease among the people.

We can understand why Jesus would go around teaching the Word of God. But why did He heal all kinds of illness and disease? The answer to this question shows us a great deal about Christ.

Jesus healed and cast out demons (4:24):

> Because He came to "save His people from their sins" (1:21). Sin ends in death, and disease represents the dying process. By dealing with one symptom of sin—sickness—Jesus declared His intention to do away with sin itself.
>
> To demonstrate that He was, indeed, "'Immanuel,' which is translated, 'God with us'" (1:23). No one has manifested such power over evil as did Jesus when He delivered men from diseases and demons. These mighty miracles show that He is the only Son of God, equal with the Father in power.
>
> To certify that He was indeed the one who could "baptize ... with the Holy Spirit" (3:11). Casting out demons and curing sickness revealed His total filling by the Holy Spirit and pointed towards the time when, after His resurrection, He would bestow the Spirit on all who would repent and believe.
>
> To prove that He was God's "beloved Son, in whom [He was] well pleased" (3:17; 12:18). He had refused to perform a miracle when Satan tempted Him in the desert, but was happy to do many public wonders in order to unveil the unique relationship He enjoyed with the Father.

To make public His earlier defeat of Satan in private (4:11). Having routed the prince of darkness, death, demons, and disease, Jesus now followed up that victory with open displays of His decisive victory over Satan.

To back up His announcement that the "Kingdom of heaven is at hand" (4:17). His deeds validated His words announcing the coming of God's royal and righteous rule.

To teach His disciples how to be "fishers of men" (4:19). These marvelous deeds of power and pity drew large multitudes to Him to hear His words.

To lay bare the compassionate core of His divine heart (20:34; Mark 1:41).

Conditions for Healing
Matthew 4:23 Part–2

And Jesus went about all Galilee, teaching in their synagogues, preaching the gospel of the kingdom, and healing all kinds of sickness and all kinds of disease among the people.

Although some people still receive miraculous healing simply through faith in Christ, most do not. The natural question is, "Why?" This passage, along with others in the New Testament, gives us several clues.

Notice that Jesus also taught the people and announced the coming of the kingdom of God. He did not simply provide miraculous cures. Let us look more closely at the connection between His words of truth and His works of mercy.

Jesus told the crowds how to be happy. "Blessed are those who hunger and thirst for righteousness; …the merciful…; … the pure in heart" (5:6–8). He warned them against anger, lust, adultery, and resentment (5:21–32, 43–48). He promised that God would provide all that we need, and told them not to worry (6:25–34).

He also commanded everyone to repent, for God's kingdom was at hand. Jesus called men and women to a radically changed life, insisting that they renounce their old ways and turn to Him in faith.

The Inauguration of the King

But what of those who are consumed with greed, envy, resentment, anger, and lust? Nowhere does the Bible promise good health to such people. In fact, we learn elsewhere that lack of reverence for God and love for other believers can lead to illness and even death (Acts 5:1–11; 1 Corinthians 11:27–34).

Jesus' brother James encourages those who are sick to call the elders of the church to pray for healing, but requires confession of sin as a condition for answered prayer (James 5:14–15).

Modern medicine has begun to uncover the mental, emotional, and spiritual roots of disease. We now know that anxiety, anger, resentment, and guilt can compromise the body's immune system, almost inviting a number of serious illnesses.

Physicians constantly remind us that lack of self-discipline can also bring on serious diseases: Poor nutrition, smoking, drinking, using drugs, lack of exercise, insufficient rest, and sex outside of marriage all carry a price tag.

Conclusion: At least one reason why Jesus does not now heal many people is that they are not following His teaching or heeding His commands to repent and believe.

When God Does Not Heal
Matthew 4:23 Part–3

And Jesus went about all Galilee, teaching in their synagogues, preaching the gospel of the kingdom, and healing all kinds of sickness and all kinds of disease among the people.

Sometimes God does not heal people because they are not following His teaching or heeding His command to repent and believe. Are there any other reasons why healing does not come? Once again, the Bible gives some clues.

> Jesus went about all Galilee: Notice that He did not go to Judea on this trip, though there must have been multitudes there suffering from illnesses of all sorts. Nor did He visit Samaria (at this time), or Rome, or Greece, or Africa, or China. Here we see God's sovereignty. It was not, apparently, the will of God that Jesus should bring healing to everyone living in His day. Only a select

group (though they were many) benefited from His mighty power. The same holds true today. God decides who will be healed, and who will not. We do not know the basis for His choice, but we believe He is always just and fair. We trust in His love precisely because He sent Jesus to save His people from their sins.

Jesus only healed those who came to Him, or were brought to Him. Our passage tells us that "Great multitudes followed Him—from Galilee and *from* Decapolis [Ten Cities], Jerusalem, Judea, and beyond the Jordan" (4:25). These crowds traveled long distances and underwent a great deal of trouble in order to get within the range of Jesus' truth and love. Perhaps we do not receive healing because we have not exerted sufficient effort.

From other places in the Scripture, we learn that God allows trouble into our lives for a variety of purposes. Perhaps He means to discipline us for disobedience; or refine us; or test our faith; or strengthen our faith through the endurance of trials; or remind us to set our hope fully on future grace when Christ returns; or keep us from pride and complacency; or demonstrate His power in our weakness by giving us sufficient ability to serve Him under great pressure (see Hebrews 12:3–11; James 1:2–4, 12; 1 Peter 1:6–8, 13; 2 Corinthians 12:7–10). At all times, however, believers in Christ can be assured that nothing—not even acute pain or chronic, debilitating disease—can "separate us from the love of God which is in Christ Jesus our Lord" (Romans 8:35–39). Indeed, we can be assured that "all things work together for good to those who love God" (Romans 8:28). For those reasons, we can "in everything give thanks" (1 Thessalonians 5:18).

5 The King's New Law

When Poverty Brings Blessing
Matthew 5:3

"Blessed are the poor in spirit, for theirs is the kingdom of heaven."

The world admires those who are "rich in spirit"—the confident, capable men and women who run the government, business, education, entertainment, and the media. We are taught to believe in ourselves, express ourselves, fulfill ourselves, promote ourselves. The self-doubting, self-effacing, self-critical do not command respect.

But Jesus promised nothing less than the kingdom of heaven [that is, the kingdom of God] to "the poor in spirit." Those who know they are spiritually poor already begin to enjoy citizenship in God's everlasting empire.

Who are the "poor in spirit"? What are they like? As always, we look first to the sacred history for the answer. Consider the example of:

David, who pleaded, "For Your name's sake, O LORD, pardon my iniquity, for it *is* great... Turn Yourself to me, and have mercy on me, for I *am* desolate [lonely] and afflicted" (Psalm 25:11, 16).

Solomon, who began his youthful kingship with a request for Divine assistance: "Now O LORD my God, You have made Your servant king instead of my father David, but I *am* a little child; I do not know *how* to go out or come in.... Therefore give to Your servant an understanding heart ... that I may discern between good and evil" (1 Kings 3:6–9).

The Gentile woman who begged Jesus to deliver her daughter from a demon: "Yes, Lord, yet even the little dogs eat the crumbs which fall from their masters' table" (15:27).

Paul, that preeminent apostle, missionary, and saint, who yet confessed, "I know that in me (that is in my flesh) nothing good dwells" (Romans 7:18).

Jesus uttered nothing new when He declared such people truly blessed, for surely He knew the seven-hundred-year-old prophecy given through Isaiah, "For thus says the High and Lofty One who inhabits eternity, whose name *is* Holy: 'I dwell in the high and holy *place*, with him *who* has a contrite and humble spirit, to revive the spirit of the humble, and to revive the heart of the contrite ones" (Isaiah 57:15).

"Happy Are the Unhappy"
Matthew 5:4 Part–1

"Blessed are *those who mourn, for they shall be comforted."*

We have no lack of causes for unhappiness. We may be sad because our investments have lost value, dashing our hopes and threatening our financial future. Failure in work or in love can provoke deep sorrow. Rejection by those who should love us leaves a deep scar. Loneliness can lead to depression, as can constant friction with family or friends. Worst of all are the death of a loved one and the death of a marriage.

In this passage, usually called The Beatitudes, Jesus gives hints of another type of mourning, however (5:3–12).

The poor in spirit mourn because of their lack of faith, hope, and love. They know they possess few inner resources to know and serve God, and this causes them sorrow.

The meek mourn when they see bullies pushing and shoving the weak out of the way. Those with more aggressive attitudes are sad when they lose their temper or act with insolence and pride, for they know this displeases their Lord.

Those who hunger and thirst after righteousness are keenly aware of their sins, and long for the day when they will be like our holy Lord. When they ponder the injustice in the world, they weep for those who are suffering.

The merciful cannot bear to see others being treated with harshness and contempt, for they remember how kindly and gently God has dealt with them.

Those who want to be pure in heart bewail their inner uncleanness, and beg God to create in them a clean heart. They wait eagerly for the day when they see God face to face, for they know that only then will they be pure, even as He is pure.

The King's New Law

The ever-present conflicts around us break the heart of peacemakers.

We can understand why those who are persecuted for righteousness' sake or for Christ and His Gospel would suffer intense pain. Their undeserved ordeal cannot but wound their hearts and make them cry out for the coming of God's kingdom.

To all these, Jesus promises comfort. This divine consolation will be complete and everlasting, which is why believers in Christ can be happy even when they are unhappy.

Exempt From Sorrow?
Matthew 5:4 Part–2

"Blessed are those who mourn, for they shall be comforted."

Followers of Jesus Christ will partake of many of the same sorrows that others experience, as we have seen. Indeed, they will have some pain that non-believers do not, for their loving hearts will break over their own sin and the ravages of evil in the world.

On the other hand, those who trust in Christ and follow Him faithfully will not have to endure certain types of bitter anguish.

Since their faith is sincere and not just superficial, they will not hear Him say, at the end of the age, "I never knew you; depart from Me, you who practice lawlessness!" (7:23)

When they read, see, or hear about miracles done by the power of Jesus, they repent of their sins and trust in Him. Thus, they will not suffer the same fate as those who saw His wonders but did not repent, and about whom Jesus said, "… it shall be more tolerable for the land of Sodom in the day of judgment than for you" (11:24).

They hear His word and bring forth works of righteousness by trusting in Him, so they will not be like "those who practice lawlessness," who will be "cast … into the furnace of fire," where "there will be wailing and gnashing of teeth" at the end of the age (13:41–42).

They try to make good use of the time and talents God has given them, so that, when Jesus returns to judge the world, they will not be "cast … into the outer darkness" (25:30).

When they see other Christians in need, they treat them as they would Jesus Himself; thus, they will not "go away into everlasting punishment" with those whose hearts were hard towards suffering believers (25:46).

In other words, they will be comforted by going "into eternal life" (25:46), where all their earthly sorrows will be forgotten. They will never be separated from the love of God.

And why is that? Because they have trusted in, and sought to follow, God's Son Jesus, who took their place as a sin offering on the Cross, where He cried out, "My God, My God, why have You forsaken Me?" (27:46).

Comfort Now
Matthew 5:4 Part-3

"Blessed are *those who mourn, for they shall be comforted."*

Believers in Christ will suffer grief along with the rest of the world, but they will also enjoy comfort, even in this life.

Will they receive back their dead loved ones? No! Will they always get a second chance, or have their losses restored? No! Or will they always understand why pain and suffering has befallen them? Again, No!

But in the midst of continuing sorrow, they will know the presence of God's consolation.

Paul, who endured more afflictions than almost any man, rejoiced because of God's abundant comfort. He knew, first, that his sufferings and subsequent experience of God's comfort would enable him to comfort others who were afflicted (2 Corinthians 1:5–7).

God also used others to bring relief to the apostle. When he was worried about the reaction of the Corinthian Christians to a strong rebuke he had sent them in a letter, the coming of his friend Titus to him with news of their continued affection brought him great comfort (2 Corinthians 7:6). He rejoiced also to learn that the Corinthians had been comforted by the Lord after they repented of their sins (2 Corinthians 7:13); we, too, can find joy when our fellow believers receive God's mercy for their transgressions.

The King's New Law

Likewise, when he learned that the Christians in Thessalonica had endured persecution without losing their faith, his soul was greatly comforted (1 Thessalonians 3:7), and this helped to strengthen him in his own sufferings. Thus, knowing how the believers in Ephesus worried about him as he languished in a Roman prison, Paul sent Tychicus to them to reassure them of his good spirits and safety (Ephesians 6:21–22).

Others can do only so much for us, however. That is why Paul urged the believers in Thessalonica who mourned the death of those close to them to comfort each other by reminding each other of the sure promise of God to raise the dead who had trusted in Christ when the Lord returns (1 Thessalonians 4:18).

Indeed, our sure source of strength amidst the trials of this life comes from the Scriptures, which contain so many words of hope from a God who can be fully trusted (Romans 15:4–5).

Divine Consolation
Matthew 5:4 Part–4

"Blessed are those who mourn, for they shall be comforted."

Loss brings grief. Major losses produce profound grief. Permanent major losses can engender lasting, inconsolable sorrow.

What does the Bible say to such pain? That the ruined relationship will be repaired? The failure undone? The loved one brought back to life? There is perhaps some hope in certain situations, but others preclude any expectation of restoration.

What then? Are we left to sink under the weight of grief, or wallow in a swamp of self-pity? Not at all!

God has words of encouragement for all those who love Him, trust in His Son Jesus, and rely on the Holy Spirit for daily strength.

We are not alone. Jesus has Himself walked the path of pain and sorrow; He knows. Even now, He prays for us, as the Holy Spirit intercedes for us within our deepest being. God cares, and He hears.

As we face, and accept as final, the agony of loss, we discover a greater gain:

"O LORD, *You are* the portion of my inheritance and my cup … In Your presence *is* fullness of joy; at Your right hand *are* pleasures forevermore" (Psalm 16:5, 11).

"The LORD is my rock and my fortress and my deliverer; my God, my strength, in whom I will trust" (Psalm 18:2).

"They are abundantly satisfied with the fullness of Your house, and You give them drink from the rivers of Your pleasures. For with You *is* the fountain of life; in Your light we see light" (Psalm 36:8–9).

"Whom have I in heaven *but You*? And *there is* none upon earth *that* I desire besides You. My flesh and my heart fail; but God *is* the strength of my heart and my portion forever" (Psalm 73:25–26).

"Neither death, nor life … nor any other created thing, shall be able to separate us from the love of God which is in Christ Jesus our Lord" (Romans 8:38–39).

The Greatest Comfort
Matthew 5:4 Part–5

"Blessed are *those who mourn, for they shall be comforted."*

Disease, discord, and death, painful as they are, represent only symptoms of a deeper disorder: Our disobedience towards God and impending doom under His righteous wrath.

That is why no sorrow compares to the agony of a violated conscience. We were created to love, and when pride, resentment, lust, greed, deceit, and idolatry defile our souls, the response can be nothing other than intense anguish.

For the same reason, the greatest comfort is reserved for those who freely confess their sins and place their trust totally in the mercy of God, who sent His Son to take the penalty we so justly deserve.

Our comfort derives from Jesus' discomfort (to employ the mildest possible term). He refused to shrink from His duty, despite intense struggle in the Garden of Gethsemane. He refused to run from His captors, answer His accusers or destroy them with a swift command to armies of angels ready to intervene. Nor would He mock His mockers by descending from the Cross. Rather, He fulfilled His destiny by absorbing in His sinless body and soul the awful anger of a

Holy God. To complete His work of redemption, He allowed Himself to descend even into the darkness of death.

Because of His courage, we receive consolation. His death defeats our despair. Faith in Him conquers our natural conviction that we could never be loved by God, whom we correctly know to be an incorruptible Judge.

"If we confess our sins, He [God] is faithful and just to forgive us *our* sins..." for "... He Himself [Jesus] is the propitiation for our sins" (1 John 1:9; 2:2).

That is why "*there* is therefore now no condemnation to those who are in Christ Jesus" (Romans 8:1). Not only so, but "God is for us" and "justifies" all who trust in Christ (Romans 8:31, 33).

Our greatest comfort comes to us by way of the cross of Jesus Christ, and can thus never be withheld or withdrawn from sincere believers.

Happy are the Humble
Matthew 5:5

"Blessed are *the meek, for they shall inherit the earth."*

We must first note that Jesus did not say, "Blessed are the *weak*." Meekness does not equal weakness; in fact, one must be inwardly strong in order to counter harsh treatment with mildness and aggressive behavior with gentleness.

Nor did our Lord promise that the meek would conquer or control the earth in this life. We all know that power, prestige, and position generally go to those who advance their own interests, manipulate or even remove others, and display boldness in asserting their claims. History is replete with examples of kings and conquerors, great and small, who gained possession of their world through power, even violence.

No, Jesus promises two things: (1) That the meek—the mild, the gentle—would (2) inherit the earth—later.

Who are the meek? Like Moses and David, when they are criticized, even threatened with death, they respond by calling upon God for vindication, guidance, and protection (Numbers 12:3; 1 Samuel 30:6). They do not burn with rage over the prosperity of the wicked; instead, they trust in the LORD, delight themselves in Him, commit their way to Him, rest in Him, wait patiently for Him, and seek to do good (Psalm 37:1, 3–5, 7), putting their hopes in God's ultimate judgment (Psalm 37:2, 9–11, 13).

The meek do not return evil for evil, or insults for insults; rather, they bless those who curse them, pray for them, and do good to those who spitefully use them (5:44).

In short, they imitate the example of Jesus, who "when He was reviled, did not revile in return; when He suffered, He did not threaten, but committed *Himself* to Him who judges righteously" (1 Peter 2:23).

Like Jesus, they may lose all that they have, including their belongings, their reputation, and their life. But like Him also, they will be rewarded in the next life, when God judges the living and the dead by Christ. In the new heavens and the new earth, where righteousness dwells, they will reign with Him and shall, with Him, possess the earth forever (2 Peter 3:13; 1 Peter 1:4).

Happy Are the Hungry
Matthew 5:6

"Blessed are *those who hunger and thirst for righteousness, for they shall be filled [satisfied]."*

We live in an age of overeating. The causes include abundant food, plenty of money, and relentless advertising. Behind all of those lies a mindset of self-gratification. "Obey your thirst," they tell us. Why? Because a full stomach brings happiness; self-denial leads to misery.

Jesus thought differently. He fasted for more than a month, at the end of which He refused to turn stones into bread to satisfy His hunger. He fed upon another kind of food: Doing the will of God (John 4:34). His goal in life was to feed others, not fatten Himself.

True happiness comes from holiness. Those who long to please God will be filled with joy and peace. Those who fast and pray so that they may not enter into temptation will be satisfied with a good conscience.

The King's New Law

If our prayers cry out for God's name to be praised, His kingdom to come, His will to be done, then He will supply our daily bread. But if we worship our own bellies we gain nothing but fat and final frustration.

Blessed are the Merciful
Matthew 5:7 Part–1

"Blessed are *the merciful, for they shall obtain [receive] mercy."*

Jesus continues His description of those who are really happy and to be admired by pointing out the reward coming to those who are merciful.

What does "merciful" mean?

We can see the face of mercy by looking at the way Jesus responded to people who cried out to Him in desperate need.

On two different occasions, a pair of blind men called to Him, "Son of David, have mercy upon us!" (9:27; 20:30). Both times, Jesus asked them what they wanted from Him, not because He did not know their condition, but to give them an opportunity to express their faith that He could heal them. Once they had made their request, He gave them sight.

While Jesus was staying in a house outside of Israel, a non-Jewish woman came to Him in tears, "Have mercy on me, O Lord, Son of David! My daughter is severely demon-possessed." After testing Her faith, Jesus delivered the woman's little girl from the demon (15:21–28).

A distraught father knelt down before Him, saying, "Lord, have mercy on my son, for he is an epileptic and suffers severely" (17:15). Immediately, Christ healed the man's son.

How did Jesus manifest mercy? By meeting the needs of people in deep trouble. He saw their helplessness; He heard their cry of pain; He pitied them in their distress; He took action that brought them relief from suffering.

He wants us to do the same.

What is God Like?
Matthew 5:7 Part–2

"Blessed are *the merciful, for they shall obtain [receive] mercy."*

While on earth, Jesus demonstrated mercy by meeting the needs of people in deep trouble.

In doing so He was only following the pattern laid down for us in the Old Testament, where God is pictured as full of mercy.

Take, for example, the LORD's self-revelation on Mount Sinai after Moses asked to see His glory. Though no man could look directly upon God and live, Moses was granted a stunning verbal description of Yahweh:

"The LORD [Yahweh], the LORD God, merciful and gracious, longsuffering, and abounding in goodness and truth, keeping mercy for thousands, forgiving iniquity and transgression and sin" (Exodus 34:6–7).

In one form or another, this same collection of words occurs at least six times in the Old Testament. Clearly, God wanted to impress upon His people the core of His nature. As John would later write, "God is love" (1 John 4:8).

The people of Israel had offended their Lord by making a golden calf and worshiping it with wild revelries and debauchery. Instead of exterminating them, however, God forgave them at Moses' request.

Thus, God displayed His mercy as forgiveness of "iniquity and transgression and sin" (Exodus 34:7).

Blessed are all those who imitate our gracious God!

Pardon—or Perish!
Matthew 5:7 Part–3

"Blessed are *the merciful, for they shall obtain [receive] mercy."*

We have seen that mercy involves pity for those in need, plus action to relieve that need. Since our greatest need is for forgiveness, God shows His mercy primarily by pardoning our sins.

Without such pardon, we are lost. We have offended God in a variety of ways—by thought, word, and deed. We have not loved Him with

The King's New Law

all our heart, soul, mind and strength; nor have we loved our neighbors as ourselves. We have neglected our duties and committed countless crimes against His holy law. Nor can we change ourselves.

Thus, when Jesus promises mercy to those who are merciful, He is offering to solve our greatest problem—alienation from a holy God. If only we can show mercy to others, then we can be sure of receiving similar treatment from our Maker and Judge.

Here we encounter at least two huge difficulties, however: First, we are simply not naturally merciful! On the contrary, we possess hearts that are indifferent to the suffering of others. When people offend us, we seldom forgive, and almost never forget. We harbor grudges and even bitterness (even though we usually deny that unpleasant fact).

Furthermore, the Bible teaches that no one can be justified by doing what God's law requires. We are saved by grace, through faith, not by our own works, including any work of mercy we might be able to squeeze out of our hardened hearts.

So what does Jesus mean here? Doesn't He know that we cannot be merciful? Or that we can never earn God's forgiveness by anything we have done?

Of course He knows! Thus, we must seek an explanation for His teaching. As we consider other teachings of His—such as, "Blessed *are* the poor in spirit" (5:3), and "blessed *are* those who mourn" (5:4)—we see that a merciful attitude comes naturally to those who themselves have been forgiven by God.

In His parable about the unmerciful servant (18:21–35), Jesus shows that the person who has himself been forgiven an unpayable debt (like the one we owe to God) is expected to treat his debtors with similar kindness. If he does not, that means that he does not appreciate the mercy he has received.

Here is the point: Being merciful to others proves that we have known the mercy of God. This builds our confidence that, at the Last Judgment, we too shall receive full and final pardon for all our sins.

How to Become Merciful
Matthew 5:7 Part–4

"Blessed are *the merciful, for they shall obtain [receive] mercy."*

God commands us to show pity to others in need, and pardon to those who have offended us. But our hearts resist this order. We find it hard to feel others' pain, and even harder to forgive their past misdeeds. If we dared to admit it, we would confess that we think that, somehow, they deserve what they are suffering, and certainly do *not* deserve our clemency.

How, then, can we soften our hearts and unlock the storehouse of our love?

First, we should consider our own condition. Are we any better than they, really? Could not the same troubles have befallen us? And have we not committed sins as serious as theirs—or even worse?

One look at the righteous law of God should suffice to unmask our desperate condition in God's eyes. We have not worshiped Him as God, or given Him thanks. We have sought happiness and "life" from created things and people rather than from our Creator. We have spurned His commands and not believed His promises.

Nor have we treated others as we would want to be treated ourselves. Instead of love; lust, greed, envy, and even malice have ruled in our innermost thoughts. How seldom do we sacrifice for the good of those around us! How often do we criticize them and withhold affection from them!

And yet, when we recognize our wrong-doing and return to God in sincere repentance and trust in Christ as the Lamb of God who died in our place, our heavenly Father receives us with open arms. He forgives our sins and cleanses us from the stain of guilt. He welcomes us into His fellowship with overflowing affection. He even supplies us with the Holy Spirit when we cry out for help.

Just thinking about the way God constantly treats His needy but unworthy children will give us perspective. Looking at the way Jesus died for us, we shall not close up our hearts against others in need, even though—like us—they do not deserve any relief. When we were helpless, God sent His Son as a sacrifice for us; when we were sinners, Christ died for us.

One glance at the cross of Jesus should be sufficient to melt our icy hearts and unleash our affections for others in difficulty. Pondering the price God paid to forgive us should prod us to extend mercy freely to those who have hurt us.

"And be kind to one another, tenderhearted, forgiving one another, even as God in Christ forgave you" (Ephesians 4:32).

Keep Your Eyes on the Target
Matthew 5:8

"Blessed are the pure in heart, for they shall see God."

What is purity of heart?

Positional purity comes when we fully trust in Christ for the forgiveness of sins; our hearts are then purified by faith (Acts 15:9; Hebrews 10:2; 1 Peter 1:22). As we confess our transgressions daily and ask for God's pardon through Christ, we are cleansed from the stain of sin (though not delivered from its indwelling presence) and thus authorized to enter into the presence of a holy God (Hebrews 9:14; 1 John 1:7, 9).

Practical purity is an ongoing, life-long process of purging our hearts from sinful affections and pursuing that holiness without which no one can see God (Hebrews 12:14). As pilgrims progressing towards their heavenly home, the pure in heart do not burn with anger (5:22); lust after the other sex (5:28); hope to replace one spouse with another (5:32); or plot revenge (5:39). Aware of their own faults, they do not hold grudges or trust in their own righteousness (5:6, 14–15; 7:1–6).

Purity of heart makes war on all hypocrisy or outward piety that looks to be seen (6:1–2, 5, 16). Rather than being obsessed with money, food, and clothing, the pure in heart seek first the kingdom of God and His righteousness (6:19–33). Meditating upon their returning Savior, they seek to be pure, just as He is pure (1 John 3:3)

They turn their eyes from the cares and idols of this life, fixing their focus instead upon God's love (5:45); future justice (6:4, 6, 18); and fatherly care for them (6:7–8, 32). They ponder the words of Christ so much that obedience follows (7:24). In joy and sorrow, plenty and want, they turn to God in prayer (6:9–13). All this they do only by the sanctifying power of the Holy Spirit (Romans 8:13; 1 Peter 1:2), who is given generously to all who continue to trust in Christ (John 7:39; Galatians 3:5; Titus 3:5–6), as they meditate constantly upon the Word of God (Psalm 119:9, 11; 1:2; John 8:32; 15:7).

Because they fix their eyes upon God, even in this life the pure in heart catch glimpses of Him. With the eyes of faith, they "see" His pardon and mercy; His generous provision and protection; His power and His presence.

This practical purity will in this life always be only *partial* purity.

The day will come, however, when we shall "see Him as He is," in the "dazzling brilliance of the beatific vision" which has been the longing and the hope of all the saints throughout the ages (1 John 3:2; D.A. Carson).

How to Be a Peacemaker Part–1
Matthew 5:9

"Blessed are the peacemakers, for they shall be called sons of God."

Becoming a peacemaker requires, first, certain *attitudes*. Jesus described these in the Beatitudes which precede this one:

Poverty of spirit: If we recognize that we have no inherent righteousness or virtue, then we shall approach others with humility, relying only on God to change them and bring reconciliation.

Mourning for sin: Those who are sorry and sad for their own faults and failings, and who weep for the effects of sin upon others, will communicate sympathy and understanding. This will gain them a hearing.

Meekness: The arrogant and assertive rarely succeed in making peace. The humble, quiet, patient person will be more likely to have a positive impact. Trusting in God rather than in himself, he will not seek to assert his rights but to see God's will done.

Hunger and thirst for righteousness: A clear passion for justice and what is right will more often gain respect and cooperation. If, on the other hand, we insist on our own rights or seek some advantage for ourselves or another party, reconciliation will elude us.

The King's New Law

Compassion and mercy: No one who condemns or criticizes others can expect to conquer resentment, bitterness, and conflict. Only those who are aware of how much they have been forgiven by God will be able to persuade others to pardon their enemies.

Purity of heart: Motives are crucial. If we seek our own advantage—power, or prestige, or possessions, or pleasure—others will not listen to us or accept our attempts to make peace. If we are pursuing only the kingdom of God, we shall see more clearly and speak more persuasively.

How to Be a Peacemaker Part–2
Matthew 5:9

"Blessed are the peacemakers, for they shall be called sons of God."

We have seen that peacemakers must have certain *attitudes*. Now let us look at the *actions* of peacemakers towards those who have done them harm:

Forsaking anger: Jesus taught that anger can be as serious an offense as murder (5:21–22). Those who desire peace will eradicate anger from their hearts by forgiving those who have hurt them (6:12, 14–15).

Taking the initiative: The Lord commanded that we go to anyone who has anything against us and seek reconciliation right away, even before we come to worship (5:23–25). We are not to wait for him to come to us.

Refusing to fight: It takes two to quarrel. Disciples of Christ should be willing to suffer personal wrong rather than retaliate (5:38–39).

Going the extra mile: Not only should we recoil from revenge; we should accede to the demands of those who would exploit us and give them even more than they seek (5:40–42).

Loving our enemies: These actions should flow from a heart of love (5:43–48). Love will lead us to bless those who curse us, do good to those who hate us, and pray for those who exploit and even persecute us.

Reforming ourselves: Outrage towards another for his wrongdoing should be turned into introspection to see how we have been guilty of a similar, or even the same, offense (7:1–6). Only then shall we see clearly enough to rebuke the one who has hurt us.

Praying for God to act: Of course, we cannot do any of this without God's intervention in our lives. Nor can we hope to influence others by our own example or exhortations unless God works in their hearts. Jesus therefore commands us to "Ask" (or, in the Greek, "Keep on asking"). And He promises that if we do so, we shall receive (7:7–12).

How to Be a Peacemaker Part–3
Matthew 5:9

"Blessed are *the peacemakers, for they shall be called sons of God."*

We cannot avoid conflict and hurt, but we can seek to conquer bitterness and estrangement.

When someone offends us, what should we do?

After checking our attitudes and beginning to act as Jesus commanded in the Sermon on the Mount, we need to go to the person with whom we are angry in honest confrontation.

Speaking through Moses, God said, "You shall not hate your brother in your heart. You shall surely rebuke your neighbor .... You shall not ...bear any grudge against the children of your people, but you shall love your neighbor as yourself: I *am* the LORD" (Leviticus 19:17–18).

Paul reflected this approach when he taught (quoting Psalm 4:4), "'Be angry, and do not sin': do not let the sun go down on your wrath" (Ephesians 4:26).

In other words, we must not bury our anger in our heart, where it will become a grudge, then bitterness, then hatred. When we cannot get over an offense through prayer and self-examination, then we must speak frankly with the one who offended us. To speak is to love; to keep silent is to foster enmity.

Here we need to avoid two errors. On the one hand, we should not go to anyone else (as we often do!). No, as Jesus taught in another place, "... if your brother sins against you, go and tell him his fault between you and him alone" (18:15). If he will not hear us, then we should

The King's New Law

take one or two others with us to try to become reconciled with him. Under no circumstances should we first slander him behind his back.

The other thing to avoid is pride. "If a man is overtaken [caught] in any trespass, you who *are* spiritual restore such a one in a spirit of gentleness, considering yourself lest you also be tempted" (Galatians 6:1). In our rebuke, we need to speak with humility, knowing that we, too, have offended God countless times.

If we only followed these simple guidelines, how much heartache could be prevented!

Jesus the Peacemaker
Matthew 5:9

"Blessed are the peacemakers, for they shall be called sons of God."

The reason why peacemakers will be called sons of God is that their attitudes and actions resemble those of the Son of God, Jesus. Their lifestyle declares that they have a living relationship with the ultimate Peacemaker, in whose steps they follow. They resemble their heavenly Father, who sent Jesus to make peace.

How did Jesus bring peace on earth (Luke 2:14)?

> He delivered people from the torment of disease. His ministry of healing brought relief and comfort to those afflicted with leprosy, lameness, blindness, fever, bleeding, and a host of other ailments, including death on a few occasions.

> He rescued people from the domination of demons.

> He formed a new fellowship of people of all sorts, who found in Him a kind of peace with others that was new in the world.

> He proclaimed the forgiveness of sins with all the authority of God Himself. Indeed, this was His greatest act of reconciliation, for it broke down the wall separating us from God and abolished the enmity between us and our Maker and Judge.

When the disciples of Christ demonstrate practical kindness; forgive their enemies; and pass on the Good News of peace with God through faith in Jesus, they show that they are "sons of God."

The Price of Peace
Matthew 5:9

"Blessed are the peacemakers, for they shall be called sons of God."

What does peace cost?

Local governments spend a great deal of money to maintain peace and safety in the community. The amount expended on national defense to prevent war is incalculable.

What does personal peace cost?

We must first try to estimate what it cost Jesus to bring about reconciliation between God and sinful humanity.

First, He had to become a man. That required emptying Himself of some of His divine privileges and glory in order to come to this earth in human form. Born of a woman, He lived among sinful men and women as an ordinary citizen of Roman-occupied Palestine.

After He began preaching, He endured constant criticism and opposition. His enemies dogged His steps, always looking for a chance to capture and kill Him. He was daily reviled by wicked, corrupt men. Even His family did not understand or support Him in His mission.

Becoming a man was not enough, however. The core of His mission was to die as a sacrifice for the sins of others, so that they could have peace with God.

At the end, He was betrayed by one of His inner circle, arrested, denied by His closest friend, and handed over to an incredibly cruel death. On the Cross, as the blood dripped from excruciatingly painful wounds in His hands and feet, He heard the mockery and scorn of the crowd.

Worst of all—far more agonizing than anything He had already suffered—was the utter desolation He felt when His own Father hid His face and poured out the divine wrath upon Jesus, who absorbed the fury of a Holy God so that we might know His favor as our Father.

That is what it cost Jesus to bring us peace with God and with each other, now and forever.

Should we be surprised if following in His steps in order to make peace should carry a price tag?

Salt and Light
Matthew 5:13–14

"You are the salt of the earth... You are the light of the world."

Salt and light—two indispensable elements of life.

Salt preserves from decay and corruption, and it adds flavor to foods. Before refrigeration, its use was mandatory to prevent spoilage of meat. Light provides illumination so that we can see clearly. Without it, we stumble in the darkness.

This world needs both. Without the presence and consistent followers of Christ, the natural tendency of men towards moral corruption will go unchecked, as a visit to any society where Christians are few will confirm.

Without the light which believers in Christ bring by their good works and true words, the deception and delusion found everywhere will only deepen into deadly darkness. We have seen this in America as the witness of Christians has grown progressively weaker in recent decades.

Jesus, therefore, reminded His disciples that salt is worthless if it loses its distinctive savor. In itself, salt cannot change its properties, but the kind used in ancient Palestine included other elements that could degenerate and rob it of its saltiness. Then people cast it onto footpaths to prevent plants from growing there. Likewise, light is no use if a basket covers the lamp.

God has set His people in this world as a "city that is set on a hill" which cannot be hidden (5:14). People know who they are, and watch constantly to see how they behave.

The Father's intention is to use His children to retard the decay of society and to provide light to expose sin and to point the way to righteousness.

Believers in Christ, therefore, cannot withdraw from the world in some "holy huddle." Nor can they hope to disguise their faith from others. The question is: Will we be known for our distinctive, God-centered lifestyle, or will we be just like everyone around us?

The way we spend our time, use our money, and react to success and failure will send a message to the world. Do we really believe that this life is not the end, and that our true reward comes later? Do we live for the now, or for eternity? Do we seek first God's kingdom and His righteousness, or are we caught up in the worship of Mammon?

How blessed are those Christians whose lives proclaim their true loyalty to God! They will make a positive impact on society and thus bring honor to their Father.

Whose Glory?
Matthew 5:16

"Let your light so shine before men, that they may see your good works and glorify your Father in heaven."

We do everything for a purpose. One common goal is to make ourselves look good. We act in order to impress others. In Jesus' words, we "receive honor [glory] from one another…" (John 5:44).

That is why many religious—and even most non-religious—people do charitable deeds "to be seen" by other people (6:1). Jesus rebukes that type of behavior and urges His disciples to help others in secret, so that only God will see.

Does that conflict with His teaching that we should do good works so that others will glorify God? No!

God alone deserves glory. As creator, sustainer, and judge of this world, He expects us to give all honor and praise to Him. Instead, says Paul, men "did not glorify *Him* as God, nor were thankful" and "worshiped and served the creature rather than the Creator" (Romans 1:21, 25).

As the *Westminster Catechism* rightly says, "The chief end [goal] of man is to glorify God and enjoy Him forever." One way we do that is by performing works that reflect the character and will of God. That is what Jesus did when He healed the sick, who—along with the crowds—almost always responded by praising God (9:8; etc.).

Another way is to do our good works "so that"—or, "in such a way that" God the Father is glorified. In other words, we imitate the goodness of God in our conduct in such a manner that those around us end up praising Him.

We do not have to be rude and refuse all appropriate compliments, but we should receive praise humbly and, when possible, give direct glory to our Father.

That means that we shall have to let them know that we trust in God as our "Father in heaven" through Jesus His Son. We must also speak and act in such a way that we refer all praise to God. When the crowds thought that the apostles had worked a miracle by their own power, they were quick to give all the credit to God (Acts 3:12–13; 14:8–18).

Finally, when we serve our Lord, we must either speak His words or rely on His strength, "that in all things God may be glorified through Jesus Christ, to whom belong the glory and the dominion forever and ever. Amen." (1 Peter 4:10–11).

Jesus and the Old Testament
Matthew 5:17

"Do not think that I came to destroy the Law or the Prophets. I did not come to destroy but to fulfill."

Since Jesus' own day, many have believed the He stood in opposition to the Hebrew Bible—the "Law and the Prophets." His teaching in the rest of the Sermon on the Mount, with its "antithesis"—"You have heard that it was said to those of old .... But I say to you..." (5:21–22); His violation of the complex rules which the Pharisees had added to the command to observe the Sabbath; His apparent disregard for some regulations regarding ritual purity—all have led people to think that Jesus came to abolish the Old Testament.

But He did not. Instead, He came to "fulfill" every single word contained in the Scriptures. By His blameless life He fulfilled all the demands of the Law; by His death on behalf of sinners He satisfied the penalty prescribed by God for sin.

When He offered Himself on the Cross as a sacrifice, He fulfilled all the purpose of the entire sacrificial system, namely, to bring sinful men into fellowship with a holy God. He was the temple of God, for the Lord dwelt in Him fully; He was the "Lamb of God" (John 1:29) who took away the sin of the world; He was the High Priest as He offered Himself as a perfect sacrifice, good for all time.

All prophecies and predictions found their fulfillment in Him, too. His powerful ministry of healing; His command over the wind and the waves; His resurrection from the dead; His declaration that all authority in heaven and on earth have been given to Him (28:18)—these declare Him to be the promised King, the Son of David.

Prophets had told of a time when God would establish a New Covenant with His people. He would give them a new heart and place His own Spirit within them, so that they could begin to obey His laws. When Jesus poured out His own Spirit upon the believers at Pentecost, this New Covenant power transformed their lives. The Spirit has been changing those who "hunger and thirst for righteousness" (5:6) ever since.

Some promises remain to be fulfilled, of course. We shall not see Jesus reign visibly on earth in all His royal splendor until He returns to judge the living and the dead and to establish a New Heaven and a New Earth.

Until then, we honor the Old Testament as He did. Though we are freed from the Mosaic Law as law, we receive all the Hebrew Bible as the words of God, and we seek to follow the example of Him who clarified its great commandments to love God and to love our neighbor as ourselves. Most of all, we place our trust in the Word of God, who became a man that we might know the God whose Spirit inspired all the prophets of old.

Practice What You Preach!
Matthew 5:19

"Whoever therefore breaks one of the least of these commandments, and teaches men so, shall be called least in the kingdom of heaven; but whoever does and teaches them, he shall be called great in the kingdom of heaven."

With these words, Jesus teaches several powerful truths:

Practice precedes preaching: Unless we "walk the walk," we should not try to "talk the talk." That does not mean sinless perfection, but a sustained effort to know and to do God's will with a humble heart.

Greatness consists in goodness: Not prestige, or power, or position, or possessions, but consistent discipleship, will earn one the title of "great in the kingdom of heaven." How many seek success, but not sanctification!

The "Old Testament" continues to be relevant: "These commandments" probably refers to the teaching of the entire Old Testament ("the Law or the Prophets" referred to in 5:17), as fulfilled and interpreted by Jesus. Though we do not have to observe aspects of the Mosaic Covenant that were abrogated by the teaching and saving work of Christ, we are to honor the whole Bible as God's Word, and follow the principles revealed in the Old Testament, as well as the precepts in it which are confirmed by Christ and the Apostles. Likewise, we are to believe its history and its prophetic promises.

"Little" things matter: We have no authority to decide which of God's commands carries more weight than others. Each one claims our total obedience and our attention in teaching others. Resentment, greed, and a bad temper incur as much guilt as murder and adultery and theft, and our speech should reflect "the whole counsel of God" (Matthew 28:20; Acts 20:27).

Doers must be teachers, too: It is not enough simply to honor the commandments of God. We must also seek to instruct others. All of our words should be for the purpose of bringing others to Christ, or building them up in Christ (Matthew 12:37; Colossians 4:5–6; Ephesians 4:25, 29).

May God give us grace, forgiving our sins and filling us with the Spirit of holiness!

An "Impossible" Standard
Matthew 5:20

"For I say to you, that unless your righteousness exceeds the righteousness of the scribes and Pharisees, you will by no means enter the kingdom of heaven."

The Pharisees were known as the most "righteous" people of their time, but Jesus tells His disciples that their righteousness must surpass that of these noted teachers of the Law.

In the rest of the Sermon on the Mount, and later in Matthew's Gospel, we find an explanation for this requirement.

To enter the kingdom of heaven, our righteousness must be:

Inner as well as outer. Not just murder and adultery, but resentment and lust, must be banished from our hearts; divorce is not an option, nor is remarriage after divorce (5:21–32).

Positive as well as negative. It is not enough not to lie under oath; we must not swear oaths at all. "Just" retaliation is ruled out, and must be replaced by generosity (5:33–42).

Extended to the "good" and the "bad." We are to love not only our neighbor, but our enemy as well, just as God has loved us (5:43–48).

Hidden from others. Public practice of piety will bring the praises of men, but God will only reward religious acts done in secret and for His approval (6:1–18).

Focused on God and not on this world. We are to seek first His kingdom and righteousness, not material wealth or even security (6:19–34).

To enter the kingdom of heaven, we must do the will of God the Father (7:21).

But no one can measure up to this standard! That is why Jesus tells us that "unless you are converted and become as little children, you will by no means enter the kingdom of heaven" (18:3).

In other words, as He said to Nicodemus, a member of the Jewish ruling class, "You must be born again" (John 3:3, 5, 7).

Or, as Paul wrote, we must trust in Christ, so that we might have the "righteousness which is from God by faith" (Philippians 3:9).

Only then will our "righteousness" exceed that of the Pharisees; only thus shall we enter into the eternal kingdom of God.

Murder in the Cathedral
Matthew 5:21–22

"You have heard that it was said to those of old, 'You shall not murder...' But I say to you that whoever is angry with his brother without a cause shall be in danger of the judgment. And whoever says to his brother, 'Raca,' shall be in danger of the council. But whoever says, 'You fool!' shall be in danger of hell fire."

Most of us do not commit murder. But we allow anger and resentment to fester in our hearts. Our spite and bitterness then find expression in words of contempt and curse.

Jesus knew the source of murder, and exposed the sin in all of us. Our hearts, which are supposed to welcome the Lord as King and Savior, harbor instead the hatred that we feel towards those who offend us. Rather than being the scene of worship and adoration, our inner being plays host to malice and malignant intent.

In other words, though murder does not take place in the marketplace outside, it occurs in the sanctuary of our souls.

Jesus not only traces the trail of homicide into the recesses of our mind. He also follows the steps of the convicted criminal to the courtroom and then to the courtyard, where the firing squad stands ready to execute the guilty. They cock and aim their rifles, awaiting the command to fire.

But wait! A message from the King! "Don't shoot! My Son will take the place of the convicted killer." The crowd which had gathered for the execution parts as the Prince strides forward to the stake. The soldiers cannot believe their eyes. Yet they must obey this order from the King.

A few of the Prince's companions carry away the body with sobs of grief. The quiet multitude returns home in disbelief. What kind of King would allow His own Son to die so that a wicked murderer could go free? What would move a Prince to forsake the royal palace for a punishment He did not deserve?

The Process of Peace
Matthew 5:23–24

"Therefore if you bring our gift to the altar, and there remember that your brother has something against you, leave your gift there before the altar, and go your way. First be reconciled to your brother, and then come and offer your gift."

After warning us of the eternal consequences of resentment, Jesus instructs us in how to be reconciled with someone whom we have offended.

Notice carefully: Jesus does not tell us how to deal with someone who has offended us (that will come later, in 18:15–20). No, His concern here is with those whom we have hurt.

Why? Is it because He wants us to protect others from the deadly effects of anger against *us*? Knowing how dangerous it is for someone to harbor resentment, we should place their spiritual welfare ahead of our own. Therefore, before we worship God, we must do what we can to become reconciled with those who are upset with us, so that *they* might be reconciled to the Lord!

Jesus has taken the command, "You shall not murder" to a new depth. Not only are we not to hate others, or harm them by word or deed, but we are to seek to rescue them from the peril of hating or hurting us!

In other words, we must seek the spiritual health of others, even before our own enjoyment of worship towards God.

When we consider that someone may have something against us because we treated them badly, and that we probably offended them because we did not love them enough to be kind and gentle, then Jesus is here commanding us to pursue people whom we do not really like with an active love that will stop at nothing less than reconciliation.

Of course, the Lord would not tell us to do something that was bad for us. In the last two verses of this paragraph (5:25–26), He warns that unless we do make friends with our adversaries (those whom we have angered), then they will probably pursue us with hatred until they have harmed us as much as possible.

Can you imagine how much better this world would be if we all followed the teachings of Jesus?

Does Hell Exist?
Matthew 5:22

"But whoever says, 'You fool!' shall be in danger of hell fire."

Though many religions believe that there is a place of punishment after this life, most people today do not think that there is a hell. They use that word only to curse someone or to describe a particularly unpleasant experience in this life.

Christians will turn to the Bible for the answer to this question. They will especially want to know what Jesus said about hell.

He promised great "reward in heaven" for those who are persecuted for His sake (5:11–12). He warned that no one whose righteousness does not surpass that of the religious leaders of His day would "enter the kingdom of heaven" (5:20).

But He also said that some people would go to hell. Today's text declares that those who curse someone are liable to the "hell of fire" (literally). "Hell" translates a word which referred to a garbage dump outside of Jerusalem that burned continually, and which had come to represent the place of punishment after death in Jewish speech.

Jesus further taught that "If your right eye causes you to sin, pluck it out and cast *it* from you; for it is more profitable for you that one of your members perish, than for your whole body to be cast into hell" (5:29). As if for emphasis, He repeated that warning about the whole body going into hell in the very next sentence.

He spoke of one who could "destroy both soul and body in hell" (10:28), and implied clearly that the religious leaders of His time would not "escape the condemnation of hell" (23:33).

Changing the metaphor, Jesus also warned of an "outer darkness" where there will be "weeping and gnashing of teeth" (8:12; 25:30).

Clearly, Jesus believed in a hell. It is a "place" of judgment, fire, and unutterable sorrow. Anything—even losing an eye or a hand—is better than being cast into such a condition of torment. No one is to be feared more than the one who has authority to consign people to that punishment (10:28).

At the end of the Sermon on the Mount, the Lord urges His hearers to strive to "enter by the narrow gate; for wide *is* the gate and broad *is* the way that leads to destruction, and there are many who go in by it.

Because narrow *is* the gate and difficult *is* the way which leads to life, and there are few who find it" (7:13–14).

May we all heed these words of the Son of God!

The Sanctity of Sex
Matthew 5:27–28 Part–1

"You have heard that it was said to those of old, "You shall not commit adultery." But I say to you that whoever looks at a woman to lust for her has already committed adultery with her in his heart."

To understand Jesus' teaching about sexual sin, we must first consider what the Bible says about sex and marriage. For that, we shall turn to the opening chapters of the Bible:

On the sixth day of creation, "God said, 'Let Us make man in Our image, according to Our likeness…' So God created man in His *own* image; in the image of God He created him; male and female He created them.… Therefore a man shall leave his father and mother and be joined to his wife, and they shall become one flesh" (Genesis 1:26–27; 2:24).

In some way that we cannot fully understand, God is both one and more than one; that is why He can say, "Let *Us* create man in O*ur* image." This unity/plurality is evident even in the first chapter of Genesis. For example, the Hebrew word translated "God" is a plural form, but it takes a singular verb (such as "created" in Genesis 1:1). Likewise, the Spirit of God and the Word of God both appear in the process of creation (Genesis 1:2–3).

In the New Testament, these hints of a unity and plurality in God become the clear statements that God is Father, Son, and Holy Spirit—one God, yet somehow three.

Likewise, man is both one and more than one, man and woman in one unity called "man." Thus, it seems that part of the image or likeness of God is our unity and plurality.

We are two—male and female, man and woman—and yet we are one "man." In marriage, this unity becomes visible: "The two shall become one flesh." Marriage, therefore, and especially sexual relations within marriage, reflects the image of God in man.

The King's New Law

Furthermore, in many passages in the Bible, God is pleased to refer to Himself as husband of His people (the classic text is Ephesians 5:22–33, but there are more). That is another reason why marriage is central to God's plan for the world, and why sex within marriage receives so much emphasis in God's Word.

In short, sex is sacred because it expresses and strengthens the unity of two persons created in the image of God, who is Himself both one and more than one. And sex is sacred because marriage itself is sacred.

The Purposes of Sex
Matthew 5:27 Part–2

"You shall not commit adultery."

We have seen that sex within marriage is sacred. Now let us look at some of the purposes for which God has bestowed the gift of marriage upon men and women:

To reflect the unity and plurality within God Himself, especially as the "two ... become one flesh" (19:5).

To mirror the relationship of Christ with His people, through the loving leadership and sacrificial service of the husband and the submissive subordination of the wife (Ephesians 5:22–33).

To provide intense pleasure and mutual delight (Genesis 2:23; Song of Solomon).

To glorify our Father in heaven through the procreation of godly children, who bring great joy to their parents as they as they grow up to walk in the truth (Genesis 1:28; Proverbs 15:20; Malachi 2:15; 3 John 4).

To afford intimate personal knowledge of another human being created in the image of God (Genesis 4:1).

To train His people in love and service in an atmosphere of forgiveness and forbearance (Ephesians 4:1–3, 32; 5:1–2, 21–33).

To provide a haven for other pilgrims and a home for the church (Romans 16:5; 1 Timothy 3:2; Titus 1:8).

To train leaders for the church of Christ (1 Timothy 3:5, 12).

To protect us against sexual temptation by giving a legitimate outlet for sexual desires (Proverbs 5:15–23; 1 Corinthians 7:2).

Clearly, such a precious gift must be cherished and carefully guarded!

The Power of Sex
Matthew 5:27 Part-3

"You shall not commit adultery."

No one needs to be reminded that the mutual attraction of men and women for each other contains great power, both for good and for ill.

Between husband and wife, it can:

> Cause a man "to leave his father and mother and be joined to his wife," thus dissolving what was previously his closest human bond and creating a new, even more intimate one (Genesis 2:24).
>
> Create great energy and joy (Psalm 19:5; Isaiah 62:5).
>
> Bring new life into the world.
>
> Inspire great sacrifices, which point towards the sacrifice of Christ for His church (Ephesians 5:25).
>
> Fill the world with poetry and song (Song of Solomon; Psalm 45).

Outside of marriage, however, the destructive power of sexuality can lead to:

> Jealousy (Proverbs 6:34; 27:4).
>
> Violence (Genesis 19:5–8; Proverbs 6:33).
>
> Disgrace (Proverbs 6:33).
>
> Shame (Proverbs 5:12–14).
>
> Deadly disease (Proverbs 5:11; Romans 1:27).
>
> Ruin of relationships (2 Samuel 11:2–5; 2 Samuel 13:1–20).
>
> Physical death (Proverbs 2:18; 5:4; 7:22–23).
>
> Spiritual death (Proverbs 6:32; Matthew 5:29–30).

We can understand why the Apostle Paul wrote, "Flee sexual immorality.... glorify God in your body, and in your spirit, which are God's" (1 Corinthians 6:18, 20).

The Perversions of Sex
Matthew 5:27 Part–4

"You shall not commit adultery."

God has given men and women a strong attraction for each other. This desire exceeds almost all others that we have, and can lead either to great joy or bitter sorrow.

Since the fall of man, we have struggled with evil urges that threaten to bring us mental, physical, and spiritual ruin. These passions are not only powerful, but deceptive. They cloud our minds and make us blind to reality, including the truth about sex and its purposes.

As a result, we allow ourselves to be seduced into unlawful activity, and often we do not know that we are violating the will of our Creator. To be very clear, the Scriptures plainly tell us what attitudes and activities count as perversions of God's intention for sexuality:

> Lust, and therefore anything that incites us to evil desires, such as immodest clothing or lascivious behavior (5:28).
>
> Premarital sexual relations (fornication) (Exodus 22:16–17; Leviticus 19:20; Deuteronomy 22:13–21).
>
> Marital infidelity (adultery) (5:27).
>
> Divorce (5:31–32).
>
> Remarriage after divorce (Matthew 5:31–32; Mark 10:11–12; Luke 16:18; Romans 7:1–3).
>
> Incest (Leviticus 18:1–18).
>
> Homosexual activity (Leviticus 18:22; Romans 1:26–27; 1 Corinthians 6:9).
>
> Bestiality (Exodus 22:19; Leviticus 18:23).
>
> Rape (Deuteronomy 22:25–27).

May God give us grace to live according to His will, and may He forgive our transgressions against His holy laws!

The Power for Purity
Matthew 5:29–30

"If your right eye causes you to sin, pluck it out and cast it from you.... And if your right hand causes you to sin, cut it off and cast it from you; for it is more profitable for you that one of your members perish, than for your whole body to be cast into hell."

God requires purity of heart in order for us to be saved and thus to see Him (5:8). But our hearts rebel against His laws and wander away in idolatry, covetousness, and lust. The penalty for persistent indulgence in lust is eternal hell, as Jesus teaches here.

What can we do to avoid condemnation? More importantly, how can we please our God and fulfill His holy purposes in our lives? Where can we find power for purity?

First and foremost, we must admit our spiritual poverty, mourn over our inherent rebellion, meekly submit ourselves to God's will, and "hunger and thirst for righteousness" (5:3–6). In other words, we must desire holiness and hate sin so much that we will do anything, pay any price, to pursue purity.

Then we need to focus our attention on God's Word rather than on the world. "How can a young man cleanse his way? By taking heed according to Your word.... Your word I have hidden in my heart, that I might not sin against You" (Psalm 119:9, 11).

As we meditate upon God's truth in the Scriptures, we should pray for God to "create in [us] a clean heart ... and renew a steadfast spirit within [us]" (Psalm 51:10). Self-control comes from the work of the Spirit in our lives, and we can ask for this miracle, trusting God to demonstrate His power and pity by transforming us (Galatians 3:5; 5:19, 22–23).

Of course, we cannot hope to break free from lust unless we avoid all occasions of temptation. The father (representing God) in Proverbs warns his son to "remove your way far from her [the seductive woman] and do not go near the door of her house" (Proverbs 5:8). Movies, TV programs, videos; people, places, activities—whatever tempts us to lust must be avoided at all costs.

Finally, we can find strength in the prayers of a spiritual partner of the same sex. "Bear one another's burdens," advises Paul, who almost

The King's New Law

always had one or more brothers with him to strengthen him (Galatians 6:2). Praying for each other and holding each other accountable will enable us to stand firm.

If we do fall, then we need to confess our sins to God, who "is faithful and just to forgive us *our* sins and to cleanse us from all unrighteousness [i.e., guilt]." "The blood of Jesus Christ His Son cleanses us from all [the guilt of] sin" (1 John 1:9, 7).

Defeating Divorce Part–1
Matthew 5:31–32

"Furthermore it has been said, 'Whoever divorces his wife, let him give her a certificate of divorce.' But I say to you that whoever divorces his wife for any reason except sexual immorality [lit. fornication] causes her to commit adultery; and whoever marries a woman who is divorced commits adultery."

As in our own time, so in Jesus' day, divorce was rampant. Among Jews, the only question was, For what cause could a man put away his wife? (See 19:3.) But Jesus had an entirely different approach.

He acknowledged that God had instructed Moses to regulate divorce in order to protect the rejected woman and to preserve the sanctity of marriage (Deuteronomy 24:1–4). But He insisted the divorce was not God's original intent (19:8).

Here, He states two things quite plainly:

> There is only one legitimate ground for divorce, and that is "fornication." Scholars have debated the meaning of the word translated here as "fornication." Some believe it means any sort of sexual sin, including marital infidelity. Though that is sometimes the word's meaning in Paul and other writers, Matthew *always* distinguishes "adultery"—sexual sin committed by married people—from "fornication." The best interpretation seems to be that fornication refers to premarital sexual sin. Joseph, for example, was about to break his engagement with Mary when he discovered she was pregnant (1:18–19). Since an engagement was considered binding, breaking it was equivalent to divorce. Thus, according to Jesus, only premarital sexual sin, discovered after

engagement, makes divorce legitimate.

After divorce there can be no remarriage. Though in this passage only the husband is prohibited from marrying a divorced woman, Mark records Jesus' words; "… if a woman divorces her husband and marries another, she commits adultery" (Mark 10:12). To emphasize this point, Jesus repeats His prohibition of divorce and remarriage in Matthew 19:4–9, and both Mark (10:5–12) and Luke (16:18) record His teaching on the subject.

May God give us grace to ponder the words of our Lord very carefully.[*]

Defeating Divorce Part–2
Matthew 5:32

"But I say to you that whoever divorces his wife for any reason except sexual immorality [fornication] causes her to commit adultery; and whoever marries a woman who is divorced commits adultery."

From the context of this saying, we find insight into the causes and nature of divorce.

Those who initiate divorce have forgotten to be poor in spirit; they do not mourn over their own sins; they are not meek, submitting their happiness to the will of God and accepting His providence in their lives; they do not hunger and thirst for righteousness; nor do they show mercy towards their spouse; they have allowed their heart to be filled with impure thoughts; they do not seek to be peacemakers; they are not willing to suffer for the sake of doing what is right; and they are not looking for a heavenly reward—they want happiness now (5:3–12).

Divorce arises when we do not focus our thoughts upon the abiding law of God (5:17–20); when we do not seek reconciliation with those whom we have offended (5:21–26); and, often, when we have allowed ourselves to long for someone else (5:27–30).

Divorce, like murder and adultery, starts in the heart. Indeed, it is essentially a sin of the heart, as Jesus teaches when He explains that

---

[*] For more on this, see the two articles on divorce and remarriage at chinainst.org. (Go to "More Information: Christianity.")

the regulations for divorce in the Old Testament were given "because of the hardness of your hearts" (19:8). In the Bible hardness of heart almost always leads to eternal separation from God (Romans 2:5).

When we are willing to break a solemn promise (5:33–37); refuse to turn the other cheek to those who "strike" us (5:38–42); will not love our enemies, as God has loved us, His enemies (5:43–48); fail to pray (6:9–13); run after material wealth rather than seeking God's kingdom (6:19–34); judge others without looking carefully at our own faults (7:1–6)—then we shall be powerless to resist the urge to gratify our own lusts and inflict irreparable harm on our spouse by seeking divorce.

Indeed, divorce usually begins before marriage, with the assumption that it is better to get than to give; better to be served than to serve; better to seek the pleasures of this world than to pursue holiness and the kingdom of God; better to follow our own ways rather than the will of God.

At the root, the impulse to divorce issues from unbelief. We do not trust that God's ways are right, or that His will is good for our lives. We do not believe that His grace is sufficient for us, or that His power will transform all who continue to trust in the one who raised Jesus from the dead (Ephesians 1:19–21).

Defeating Divorce Part–3
Matthew 5:32

"But I say to you, whoever divorces his wife…; and whoever marries a woman who is divorced commits adultery."

Looking more closely at the immediate context of Jesus' words, we see that divorce moves in two directions: Away from our current marriage, and towards another, "better," one. Even if they have no one else in mind, most who divorce do so with the expectation of remarriage to someone more suitable.

Let us look at the first direction: Those who contemplate divorce want to distance themselves from their current spouse. They look for the death of the marriage. In fact, they may long for the death of their mate! Sometimes that desire manifests itself in fantasy ("If my husband died, then I could remarry…"), and sometimes in an exaggerated fear ("I'm so afraid he is going to die of a heart attack!").

Usually, there are two reasons why we might want our marriage to dissolve: *denial* and *damage*.

When our spouse denies us something we think we need, then we become very angry. We may perceive this as hurt, but it quickly turns to resentment, even bitterness. Just as murder issues from the heart (5:21–22), so the urge to kill our marriage comes from deep dissatisfaction.

If a wife does not receive affection, or attention, or care, or provision, or leadership from her husband, she will lose heart. After a long period of unmet expectations, she loses hope. Along the way, she has lost whatever love she may have initially had for him.

The husband goes through a similar process if his wife denies him sexual satisfaction, either by withholding herself or by becoming unattractive to him. Men desire respect and admiration almost as much as they do sex. If she also does not afford him companionship or support in his work, and if she neglects her domestic duties, resentment and bitterness will build in his heart, too.

If *damage* is added to denial, then the reaction will be even worse. Utter abandonment (perhaps through irresponsibility) and outright meanness (in words or deeds) will crush a woman's spirit and cause her to want to run away. Likewise, criticism and contempt will so enrage a man that he will distance himself as much as possible from his wife.

The remedy? Jesus told us to pursue reconciliation (5:23–26; 18:15–16). He taught us to turn the other cheek (5:38–42), and to love our "enemies," blessing them, doing good to them, and praying for them (5:43–48). Above all, He commanded us to forgive, just as God has forgiven us (6:12, 14–15).

Defeating Divorce Part–4
Matthew 5:31–32

"Whoever divorces his wife...; and whoever marries a woman who is divorced commits adultery."

Divorce moves in two directions, as we have seen: *Away* from the current spouse, and *towards* someone else who seems better. People contemplating divorce long for the *death* of their marriage and are filled with *desire* for another, "better," one.

Not all those who want to dissolve their marriage have an alternate lover, though many do. Others entertain fantasies of someone more loving, caring, attractive, and desirable. In either case, they are victims of self-deceit (and maybe actual deceit by the new lover).

They vainly believe that they made a mistake with the first partner, and that there is another person more suited for them. They consider only the attractive qualities of their real or imagined future spouse. Just as they did when in love the first time, they imagine that they have found the right person, one who will make them happy. They overlook the faults and failings of the prospective replacement for their now-unattractive spouse.

What they forget is that romantic love is based on an illusion. Charm and beauty in a woman lead a man to believe that she is good and kind and sweet, and will be cooperative. Kindness, attentiveness, and competence in a man create the conviction in a woman that he will love her as her current husband does not. Or, if the new man lives only in her mind, she fantasizes life with someone who does not exist, and could not.

The brutal fact is that we are all sinners! We are self-centered, proud, lazy, lustful, and consumed with our own covetous cravings. These selfish desires hinder—or prevent—us from loving another as we should (Galatians 5:16–21). Thus, both we and anyone we marry will struggle with constant conflict. It does not matter who lives with us, for two sinners in one house will inevitably collide.

That is perhaps one reason Jesus spoke of divorce after He taught that adultery proceeds from lust in the heart (5:27–30). He knew that only contentment with God's provision, including our current mate, will enable us to love the person in front of us and avoid illusory alternatives.

The remedy? To focus on our own faults, not those of our spouse (7:1–6). To pray for God to change both us and them (6:9–13; 7:7–12). To hunger and thirst for righteousness, not earthly "happiness" (5:6; 6:33). To trust God as our heavenly Father, who will provide all we really need (6:8).

Defeating Divorce Part–5
Matthew 5:31–32

"Whoever divorces his wife ... causes her to commit adultery; and whoever marries a woman who is divorced commits adultery."

If divorce is not an option, what does God want us to do with an unhappy marriage? Does He just want us to suffer without relief? Is He cruel and sadistic? Does He not want us to be happy in this life?

Let us return to basics. God has created us to know and love Him. Our purpose in this life is to live for His glory, especially the glory of His grace (Ephesians 1:6, 12). He does not intend for us to enjoy a pain-free existence on this earth, but allows us to suffer in many ways.

We may have a bodily illness, as Paul's "thorn in the flesh" may have been (2 Corinthians 12:7). Sooner or later, "all who desire to live godly in Christ Jesus will suffer persecution" (2 Timothy 3:12). We may have to watch loved ones fall ill and die.

And we may just face constant frustration in relationships, including marriage, because we live in a world that has been "subjected to futility [frustration]" because of the Fall (Romans 8:20).

God has many purposes for suffering. These include refining our faith and exposing its genuineness (1 Peter 1:6–7). Perhaps He wants to round out our faith, by causing us to trust Him in new ways, or maybe He intends to make us more patient (James 1:2–4).

Since we are still burdened with what Paul calls the "flesh," we wrestle with evil passions and desires. Usually, we are unaware of these, but a close relationship like marriage, in which our wants conflict with those of another, brings them out. Only then can we see just how sinful we are.

Remember that God's ultimate goal is to make us holy, as He is holy (Ephesians 1:4; 1 Peter 1:16). He will use any means to accomplish this end. Because of the deceptiveness of the heart, we do not recognize our inner idols until someone deprives us of them. God liberates us from bondage to false "gods" by bringing our idolatry to light so that we can repent, receive forgiveness, and be transformed.

Above all, our Lord has called us to follow in the footsteps of Jesus, who suffered innocently (1 Peter 2:21). How can we demonstrate the unconditional love of Christ to others unless we are forced to love the unlovely, even when it hurts? Marriage offers us the ideal opportunity to imitate our suffering Savior!

Reliable Speech
Matthew 5:33–37

"Again you have heard that it was said to those of old, 'You shall not swear falsely, but shall perform your oaths to the Lord.' ... But let your 'Yes' be 'Yes,' and your 'No,' 'No.' For whatever is more than these is from the evil one."

Jesus continues His authoritative interpretation of God's moral law by forbidding all unreliable and unnecessary speech.

First, he counters the current silly practice of swearing an oath by heaven or earth, Jerusalem, or even one's head—all in an effort to avoid using God's name in vain (5:34–36) or promising to give something to God, and then not fulfilling that obligation (see Leviticus 19:12; Numbers 30:2; Deuteronomy 23:21, 23).

Our Lord goes further than that, however.

He also forbids all frivolous oaths; then all superfluous ones. "Let your 'Yes' be 'Yes.'" That is enough.

Some Christians believe that Jesus here prohibits us from taking an oath in court, or even making a marriage vow, but most interpreters think that Jesus means only to emphasize the necessity of saying only what we mean and know to be true.

Our words should be trustworthy.

When we sign the tax return, it should be fair and accurate.

When we endorse a check, there should be money in the bank.

When we put our name to a credit card bill, we should be able to pay it.

When we promise to do something, we should fulfill our promise. Our commitments should come from a sober sense of what we can actually perform.

That includes marriage vows, which are solemn pledges made before God in the presence of human witnesses.

In fact, it encompasses all our speech: Everything we say should be fully accurate and trustworthy. No more, no less.

May God give us grace to avoid making commitments that we cannot keep, and to speak only what we know to be true!

Words that Count
Matthew 5:37

"But let your 'Yes' be 'Yes,' and your 'No,' 'No.' For whatever is more than these is from the evil one."

Jesus had told His disciples not to swear oaths falsely and not to swear frivolously, by invoking heaven, earth, Jerusalem, or one's own head, as contemporaries did.

With these two principles, He puts boundaries on the use of our tongues.

On the one hand, we are to avoid falsehood and speak only the truth. As an extreme case, He forbids us to make an affirmation that we know is false. By extension, He forbids also breaking promises we have made.

In other words, our words must be reliable. They must be true and trustworthy. If we state something, it should be accurate. If we make a commitment, we should honor it.

Followers of Jesus will keep their marriage vows. They will swear to their own hurt and not change (Psalm 15:4). They will not renege on a contract. They will not undertake obligations lightly, but they will fulfill those they do undertake.

On the other hand—and as a condition for keeping our word—we are to avoid unnecessary speech.

Jesus' brother James, whose short letter often echoes the Sermon on the Mount, admonished, "... let every man be swift to hear, slow to speak, slow to wrath" (James 1:19), and pointed out the evils caused by an unbridled tongue. Indeed, he says that "If anyone among you thinks he is religious, and does not bridle his tongue but deceives his own heart, this one's religion *is* useless" (James 1:26).

Paul urged the Ephesian Christians, "Let no corrupt word proceed out of your mouth, but what is good for necessary edification [building others up], that it may impart grace to the hearers" (Ephesians 4:29). He also warned against the dangers of coarse jesting (Ephesians 5:4).

Nine hundred years earlier, King Solomon had advised, "Let your words be few" (Ecclesiastes 5:2). More pointedly, he observed that "a fool ... multiplies words" (Ecclesiastes 10:14); "... He who has knowledge spares his words .... Do you see a man hasty in his words? *There is* more hope for a fool than for him" (Proverbs 17:27; 29:20).

In sum: Avoid false and frivolous speech, and we shall avoid a great deal of folly.

The Other Cheek, The Second Mile
Matthew 5:38–42

"You have heard that it was said, 'An eye for an eye and a tooth for a tooth.' But I tell you not to resist an evil person. But whoever slaps you on the right cheek, turn the other to him also.... Give to him who asks you and from him who wants to borrow from you do not turn away."

Jesus' teaching runs counter to every impulse in the sinful human heart! Before we reject His words as totally unrealistic for life in our world, we need to try to understand what He meant.

The Lord does not here address the questions of war and peace, nor is He denying the authority of the state to punish evildoers. Both Jesus and His apostles always upheld the police powers of those in authority (22:21; John 19:11; 1 Peter 2:13–14).

Nor is Jesus telling us to give in to persistent and dangerous physical abuse in the home, or to encourage begging on the street.

No. Jesus here confronts our tendency to exact revenge. The original law of retribution (*lex talionis*) in the Old Testament forbade inflicting more damage than one had suffered (Exodus 21:24). But Jesus goes further: He forbids His disciples from taking any revenge at all for personal insult and injury.

A slap on the face hurts, and usually constitutes an insult. Turn the other cheek! Someone takes your possessions; do not go to law about it. If he infringes upon your liberty, give more than he demands. Freely give to those who ask.

Imagine what would happen if we actually lived this way! Street violence would drop; divorce rates would plummet; family feuds would disappear; thousands of tort lawyers would have their income radically—and rightly!—reduced.

It is not a matter of overlooking insult and injury while you seethe inwardly, waiting for the time when you can repay the one who hurt you.

No! Jesus would have us "overcome evil with good," and not be overcome by evil, or by our response to it (Romans 12:21). He wants us to be free from resentment, the lust for revenge, and the tyranny of insisting upon our own petty rights.

In other words, He is saying, "Follow Me!"

Who is the Real "Enemy"?
Matthew 5:44–45 Part–1

"But I say to you, love your enemies, bless those who curse you, do good to those who hate you, and pray for those who spitefully use you and persecute you, that you may be sons of your Father in heaven; for He makes His sun rise on the evil and on the good, and sends rain on the just and on the unjust."

Jesus' words strike to the core of our hearts. He exposes our inability to love the unlovely, much less to love those who hate us or hurt us. In the previous verses, He told His disciples not to resist one who is evil. Now He demands something even harder: An active attitude of kindness for those who are mean or uncaring towards us.

His reason? That we may be like our Father in heaven, who bestows earthly benefits on "good" and "bad" people alike. If we think about it, God has treated us the way Jesus tells us to treat others: "... when we were enemies we were reconciled to God through the death of His Son" (Romans 5:10). How can we do less for others?

Perhaps more than any other command, this requirement that we love those who do not love us, or who do not treat us well, demonstrates just why we needed Christ to die for us. More than that, our ongoing difficulty in loving the unlovely proves how much we stand in need of daily forgiveness by God.

How do we usually respond to those who do not love us? By withdrawal, coldness, anger, bitterness, resentment. Does this not reveal the essential lack of love in our own hearts? Does that not disqualify us from a critical attitude towards our "enemies"?

Notice the application of this teaching to marriage and family relationships. So often, we are disappointed and hurt when those closest to us do not satisfy our desires for affection and care. But then our response puts us into the same category! In fact, perhaps they are not as good to us as we would like partly because we have in some way also disappointed them?

Jesus will not let us linger in the realm of self-pity; He absolutely forbids self-righteousness. He will have our full obedience, preceded by our humble admission that we, too, are "enemies" who desperately need His constant love.

My Enemy—My Friend
Matthew 5:44 Part–2

"But I say to you, love your enemies..."

Actually, my "enemy" is my friend. Think about it:

When someone mistreats me, my reaction reveals the state of my heart. All too often, I respond with anger. If my anger were only outrage because God's holiness had been violated, there would be no sin. Usually, however, other forces are at work, such as pride, selfishness, fear, self-protection, ambition, passion, and the like. Had my goals not been blocked or my idols assaulted, I would not have known how much I love this world and how little I love God and the people He has put around me.

Christ the King

With the motives of my heart thus unveiled, I see my sin more clearly. My conscience rebukes me, the Spirit of God convicts me of wrong, and I fly once more to Christ for mercy. A deeper awareness of my spiritual poverty and perilous position before God impels me to the throne of grace, where I discover more of God's forgiveness than I had known before.

Contemplating both God's command that I love my "enemy," and my utter inability to obey, I ask for divine assistance. Little by little—and sometimes all at once—God's mighty Spirit transforms the beast inside me into something less wild and wicked, something with a bit more patience, kindness, and forbearance. God thus demonstrates His immense power to change sinners, and receives even more praise.

Then again, my "enemy," by taking away what I hold dear or preventing me from gaining something I cherish, gives me an opportunity to loosen my grip on what is visible, and pursue what is invisible. His unjust action forces me to seek first the kingdom of God and His righteousness, for I can no longer find satisfaction in anything else.

Just as I cannot know how much the things of this world imprison me until I am deprived of what I so fervently desire, so I can only discover the riches of God's goodness and abundance when I pursue Him with the intensity of a starving beggar. "Rich" men do not "need" God; they are full and satisfied. Only the "poor" seek—and find!—Him in all His wealth of wisdom, power, and love. By making me "poor," my enemy has opened the door for me to enter the treasury of the Lord.

Large portions of the Bible are now illuminated to me. The Psalms, with their urgent cries for deliverance; the history of the early church and the epistles of the Apostles; but most of all, the Passion narratives at the end of each Gospel. Of course, there is no way that I can feel what Jesus felt in front of the jealous Jewish leaders, with His friends in fearful flight. The distance between His deity and my humanity, and His purity and my perversity, prevent me from tasting the bitterness of the cup He drank on the Cross.

Nevertheless, without intending to, the person who hurts me, even hates me, has brought me into a closer, richer, and everlasting communion with Christ.

Thus, my enemy is my best earthly friend.

What is "Love"?
Matthew 5:44–45 Part-3

"But I say to you, love your enemies…"

When Jesus tells us to love our enemies, what does He mean?

Ordinarily, we think that "love" means to feel affection and admiration for others whom we consider lovable or attractive; it feels good to be with them. They treat us well, so we reciprocate, with pleasure.

Notice how Jesus describes love in this passage, however. He calls upon us to bless those who curse us; do good to those how hate us; and pray for those who spitefully use us and even persecute us. In the following verses, He reminds us that God sends sunlight and rain upon the evil and the good, the just and the unjust alike (5:45).

In other words, Jesus here defines love as action, not attitude. To bless them—to speak kindly to them; to do good; to pray. Elsewhere, He will emphasize the necessity of inner forgiveness towards those who have mistreated us (6:14–15; 18:35), but here, when ordering us to "love" our enemies, He concentrates upon our words towards them; our deeds to them; and our prayers for them.

Does this not place Jesus' imperative more within our reach? At the moment, He is not commanding us to enjoy, to admire, or to feel good about hateful people. No, He is only asking us to treat them kindly, despite their meanness toward us.

Of course, this is already far too difficult for most people. We usually find it nearly impossible to return cursing with blessing; harm with help; persecution with prayer. Still, we should note that Jesus is not asking us to pretend to have warm feelings towards those who have treated us with coldness or even cruelty. He is only requiring us to be kind.

As we shall see in the next verses, He points us to the example of God the Father, which reminds us that He has treated us, His former enemies, with infinite kindness and mercy.

Imitating God's Love
Matthew 5:46–48

"For if you love those who love you, what reward have you? Do not even the tax collectors do the same? And if you greet your brethren only, what do you do more than others? Do not even the tax collectors [some manuscripts read "Gentiles"] do so? Therefore you shall be perfect, just as your Father in heaven is perfect."

Jesus concludes His teaching on love for our enemies by calling us to the highest possible standard: God's own "perfect" love. He had already spoken of God's utter fairness in the dispensing of earthly blessings, since He sends sunlight and rain to both the evil and the good, the just and the unjust.

Now Jesus gets to the heart of the matter. Why do we "love"—think or act kindly toward—others? Generally, because we receive, or hope to receive, some benefit from them. We love those who love us, that is, who are good to us. We love those who are friendly to us. In short, we love those who are lovable. This sort of love is natural and unforced; it is a response to love that has been given us.

What happens, however, when we encounter unkindness, abuse, even hatred? We respond with anger, leading to withdrawal or even hostility. Is this not why so many marriages fall apart? The person who once was so attractive to us now seems like an enemy. What has happened? Our spouse has failed to return our love, or perhaps has acted selfishly, thoughtlessly, even with meanness toward us.

Our "natural" response at that point, as we have seen, is to respond in a similar way.

But Jesus expects something better from His disciples: They are to be "perfect" like their heavenly Father. What does this mean? Not that we can, in this life, attain moral perfection. He has already made that clear in the previous sections of the sermon, and the Lord's Prayer will remind us that we need daily to ask forgiveness for our sins (5:3, 6, 7, 21–30; 6:12).

No, Jesus commands only that we should love all people, even the unlovely, just as God our Father distributes His blessings to all. Indeed, if they pay attention, Jesus' hearers will realize, if they have not already, that they are "evil" and the "unjust," upon whom God has

The King's New Law

bestowed manifold mercies. Our love is only a reflection of His, and a response to it.

In that sense, we can be "perfect"—that is, complete in our love for others—in this life, but only as we rely entirely on the power of God's Spirit dwelling in us, and only as we meditate constantly upon God's manifold mercies to us. Final and full moral purity will come when Christ returns to raise us up to glory, but only then. Indeed, Jesus' command to be "perfect" constitutes an implied promise for those who hunger and thirst for righteousness (6:5; Romans 8:29–30; Ephesians 1:4; 1 John 3:2).

Christ the King

6 The King Points Us to His Father

Secret Service
Matthew 6:1–4

"Take heed that you do not do your charitable deeds before men, to be seen by them. Otherwise you have no reward from your Father in heaven."

Now Jesus turns from misinterpretations of the Law of God by the scribes and the Pharisees to hypocritical practices of which they were guilty. His goal: To explain what He meant when He said, "Unless your righteousness exceeds that of the scribes and Pharisees, you will by no means enter the kingdom of heaven" (5:20).

Unlike hypocrites in every age, followers of Christ must not practice their piety before men, in order to be seen by them. Instead, they must seek the favor of God alone.

Jesus assumes that we will do good deeds, works of charity that provide practical help to others in need. We shall read later that He counseled the rich young ruler to sell all his possessions and give them to the poor (19:21). He told a powerful parable about the final judgment, when we shall be evaluated according to whether we provided our fellow Christians with food, drink, shelter, clothing, and visits to the sick and imprisoned (25:34–40).

But we absolutely must not offer any service in order to show off; we must not seek to impress others with our goodness. Only God must know what we have done for others. Indeed, we should be so unselfconscious about our good deeds that our left hand must not know what the right hand is doing! Unlike the self-promoting religious leaders of Jesus' day—and countless others since them—we must eschew any attempt to seek the praise of men. If we do, then their approval is all we shall reap as a reward.

On the contrary, Jesus commands us to serve in secret, where only the omniscient God can see what we are doing. To that command our Lord adds a promise, "And your Father who sees in secret will Himself reward you openly" (6:3; see also 16:27, Romans 2:5–11, Galatians 6:6–8, Ephesians 6:8, Psalm 62:12).

That reward will come on the last day, when charitable Christians will receive everlasting life as their recompense, and will hear their Master say, "Well *done*, good and faithful servant" (25:23). Is that not reward enough?

Jesus Prayed
Matthew 6:5

"And when you pray…"

Jesus assumed that His disciples would draw near to God in prayer. He did not debate such issues as why we should pray if God knows everything, or tell us why God sometimes does not give us what we want. He simply taught His people how to pray.

He also set us an example. Though He was the eternal Son of God, equal with the Father in power and glory, yet as a man He humbly offered His requests to God. In other words, He practiced what He preached about prayer.

He did not pray so that others could see, but withdrew to the wilderness or some other deserted place. Sometimes, He prayed at night, presumably to have privacy. Nor did He multiply needless words. In the Garden of Gethsemane, when facing His greatest trial, He simply asked to be kept from suffering God's wrath if that were possible, but otherwise that God's will be done (26:39, 42).

Jesus prayed for himself, and He prayed for others, but He prayed particularly for God's name to be glorified (John 12:28).

Jesus prayed before He chose His twelve disciples. He prayed that the Father would raise Lazarus from the dead. He requested protection from total apostasy for Peter. In His great "Highly Priestly Prayer" recoded in John 17, He asked the Father to keep the disciples from the Evil One; give them unity; sanctify them by His word; and bring them into glory.

He prayed with great intensity, especially on that last dreadful night when He knew He had been betrayed and would soon face the hatred of His enemies. The agony of His intercessions brought blood out through His pores. This was no parlor game; it was spiritual warfare with a deadly foe. That is why He "offered up prayers and supplications, with vehement cries and tears…" (Hebrews 5:7)

The Father heard and answered the prayers of Jesus "because of His godly fear" (Hebrews 5:7). Not only all throughout His life (John 11:41–42), but also at the end. No, the cup of God's wrath did not pass from His lips. But God's will was accomplished: Jesus was granted strength to complete the work of salvation by going all the way up to the Cross and then staying there until He had fully satisfied the righteous anger of God against sinful men.

This Jesus is the same one who said, "when you pray." Jesus prayed. Let us follow in His steps to the quiet place where a gracious Father waits to meet a humble, trusting soul.

Why Pray?
Matthew 6:6 Part–1

"But you, when you pray, go into your room, and when you have shut your door, pray to your Father who is in the secret place; and your Father who sees in secret will reward you openly."

In one sentence, Jesus tells us why to pray: God will reward us. In other words those who pray to God receive some sort of benefits. The letter to the Hebrews puts it this way: "He who comes to God must believe that He is and that He is a rewarder of those who diligently seek Him" (Hebrews 11:6).

Does this mean that God always answers our prayers in the way that we would wish or expect? No! Paul prayed without success three times for his thorn in the flesh to be removed (2 Corinthians 12:8–9). James says we can fail to get what we request because we "ask amiss" (James 4:3).

Even Jesus' plea in the Garden of Gethsemane that "this cup pass" from Him was denied (26:39–44), though God granted His desire that "Your will be done."

Nevertheless, Jesus says, "Ask, and it will be given to you …. If you then, being evil, know how to give good gifts to your children, how much more will your Father who is in heaven give good things to those who ask Him!" (7:7, 11)

What kind of reward awaits those who pray?

First, God may give us what we ask, as Jesus said in the words quoted above. After all, why would He instruct His disciples in prayer, even telling them what sort of things to seek from God, if the Father had no intention of responding?

Second, the Lord may give us "exceedingly abundantly above all that we ask or think" (Ephesians 3:20), as He did for young King Solomon (1 Kings 3:5–13). Jesus not only healed a paralytic, but forgave his sins (9:2).

Third, our wise and loving Father may give us something other, but far better, than what we request. Though Paul's thorn was not removed, yet he received the promise of God's grace each day and the ongoing demonstration of God's power through his weakness (2 Corinthians 12:9–10). Jesus did not arrive in time to heal Lazarus, as his sisters desired, but waited until He could demonstrate His might by raising their brother from the dead (John 11:1–44).

Most of all, however, prayer brings us into communion with our God. We draw near to Him in prayer, by faith in His word. "Whom have I in heaven *but* You? And *there is* none upon earth *that* I desire besides You.... But *it is* good for me to draw near to God [or, "the nearness of God is my good"]" (Psalm 73:25, 28).

Through prayer we enjoy intimacy with God through Jesus Christ, by the Holy Spirit. What greater reward could there be?

Talking to Your Father
Matthew 6:6 Part–2

"Pray to your Father who is in the secret place; and your Father who sees in secret will reward you openly."

Followers of Jesus Christ have a unique privilege: They may know God as Father.

Though the Old Testament refers to God as the Father of Israel as a nation, almost nowhere do we find pre-Christian Jews referring to God as their own personal Father. When Jesus came, He brought with

The King Points Us to His Father

Him the revelation that the Maker of the universe, the Ruler of the kings of the earth, the Savior of His people, is a heavenly Father.

Jesus also told us what kind of Father our God has shown Himself to be:

"In secret": God is invisible. He is a Spirit, without a body. He cannot be known except by self-revelation. That is why reason and religion cannot lead us to God. He can only be known through His Word and Spirit as these come to us from God alone.

"In heaven": He is a transcendent God. Though we are made in His image, and thus like Him, in many ways, He far exceeds us even in those qualities which we share with Him, such as intelligence and goodness. He possesses infinite power, wisdom, and authority. He governs the world according to His own good purposes, with none to hinder Him. He dwells in unapproachable light, for He is righteous, holy, and pure.

All knowing: He knows what we need even before we ask. He also knows what is best for us, and how and when to grant what we need (6:8, 32).

Generous: Otherwise, why would Jesus say, "Your Father ... will reward you"? Later, He told the disciples that will "give good gifts to those who ask Him" (7:11). He seems to enjoy showering presents upon His children on earth. He gives "exceedingly abundantly above all that we ask or think, according to the power that works in us" (Ephesians 3:20).

To know this God as Father, through faith in Jesus His Son, is eternal life (John 17:3). To draw near to Him in open and unhindered communication is the greatest privilege on earth!

Whom Does God Reward?
Matthew 6:6 Part–3

"Your Father who sees in secret will reward you openly."

According to Jesus, those who perform good works in order to be seen by others, and thus to gain glory, will receive a reward. They get what they want: Glory from men. "They have their reward," Jesus wryly remarks. In other words, they have already gained what they sought, which is a good reputation on earth.

On the other hand, those who give to the poor or who pray to God in secret get a better reward. Since they are seeking only to please God, not men, they allow only Him to know what they are doing. In return, He will reward them.

He will answer their prayers and grant to them all that they really need. He will draw them ever deeper into intimate communion with Himself. He will give them peace of mind, since they know that He will take care of them. Finally, He will give them an inheritance in the eternal kingdom when Jesus returns to establish a new heaven and a new earth.

So, let us look deeper at these people whom God rewards.

They seek glory from God, not men. They are not looking for "face" or reputation among fellow sinners. They do not have their eyes focused on what is seen, but on Him who is unseen. They seek an eternal, rather than a temporary, happiness.

What drives them? How can they escape the constant pressure to please people and not God?

In one word, faith! They believe God's word, especially His promises. They trust that He will do what He has said He will for those who rely on Him alone. They believe that He is a rewarder of those who seek Him (Hebrews 11:6). They walk by faith, not by sight (2 Corinthians 5:7). They shut out the noises of this world and enter into their private place of quiet contemplation; there, they hear the still, small voice of God (1 Kings 19:12).

They are poor in spirit; they mourn their sins; they are meek before God, demanding nothing but His presence and favor; they hunger and thirst for righteousness. They trust not in themselves or in other finite and fallen creatures, but in the Creator, Sustainer, and Redeemer of the world.

They come to God empty handed, with nothing to offer but their poverty and their praise. They look to Him and to Him alone. As a handmaiden looks to her mistress, so they look to their God—for direction, provision, protection. They lean on Him, rely on Him, depend on Him, trust in Him.

These are the ones whom God richly rewards!

Brief History of Prayer
Matthew 6:7a

"And when you pray..."

Jesus assumed that His disciples would pray, because they were Jews. Ever since their great ancestor Abraham, the Hebrew people had learned to call upon their God for help in time of need.

Abraham prayed for the innocent people living in Sodom and Gomorrah (Genesis 18). His grandson Jacob begged for protection from his angry brother (Genesis 32:11). Faced with a daunting task, Gideon asked for guidance (Judges 6:22, 36–39). Barren Hannah asked for a child (1 Samuel 1:10).

King David responded to God's promise of an everlasting dynasty with thanksgiving and petition (2 Samuel 7). His son Solomon asked for wisdom, and received that plus long life and wealth (1 Kings 3:5–14). King Hezekiah received healing and extra years by simply asking God (2 Kings 20:1–8).

The list goes on and on. Repentant Manasseh and Jonah were delivered from the full penalty for their disobedience. Ezra and Nehemiah found wisdom, strength, protection, and provision to rebuild fallen Jerusalem. Daniel received supernatural revelation.

The Old Testament is filled with prayer, notably in the Psalms, but also throughout the length and breadth of the histories and prophets.

Why? Because God enjoys giving good gifts to His people. He knows what we need, but likes to have us ask Him for it anyway. Indeed, He commanded Israel to pray: "Call upon Me in the day of trouble; I will deliver you, and you shall glorify Me" (Psalm 50:15). God receives honor when we call upon Him to demonstrate His power and His pity. More glory comes to Him when we praise Him for His answers to our humble, believing requests.

No wonder Jesus assumed that His disciples would pray!

Whose Name?
Matthew 6:9

"Our Father in heaven, hallowed [sanctified, set apart, honored] be Your name."

For whose name do I live? Mine, mostly. From dawn to dusk, I labor that my name may be honored among men. I seek a good reputation. I hide my faults and highlight my virtues. I bristle with irritation when others even hint that I may be either incompetent or wrong.

But that way leads to frustration and ultimate failure, because I am both finite and fallen. Reality mocks my efforts to establish a name for myself.

There is a better way: To live for God's name. To seek His reputation, His honor, His glory, in all that we do.

After all He deserves praise and adoration. He does nothing wrong and all things right. He is great and He is good. His judgments are just and His mercy endless. He has created a stunningly beautiful and ordered world and given us the faculties to behold His power and wisdom in what He has made. The whole universe is full of His glory.

To live for Him, speak of Him, obey Him, follow Him, imitate Him—what a noble cause! What an energizing, unifying motive for all of life! What a way to joy and peace, without frustration, forever!

"Father in heaven, hallowed be Your name!"

What Is God's Will?
Matthew 6:10

"Your will be done, on earth as it is *in heaven."*

How can we know what God wants us to do? Are there any reliable clues to His will for our lives? Certainly! Here are a few basic ingredients:

> Suffering: "For to you it has been granted on behalf of Christ, not only to believe in Him, but also to suffer for His sake" (Philippians 1:29). "Therefore, since Christ suffered for us in the flesh, arm yourselves also with the same mind [purpose]" (1 Peter 4:1). Note:

The King Points Us to His Father

We are not to suffer for doing wrong, but for doing what is right (1 Peter 4:15–16).

Sacrifice: "I beseech you therefore, brethren, by the mercies of God, that you present your bodies a living sacrifice, holy, acceptable to God" (Romans 12:1).

Self-denial: "And he who does not take his cross and follow after Me is not worthy of Me" (10:38). "If any one desires to come after Me, let him deny himself, and take up his cross daily, and follow Me" (Luke 9:23).

Sanctification. "For this is the will of God, your sanctification: that you should abstain from sexual immorality" (1 Thessalonians 4:3). Any sex before or outside of marriage cannot be God's will for us, nor any intimate relationship with anyone other than one's spouse if we are married.

Service: "As each one has received a gift, minister it to one another, as good stewards of the manifold grace of God" (1 Peter 4:10). "Through love serve one another" (Galatians 5:13). "Let each of you look out not only for his own interests, but also for the interests of others" (Philippians 2:4).

Submission: "Therefore submit to God. Resist the devil and he will flee from you" (James 4:7). "Therefore humble yourselves under the mighty hand of God, that He may exalt you in due time, casting all your care upon Him, for He cares for you" (1 Peter 5:6–7).

Satisfaction: "In everything give thanks; for this is the will of God in Christ Jesus for you" (1 Thessalonians 5:18).

Now we see why Jesus told us to pray, "Your will be done," for none of these attitudes and actions come naturally to us. We need the grace of God to know and do His will.

Here also we have the perfect example, however. In the Garden of Gethsemane, facing such horrible physical, mental, and spiritual pain that we cannot even imagine, Jesus prayed, "Nevertheless, not as I will, but as You *will*" (26:39).

God heard His prayer, and He will hear ours, so let us pray daily, "Your will be done."

Asking for Bread
Matthew 6:11

"Give us this day our daily bread."

Jesus here teaches His disciples to ask their heavenly Father for all their material needs. Notice that:

> We are told to *pray* for what we need. That does not mean that we do not plan or work for the necessities of life. But we must not worry about them (as we so often do!). Jesus said, "… do not worry, saying, 'What shall we eat?' or 'What shall we drink?' or What shall we wear?'… But seek first the kingdom of God and His righteousness, and all these things shall be added to you" (6:31–33). Nor must we think that our efforts will automatically bring results. "Every good and every perfect gift is from above, and comes from the Father of lights…" (James 1:17).

> We are told to pray for "our *needs*, not our greeds" (D.A. Carson). Necessities, not luxuries. Bread, not champagne and caviar. God does not promise to provide the biggest house, newest car, most fashionable clothes, or most expensive vacations. "And having food and clothing, with these we shall be content. But those who desire to be rich fall into temptation and a snare, and *into* many foolish and harmful lusts which drown men in destruction and perdition" (1 Timothy 6:8–9).

> We are to ask for *daily* provision. "… do not worry about tomorrow, for tomorrow will worry about its own things. Sufficient for the day *is* its own trouble" (6:34). Like the Israelites in the wilderness, we must look for no more than what we require each day.

If we ask with this attitude, we can be sure that our Father, "who knows the things [we] have need of before [we] ask Him," will, like any good father, give us every "good gift" (7:11).

How to Receive Forgiveness
Matthew 6:12

"And forgive us our debts, as we forgive our debtors."

Having taught us how to ask for what usually most concerns us—our material needs—Jesus now shows us how to pray for what most concerns Him—our spiritual needs. After all, the angel said that Jesus came to "save His people from their sins" (1:21). Knowing that there is one "who who is able to destroy both soul and body in hell" (10:28), He tells us how to become reconciled with the Judge of all mankind.

For we have offended a holy God, and He has declared that "the soul who sins shall die" (Ezekiel 18:4). We owe Him a debt which we can never repay. Only if He forgives this debt can we escape eternal punishment.

But Jesus knew that He would pay that price; He would redeem His people by His own blood; He would satisfy God's righteous anger by offering Himself as a sacrifice for sin. Thus, He authorized His followers to approach God as Father, simply asking for pardon.

It is that simple! All we have to do is admit, and renounce, our sins (repent), and trust in Christ as the "Lamb of God who takes away the sin of the world" (John 1:29) (believe the Gospel), and we shall be saved from God's wrath.

How, then, should we pray for forgiveness?

> With humility, not trying to hold on to any shred of righteousness, for we have none (Romans 3:21–24; 7:18; Philippians 3:9).

> With childlike trust in God's promise. "If we confess our sins, He is faithful and just to forgive us our sins" (1 John 1:9).

> With charity towards those who have hurt us. Remember the clause, "As we forgive our debtors." God does not forgive us *because* we forgive others; His pardon comes without cost to us. But His mercy falls only upon those who realize their own sins and receive His grace. The sure sign of whether we have true repentance and faith is whether we can sincerely forgive those who have offended us.

"And be kind to one another, tender-hearted, forgiving one another, even as God in Christ forgave you" (Ephesians 4:32).

Temptation and Prayer
Matthew 6:13

"And do not lead us into temptation..."

Why does Jesus teach His disciples to pray like this?

Because He knows that Satan prowls around, "like a roaring lion, seeking whom he may devour" (1 Peter 5:8). Meanwhile, we are vulnerable to the enemy's wiles, because "the spirit indeed *is* willing, but the flesh *is* weak" (26:41) Indeed, in our flesh "nothing good dwells" (Romans 7:18).

Jesus knows, too, that "the Lord knows how to deliver the godly out of temptations" (2 Peter 2:9). We can "be strong in the Lord, and in the power of His might" (Ephesians 6:10)—but *only* in the Lord, not in ourselves. Thus, we pray for divine help.

What does Jesus teach them to pray? That we may not be led into temptation, as He was in the wilderness. He has borne the fury of Satan's attacks. He knows the subtle arguments which the devil uses to divert our eyes from God, disbelieve His Word, doubt His promises, and disobey His commands.

How does He want us to pray these words? With alertness: "Watch and pray, lest you enter into temptation," He warned His sleepy disciples in the Garden of Gethsemane (26:41). When we are hungry, as He was in the desert; or tired, as His followers were in the Garden, then we must be especially alert.

We need to be aware of our own particular, personal weaknesses, and to pray with special fervor when these appear. More than that, we must stand guard at all times, "because the days are evil" (Ephesians 5:16). No one enjoys immunity from Satan's wiles, not even the most mature believer. "Therefore let him who thinks he stands take heed lest he fall" (1 Corinthians 10:12).

Nor should we ask to be kept from temptation if we are rushing headlong into it! "Flee from idolatry;" "Flee sexual immorality" warns the Apostle (1 Corinthians 10:14; 6:18). Jesus Himself states the issue starkly: "If your right eye (or hand) causes you to sin, pluck it out (or cut it off) and cast *it* from you; for it is more profitable for you that one of your members perish, than for your whole body to be cast into hell" (5:29–30).

The King Points Us to His Father

Oh, may we learn to pray as Jesus did, with bloody sweat, that the Lord's will be done, and that we be delivered from temptation and sin!

Deliver Us from Evil
Matthew 6:13

"But deliver us from the evil one."

What is the evil from which we need deliverance? In Matthew's Gospel alone, we encounter wicked, murderous kings; illness of all sorts; demonic influence; and sin. Behind all these lurks Satan, who is called "the evil one."

Thus, it does not matter whether we translate the original Greek "from evil" or "from the evil one"—both are possible—because all evil is somehow related to sin, and all sin has some connection with Satan.

Why should we pray for deliverance? Because evil is bad! The Bible insists upon the radical distinction between good and evil; virtue and vice; light and darkness; life and death; God and Satan. With wickedness, there can be no truce, cease-fire, peace treaty, or even negotiations. Jesus came to "save His people from their sins," and to "destroy the works of the devil."

We ask God to save us from evil because we cannot save ourselves. Even with marvelous advances in medical science, illness often leads to disability and death. Tyrants still oppress and kill. And, despite the doubts of skeptical (and inexperienced) moderns, evil spirits still harass and even possess people. Worst of all, sin holds sway in our hearts unless and until Jesus comes to set us free.

We pray for liberation from evil because God can save! He made the world through His mighty Word, who became the God-man Jesus, the Christ. Jesus healed the sick and cast out demons. He defeated Satan on the Cross and rose victoriously to ascend to God's right hand, from whence He rules the entire universe for the sake of the church. Someday, He will return in glory and create a new heaven and a new earth, where righteousness dwells.

How, then, should we offer this prayer to God? With persistence, until He hears and answers. With faith, that He is both willing and able to save. With thanksgiving for past deliverances. And with praise, for the decisive victory in the war against evil has already been won at the Cross and the resurrection of Christ.

Fruitful Fasting
Matthew 6:16–18

"Moreover, when you fast, do not be like the hypocrites, with a sad countenance. For they disfigure their faces that they appear to men to be fasting. I say to you, they have their reward. But you, when you fast, anoint your head and wash your face, so that you do not appear to men to be fasting, but to your Father who is in the secret place; and your Father who sees in secret will reward you openly."

At least some Pharisees fasted twice a week, abstaining from food as a spiritual exercise (Luke 18:12). Moses and Elijah fasted for forty days; David, Daniel, Nehemiah and others fasted for shorter periods of time; and the whole nation was called to fast on the Day of Atonement (Exodus 34:28; 1 Kings 19:8; Daniel 10:2–3; Nehemiah 1:4; Leviticus 16:29–31).

Jesus fasted for forty days in the wilderness (4:1–2), and the Apostles sometimes fasted at critical times (Acts 13:2–3; 14:23). It seems that Jesus assumed His disciples would abstain from food for shorter or longer periods of time, as expressions of contrition, devotion to God, and waiting upon the Lord for guidance.

Throughout the centuries, some Christians have found fasting to be a helpful way to focus on God in prayer, and to discipline the body against sinful habits (see 1 Corinthians 9:24–27). At least in America today, such a practice might be one way to combat the epidemic of obesity!

But—and here is the main point of Jesus' teaching—we must never engage in any religious act in order to be seen by others or to gain their approval. As with charitable giving, our fasting must be done in secret, where only God sees. In other words, when you fast, don not tell anyone!

And, like giving to those in need, secret fasting will yield the fruit of God's attention and approval, and He will reward us for our self-denial. The results may be seen in greater victory over sin, but they will surely receive God's commendation and recompense on the last great day of judgment, when all those who love the Lord will receive an imperishable wreath of glory.

Only One Master
Matthew 6:19–24

"Do not lay up for yourselves treasures on earth ...; but lay up for yourselves treasures in heaven.... For where your treasure is, there your heart will be also.... You cannot serve God and mammon [money]."

Most of us spend our lives investing in this world's goods. All day long, we plan, work, and worry about getting enough possessions to live and even to live comfortably. In the process, we often neglect God and His kingdom.

Jesus shows us the folly of such shortsightedness. For one thing, all earthly treasures will either decay or be stolen from us. Furthermore, the pursuit of things steals our heart and blinds our eyes to spiritual realities. Finally, we end up in bondage to a master who cannot satisfy and who cannot save us from eternal death.

The alternative? Lay up treasures in heaven. But how? Jesus told the rich young ruler to "sell what you have and give to the poor ... and come, follow Me" (19:21). He instructed His disciples to care for the physical needs of other believers as if they were doing it to the Lord Himself (25:31–46).

Paul warned those who were rich not to be proud, "nor to trust in uncertain riches but in the living God .... *Let them* do good, that they be rich in good works, ready to give, willing to share, storing up for themselves a good foundation for the time to come..." (1 Timothy 6:17–19).

The way to avoid being obsessed by a passion for prosperity is to know that "we brought nothing into *this* world, *and it is* certain we can carry nothing out. And having food and clothing, with these we shall be content. But those who desire to be rich fall into temptation and a snare, and *into* many foolish and harmful lusts which drown men in destruction and perdition" (1 Timothy 6:7–9).

How, then, should we use our money? Give as much as possible to the work of the Gospel; relieve the needs of poor believers; care for our families; avoid extravagance and waste; invest wisely, not seeking quick or inordinate profits, but attempting to be wise managers of what God has given us.

Above all, we should "seek first the kingdom of God and His righteousness," knowing that "all these things [i.e., our daily needs] shall be added to" us in God's good time (6:33).

The bottom line: We must choose between two masters: God, or Mammon.

Mammon's Wages
Matthew 6:25

"Therefore I say to you, do not worry about your life, what you will eat or what you will drink; nor about your body, what you will put on."

When the Bible puts a "therefore" at the front of a sentence, we must ask, "Why? What does this sentence have to do with the previous words?"

In this case, the question is, What connection does the command not to worry have with the observation that "You cannot serve God and Mammon" (6:24)?

At the start of this section on our attitude towards earthly possessions, Jesus said, "Do not lay up for your selves treasures on earth..." (6:19) and then had given several reasons:

All earthly "treasures" will either rot or be stolen. They dominate our thoughts and thus our heart. Focusing on them will plunge us into darkness, leading us to make foolish decisions. In the end, we shall be slaves of the love of money, worshipers of Mammon. And Mammon pays bad wages!

"THEREFORE," continues Jesus, don not worry about material things. He will go on to add several more reasons not to be eaten by anxiety for the future, but the "therefore" should be enough to remind us that Mammon—money and what it can buy—does not deserve our loyalty, much less our love. This "god" is a useless idol, unable to help us, and fully capable of inflicting great harm upon his devotees.

We see, then, that we will worship and serve either God or Mammon. If we choose the latter course, we shall be plagued with worry every day of our lives, and Jesus wants to deliver us from such bondage.

Indeed, Jesus came to "save His people from their sins" (1:21). He opened the Sermon on the Mount with the so-called Beatitudes, which describe the truly happy, prosperous, "fortunate" person. God sent His Son so that we might have life, true life, abundant life, instead of the misery that imprisons all who are slaves to error and idolatry. Jesus came to set us free from worry and anxiety. Shall we not accept His invitation?

First Things First
Matthew 6:25

"Therefore I say to you, do not worry about your life, what you will eat or what you will drink .... Is not life more than food...?"

Notice the flow of Jesus' thought: First, He pronounced a blessing on those who "hunger and thirst for righteousness." Next, He told His disciples to ask their heavenly Father, "Give us this day our daily bread." Then He instructed them in fasting, which is one way of expressing our desire for spiritual nourishment. After warning against seeking this world's goods more than God, He now urges them not to worry about food and drink.

His reason? "Is not life more than food?" First and foremost, we should long for that which sustains our soul, desiring spiritual food for what does not perish more than physical food for our mortal body.

As Jesus told those whom He had fed by the side of the lake, we are not to be obsessed with getting "the food which perishes, but" aim first to acquire by faith "the food which endures to everlasting life, which the Son of Man will give" us (John 6:27).

Our current sinful body will die, but the soul will survive for eternity. The question is, In what state? Where? In hell, or in heaven? In outer darkness, or in everlasting light? Eternally alienated from God our Maker, or enjoying endless happiness with Him?

That is why Jesus warned His followers, not to "fear those who kill the body but cannot kill the soul. But rather fear Him who is able to destroy both soul and body in hell" (10:28).

Happiness comes from aiming at the right goals. Finding eternal life ought to be our highest priority. Everything else is secondary.

"Blessed are those who hunger and thirst for righteousness, for they shall be filled" (5:6). After all, "Is not life more than food?"

How Much Are You Worth?
Matthew 6:26

"Look at the birds of the air, for they neither sow nor reap nor gather into barns; yet your heavenly Father feeds them. Are you not of more value than they?"

But we still do need to eat in order to live. Jesus knows that, and so He points to the birds: "Look at the birds of the air ... your heavenly Father feeds them. Are you not of more value than they?"

In other words, if God provides for the little birds that fill the sky, He will certainly take care of His children—all those who trust in Him.

Does this mean we should, like the birds, "neither sow nor reap nor gather into barns?" Not at all. God expects us to work for our meals, just as the birds seek their food in various ways (see 2 Thessalonians 3:6–10). But we should not *worry* about having enough to eat. The contrast is not between activity and idleness, but between work and worry.

So, as we go about our daily tasks, we can do so with thanksgiving for all God has given us, and confidence that He will continue to meet our needs.

The King Points Us to His Father

Useless Worry
Matthew 6:31–32

"Therefore do not worry, saying, 'What shall we eat?' or 'What shall we drink?' or 'What shall be wear?' For after all these things the Gentiles seek. For your heavenly Father knows that you need all these things."

Jesus continues His argument against worry.

"Therefore" points to the reasons He has already given: If God takes care of the bird of the air, and clothes the grass of the field, will He not also provide for human beings created in His own image, who are of far greater value? Of course!

He repeats the warning against worrying about food and clothing, adding two more reasons:

First, "Gentiles"—that is, those who do not know God—are obsessed with these things. Around the world, in every culture, the pursuit of physical survival consumes the thought, time, and energy of almost everyone. They are all more or less "seeking" the things that make life possible. That is, putting food on the table and clothes on our body outranks all other goals in our list of priorities.

In some societies, like ours, people have gone beyond focusing on necessities to a passion for pleasure and self-indulgence. Who really needs a luxury car, the latest fashion-designed clothes, or a house filled with more rooms than they can use?

Jesus' second reason goes deeper: Our Father in heaven knows that we need food and clothing to survive. Here Jesus assumes the truth of what He said before, that God will take care of His children (6:26, 30). If an earthly father knows what his children need, he will do all he can to provide for them. *How much more* will our Father in heaven take care of us?

Jesus rebukes His followers for their "little faith" (6:30). Does that apply to us as well?

How much time and energy do we expend on figuring out ways to acquire material possessions? We need to work for a living, of course. That is part of being human. "If anyone will not work, neither shall he eat," warned Paul (2 Thessalonians 3:10). But Jesus is not talking about making legitimate efforts to care for our physical existence.

What He warns against is not work, but worry. Worry can literally make you sick. By not trusting in God to take care of us, we fall back upon our own limited resources. We think and act as if we are fatherless orphans, who must scrape and fight and scratch for every morsel we can find. That inner fear wears us out, and makes us loveless and joyless.

How much better to consider who we are: Not "Gentiles" without God, but beloved children of a gracious and generous heavenly Father, who not only knows what we need but holds in His omnipotent hand all the wealth required to provide for every one of His children.

First Things First
Matthew 6:33 Part–1

"But seek first the kingdom of God and His righteousness, and all these things shall be added to you."

Instead of focusing on bodily needs, Jesus commands us to set our hearts and minds on the kingdom and righteousness of God above all.

He had earlier told them to pray, "Your kingdom come" (6:10). The kingdom of God is His reign and rule over the universe, and especially over men and women. Our heart's desire should be for God to have His way in our lives and in the lives of others. That includes, of course, "Your will be done," as Christ prayed in the Garden of Gethsemane (26:42). More than anything else, we must long for God to exercise His sovereign sway.

His "righteousness" has been variously interpreted. Some think Jesus refers to the justice for all which God will bring on the last day, and for which we must work even now. Others believe that it means that righteousness which God confers by grace to all who trust in Christ for salvation. These are both true, of course.

Probably, however, the main meaning here is that personal righteousness—holiness, virtue—which Jesus had told His disciples must surpass even that of the Pharisees, as a requirement for entrance into God's kingdom (5:20).

The King Points Us to His Father

In any case, the Lord requires that we hunger and thirst for righteousness (5:6), even to the point of being willing to suffer for it (5:10). Nothing—not even an eye or a limb—must come before our pursuit of moral likeness to God Himself, who alone is fully righteous (5:29–30). Like Jesus Himself, we must be willing to forsake all to follow God's way, even if it leads to Golgotha (10:37–39).

After all, that is what Jesus meant when He said to the first disciples, "Follow Me" (4:19). He had Himself submitted to baptism by John in order to "fulfill all righteousness" (3:15), and He had refused to let Satan deflect Him from the path of obedience to God the Father (4:1–10). As the writer of the Letter to the Hebrews said, Jesus preferred to suffer rather than give in to temptation (Hebrews 2:18).

How about you? What is your main goal in life? To feed and fulfill yourself, or to follow in the steps of Him who sought, first and foremost, the kingdom of God and His righteousness?

Longing for the Kingdom
Matthew 6:33 Part-2

"But seek first the kingdom of God and His righteousness, and all these things shall be added to you."

What does it mean to seek first the kingdom of God?

We seek God's kingdom when we:

Listen to the voice of the King (Psalm 45:2).

Delight in the beauty of the King (Psalm 45:2).

Pray for the victory of the King (Psalm 45:3–5).

Praise the King at all times (Psalm 145:1–3).

Proclaim the mighty acts of the King and the glory of His kingdom (Psalm 145:4–7, 10–12).

Esteem the kingdom more highly than every other precious thing (13:44–46).

Obey all the commands of the King (7:24; 28:20).

Preach the Gospel of the kingdom to all nations (24:14; 28:18–20).

Long for the coming of the kingdom in all its fullness (6:10).

God's Righteousness
Matthew 6:33 Part–3

"But seek first the kingdom of God and His righteousness, and all these things shall be added to you."

We have seen that the righteousness of which Jesus here speaks refers to that practical obedience to His commands which our Lord said was necessary for admission to the kingdom (5:20). To seek for God's righteousness, therefore, is a necessary corollary of seeking His kingdom, for He is the righteous King who requires that His subjects obey and imitate their Ruler.

Earlier in the Sermon on the Mount, Jesus told His disciples what this sort of righteousness looks like:

Renouncing anger (5:21–26).

Making war on lust (5:27–30).

Remaining faithful to one marriage partner for life (5:31–32).

Avoiding impious and insincere oaths, and speaking simple truth (5:33–37).

Giving to the unworthy (5:38–42).

Loving the unlovely and the unloving (5:43–48).

Giving generously, but in secret, for God's eyes only (6:1–4).

Praying privately, in faith, to our Father in heaven (6:5–13).

Forgiving our enemies (6:14–15).

Fasting for God's pleasure alone (6:16–18).

Laying up treasures in heaven, not on earth (6:19–21).

Worshiping God, not Mammon [money] (6:22–24).

Forsaking all worry as we trust God to provide (6:25–32).

These are the things for which we should hunger and thirst every day (5:6).

Seeking God's Righteousness
Matthew 6:33 Part–4

"But seek first the kingdom of God and His righteousness, and all these things shall be added to you."

How, then, can we seek the righteousness of God? What practical steps do we take?

From the Gospel of Matthew, we see that those who desire to "fulfill all righteousness" will identify with sinners, as Jesus did at His baptism (3:15). With repentant hearts they will receive baptism (28:19). They will put their trust for salvation in Christ alone, who came to "give His life a ransom for many" (20:28).

Having been baptized, they will do their best to "observe all things that [He] has commanded" them to do (28:20). First, however, they will try to understand His will by listening to His words (7:24; 28:20). In imitation of Jesus Himself, they will study the Old Testament, that they may use its words to resist the temptations of Satan (4:4, 7, 10). Like the early disciples, they will attend to the teachings of Christ (5:2 ff.), and as did the believers after Pentecost, they will devote themselves to the instructions of the chosen Apostles (28:20; Acts 2:42).

But they will not be hearers of the Word only, but also doers, knowing that only those who hear and do are building upon a solid foundation (7:24–25). They will forsake all to follow Christ (4:19–23; 9:9).

In their fight against indwelling sin, they will spare no pain to gain the victory (5:29–30). Like their Lord, they will pray, "Your will be done," even if the answer to that prayer leads to Golgotha (6:10; 26:39, 42).

Knowing that they cannot follow Jesus alone, and that they have been called into a worldwide fellowship of disciples, they will join others in remembering the death of Christ (26:26–28). When they are rebuked by other believers for doing wrong, they will listen and change (18:15–17).

And at the end of the day, aware that they have failed to follow Christ as they should, they will pray, "Forgives us our debts [trespasses]" (6:12, 15).

While others are panting after possessions, prestige, position, and pleasure, they will be consumed by one pure and holy passion, to know and follow after Jesus Christ their Lord.

Christ the King

Impossible Standard?
Matthew 6:33 Part–5

"But seek first the kingdom of God and His righteousness, and all these things shall be added to you."

Jesus has told His disciples that their righteousness must exceed that of the scribes and the Pharisees if they want to enter the kingdom of heaven (5:20). In the Sermon on the Mount, He lays out the basic principles of this sort of righteousness, as we have seen.

Does He mean for His followers actually to attain to the necessary degree of righteous conduct that He has taught them? Scholars debate this question, and for good reason.

On the one hand, Matthew's Gospel contains many indications that there are some who can, even in this life, properly be called "righteous." Joseph was a righteous man (1:19), as was Abel (23:35). God sends rain on the righteous and the unrighteous (5:45).

Those who receive a righteous man will receive and appropriate reward (10:41). Though they may not be aware of what they are doing, followers of Christ who serve other believers will be called "righteous," and will later enter eternal life (25:46), where they will "shine forth as the sun in the kingdom of their Father" (13:43).

Likewise, Jesus refers often to "good" people who bring forth "good fruit" by doing "good works" (5:16, 45; 7:17–18; 12:35).

On the other hand, Jesus told the rich young ruler that "no one *is* good but One, *that is,* God" (19:17). He Himself came to "fulfill all righteousness" by being identified with sinners in His baptism (3:15). He taught His disciples to pray daily, "Forgive us our debts"—by which He meant our sins (6:12).

He came to "save His people from their sins" (1:21), not just by teaching, but by His death on the Cross as a "ransom for many" (20:28). His suffering and death, which Matthew uses two full chapters to narrate, inaugurated a new covenant by His blood, which was shed for "the remission of sins" (26:28).

Here, then, we see the "already" and the "not yet" of God's kingdom. Disciples of Christ are already children of God who, by God's power, can do good works and, to a significant degree "observe all" that Jesus has commanded us (28:20). On the other hand, we are still sinners in need of daily forgiveness. We are not yet fully obedient or

The King Points Us to His Father

righteous. We must wait until He returns before we "shine forth" like the sun.

That is why we must constantly seek the coming of the kingdom and the righteousness of God, trusting in Jesus to save us fully from our sins.

Christ the King

7 The King's Narrow Highway

Dealing with "Dogs" and "Pigs" Part–1
Matthew 7:1–12

"Judge [condemn] not, that you be not judged [condemned].... Therefore, whatever you want men to do to you, do also to them, for this is the law and the Prophets."

Though usually treated separately, these twelve verses all go together, and provide practical instruction on how to deal with difficult people.

What should I do when I notice that my "brother" has a fault?

First, I must not condemn him. I may "judge" that his action or attitude is wrong; this type of moral evaluation must be made by anyone with a conscience. But I may not play the role of God and consign him to punishment (unless I am an officer of the law confronting a criminal). That is, I must not assume a self-righteous, prideful posture towards the one whose actions I think wrong.

Otherwise, I shall have to face God's judgment. He will use the same standard to measure me that I use to measure others. Those around me may do the same, if they hear me criticizing someone.

So, before I say anything to my brother, I must examine myself, to see whether I, too, have a similar fault. In fact, I shall find that I am also guilty of failing to measure up to God's perfect standards. To my surprise, I will discover that I have a "plank" in my eye, compared to the little "speck" in my brother's eye.

Then, I need to get rid of the "plank" in my own eye, so that I can see clearly enough to help my brother get the "speck" out of his eye. How do I do that? By prayer! If I earnestly ask God to forgive me and to change me, as Jesus had taught His disciples earlier (6:12–13), He will surely answer me.

Dealing with "Dogs" and "Pigs" Part–2
Matthew 7:1–12

"Do not give what is holy to the dogs; nor cast your pearls before swine..."

These words are usually interpreted to mean that we should not share God's Word with people who do not want to listen. Other passages in the Bible do contain that wise counsel, but perhaps Jesus is saying something else here.

More likely, the Lord has seen into our self-righteous, critical heart when we observe someone with a fault that we do not like. We become proud and arrogant. We look down on the one who has offended our standards of right and wrong (or even of taste!). In our eyes, our brother seems contemptible, even despicable.

To the Jews of Jesus' day, pigs (swine) and dogs were loathsome. The Law of Moses forbade eating or raising pigs, and dogs were known only as slinking, skulking scavenger, not beloved pets.

With a kind of exaggeration often seen in the Sermon on the Mount, Jesus imagines that I am so disgusted with my brother that he seems almost like a pig or dog—ugly, gross, and low—in my eyes.

On the other hand, the advice, or even rebuke, that I have to offer is "holy" and precious. Holy, because I want to share my understanding of God's righteousness with him. Precious, because I consider my insights as "pearls of wisdom" for my benighted neighbor.

Always the insightful psychologist, Jesus shrewdly warns us against correcting an erring person with that kind of attitude. If I do not communicate respect for the person whom I hope to help improve, he will not only trample my "pearls of wisdom" under his feet (like a pig), but turn on me and bite me (like a dog). He will, in other words, act the way I think he his!

Better to keep silent for a while, except to pray to God for wisdom and grace to see my own "plank" and get it out of my eye!

Dealing with "Dogs" and "Pigs" Part–3
Matthew 7:1–12

"Ask, and it will be given to you... Therefore, whatever you want men to do to you, do also to them, for this is the law and the Prophets."

We have come now to the only effective way of dealing with difficult people, whose attitudes and actions seem wrong to us.

We have already seen that we should first examine ourselves and ask God to show us the more serious flaw of which we are probably guilty. Meanwhile, we should avoid criticizing our brother with a proud and condescending heart.

Instead, we should pray to God. Ask Him for insight into your own words and deeds. Beg Him to show you how you are guilty of an offense similar to (though perhaps not exactly the same as) the one you find so irritating in your neighbor. He will answer that prayer, and often quite quickly!

Once you have seen your own sin, beg for forgiveness and for God to transform you. Keep on asking, seeking, knocking, and the Lord will surely grant your request, though the process may take time.

Perhaps most of us find it almost impossible to believe that God would change us, or a person whom we consider unlovely, or the situation between us and that person. But Jesus has commanded us to love our enemies (5:44); surely we can trust the Father to enable us to fulfill His commands! Jesus has also reminded us that our Father is in heaven; the kingdom, power, and glory are His; He hears and answers prayer (6:6, 9, 13).

Now the Lord assures us of God's fatherly love towards all who trust in Christ, and reminds us that even human fathers, who are selfish, give good gifts to their children. How much more will our heavenly Father answer our prayers for wisdom, humility, patience, and love towards those who hurt us!

Reviewing this entire process, we find that it is just what we would want others to do with our faults. Do we respond well when people criticize us harshly, as if they had no faults of their own? No! Usually, we reject their exhortations and even respond with our own criticism of their behavior—just like "dogs" and "pigs"!

We would rather have others set us a good example and pray for us before they point out one of our flaws.

"Therefore, whatever you want men to do to you, do also to them, for this is the Law and the Prophets."

The Road Less Traveled
Matthew 7:13–14

"Enter by the narrow gate; for wide is *the gate and broad* is *the way that leads to destruction, and there are many who go in by it. Because narrow* is *the gate and difficult* is *the way which leads to life, and there are few who find it."*

As He begins the conclusion to the Sermon on the Mount, Jesus lays before His disciples—and before us—a stark choice.

There are two gates; two paths [ways]; and two destinations. Only two.

One gate opens wide, and leads to a broad, well-traveled road. You would meet most of your friends and co-workers on it, all heading in the same direction.

The other gate is narrow, and opens onto a difficult path, with few travelers. You might feel a bit lonely at times as you trudge along this upward journey.

The first road is easy to find, easy to follow. Just go with the crowd. The requirements are simple: Do what everyone else does, without questioning. Accept the current fads; follow the trends; repeat the slogans. Pursue personal happiness; acquire wealth; indulge your desires. Live for now, for self.

The second path, much harder to discern, also demands more. You will have to search diligently for it, and watch your step as you go. Pilgrims on this way listen to God's Word, not to the world. They refuse to be conformed to this age. Seeking first the kingdom of God and His righteousness, they deny themselves, seeking a future reward.

Those who enter the narrow gate commit themselves to humility; they are poor in spirit, mourning for their sins. Aware of their own shortcomings, they treat others with meekness and mercy. Because they hold to a strict standard—nothing less than the imitation of God—they are slow to pronounce judgment on people who rub them the wrong way. Instead, they pray for God to pity and transform both them and their neighbors.

Most of all, they trust not in their own goodness but in the grace of God, which they find daily in Jesus, the only Son of God.

This alternative route winds through many valleys, climbs steep mountains, and traverses difficult terrain. Dark forests and dusty deserts, filled with wild animals, will make you wonder whether you have gone astray. After an arduous journey, however, you will reach your destination: Eternal life with God and with His Son, Jesus, the Way, the Truth, and the Life.

The more popular path leads its many followers through popularity, pleasure, prestige, power, and possessions—for a while. Then suddenly the crowd turns a corner and falls off a cliff, plunging to an endless death.

Which way will you go?

Beware of False Prophets
Matthew 7:15–23

"Beware of false prophets, who come to you in sheep's clothing, but inwardly they are ravenous wolves. You will know them by their fruits.... Not everyone who says to Me, 'Lord, Lord,' shall enter the kingdom of heaven, but he who does the will of My Father in heaven."

After we enter the narrow gate and start on the difficult way, we need to choose our guides carefully. Many will seek to influence us. Some will appear to be sincere and orthodox, but will conceal their true false character.

So, we must not only listen to their words, but look at their works.

Even though they claim to speak God's Word, even to prophesy, we should not necessarily trust them. They might work miracles in the name of Jesus, but that does not prove them genuine, either.

How shall we tell the true from the false? Their "fruits"—their own conduct and the conduct of those who follow them.

Look first at the preachers themselves: Are the humble? Or do they draw attention to themselves? Does criticism of others, especially other Christian leaders, often drop from their lips? Or do they try to be charitable in their judgments, pointing out errors with caution and compassion?

Do they take advice and submit to authority? Any leader or teacher, who will not allow others to evaluate his ministry, including his use of money, should arouse suspicion. Before accepting the guidance of a "prophet" or worker of miracles, inquire into his family life, to see how he manages his household, loves his wife, and brings up his children.

Then examine carefully the preacher's message. Does it focus on the cross of Christ? More specifically, does he call believers to take up their cross and follow Christ in daily self-denial? Jesus insisted upon holiness; so should all who teach in His name.

Finally, without being judgmental, we should assess the lives of those who admire and adhere to any Christian teacher. If we find them earnestly hungering and thirsting for righteousness, conscious of their spiritual poverty apart from Christ and mourning over their sins, that is a good sign.

The faithful preacher of the Gospel will encourage his hearers to trust in God at all times and for all things. Pointing them away from self-reliance and self-righteousness, he will turn their attention to the Lord who rose, ascended, and even now intercedes for them. A mixture of solemn sorrow over sin and holy joy over God's grace will indicate solid, healthy instruction from the pulpit.

Of course, the key component in evaluation will be fidelity to the Word of God. Any subtraction from it, addition to it, or distortion of it should alert us that we are dealing with men who do not deserve our attention.

The Only Solid Foundation
Matthew 7:24–28

"Therefore whoever hears these sayings of Mine, and does them, I will like him to a wise man who built his house on the rock: and the rain descended, the floods came, and the winds blew and beat on that house; and it did not fall, for it was founded on the rock. But everyone who hears these sayings of Mine, and does not do them, will be like a foolish man who built his house on the sand: and the rain descended, the floods came, and the winds blew and beat on that house; and it fell. And great was its fall."

Jesus concludes the Sermon on the Mount with the most heartening assurance along with a very sobering warning. His "therefore" will guide our interpretation: Clearly, the Lord intends for us to think back over the previous three chapters.

The promise: Those who not only hear but do His words will have a solid foundation; nothing will deprive them of security.

So, those who heed Jesus' teachings will inherit the kingdom of heaven; receive comfort in sorrow; inherit the earth; be fully and finally satisfied; receive mercy from God; see God; be justly called "sons of God"; receive a great reward in heaven (5:3–12, 45).

Observing their conduct, others will glorify their heavenly Father (5:16). Those who teach and keep God's Word will be called great in the kingdom of heaven (5:19). Their secret charitable gifts, prayers, and fasting will receive a reward (6:1–1; 7:7–11). All their legitimate needs will be provided (6:25–33). They will enter into eternal life and be safe from all spiritual calamity (7:14, 24–25).

On the other hand, everyone who hears the words of Christ but does not obey them face a fearful prospect:

They will not enter the kingdom of heaven; they will be in danger of hell fire; in fact, be cast into hell (5:20, 22, 29–30). If they seek to please other people rather than God, they will achieve their goal—and no more (6:2, 5, 16). If they spend all their energy amassing treasure on earth, they will see it destroyed or stolen from them (6:19), and their days will be lived in darkness (6:23).

Self-righteously judging others, they too will be judged by the same merciless standard (7:1–2). Their end will be destruction, accompanied by truly awful words of the Lord, "I never knew you; depart from Me, you who practice lawlessness" (7:13, 23).

The crowds who heard Him realized that He spoke with unique authority. Will we bow before that authority with faith and fear?

8 The King's Authority over Evil

Willing and Able
Matthew 8:1–4

"Lord, if You are willing, You can make me clean."

Huge crowds followed Jesus to hear His teaching. Of those multitudes, Matthew records only one individual who came and spoke with Jesus. What set him apart from the others?

He was a leper, afflicted with some loathsome skin disease. According to the Law of Moses, he was "unclean." That is, he could not enter the Temple to worship God, and he had to keep away from other people. In that sense, he was "set apart" from others.

But he had another quality that made him even more distinctive: His faith. Notice:

> He came out of the crowd to Jesus. He eagerly and actively sought Jesus.

> He worshiped Jesus. Others might marvel at the teaching of Christ (7:28–29), but this man saw beyond the words to the Word of God made man. He somehow knew that Jesus was more than a man; He was the Lord. Moses' law forbade the worship of anyone but Yahweh, the one true and living God. This leper discerned that Jesus was, in some sense, equal with God.

> He believed in Jesus' power. "If You are willing, You can make me clean." In his eyes, Jesus had the power to take away his awful disease. And since, ritual uncleanness kept him from approaching God in worship, this "cleansing" would also bring restoration of fellowship with the Father and thus with other people as well.

> He believed in Jesus' love. Otherwise, why would he have summoned up the courage to step out of the crowd, who would have shunned and despised him, and approach Jesus? He must have seen that Jesus, who had just spoken of the Father's willingness to give good gifts to His children (7:11), would do the same to all who asked.

He submitted to Jesus' authority. "If You are willing..." He did not presume to know the will of God. He did not demand healing. He merely expressed his utter trust in the greatness and goodness of Jesus.

His faith found an immediate reward. Unlike others, Jesus touched the man. With that contact came healing words, "I am willing; be cleansed." Instantly, the man's skin took on the soft freshness of that of a little baby. A mighty miracle had come in response to simple faith, so that he now could approach God and live among men.

What about us? Do we believe that Jesus is the divine Son of God, our only Savior? Do we trust that He will answer our prayers for fellowship with God through cleansing from sin? Do we have confidence that He can remove obstacles between us and others also?

If so, let us come to Jesus with the same words, "Lord, if You are willing, You are able."

The "Power" of Faith
Matthew 8:5–13

"Go your way; and as you have believed, so *let it be done for you."*

A Roman centurion came to Jesus, "pleading with him, saying, 'Lord, my servant is lying at home paralyzed, dreadfully tormented." Jesus responded with an offer to "come and heal him," but the soldier declined the offer, on two grounds:

First, "Lord, I am not worthy that You should come under my roof." He knew himself to be a sinner, and sensed that Jesus transcended other "teachers" in holiness, so much that his home was unworthy to have Jesus as a guest.

Second, he believed that Jesus did not need to come. "Only speak a word, and my servant will be healed." He trusted not only in Jesus' purity, but in His power. As a soldier, he understood authority, and knew the effect of a simple command. Assuming that Jesus possessed supreme authority, even over a deadly disease, he asked only for Him to issue an order; the healing would follow immediately.

The King's Authority over Evil

How did Jesus respond? He commended the man's faith, declaring it to be greater than any He had seen so far among the Jews. Drawing out the implication of that fact, He pronounced salvation for many Gentiles and judgment for many unbelieving Jews. Finally, He sent the man away with the words quoted above, "As you have believed, *so* let it be done for you."

Sure enough, the centurion returned home to find his servant well.

What do we conclude from this incident? That any sort of faith will work miracles? No! This man's trust in Christ contained key components: A belief in the goodness of God; an awareness of his own sin; confidence in the power of God; submission to the authority of Jesus. Notice, too, that he asked not for himself, but for his servant, showing his unselfish love and compassion.

That sort of faith will not fail to bring "results"! We must of course, leave the precise details of those "results" in the hand of God, who alone knows what is best for us and most conducive to His glory. Still, this ancient Roman soldier has left us a pattern to follow as we seek to trust God's grace towards us in Christ.

Jesus Heals
Matthew 8:14–15

Now when Jesus had come into Peter's house, He saw his wife's mother lying sick with a fever. So He touched her hand, and the fever left her. And she arose and served them.

When Jesus announced, "the kingdom of heaven is at hand" (4:17), He backed up this declaration with words and with deeds. He taught about the life of the kingdom, and He demonstrated the power of the kingdom, and thus added credence to His claim to be the coming King, the Messiah.

The healing miracles of Jesus reveal both His pity and His power. He cares for the welfare of those whom He has made, and He is able to deliver them from all their troubles.

We must avoid two errors when thinking about the healing work of Jesus today.

Christ the King

On the one hand, we cannot believe all—or even most—of the extravagant, usually exaggerated, often self-promoting, and extremely profitable advertisement of widespread healing by televangelists and itinerant ministers of the "health and wealth" message. Widespread fraud and deception mar these ministries, which are often also marked by luxurious lifestyles and sloppy accounting (to put it kindly). Healings resulting from prayer are considered "miraculous" precisely because they are relatively rare displays of God's creative and redemptive power.

On the other hand, we should not fall into the trap of "Christian Deism" that restricts the wonder-working power of God to the age of Christ and the Apostles. Not only does this sort of theology rest upon very shaky exegesis, but it defies the experience of untold numbers of believers around the world and throughout the ages. This writer has personally witnessed medically-attested miracles of healing through prayer. Jesus heals today.

Jesus healed Peter's mother-in-law not in order to draw attention to Himself, or to attract donors, but that He might show His love for Peter and for her. She obviously felt that love, for after her recovery, she "arose and served them."

That is also a reminder to those of us who enjoy good health: Our lives belong to God, who calls us to love Him and those around us. May we all devote ourselves to the health and welfare of others, and not to our own pleasure, prestige, or profit!*

---

* For more on Jesus' healing ministry and its relevance for today, see my book, *The Lord's Healing Words* available from AuthorHouse.com; all proceeds go to China Institute.

The King's Authority over Evil

Demons Defeated
Matthew 8:16

When evening had come, they brought to Him many who were demon-possessed. And He cast out the spirits with a word, and healed all who were sick...

Right after His baptism, Jesus had been driven by the Holy Spirit into the wilderness, where Satan tempted Him (4:1–11). Having overcome the devil's clever wiles, Jesus returned to Galilee "in the power of the Spirit" (Luke 4:14) and began His ministry of preaching, teaching, healing, and deliverance from evil spirits (4:23–25).

Matthew now relates how Jesus not only cured Peter's mother-in-law but also cast out demons from those who were brought to Him for deliverance.

The King has come! The kingdom of God is at hand! Satan, in whose power the world had lain in darkness for millennia, has not been able to deflect the Son of God from His mission. The light of truth dispels darkness. The love of God brings healing to the sick. And the powerful word of Christ expels demons from tormented souls.

No wonder the crowds flocked to Him! Is it strange that they sought out this Man, who not only "taught as one having authority" (7:29), but exercised that same authority over evil spirits?

That same authority empowers even the simplest believer today not only to resist the wiles of Satan (James 4:7; 1 Peter 5:9), but to bring freedom to those who are held captive by him and his wicked minions (Mark 16:17).

Though deprived of his former power to accuse and to deceive (Luke 10:18; John 12:31; Revelation 12:10; 20:3), Satan still "prowls around, like a roaring lion, seeking whom he may devour" (1 Peter 5:8). His evil servants, likewise, can still cause great trouble, inflicting illness and leading astray through idolatry and false teaching (Luke 8:36; 13:16; 1 Corinthians 10:20; 1 Timothy 4:1).

What a great comfort to know that those who are in Christ have the Spirit of God within them, and can call upon the authority of their Lord and Savior to resist the devil and to cast out demons with a word of command!

Why He Came
Matthew 8:16–17

When evening had come, they brought to Him many who were demon-possessed. And He cast out the spirits with a word, and healed all who were sick, that it might be fulfilled which was spoken by Isaiah the prophet, saying: "He Himself took our infirmities and bore our sicknesses."

Why did the eternal Word of God, the unique Son of God, who was equal in dignity, might, and being with the Father and the Spirit, leave the glories of heaven above to descend to this grubby earth?

What motivated Him to become a little baby in a small town in a backwater province of the mighty Roman Empire, with obscure parents lacking prestige, power and abundant possessions?

Thousands of weighty tomes could not adequately answer this question, but this short passage from Matthew provides at least one small clue: He came to save us from "all our sins and sorrow."

Though not every sickness is the result of any particular sin (John 9:3), illness does come from the penalty for sin which God pronounced upon Adam and Eve: "In the day that you eat of [the tree of the knowledge of good and evil], you shall surely die!" (Genesis 2:17). Every ailment of the body, including fatigue, weakness, and disease, points toward that final dissolution into dust that we call death.

Now Jesus came to "save His people from their sins" (1:21)—from the penalty, power, and finally even the presence of sin itself. When He healed the sick and delivered the demon-possessed, the beginnings of this salvation proved that His kingdom of light, life, and liberty was advancing to inevitable and total victory.

In short, He came to take upon Himself our infirmities and bear our sicknesses, as Isaiah had foretold long before His incarnation (Isaiah 53:4). By taking our sins and placing them upon Himself, He gained the authority to heal those who were brought to Him from these effects of disobedience and bitter foretastes of its ultimate penalty, death itself.

How shall we adequately honor the one who divested Himself of all the comforts of heaven to deliver poor sinners from the consequences of rebellion against our most holy Creator and Lord? Let us offer to Him daily our unfeigned praise, thanksgiving, worship, and heartfelt love.

No More Sickness?
Matthew 8:16b–17

And He ... healed all who were sick, that it might be fulfilled which was spoken by Isaiah the prophet, saying:
"He Himself took our infirmities
And bore our sicknesses."

Jesus healed all whom He touched for that purpose, and Matthew connects this with the famous prophetic passage in Isaiah in which the coming Servant "bore the sin of many" (Isaiah 53:12; see also Isaiah 53:5–6).

Does that mean that the atoning work of Christ on the Cross not only brings full and instant forgiveness to all who trust in Jesus, but also ensures complete and immediate healing for all who pray in faith?

After all, Peter writes, referring to the same prophecy in Isaiah, that by His "stripes [wounds] you were healed" (1 Peter 2:24). And the Psalmist declares that Yahweh "heals all your diseases" (Psalm 103:3).

This view faces two major problems, however. First, most of the people who ask in full faith for healing go away as ill as they were before. Despite many inflated claims by televangelists and itinerant "health and wealth" preachers that we can simply "name it [whatever it is we want from God] and claim it," the fact is that this assertion lacks evidence.

On the contrary, the experience of Christians throughout the ages, including our own time, testifies to the continuing presence of sickness, even for those with the strongest faith.

Second, Paul, who certainly had the apostolic gift of healing, wrote, "Trophimus I have left in Miletus sick" (2 Timothy 4:20). Furthermore, he taught explicitly that "the whole creation groans and labors with birth pangs together until now. Not only *that*, but we also... groan within ourselves, eagerly waiting for the adoption, the redemption of our body," because of the "sufferings of this present time" (Romans 8:22–23, 18).

And Peter precedes "by whose stripes you were healed" with the explanation that Christ died for us so that "we, having died to sins, might live for righteousness," and follows it with, "For you were like sheep going astray, but have now returned to the Shepherd and Overseer of your souls" (1 Peter 2:24–25).

We must await the resurrection of our bodies for full healing of all disease. Meanwhile, we rejoice that the Shepherd of our souls has freed us from the penalty and power of sin, the ultimate root of all illness and of death itself.

The Cost of Discipleship
Matthew 8:18–22

"Foxes have holes and birds of the air have *nests, but the Son of Man has nowhere to lay* His *head.... Follow Me, and let the dead bury their own dead."*

These two statements by Jesus must have stunned the would-be followers who had come to Him.

The first man eagerly offered his allegiance: "Teacher, I will follow You wherever You go" (8:19). Perhaps he had heard of Jesus' call to the original disciples, "Follow Me!" Certainly, he had seen the crowds following Jesus because of His teaching and healing ministry.

Why did Jesus apparently discourage him by stating so starkly the demands of discipleship? Maybe the Lord saw that the man did not appreciate how much he would have to give up in order to follow Jesus. He would lose security, stability, and self-sufficiency. Was he ready to give up material comfort and convenience, not to mention financial prosperity?

The second man was already, in some sense, a "disciple" (8:21), but he wanted to wait until he had buried his father before joining the wandering band who accompanied Jesus. It is possible that his father had not even died yet; otherwise he would have already gone home to bury him. Maybe he was just putting future family considerations ahead of present commitment to Christ.

How about us? Do we see Jesus as Lord of heaven and earth, and Lord of our lives also? Are we prepared to lay down both material comfort and family considerations, if necessary? Jesus will never call us to waste money or desert a spouse or children, but He does insist that we put Him first in our lives.

The King's Authority over Evil

Jesus Calms Our Storms
Matthew 8:26 Part–1

But He said to them, "Why are you fearful, O you of little faith?" Then He arose and rebuked the winds and the sea, and there was a great calm.

The disciples had followed Jesus into a little boat and out onto the Sea of Galilee. Suddenly a huge storm arose and the waves threatened to swamp the boat. Meanwhile, Jesus was calmly sleeping. Terrified, Jesus' disciples woke up, shouting, "Lord, save us! We are perishing!"

To their utter amazement, Jesus uttered two rebukes, one to them for their fear, and another to the wind and the waves, which immediately settled into a great calm.

Why did Jesus speak so harshly to these frightened men? Did they not have cause to be afraid? Was He simply annoyed that they woke Him up from a rest which He obviously desperately needed after His strenuous labors? Should He not have commended them for their obvious confidence that He could save them from drowning? What is going on here?

Perhaps the key lies with the presence of the Lord in their little boat, into which He had led them out into the deep waters. Despite the raging gale and crashing billows, He slept soundly in the tossing craft and soaking waters.

Maybe He wanted them to realize that if they followed Him, they would be safe—not from trouble, but from ultimate danger. If they thought He had the power to rescue them from capsizing, they should have known that His very presence was their guarantee of safety.

How like them we are!

We allow the gales of life to scare us into thinking that Jesus is "asleep"—unaware of our difficulties and even danger. He seems so far away, so unconcerned with our problems and perils. We even complain when He does not seem to care enough about our troubles to deliver us from them.

Who knows? If they had waited a bit longer, maybe Jesus would have awakened on His own and stilled the storm. Perhaps the tempest would have quieted down as quickly as it had arisen. Lacking faith in the security of their proximity to Christ, they panicked.

Christ the King

Had they pondered the power of His healings (4:23–24; 8:14–16), the authority of His teachings (7:24–29), and the meaning of His self-chosen title, "Son of Man" (8:20; see Daniel 7:13–14), they would have understood that He was Immanuel—God with us—and would have found peace in His mere presence.

Calming the Storm
Matthew 8:26–27 Part–2

Then He arose and rebuked the winds and the sea, and there was a great calm.

Following their Master, the disciples got into a boat and launched out into the Sea of Galilee. Jesus, exhausted from a full day of teaching and healing, fell asleep in the stern. Suddenly, a fierce storm arose and threatened to sink the boat.

Afraid for their lives, the disciples cried out to Jesus for help. He awoke, rebuked them for their lack of faith, and stilled the raging sea and wind with a simple command.

From this brief narrative, we learn that:

> Disciples of Christ will sometimes encounter danger as a result of obeying His command. As He promised, "In the world you have tribulation [trouble]" (John 16:33).
>
> When we do face suffering, we can be sure that Jesus understands, for He, too, was a man. He knew hunger, thirst, fatigue, and extreme emotional pain. He knows.
>
> He was more than a man, however. Jesus is also God, equal with the Father and the Spirit. Thus, He could command the tempest to be quiet, and the winds and waves obeyed His voice.
>
> Thus, we can trust Him to still the storms in our life, too. When we are overwhelmed by disease, or destitution, or desertion, or danger, or even despair, we can call out to Him to save us.

He is willing, and He is able. Shall we not trust Him to restore peace to our troubled hearts?

The King's Authority over Evil

Who is this Man?
Matthew 8:27

"Who can this be, that even the winds and the sea obey Him?"

That same question confronts us today: Just what kind of a man was Jesus?

As we read Matthew's Gospel, we find that Jesus was:

Just like us: He was born as a little baby, and His human body, like ours, required sleep after exhausting labor.

Jealous for God and His glory: He would not succumb to Satan's attempts to disobey His Father or glorify Himself (4:1–10).

Passionate for purity: Not only did He refuse to fall into sin, but He called everyone to repent, and enjoined upon His followers a standard of complete holiness (4:17; 5:3–7:27).

Zealous for God's kingdom: His opening words were, "…the kingdom of God is at hand" (4:17, 23), a message He preached wherever He went.

A charismatic leader: When He said, "Follow Me!" men left all to obey (4:18–22).

Persuasive as a speaker: Multitudes listened with rapt attention to His every word and acknowledged His unique eloquence (7:29).

Permeated with pity: He healed the sick, delivered the demon-possessed, rescued those in danger (8:14–16, 26).

Courageous enough to rebuke: Would-be followers were urged to count the cost of discipleship; His own disciples were chided for their unbelief (8:19–22, 26).

Possessed of immense, even infinite, power: He ruled over disease, demons, and the destructive power of winds and waves.

More than a mere man: Even if we had read no further in Matthew, we would know by now that He was born by the power of the Holy Spirit working in His mother Mary (1:20); designated by God the Father as His unique Son (3:17); and the mysteriously divine Son of Man prophesied by Daniel (8:20; Daniel 7:13–14).

In short, this Man from Galilee is also Immanuel, God with us, the only one who can "save His people from their sins" (1:21, 23).

As such, He merits our awe, reverence, complete confidence, and total submission.

Dealing with Demons Part–1
Matthew 8:32

And He said to them, "Go." So when they had come out, they went into the heard of swine. And suddenly the whole herd of swine ran violently down the steep place into the sea, and perished in the water.

This striking story (8:28–34) illustrates several key truths about demons.

They are dangerous. Evil spirits had horribly tormented these two men, so that they lived among tombs, far from human society. From Mark's Gospel (Mark 5:1–20), we learn also that the demons caused the men to cry and cut themselves. The unclean spirit also gave the men such strength that they could not be bound, even by chains. In fact, the horrendous power of these demons later impelled an entire herd of pigs to hurl themselves to destruction.

They are defective in their faith. Though they confess Jesus to be the Son of God, they do so with fear, not faith. As Jesus' brother James would later write, "…the demons believe—and tremble" (James 2:19). They acknowledge Jesus as Lord, but not with love or trust. On the contrary, their wickedness rightly arouses terror when they encounter the Holy Son of God. Their belief consists only in intellectual assent to the truth.

Their defeat is certain. Despite their supernatural power, they are no match for Jesus. One simple command from Him, and they are expelled and sent into a herd of hogs. Indeed, casting out evil spirits formed a key component of Jesus' earthly ministry (8:16). He had come announcing the in-breaking of the Kingdom of God (4:17). When the King arrives, He drives out His enemies.

We too can defeat evil spirits. Through faith in the now-risen Christ, we can be "strong in the Lord, and in the power of His might" (Ephesians 6:10). From earliest days, believers in Jesus as Lord have been able to exorcise evil spirits from afflicted souls and have won victory over their deceptive influence in their own lives.

All we need for victory is a faith that moves beyond intellectual assent to the Lordship of Jesus to a sincere love for Him and trust in His saving grace.

The King's Authority over Evil

Dealing with Demons Part–2
Matthew 8:32

And He said to them, "Go." So when they had come out, they went into the herd of swine.

Although demon possession is rare, we should be prepared to expel evil spirits if necessary. From this account, as well as the longer one in Mark's Gospel (Mark 5:1–20), we may derive certain guidelines:

Recognize the presence of evil spirits. Genuine demon possession may be characterized by certain symptoms: Inner turmoil; self-destructive behavior; violence towards others; extraordinary strength; an extreme reaction to the presence of Christians or to the name of Jesus; multiple personalities; and speaking with another voice.

Refuse to enter into dialogue with the evil spirit. These spirits sought to engage Jesus in a conversation, perhaps even to "bind" Him with an oath, but He would not fall into their trap. Remember, demons are servants of Satan, the supreme liar.

Reveal the name of the demon(s). In this case, their name was Legion, the title for a Roman army division, for they were many. Knowing the name is not always necessary, but it can be useful.

Rebuke the demon(s) in the name of Jesus Christ. A Simple command will do. There is no need to shout or engage in prolonged wrestling in most cases, but you must insist upon the authority of Christ over the evil spirit(s) and believe that the name of Christ will win the victory.

Require the demon(s) to leave the person whom they possess and send them elsewhere. Many exorcists now command them to go to Jesus, who knows how to deal with them, as He did in this case.

Even the youngest believer, when confronted with evil spirits, can invoke the all-powerful name of Christ and rely on His supreme authority to drive out evil spirits from anyone whom they have possessed.

Dealing with Demons Part–3
Matthew 8:28

... there met Him two demon-possessed men, coming out of the tombs, exceedingly fierce, so that no one could pass that way.

The word translated "demon-possessed" really means "demonized"—that is, subject to the activity of demons. In this case, the demons actually "inhabited" the men, so "demon-possessed" is the correct meaning. Indeed, many of the Gospel accounts of demons do involve such infestation, which can only be cured by casting out the demon.

In this case, the demons caused, as we have seen, mental torment, social alienation, and self-destructive behavior.

Sometimes, however, demons cause other damage. Jesus delivered people whom evil spirits had rendered ill, deaf, mute, crippled, deformed, and subject to seizures.

We should not think that evil spirits inflict only physical or emotional damage, however. Paul warns against those who heed "deceiving spirits and doctrines of demons" (1 Timothy 4:1). Since Satan is the "ruler of demons" (9:34), we should not be surprised that his servants engage in the sort of deception he always has.

That is why the same Apostle says that our conflict is not "against flesh and blood, but against the principalities, against powers, against the rulers of the darkness of this age, against spiritual *hosts* of wickedness in the heavenly *places*," and urges us to "stand against the wiles of the devil" (Ephesians 6:12, 11).

In other words, whenever we are tempted to disbelieve or disobey the Word of God as revealed in the Bible, the devil and his army of demons are at work.

Then our task is not to cast out an evil spirit, but to stand firmly on the truth of God. The enemy seeks to mislead us, and thus to control us. These tactics are more subtle, and thus more dangerous.

To deal with demons effectively, therefore, we must recognize their various types of attack, and respond appropriately. Most of the time, that means putting on the "whole armor of God" (Ephesians 6:10–20) and resisting spiritual foes with the Word of God, relying in faith on the Spirit of God, as we pray to God the Father in the name of Jesus.

9 The King's Compassion

Faithful Friends
Matthew 9:1–8

Then behold, they brought to Him a paralytic lying on a bed. When Jesus saw their faith, He said to the paralytic, 'Son, be of good cheer; your sins are forgiven you."

This man could not walk. Doubtless, He had heard about Jesus' healing ministry. It seemed that everyone who could get to Jesus would be cured.

But how could he make his way into the presence of this mighty healer? He could not even take one step out the door. Besides, as we know from Mark's Gospel (Mark 2:3–12), Jesus was inside a house, surrounded by such a large crowd that the door was blocked.

Did He share His desire and his despair with His friends? Or did they simply realize what He needed and take action? We do not know. Nevertheless, we see how much they cared for him. They carried him on his pallet to the house where Jesus was working miracles.

Seeing the entrance blocked, they did not give up, but took their friend up onto the roof, which was probably covered with thatch or movable tiles. Determined to bring their friend into the saving presence of Christ, they removed a section of the roof and lowered him down into the room, right in front of the Lord!

All of this took not only devoted love for the crippled man, but great faith in Jesus. Apparently, these men believed that Jesus not only could heal a paralyzed man, but would do so. All they had to do was present the man to Christ, and He would do the rest.

What about us? Do we care about those around us who are, in one way or another, "paralyzed"—perhaps by ignorance of the Gospel? Are we willing to expend great effort to "carry" them into the presence of Christ?

For example, will we gather a group to pray for our friends? Do we care enough to invite them to church or to a Bible study? Remember, it is not our goodness, but the greatness of Christ, who can save those whom we love. All we have to do is expose them to the word of the Gospel, and pray for the Spirit to work in their hearts.

Then we can trust God to do His perfect will in them.

Christ the King

Our Main Need
Matthew 9:2

Then behold, they brought to Him a paralytic lying on a bed. When Jesus saw their faith, He said to the paralytic, "Son, be of good cheer; your sins are forgiven you."

What a strange thing to say! Here lies a man who cannot walk, and Jesus tells him to cheer up, because his sins are forgiven.

Does our Lord not know that a crippling disability grips his entire life, keeping him for work, from friends, perhaps even from worship?

Yes, Jesus knows all that, and more. He realizes that paralysis of the soul brings even greater affliction. It is one thing not to be able to go see your friends, but not being able to approach God because of sin is far worse.

The healthiest, most active person will someday succumb to a final illness and be laid onto a bed from which he will never rise. But the unforgiven sinner will be cast into what Jesus earlier called "hell fire"—an eternity of torment, anguish, and alienation from God.

We do not know whether any particular offense against God caused this man's paralysis, but we do know that all sickness comes ultimately from sin, and will lead to death.

Thus, seeing this disabled man before Him, Jesus at once dealt with his greatest need: Forgiveness.

"Cheer up! Though in this life you may never walk, you will, on the last day, rise up to eternal life, clothed with a glorious body. From that time forward, you will run with the gazelles on the mountain tops and leap with everlasting joy. You will at any time be able to approach God and know His love and pleasure."

"Cheer up! Whatever sins you have committed—self-pity, self-indulgence, self-righteousness—are pardoned."

God the Father will speak the same words of comfort today to all who believe in His Son Jesus as sacrifice and savior.

"In Him (Jesus) we have redemption through His blood, the forgiveness of sins" (Ephesians 1:7).

Who Can Forgive?
Matthew 9:2–3

"Son, be of good cheer; your sins are forgiven you." And at once some of the scribes said within themselves, "This Man blasphemes!"

Who has the authority to forgive sins? We have offended a holy God, who must judge wickedness and rebellion. No mere man pronounces forgiveness of sins to another in the name of God.

But Jesus was not ordinary man, as this passage indicates.

First, He called the man, "Son." Since Jesus Himself was only about thirty years old at this time, and we have no evidence that the paralytic was a youth, this form of address hints at a sense of authority on Jesus' part.

Then, He pronounces forgiveness. Nowhere in the Bible do we have anyone else—not Moses, not any of the prophets—simply telling a sinner that his sins were forgiven. Jesus well knew that only God can pardon offenders against His holy law.

Jesus points further to His extraordinary status by saying, "But that you may know that the Son of Man has power on earth to forgive sins…"

Though "Son of Man" could have several different meanings, on Jesus' lips it almost certainly refers to the Son of Man in Daniel, who "was given dominion and glory and a kingdom, that all peoples, nations, and languages should serve Him. His dominion *is* an everlasting dominion" (Daniel 7:14).

Finally, the Lord confirmed His authority to forgive sins by healing the paralyzed man with a simple command.

Who can forgive sins? Jesus, the eternal Son of God, who became Son of Man, "God with us" in order to "save His people from their sins" (1:23, 21).

Only Sinners Accept Jesus
Matthew 9:12

"Those who are well have no need of a physician, but those who are sick."

The Pharisees were disgusted with Jesus for dining with people whom they considered sinners. Jesus responded by telling them why He came—not "to call the righteous, but sinners, to repentance" (9:13).

As we have seen, He did not mean that the Pharisees had no sin, but that they considered themselves righteous. To use another figure of speech, they saw themselves as healthy, not needing a physician.

The tax collectors, thieves, and harlots knew otherwise. They realized their sin, and saw themselves as "sick," needing the care of a doctor. That is why they flocked to Jesus for healing and forgiveness.

But the Pharisees rejected not only those "sinners," but Jesus as well. They simply saw no need for Him. They were so obsessed with the faults of others that they could not see their own spiritual poverty and sickness.

What about us? Are we so aware of the faults of others that we remain blind to our own? Do we not see just how heinously we offend against God each day, each hour, almost each moment, as we fail to love Him with all our heart, soul, mind, and strength, and our neighbor as ourselves?

Self-righteous people not only criticize and look down upon others; they also fail to see their desperate, daily, need of Christ. They may profess to believe in Him, but they do not cry out desperately for mercy; they do not beg Him for forgiveness and the power to change.

Strange as it may seem, only "sinners" can accept Jesus! And only the self-confessed wicked can receive His grace and mercy.

Jesus Accepts Only Sinners
Matthew 9:13

"For I did not come to call the righteous, but sinners, to repentance."

In Jesus' day, tax collectors were hated because they served the occupying Roman army. Usually, they took more than the law required, in order to enrich themselves.

Thus, when Jesus called Matthew, a tax collector, to follow Him, the Pharisees were probably outraged.

Their anger increased when they saw Jesus eating in Matthew's home, surrounded by other notorious "sinners"—prostitutes, thieves, and the like. How could a holy man like Jesus associate with such wicked people?

Jesus first rebuked the self-righteous Pharisees, then proclaimed that He came only for "sinners," to call them to repentance (and thus to eternal life).

Did He mean that the Pharisees were not sinners? Of course not! Elsewhere He condemns them for pride and hypocrisy, among other offenses. He meant that He receives only those who *recognize* and *admit* their need for forgiveness.

That is good news for those who suffer great sorrow for their lack of love for God and for others. Jesus' treatment of Matthew and his unsavory companions demonstrates God's matchless mercy towards all those who come humbly and without excuse to Him for pardon.

The Ideal Husband
Matthew 9:15 Part–1

And Jesus said to them, "Can the friends of the bridegroom mourn as long as the bridegroom is with them?"

In response to a question about fasting, Jesus reveals something very precious about Himself: He is the long-awaited Bridegroom of Israel.

Yahweh frequently identifies Himself as the husband of Israel, His people in the Old Testament.

Psalm 45 shows Him to be a glorious King, resplendent in majesty as He rides on to endless victories.

Christ the King

Hosea the prophet declares to the northern kingdom of Israel that their worship of idols amounts to spiritual adultery against the LORD who had loved and saved them.

Later, Ezekiel proclaims the same message to the southern kingdom of Judah, and relates how God had found her as an abandoned baby in the wilderness; cleaned and clothed her; wooed her with tender words; and fed her with the finest fare.

Both of these spokesmen for Yahweh reveal His broken heart over their infidelity, His burning jealousy for their dedicated affection, and His faithfulness to His promise to be their God and Savior, despite their sins.

In the meantime, however, He cannot abide their unfaithfulness, which amounts to self-destructive folly as well as inexcusable rebellion. As King, He deserves and demands total obedience. If they refuse to heed His warnings and return to Him, He will pour out upon them His anger through plagues, locusts, and ruthless foreign invaders. They will be left naked, desolate, and despised in a barren wilderness once again.

And so it happened, again and again, until Israel was destroyed by Assyria and then Judah was taken into captivity by Babylon.

But what of the promise that God would not forget or forsake His chosen people, whom He had once sworn to love forever? Had not Zephaniah foretold a time when Yahweh would be in their midst, rejoicing over them with songs of love?

Longing for redemption from the Romans, who had occupied their land and installed a puppet Edomite as King, Israelites looked for One who would come to save. Imagine their thoughts when Jesus, in this parable and others, revealed Himself as the heavenly Husband!

The Bridegroom is Coming!
Matthew 9:15 Part-2

"Can the friends of the bridegroom mourn as long as the bridegroom is with them?"

As we saw last time, Jesus referred to the Old Testament when He called Himself the Bridegroom of His people. The New Testament picks up this theme in a number of important passages referring to Christ.

John the Baptist, when questioned about his ministry, said that he was not the long-awaited Christ, and then declared, "He who has the bride is the bridegroom; but the friend of the bridegroom, who stands and hears him, rejoices greatly because of the bridegroom's voice" (John 3:29).

Christ Himself told a parable about a wedding feast, in which the son of the king clearly refers to Jesus, the Son of God, who came to be joined to His people in an unending covenant of love. Those who reject the invitation to the wedding celebration will be cast out forever (22:1–14).

In another parable, Christ urged upon His disciples the necessity of waiting eagerly for His return, like the sudden coming of a bridegroom (25:1–6).

All these passages—and others which we shall introduce later—tell us several things:

> Jesus is Yahweh come in the flesh as the unique God-Man. By applying the title of bridegroom to Himself, our Lord clearly intends to claim the highest dignity.
>
> The sense of expectation which rises with mounting intensity in the Old Testament has given way to the gladness of fulfillment. The long-expected Messiah has come to deliver His people!
>
> As in the message of the prophets, so in Jesus we see a mixture of passionate love for His people and furious jealousy for His relationship with them. He will tolerate no rivals for our affection, and His Father will reject those who refuse the invitation to His Son's wedding banquet.
>
> But for those who do receive Him, who believe in His name, there is joy unimaginable. The happiest occasion we know—a

wedding—hints dimly at the thrilling rapture of union with Christ. We must wait, however, for the final consummation. The Bridegroom will be taken from His disciples and they will mourn for a while, longing for His return to consummate the wedding and usher us into eternal bliss.

Union with Christ
Matthew 9:15 Part-3

"Can the friends of the bridegroom mourn as long as the bridegroom is with them?"

Paul dwells at greatest length on the relationship of Christ to His bride in the justly famous passage on marriage in Ephesians 5:22–33. Jesus is the head of His body, the church. He loved her and "gave Himself for her, that He might sanctify and cleanse her with the washing of water by the word, that He might present her to Himself a glorious church, not having spot or wrinkle or any such thing, but that she should be holy and without blemish."

Even now, the Lord Jesus "nourishes and cherishes" His people like a tender, loving husband. As Christ did, Paul reaches back to the dawn of time to explain, "For this reason a man shall leave his father and mother and be joined to his wife, and the two shall become one flesh" and explains that the full meaning of marriage is to be found in the union of Christ and those who believe in Him.

Casting his eyes to the consummation of the ages, the Apostle John announces the marriage supper of the Lamb, and pronounces those who are invited blessed (Revelation 19:9). When Christ returns, His church will finally be all glorious, without any blemish, and gloriously clothed to meet her heavenly Bridegroom (Revelation 21:2).

What are we to make of this connection between marriage and the union of Christ with all believers? What can we learn about each?

> Jesus has paid the ultimate price to reconcile us to God the Father and bring us into an intimate relationship with Himself. He has demonstrated His love once and for all on the Cross. We must never doubt His unwavering, unconditional commitment to us.

He calls us to abide in Him, that our joy may be made full (John 15:1–11). We do this by listening to His voice as He speaks through Scripture, and by responding with constant and believing prayer (John 15:7). He seeks nothing less than a personal relationship with us, through the Holy Spirit Whom the Father has given us through Christ.

In this union with Christ, we can know real love. He alone can satisfy our craving for sustained and lasting affection, attention, and approval. Furthermore, He will take care of all our needs, supplying whatever is necessary for us to know and serve God. He will not keep us from the troubles of this world, but will grant us peace in the midst of them (John 16:33).

Shall we not respond to Him with our heartfelt devotion, trust, and praise?

Jesus the Bridegroom
Matthew 9:15 Part–4

"Can the friends of the bridegroom mourn as long as the bridegroom is with them?"

The disciples of John the Baptist had asked Jesus why they and the followers of the Pharisees fasted regularly, but His disciples did not.

Jesus' reply strikes at the heart of man-centered religion, with all its rules and regulations. The Jews of His day tried to get right with God by engaging in all sorts of "religious" activity, but He pointed them to a different way of life.

Jesus offered them—and us—a relationship. More than that, He presented Himself as a bridegroom, what we would today call the groom at a wedding.

Often in the Old Testament God had portrayed Himself as the husband of His people Israel (Psalm 45; Ezekiel 16; Hosea; etc.). He had chosen them, loved them, delivered them, and bound them to Himself with cords of love.

By calling Himself the Bridegroom, Jesus asserts His deity. At the same time, He invites us into a relationship with Him that surpasses even the intimacy of husband and wife.

Since we are sinners, however, we can only enjoy this common life with God in Christ because Jesus, the Son of God, died for us. "Husbands, love your wives, just as Christ also loved the church and gave Himself for her" (Ephesians 5:25).

Even now, at the right hand of the Father, the Lord Jesus, by His Spirit, "nourishes and cherishes" all who trust in Him (Ephesians 5:29).

Shall we not turn from all other would-be "lovers" and, through repentance and faith, unite ourselves to our heavenly bridegroom?

Replacing the Old with the New
Matthew 9:16–17

"No one puts a piece of unshrunk cloth on an old garment; for the patch pulls away from the garment, and the tear is made worse. Nor do they put new wine into old wineskins, or else the wineskins break, the wine is spilled, and the wineskins are ruined. But they put new wine into new wineskins, and both are preserved."

The disciples of John the Baptist had asked why Jesus' disciples did not fast like them and the disciples of the Pharisees.

Jesus' reply has two parts: First He shows that He is the heavenly Bridegroom, in whose physical presence there is no room for gloom.

Second, He contrasts the new age which He is bringing with that age that is passing away. Before His coming, religious people relied on ritual and rigorous self-denial to achieve intimacy with God. Now, they may know God through simple faith in Jesus, the heavenly Bridegroom who is God's Son.

In the new age, which Jesus came to inaugurate, God dwells with His people directly. All we have to do is repent of our sins, believe in Jesus as our only Savior, and earnestly seek to follow Him as our heavenly Husband.

After His resurrection and ascension, Jesus poured out the gift of the Holy Spirit upon all who trusted Him fully. He does so now also.

Thus, any attempt we make to earn God's approval by our own efforts, including fasting, church attendance, or religious observances, will not only fail, but actually prevent us from experiencing God.

The King's Compassion

Furthermore, for believers in Christ to try to "patch" a Spirit-led life onto the old system of religion, or to pour the new wine of the Spirit into old skins of religious and cultural practice, will ruin both the old and waste the new.

Some of these "old" things may include current features of the Christian church, such as large buildings, formal worship led by a priestly elite, academic training for ministers, as well as prescribed days and rituals, pilgrimages, relics, and "holy places." None of these characterized New Testament Christianity, and may well be blocking the work of the Holy Spirit in us today.

According to Your Faith
Matthew 9:22, 29

"Be of good cheer, daughter; your faith has made you well... According to your faith let it be to you."

A woman with a chronic hemorrhage said to herself, "If only I may touch His garment, I shall be made well" (9:21). She was right. As soon as she touched Jesus, she was healed.

Jesus immediately explained to her that not the action of her hand, but the faith in her heart, had made her well.

Later, two blind men begged Jesus to have mercy upon them. "Do you believe that I am able to do this?" He asked them. "Yes!" they replied.

"According to your faith let it be to you," He replied, as He touched their eyes, and immediately their blindness disappeared.

Why did faith in Jesus bring such results? Such trust in Jesus demonstrates a confidence in His pity and in His power. These people believed that Jesus *could* perform the impossible, and that He *would*, if only they approached Him.

Their faith showed that they believed the reports they had heard about Jesus. They considered Him to be *great* in His power, and *good* in His person.

Jesus did not promise that any sort of belief would work miracles. He commended only that sort of faith which focuses on Jesus as the Son of God, willing and able to demonstrate God's mercy and majesty towards the needy.

We, too, can approach Christ with this type of confidence. In prayer, we can ask Him to give us all that we need to glorify God on this earth. First and foremost, faith in Christ brings us forgiveness of sins. Then, as we rely on Him, we receive power to follow in His steps.

If He thinks that we need healing to serve Him more effectively, He will grant us good health. Otherwise, He will enable us to serve Him out of our weakness.

The Power of Perspective
Matthew 9:36

But when He saw the multitudes, He was moved with compassion for them, because they were weary and scattered, like sheep having no shepherd.

As He traveled around the countryside, Jesus encountered crowds of needy people. Some were physically sick; many evinced spiritual hunger. But all were dead in sin, far from God because of unbelief and rebellion.

Notice how Jesus saw them. Though He could have justly despised them for their folly, He chose instead to pity them for their suffering. He focused not on what they had done wrong, but on how they had been wronged by their political and spiritual rulers.

Thus, He was "moved with compassion for them."

Here we see into the heart of God. He could have condemned the entire world to hell for our manifold transgressions against His holy law. Rather than pouring out His righteous indignation, however, He sent His only Son to live a righteous life and then to die in our place.

As the Good Shepherd, Jesus looked upon sinners as erring sheep. His divine love impelled Him to endure untold pain in order to take our guilt upon Himself and lay down His life for us.

How about us? When we see others in trouble because of their foolishness, how do we respond? With disdain and criticism, or with compassion and a desire to help?

Labor Shortage
Matthew 9:37–38

Then He said to His disciples, "The harvest truly is plentiful, but the laborers are few. Therefore pray the Lord of the harvest to send out laborers into His harvest."

Jesus' words are just as true today as they were when He first uttered them. Multitudes perish for lack of the knowledge of God through faith in Christ. They are like sheep without a shepherd, with no one to care for them.

On the other hand, too few Christians are either willing or able to lead others into the truth. They are preoccupied with making a living, seeking the things of this world rather than the kingdom of God.

Overseas, conditions are even worse. In almost every country, masses rush headlong into spiritual destruction, with no one to show them the way to eternal life. Compounding the crisis is the lack of qualified teachers and pastors among those who do believe in Christ.

Jesus' command rings loud and clear: "Pray the Lord of the harvest to send out laborers into His harvest."

Christ the King

10 The King's Messengers

Our Commission?
Matthew 10:1 Part–1

And when He had called His twelve disciples to Him, *He gave them power* over *unclean spirits, to cast them out, and to heal all kinds of sickness and all kinds of disease.*

Jesus was moved with compassion when He saw the multitudes, "for they were weary and scattered, like sheep having no shepherd" (9:36). Observing such needs, He commanded His disciples to "pray the Lord of the harvest to send out laborers into His harvest" (9:38). But that was not all.

He immediately began to answer His own prayer, by calling and commissioning twelve of His followers to expand His own ministry.

Lets look first at what He commissioned them to do: Cast out evil spirits and heal all sorts of illness and disease, just as Jesus Himself had been doing from the beginning of His ministry (4:23–24; 8:1–17; 9:1–8, 18–35).

Why was deliverance from demons and disease so important to our Lord? Because in this way He demonstrated the truth of His primary message, which was the same message He commanded His disciples to convey: "the kingdom of heaven is at hand" (4:17; 10:7).

Long held in bondage to sin and Satan, this tired earth was now being liberated by the true King, Jesus. By the power of the Holy Spirit, He and His disciples expelled demons from anguished souls and cured the sick of all sorts of ailments.

Exorcism and healing demonstrate both the pity and the power of our God. He does care, and He can deliver!

Some Christians today doubt whether we are to ask God to work such miracles of spiritual and physical deliverance and healing. They say that these things were only for the first century, to authenticate the message of Christ and the Apostles.

But has God's pity or His power changed? And do not millions still languish in bondage to evil spirits and illness? Most doubters live in the secularized West. In Africa, Asia, and Latin America, God continues to reveal His wonder-working power and His compassionate pity when His people call upon Him in faith.

Our Call?
Matthew 10:1 Part–2

And when He had called His twelve disciples to Him, *He gave them power...*

Jesus called the disciples to Himself. That is implied in the Greek verb "called," and made explicit in Mark's account:

"Then He appointed twelve, that they might be with Him and that He might send them out to preach, and to have power to heal sickness and to cast out demons" (Mark 3:14–15).

Though we discussed the commission which Christ gave His apostles first, in reality His *calling* preceded the commission. First and foremost, He wanted them to come to Himself, to be with Him.

That is our call, too.

"Abide in Me, and I in you... He who abides in Me, and I in him, bears much fruit; for without Me you can do nothing" (John 15:4–5).

Fellowship with Christ comes before fruit-bearing.

Prayer precedes preaching.

Works must flow from worship.

Before we can heal in His name, we must hear His words.

Unless we imitate Christ, how can we lead others to Him? And how can we imitate Him if we do not have an intimate relationship with Him?

So, for the next three years, the Twelve followed Jesus wherever He went. They listened to His teaching, witnessed His mighty works, saw His matchless manner of life, and (at least some of them) stood— though at a distance—silently as grieving onlookers at His terrible agony on the Cross. Then they waited until the promised Holy Spirit came upon them to thrust them out into the world with a power even greater than that given to them during their apprenticeship.

May we follow their example, as they followed His.

Twelve Ordinary Men
Matthew 10:2–4

Now the names of the twelve apostles are these: first, Simon, who is called Peter, and Andrew his brother; James the son of Zebedee, and John his brother; Philip and Bartholomew; Thomas and Matthew the tax collector; James the son of Alphaeus, and Lebbaeus, whose surname was Thaddaeus; Simon the Cananite, and Judas Iscariot, who also betrayed Him.

Whom did Jesus call to be His delegates and messengers to the whole world? To whom did He entrust authority over the church for which He was to die?

We would have picked the rich, the powerful, the famous, the highly-educated, the well-connected.

But Jesus selected ordinary men: Four, at least, were lowly fishermen. One (Matthew) worked for the hated Roman occupation; the other belonged to a revolutionary party (Simon the Canaanite—or Zealot). We know nothing of the others, except that they were all Galileans, residents of a despised and outlying province, far from the power and prestige of Jerusalem.

What, then, *did* they have?*

> A *call* from Jesus: They were summoned by the Lord to follow Him and do His will.
>
> *Communion* with Jesus: They spent three years in His company, watching every move, hearing every word. After the Resurrection, they enjoyed His ongoing presence (28:20).
>
> *Commitment* to Jesus: They left all and followed Him, despite the danger and opprobrium. At the end of His life, they did desert Him, but after they had received the Holy Spirit at Pentecost, they re-dedicated their lives to Him and His service.
>
> *Community* with each other: They stuck together as a group, despite occasional squabbles. After the Resurrection, they lived and worked together in Jerusalem until they were sent out to spread the Good News to all the world.
>
> *Courage*: At least after Pentecost, and often before, these simple men braved danger and difficulty to follow the commands and the example of their Master.

A *commission* from the Risen Christ to make disciples of all nations (28:18–20).

As believers in Christ, we all now enjoy the same blessings they did; may we also have their commitment and courage!*

Sheep amidst Wolves
Matthew 10:16, 22, 24

"Behold, I send you out as sheep in the midst of wolves.... And you will be hated by all for My name's sake.... A disciple is not above his teacher, nor a servant above his master."

Jesus sent out His disciples with very clear instructions. He told them where to go, what to say, what to do, and how to finance their mission (10:5–11).

After that, however, He warned them that they would face fierce opposition, even deadly persecution. He did not want them to be surprised when people rejected both the Gospel message and the messengers.

The same warning applies to us. If we are faithful to the truth, the world will hate us, just as it hated Jesus (John 15:18–20). Indeed, the more closely we resemble our Lord, the more hostility will we face from certain people.

But Jesus' promises to His first disciples also apply to us. "Do not worry about how or what you should speak. For it will be given to you in that hour what you should speak" (10:19).

"But he who endures to the end will be saved" (10:22).

"Therefore do not fear them. For there is nothing covered that will not be revealed, and hidden that will not be known" (10:26).

"Therefore whoever confesses Me before men, him I will also confess before My Father who is in heaven" (10:32).

In a word, "do not fear those who kill the body but cannot kill the soul" (10:28).

---

*For much of the following I am indebted to Dr. Malcolm Webber. For the best on Christian leadership development, go to leadershipletters.com.

The Cost of Discipleship
Matthew 10:37–39

"He who loves father or mother more than Me is not worthy of Me. And he who loves son or daughter more than Me is not worthy of Me. And he who does not take his cross and follow Me is not worthy of Me. He who finds his life will lose it, and he who loses his life for My sake will find it."

Although Jesus spoke these words to the Apostles as they began their danger-filled evangelistic career, they apply equally to all believers today.

Jesus warned that the Gospel would evoke anger and hostility from many people, leading to rejection and even suffering for the Christian messenger. But those who follow Christ must forsake all competing "loves" in order to gain eternal life.

On another occasion, Jesus said, "Whoever desires to come after Me, let him deny himself, and take up his cross, and follow Me" (Mark 8:34). Between self-denial and fellowship with Jesus lies the cross. Will we take it upon ourselves?

What does it mean to take up the cross and follow Jesus? Self-denial comes first. Putting to death the evil deeds of the body (Romans 8:13). Paying any price to avoid sin (5:27–30). Serving others before, or perhaps even instead of, oneself (Romans 15:2–3; 2 Corinthians 5:15; Philippians 2:4). That leads to following Christ in the footsteps of His suffering for others (1 Peter 2:21).

Specifically, that might mean: Staying in an unhappy marriage; not responding to criticism with self-justifying remarks, much less in anger; taking a lower-paying job in order to preserve integrity; staying home to care for children. In short, to take up the cross is to crucify all the "idols" of the heart—the hopes, dreams, aspirations, and "rights" that keep us from loving and serving others.

Is it worth it? "He who loses his life for My sake will find it." We walk behind a Man who endured the Cross because of the joy set before Him, and who right now enjoys intimate fellowship with God the Father.

Christ the King

11 The King Vindicates His Herald

Who Is Greater? Part–1
Matthew 11:11

"Assuredly, I say to you, among those born of women there has not risen one greater than John the Baptist."

Jesus' evaluation of John comes through loud and clear: He was the greatest person born up to that time.

Why? Because he bravely rebuked King Herod for his adultery, and suffered imprisonment and finally death?

Or was it his firm, unbending conviction that led him to preach repentance for sin? He surely was no "reed shaken by the wind" (11:7).

Nor did he indulge in luxury, for he was not "clothed in soft garments," but "in camel's hair, with a leather belt around his waist" (11:8; 3:4).

He also exercised strict self-control, so that Jesus said that he "came neither eating nor drinking" (11:18)—referring to John's simple diet (3:4).

Like Jesus who came after him, John suffered abuse and rejection, for people said that his simple lifestyle showed that he was demon-possessed.

Though all of these qualities show John to be an extraordinary man, Jesus called him great for another reason:

"Behold, I send My messenger before Your face, who will prepare Your way before You" (11:10, quoting Malachi 3:1).

John was great, because God made him so.

In particular, John prepared the way for Jesus (11:10). Unlike other prophets, he not only predicted the coming of the Messiah, but pointed Him out when He arrived on the bank of the Jordan (John 1:29).

John looked for Christ, spoke of Christ, oriented his entire life towards Christ, and finally saw Christ.

May we be like him!

Who Is Greater? Part–2
Matthew 11:11

"Assuredly, I say to you, among those born of women there has not risen one greater than John the Baptist; but he who is least in the kingdom of heaven is greater than he."

Though John the Baptist exceeded all who went before him, he is "less" than the least of those disciples of Christ who follow the Lord to whom John pointed.

His greatness lay in his unprecedented knowledge of the Messiah. Their deeper, clearer understanding of Christ renders the followers of Jesus even "greater" than John.

Because of his courageous criticism of Herod, John was cast into prison and later beheaded. He thus did not live to see the ministry of Jesus.

John never witnessed the powerful healings and marvelous deliverance from demons which those who believed in Jesus saw. Perhaps that partly explains why he asked, "Are You the Coming One, or do we look for another?" (11:3)

Nor did John live to hear the matchless teachings of Christ about the kingdom of God (chapters 5–7, 13, 18, 24, etc.).

Most important of all, John did not have the chance to follow Jesus through His last days, as He was mocked, tried, and then cruelly crucified. When the Lord rose victoriously from the grave, only His disciples were allowed to see Him alive again.

Finally, when the day of Pentecost arrived, the promised Holy Spirit fell upon Jesus' disciples, fulfilling ancient promises and bringing them that regeneration without which no one can either see or enter the Kingdom (John 3:3, 5).

John's significance lay in his clarion call to repent, and his pointing to Jesus as the Messiah prophesied in the Old Testament. Likewise, the goal of our life is achieved when we bear witness to Christ (10:32–33; 28:18–20).

What a privilege we have, to surpass even the greatest of the Old Testament prophets as we disciple all nations!

The King Vindicates His Herald

Greater Responsibility
Matthew 11:20–22

Then He began to rebuke the cities in which most of His mighty works had been done, because they did not repent: "Woe to you, Chorazin! Woe to you, Bethsaida! For if the mighty works which were done in you had been done in Tyre and Sidon, they would have repented long ago in sackcloth and ashes. But I say to you, it will be more tolerable for Tyre and Sidon in the day of judgment than for you."

Jesus' stinging denunciation of these small towns teaches us a great deal about the coming judgment of God:

It will be terrible and total. The ancient cities of Tyre were overthrown by fierce armies; Sodom and Gomorrah, to which Jesus refers in the next verse, were wiped out by fire from heaven (Genesis 19:24–25). Jesus Himself spoke of "hell fire" (5:22); "destruction" (7:13); and of "outer darkness," where "there will be weeping and gnashing of teeth" (8:12).

It will be according to the light which we have received. Those who have been exposed to more of God's revelation will be judged more severely than those who have had less of an opportunity to know God and turn to Him (John 15:22; Hebrews 10:28–29). Thus, those people who heard Jesus' preaching and saw His miracles, but rejected Him anyway, will receive a worse punishment than the citizens of pagan cities which knew only God's general revelation and His warnings through the prophets of Israel (Romans 1:18–32; Isaiah 23).

For those who have heard the Gospel of Christ, it will be based on our response. Did we repent of our sins and turn to Him in faith? If so, we shall be forgiven of all our sins and enter into everlasting life. If, on the other hand, we harden our hearts and seek to hide our sins, not admitting them and trusting in God's grace to us through Christ, there is a "fearful expectation of judgment, and fiery indignation" (Hebrews 10:27). Greater privilege carries greater responsibility.

Sovereign Grace
Matthew 11:25–27

At that time Jesus answered and said, "I thank You, Father, Lord of heaven and earth, that You have hidden these things from the *wise and prudent and have revealed them to babes. Even so, Father, for so it seemed good in Your sight. All things have been delivered to Me by My Father, and no one knows the Son except the Father. Nor does anyone know the Father except the Son, and* the one *to whom the Son wills to reveal* Him.*"*

To understand this saying, we must consider its context. Jesus told His disciples that they would be persecuted, even killed (10:16–39). Later, He referred to the way the crowds rejected both John the Baptist and Himself (11:18–19) and pronounced woes on cities that had refused to believe in Him (11:20–24).

Now He explains why some believe in Him, and some do not. It all depends on God's sovereign grace. That is to say, God reveals Himself to some, and not to others.

We cannot know God as Father apart from faith in Jesus the Son. But we cannot know Jesus as the Son of God unless the Father opens our eyes.

For Jesus personally, this meant that He and His message would be received by only a minority and despised by the majority, who would then subject Him to terrible suffering and death. Of course, it also meant that many would receive Him and find eternal life.

Notice how He responded to this: "Even so, Father, for so it seemed good in Your sight." He submitted, even though it would lead to unspeakable agony for Him.

Shall we not also submit humbly to God's plan for our lives, even if it includes pain?

True Rest
Matthew 11:28–30

"Come to Me, all you who labor and are heavy laden, and I will give you rest. Take My yoke upon you and learn from Me, for I am gentle [meek] and lowly in heart, and you will find rest for your souls. For My yoke is easy and My burden is light."

These famous words of Jesus offer us the path to true rest of soul.

Are you laden with guilt? Jesus provides full pardon and forgiveness.

Are you weary of constantly doing what is wrong? Jesus offers progressive, and substantial, freedom.

Are you tired of trying to justify yourself by your performance? Jesus gives instant justification to all who believe.

Are you overwhelmed by the task of obeying God? Jesus sends the Spirit to transform all those who trust in Him.

Are you worn out by constant rejection from those who do not know God? Jesus, who endured the murderous hatred of wicked enemies, will comfort and strength you.

"Yoked" to Jesus, we can let Him carry the load for us. All we have to do is walk with Him by faith. For those who transfer their heavy burdens to Him, there is profound peace and real rest.

Christ the King

12 The King Counters His Critcs

Day of Rest? Part–1
Matthew 11:28–12:8

"Come to Me, all you who labor and are heavy laden, and I will give you rest."

It seems that nowadays almost everyone is tired and weary much of the time. Is there any way out of the fast lane?

Jesus promised "rest" to all who would come to Him. He offered relief from many of the stresses that sap our energy: Guilt, worry, striving to prove our worth, and legalistic religion.

For centuries, Christians have believed that observing one day a week for rest and worship offers relief from the incessant labor and toil that wears us down.

After all, after having made the world in six days, God "rested" on the seventh day. He blessed that day and set it apart as special (Genesis 2:2–3).

Later, when He gave the moral law to His people Israel at Mount Sinai, the LORD commanded them to "Remember the Sabbath day, to keep it holy. Six days you shall labor and do all your work, but the seventh day *is* the Sabbath of the LORD your God. *In it* you shall do no work" (Exodus 20:8–10).

After Jesus rose from the dead, His followers commemorated that great demonstration of His lordship by gathering on the first day of the week to worship God through faith in Him (Acts 20:7). They called it "the Lord's Day" (Revelation 1:10). Centuries later, they began to observe this day as a Sabbath, doing no work on it.

Perhaps it would be good for us to re-consider this ancient practice to see whether we, too, might benefit from it. Maybe this is one way in which Jesus provides rest to us.

Day of Rest? Part–2
Matthew 12:5–6

"Or have you not read in the law than on the Sabbath the priest in the temple profane the Sabbath, and are blameless?"

The Pharisees had criticized Jesus' disciples for plucking grain on the Sabbath as they walked through a field. Jesus first showed them that their definition of "work" was wrong.

The Mosaic Law allowed the priest to "work" on the Sabbath. It also allowed people to pick a few grains of standing wheat if they were hungry. So, His disciples were blameless

By this statement, as well as His reminder that David had been given holy bread from the tabernacle when he and his men were hungry (12:3–4), Jesus challenged the man-made tradition of the Pharisees.

He proved, from their own Bible, that two types of "work"—at least—were allowed on the Sabbath: What is necessary for worship, and what is necessary for life.

At the same time, Jesus exposed their ignorance of Scripture; their critical, judgmental attitude; their selective moral standards.

We may not hold to the same traditions as they did, but are we ever guilty of similar sins?

The King Counters His Critics

Day of Rest? Part–3
Matthew 12:5–6

"Yet I say to you that in this place there is One *greater than the temple."*

Then Jesus stunned them with a stupendous claim: That He was greater than the Temple in which the priests worked.

> He is purer than the temple, which had become defiled by hypocritical worship and mercenary activities.

> He is more permanent than the temple, for it would be destroyed and He would rise to eternal glory.

> He is holier than the temple, for in Him the fullness of God dwelt in bodily form.

> He is greater than the sacrifices, for they had to be offered daily, but He died only once.

> He is greater than the priests, for they had to sacrifice for their own sins, but He only offered a sacrifice (Himself) for the sins of others. Moreover, they all died, but He lives forever to make intercession for us.

Now, if Jesus is "greater than the temple," then He is greater than the covenant which established the entire sacrificial system. In that case, He has authority to regulate worship for His people.

Not only so, but if He is greater than the temple, then He must be the center and focus of all our worship and service. In that case, our attitude towards Him is far more important than our actions on any particular day.

The Pharisees missed that point entirely. How about us?

Day of Rest? Part–4
Matthew 12:8

"For the Son of Man is Lord even of the Sabbath."

Jesus rebuked the Pharisees for accusing His disciples of breaking the Sabbath law, because they misunderstood the Scriptures, the true purpose of the Sabbath, and His own unique person.

Now He ends this exchange with an even more radical claim: As Son of Man, He is greater even than the Sabbath. "Son of Man" refers to Daniel's vision of a Being equal with God (Daniel 7:13–14). Jesus often applied this title to Himself, plainly declaring His divine identity.

As Son of Man and Son of God, Jesus had authority even over the Law of God. He not only provided the proper interpretation of it (5:21–48), but completely fulfilled it (5:17). If He allowed His disciples to do something on the Sabbath, they were guiltless.

More than that: As Son of Man, Jesus has authority over all of time. He can determine what people do on the weekly holy day. He can also decide what we should do every other day! He is Lord of our moments and our days.

Shall we love, trust, and obey Him as Lord of every moment of our lives? Or shall we join the Pharisees in rejecting Him and His people?

Shall we seek every opportunity to draw closer to Him through worship, prayer, Bible study, and fellowship, or go our own way, do our own work, and neglect both Jesus and His people?

Day of Rest? Part–5
Matthew 12:8

"For the Son of Man is Lord even of the Sabbath."

Some Christians believe that Sunday, the first day of the week, has become the Christian Sabbath, for Jesus rose on that day. They transfer all the force of the Law of Moses dealing with the Sabbath to the Lord's Day.

In this view, we must not work on Sunday, but attend worship and feed on the Word of God together. Of course, as Jesus taught, works of mercy and of necessity are allowed.

Others say that the New Covenant has set us free from the Law of Moses. They cite passages such as Romans 14:5–6, 10–13; Galatians 3:10–14. 24–25; 4:1–10; Colossians16; to show that Christians are no longer bound by the Mosaic Covenant.

Perhaps we should hold on to a few basic certainties: The Lord God rested after working for six days, and consecrated that day. Jesus rose on the first day of the week, and Christians have always observed that day as the Lord's, reserved for His honor and service.

Those who set aside the Lord's Day for worship, rest, and deeds of kindness almost always find it to be a day of true refreshment and renewal.

When the Lord's Day has been observed with faith and joy, true religion has tended to flourish. But when it has been neglected, or observed with legalism and a critical spirit, vital spirituality becomes rare.

So let us remember one fact of central importance: The Son of Man is Lord of the Sabbath, and therefore Lord of all our moments, hours, days, seasons, and years. Shall we also not honor Him as the Lord of His special day? And shall we not cease from judging others for at least one day in seven?

Jesus the Healer
Matthew 12:13

Then He said to the man, "Stretch out your hand." And he stretched it out, and it was restored as whole as the other.

In the synagogue on a Sabbath day, Jesus was confronted by the Pharisees, who were seeking to find a way to accuse Him of breaking the Sabbath. In the previous passage (12:1–8), we read of Jesus' assertion that He—the Son of Man—was "Lord even of the Sabbath." Surely enraged by that claim, His enemies now pointed to a man whose hand fell useless at his side, withered and lifeless.

"Is it lawful to heal on the Sabbath?," they asked Jesus. The room was tense as everyone waited to see how Christ would respond. What follows demonstrated His true majesty. We see:

> The *perspicacity* of Christ: He saw clearly through their inquiry, aware that it was not just an innocent request for information, and parried with two rhetorical questions of His own. (1) Which of them would not, on the Sabbath, rescue a sheep which had fallen into a pit? (2) How much more valuable is a man than a sheep?
>
> The *penetrating logic* of our Lord, arguing from the lesser to the greater: "Therefore it is lawful to do good on the Sabbath."
>
> The *pity of the Good Shepherd*: He cared more for the crippled man before Him than for the niceties of Pharisaic tradition or the danger of the trap which they intended to spring.
>
> The *power of the Son of God*: With a simple command, "Stretch out your hand," He made the withered hand become "as whole as the other." (We might note in the process that He did no real "work" according even to the man-made rules of His enemies.)

Surely this Man is worthy of our deepest devotion and total trust!

The King Counters His Critics

Hidden Works
Matthew 12:15–16

"And great multitudes followed Him, and He healed them all. Yet He warned them not to make Him known..."

Jesus healed countless people, who were eager to let others know what He had done. Most in His position would love the publicity, but He avoided it. We want our good deeds to be widely known, but He did not. Why?

For several decades, scholars have called this the "Messianic secret." With varying interpretations, they have generally agreed that Jesus desired to keep His identity as Messiah a secret, lest the crowds misunderstand His real goal. They expected a savior to deliver them from the hated Romans, but He came to save them from their sins (1:21).

While there may be some truth in this, it cannot be all that is going on here. After all, Jesus' mighty works were done in public. There was no way to hide His miraculous cures. Word of His wondrous works spread like wildfire, attracting huge throngs. There was no "secret" about His supernatural powers.

Could it be that Jesus was practicing what He preached in the Sermon on the Mount? "Take heed that you do not do your charitable deeds before men, to be seen by them... But when you do a charitable deed, do not let your left hand know was your right hand is doing" (6:1, 3).

Of course, Jesus' works of mercy, done in the open, could not be hidden. But His essential humility, expressed in His Incarnation, life of service, and sacrificial death (Philippians 2:5–8), would explain also why He did not crave fame.

He knew who He was. He did not need to gain favor with God or with man. He sought only to glorify the Father by His truthful speech and life of humble service.

And He calls us to follow in His steps.

Christ the King

What Delights God?
Matthew 12:18

"Behold! My Servant whom I have chosen,
My Beloved in whom My soul is well pleased!"

Matthew applies this quotation from Isaiah to Jesus and His ministry. Notice:

God commands us to pay attention: "Behold!" He says. He wants us to turn our eyes to this Person in whom He especially delights.

Jesus is called God's Servant. Before Him, this title was applied to the patriarchs; Moses; Joshua; David; the prophets; and even pagan kings whom God raised up to do His will. But now the word "Servant" finds its fulfillment in the person and work of God's Son.

God has "chosen" this Servant for a special task—to "declare justice to the Gentiles" until "He sends forth justice to victory" (12:18, 20).

Before being chosen as Servant, however, Christ was God's eternal Son, His Beloved, in whom His soul delighted. (The Greek word translated "servant" also means "son.")

Consider the implications of this brief passage:

We are to focus our minds on Jesus more than on any other person, event, or thing in this world.

If the Father delights in Him, should we not also find our deepest joys in Christ?

And if God especially favors the title "Servant," does that not imply that we, too, should assume the servant role in life?

Gentle Warrior
Matthew 12:18–21

"Behold! My Servant whom I have chosen,
My Beloved in whom My soul is well pleased!
I will put My Spirit upon Him,
And He will declare justice to the Gentiles."

Quoting from the prophet Isaiah (Isaiah 42:1–4), Matthew describes the earthly ministry of Jesus:

> He was a self-conscious Servant of God. He came not to be served, but to serve (20:28); not to do His own will, but that of the Father (26:39, 42).

> He was empowered by the Holy Spirit (12:18, 28).

> He intended to declare the good news of God's just reign not only to the Jews but to all the nations—the Gentiles (8:5–12; 15:28, 29–39; 24:14; 28:19).

> He spoke in the Temple of Jerusalem, in the village synagogues, by the seaside and in deserted places, but He did not "quarrel or cry out," nor did He stir up trouble as an urban rabble-rouser, raising His voice "in the streets" (12:19).

> He acted with consummate gentleness, not breaking a "bruised reed" or extinguishing "a smoking flax" (12:20).

> He marched deliberately towards an ultimate victory, one which would vindicate the justice of God by the self-sacrifice of the only righteous Man for the sins of His people (12:20; 1:21; 20:28).

The result of such a peaceable, patient, and persistent campaign: "in His name the Gentiles will trust" (12:21).

May we not only rely on this Servant of God for our salvation, but follow in His steps of service and sacrifice for others!

The Kingdom Has Come!
Matthew 12:28

"But if I cast out demons by the Spirit of God, surely the kingdom of God has come upon you.

After Jesus delivered a man rendered blind and mute by demons, the Pharisees accused Him of casting out demons by the power of Satan.

Jesus first exposed the silliness of this charge by showing the Satan would not attack his own kingdom.

Then He highlights the true significance of His ministry of demon expulsion: By rescuing people from bondage to evil spirits, Jesus has inaugurated a new stage in the reign of God on earth.

From then on, even the simplest believer can withstand the assaults of Satan, even to the point of driving a demon out of a poor, possessed soul.

In fact, the Early Church Father Athanasius pointed to this fact as a demonstration of the deity of Christ, for only one who was truly God could exercise such power and then delegate it to His followers.

What does that mean for us today?

Just as Jesus defeated Satan by the power of the Holy Spirit, so can we. "Resist the devil, and he will flee from you" (James 4:7).

Clothed in the mighty armor of God, we can be "strong in the Lord and in the power of His might" (Ephesians 6:10), not only to withstand Satan's wiles, but to do all that God wills for us (Ephesians 6:11, 13).

The kingdom has come, because the King has come. Trusting in Him, we can overcome all of the temptations the devil may throw at us, and even expel demons from those he has fully possessed.

As citizens of this heavenly kingdom, we rejoice in His reign in and through us, even as we await the full revelation of His glory.

Binding the Strong Man
Matthew 12:29

"Or how can one enter a strong man's house and plunder his goods, unless he first binds the strong man? And then he will plunder his house."

Jesus had been casting out demons, when the Pharisees charged that Jesus did so by the power of Satan himself. After countering that accusation by showing its inconsistency and stating that the real reason for His victory over demons lay in His kingly power, Jesus now explains further:

As the "stronger" man, He has bound the "strong man," that is the devil. That is why Jesus can plunder the strong man's house by expelling demons from tormented people.

Jesus defeated Satan in the wilderness (4:1–11). Afterward, He began His ministry of teaching, preaching, healing, and deliverance with the words, "Repent, for the kingdom of heaven is at hand" (4:17).

In other words, His power to heal and His proclamation of the truth, along with His casting out of evil spirits, demonstrate that He, the true and final King, has come, bringing with Him deliverance from evil of all sorts.

When the Seventy disciples had returned from their triumphant tour of ministry, exclaiming that "even the demons are subject to us in Your name," Jesus told them where that authority came from: "I saw Satan fall like lightning from heaven" (Luke 10:18).

John records that event in these words: "The great dragon was cast out, that serpent of old, called the Devil and Satan, who deceives the whole world; he was cast to the earth, and his angels were cast out with him" (Revelation 12:9). The context makes clear that this took place after the birth of Christ.

Thus, we do not need to "bind" Satan or any demons now. We may simply claim the power of the crucified and risen Christ as we preach and heal and resist evil in His name.

In other words, we serve the really Strong Man, Jesus!

Christ the King

Only Two Options
Matthew 12:30

"He who is not with Me is against Me, and he who does not gather with Me scatters abroad."

There is no middle ground; no neutral stance; no third way.

We go with the Magi, to worship the Baby Jesus, or with Herod, to kill Him.

We stand with John the Baptist, who honored Jesus as the Christ, or with Satan, who tried to deflect Him from the path to Golgotha.

We walk with the four fishermen, who followed Jesus as Master, or with the Pharisees, who stalked Him as prey.

Indeed, Jesus made this solemn pronouncement after the Pharisees had ascribed the expulsion of a demon to the ruler of the demons, Satan himself (12:24).

Throughout Matthew's Gospel, this theme recurs repeatedly, as we have already seen.

There are the hypocrites (Pharisees) who practice their piety before men, in order to be seen by them; and the true disciples, who seek God's favor alone (6:1–18).

"No one can serve two masters; ... You cannot serve God and mammon" (6:24).

"Wide *is* the gate and broad *is* the way that leads to destruction, and there are many who go in by it. Because narrow *is* the gate and difficult *is* the way which leads to life, and there are few who find it" (7:13–14).

We shall build our lives upon the rock of Jesus' teaching, or the sands of folly (7:24–27).

We shall take up our cross to follow Christ, and find life; or seek the "life" in this world, and endure eternal death (10:38–39).

The good tree bears good fruit; the bad tree bears rotten fruit, or none at all (12:33).

Our words will either build others up in faith, hope, and love, or they will be idle and corrosive (12:36; Ephesians 4:29).

We either redeem the time, or waste it (Ephesians 5:16).

Which will it be for us today, tomorrow, and always?

What Sins Can be Forgiven?
Matthew 12:31

"Therefore I say to you, every sin and blasphemy will be forgiven men, but the blasphemy against *the Spirit will not be forgiven men."*

We must take both parts of this statement very seriously. Lets start with the warning.

There is a sin which cannot be forgiven. This "blasphemy *against* the Holy Spirit" renders one incapable of salvation, now or in the age to come (12:32).

The Pharisees obviously committed this unpardonable transgression when they said that Jesus was casting out demons by the power of Satan, not God. Jesus countered by insisting that His exorcisms were worked by the power of the Holy Spirit.

The Pharisees' sin apparently consisted in their total rejection of the ministry Jesus came to do, which was in fact good. Thus, they placed themselves beyond the range of Jesus' saving grace, for they rejected the essence of His ministry, which was salvation from sin and its effects.

Those who, like Paul, at first did not believe in Jesus but later repented could be forgiven. On the other hand, those who did not even want the kind of deliverance Jesus came to bring, and who in fact considered it satanic, would not even ask forgiveness, for they did not consider themselves wrong before God.

What about the promise? How wonderful and comprehensive it is! "Every sin and blasphemy will be forgiven"! Dishonoring parents, adultery, murder, stealing, lying, covetousness, not loving and serving God—all these can be covered with the blood of Jesus, who came to "save His people from their sins" (1:21).

Traitors and prostitutes, adulterers and thieves, even Matthew the tax collector and Peter the coward, knew the grace of God through faith in Christ Jesus.

And so can we, as long as we truly repent and trust in Jesus each day.

Who are the True Christians?
Matthew 12:33

"Either make the tree good and its fruit good, or else make the tree bad and its fruit bad; for a tree is known by its fruit."

Much confusion surrounds the name "Christian." Does it refer to those who go to a "Christian" church? Or to those who simply profess faith in Jesus Christ? Or does "Christian" describe those whose lives reflect, to a substantial degree, their faith in Christ?

Jesus had warned against false prophets, saying, "You will know them by their fruits" (7:16). Immediately after that, He declared, "Not everyone who says to Me, 'Lord, Lord,' shall enter the kingdom of heaven, but he who does the will of My Father in heaven" (7:21).

In this passage, He continues His rebuke of the Pharisees, whom everyone considered to be very religious, and who considered themselves to be righteous. Jesus saw them differently. Both their works and their words proved them to be hypocrites.

Likewise, today many people say they believe in Jesus Christ as Lord, but how many live accordingly? What "fruit" do they bear in daily life?

A "good tree"—that is, a true believer—will sink its roots deep into God's Word each day, and soak that reading with prayer. He or she will bear the "fruit" of humility, trust in God alone, and love towards others (John 15:1–10; Galatians 5:22–24).

While working hard to complete the tasks set before him, a real Christian sets his hope on the next life, and does not live for success or satisfaction in this life. People will notice the relative absence of pride and passion, and the greater degree of unselfish service towards God and others in the life of one who sincerely trusts in Christ.

What kind of "tree" are you?

The Hissing of Snakes
Matthew 12:34

"Brood of vipers! How can you, being evil, speak good things? For out of the abundance of the heart the mouth speaks."

The Pharisees had accused Jesus of casting out demons by the power of Satan (12:24). In other words, they had labeled the good work of Christ, done by the power of the Holy Spirit, as evil.

They should have known better, for Jesus had given them plenty of evidence that He was the Son of God, empowered by the Spirit of God. Their criticism of Him, therefore, demonstrated that they were allies of the devil, "that serpent of old" (Revelation 12:9).

Jesus had heard the hissing of God's inveterate enemy in the wilderness (4:3–10), and recognized his voice in the words of the Pharisees. That is why He called them, "brood [offspring] of vipers."

Then He went to the root of the matter: Since they were, like Satan, wicked to the core, how could they utter anything good?

The condition of the heart determines the character of our speech. To put it another way, our words reflect our inner nature. This especially applies to what we say about others, and particularly about God and His Son, Jesus.

Now is the time to examine our heart, using our tongue as a standard. Are we critical of others? Do we express unbelief in God's goodness? Are our lips filled with praise and thanks to our heavenly Father for His grace to us and to others who believe in Christ?

What is our "native tongue"? What kind of "abundance" fills our inner self? In other words, whose children are we?

Only Two Options
Matthew 12:35

"A good man out of the good treasure of his heart brings forth good things, and an evil man out of the evil treasure brings forth evil things."

Notice the stark contrasts which Jesus places before us: Good man/good heart/good words *vs.* Evil man/evil heart/ evil words.

The Greek word for "good" used here refers to that which is good in itself and helpful to others. The word for "evil" denotes an active, malevolent meanness, and refers often to Satan himself, "the evil one." This type of "evil" is intrinsically bad and also brings harm to others.

There are only two kinds of people, each with a characteristic set of motives and mental habits. Jesus certainly does not mean that a "good" person is without sin, for He has already told us to pray daily, "Forgive us our debts" (6:12).

A "good man" is one who has received a new heart from God through the work of the Holy Spirit; he has been born again from above (John 3:3, 5). Though still capable of sin, he is nevertheless on the right path, seeking God, and trusting in Jesus Christ. The "evil man" does not know God and walks on a road that leads to destruction.

Likewise, there are only two types of words: All that we say or hear is either helpful or harmful. Words either build, or destroy; feed, or poison; heal, or wound; enlighten, or mislead; encourage, or discourage.

"Create in me a clean heart, O God, and renew a steadfast spirit within me" (Psalm 51:10).

"Let the words of my mouth and the meditation of my heart be acceptable in Your sight, O LORD, my strength and my Redeemer" (Psalm 19:14)

Weighed Words
Matthew 12:36–37

"But I say to you that for every idle word men may speak, they will give account of it in the day of judgment. For by your words you will be justified, and by your words you will be condemned."

What an awful prospect! On the last day, when the books are opened and our actions are weighed in the balance, our words will bring justification [acquittal] or condemnation.

Why is that? Because, as we have seen, we speak from the heart (12:34–35). The Pharisees revealed their inner wickedness when they accused Jesus of casting out demons by the power of the devil (12:24).

By contrast, those who confess faith in Christ before men will be commended to the Father by Christ on the Last Day, for their words will have confirmed their commitment to Jesus (10:32).

But what are "idle" words? In short, anything that is "corrupt" [rotten, useless], that does not build others up in faith, hope, and love; that does not "impart grace to the hearers" (Ephesians 4:29).

That includes, of course, "filthiness, foolish talking, coarse jesting," as well as bitter, angry, contentious, and blasphemous speech (Ephesians 4:31), as well as "empty words" that deceive people into thinking that our actions will not be punished (Ephesians 5:6).

The Israelites died in the wilderness because they spoke words of complaint (1 Corinthians 10:10), and Moses was barred entry to the Promised Land for his angry outburst in response (Numbers 20:12).

That is why we should be "swift to hear, slow to speak, slow to wrath" (James 1:19).

"Let the words of my mouth, and the meditations of my heart be acceptable in Your sight, O LORD, my strength and my Redeemer" (Psalm 19:14).

Weighty Words
Matthew 12:37

"For by your words you will be justified."

If "idle" words will be found empty and worthless on the Last Day, what sort of words will receive approval?

"But let your 'Yes' be 'Yes', and your 'No,' 'No'" (5:37). Honest words of conviction and commitment, followed by consistent behavior, will be accepted by the one who Himself was the "Amen," the true and faithful Word of God.

"In this manner, therefore, pray: Our Father in heaven..." (6:9). "Vain repetitions" carry no weight in prayer. "Many words" uttered without true faith and heartfelt confidence will not be heard by God (6:7). But prayers based upon the teaching of Christ and His apostles will certainly have effect.

"Not every one who says to me, 'Lord, Lord,' shall enter the kingdom of heaven, but he who does the will of My Father in heaven" (7:21). Only those professions of allegiance to Jesus that are backed up by performing the will of God, as revealed by the words of Jesus (7:24), will bring entrance into the eternal kingdom.

"Therefore whoever confesses Me before men, him I will also confess before My Father who is in heaven" (10:32). A simple, sincere expression of faith in Jesus Christ will be met with Christ's corresponding affirmation of the speaker to God the Father and Judge.

"Go therefore and make disciples of all nations, baptizing them in the Name of the Father and of the Son and of the Holy Spirit, teaching them to observe all things that I have commanded you" (28:19–20). Words that proclaim the Gospel of salvation by faith in Jesus Christ, and that instruct believers to keep all of the commands of Christ, will also find favor on the day of judgment.

May our words be "weighty" and "worthy"!

The Case for Christ
Matthew 12:39

But He answered and said to them, "An evil and adulterous generation seeks after a sign, and no sign will be given to it except the sign of the prophet Jonah."

Despite all the miracles of healing and exorcism, His matchless teaching, and His sinless life, the Pharisees still demanded from Jesus some proof of His authority!

He rebuked them in two ways: By calling them "an evil and adulterous generation" and by denying to them any "sign" other than His resurrection. (As He explained immediately, "the sign of Jonah" refers to his "resurrection" from the belly of the great fish, which is a type of the resurrection of Jesus from the grave.)

They were "evil" because they hated God's only Son and the salvation He brought. He called them "adulterous" because their hearts had wandered from God. Instead, they worshiped their own righteousness, which was a sham.

They could not believe in Christ, because they would not. They had their own ideas of what the Messiah would be like, and Jesus did not fit their mental image. They could not discern God's love in His actions, or truth in His teachings.

What about us? Do we seek some sort of proof from God that Jesus is Savior and Lord? Do we demand a "sign" from heaven to convince us that God's love is found in Christ?

Let us remember that the ultimate proof of God's love for us consists in Christ's death for the ungodly (Romans 5:8). And the decisive indication that His death was a sacrifice accepted by God lies in His resurrection.

No matter what our circumstances, trials, troubles, and suffering, to look any further is to join the Pharisees, and to miss God's blessing.

Greater than Jonah
Matthew 12:40–41

"And indeed a greater than Jonah is here."

After rebuking the scribes and Pharisees for seeking some sign to authenticate Jesus' authority, He refers them to the greatest "proof" of His person and work: His resurrection from the dead (12:40). Then Jesus both compares and contrasts Himself with the prophet Jonah:

He is like *Jonah* in that He startled everyone by appearing alive after being presumed dead. Jonah came out of the belly of the great fish, and Jesus came out of His tomb.

Jonah had preached a message of repentance to the people of the great pagan city of Nineveh, in Assyria. Jesus, likewise, began His ministry with a command to "Repent, for the kingdom of heaven is at hand" (4:17).

On the other hand, Jesus is unlike Jonah:

> The Old Testament prophet was the son of Amittai (Jonah 1:1). Jesus called Himself "Son of Man," referring not only to His human nature, which was like ours in every respect but sin (Hebrews 2:14; 4:15), but also to His divine nature, foretold by the great prophecy in Daniel 7:13–14.

> Jonah did not really die, but was preserved alive in the stomach of the great fish. Jesus was truly killed on the Cross. When He emerged from the tomb, it was a real resurrection from death (16:21).

> Jonah preached repentance to people of a limited locale, and the change in the Ninevites proved to be temporary, for their nation later turned and attacked both Israel and Judah. Jesus commanded His disciples to preach a message of "repentance and remission of sins ... in His name to all nations" (Luke 24:47). Their obedience produced a church in Nineveh itself that took the Good News even to China in the 7th century A.D. Though greatly reduced, the Syrian church remains to this day.

Shall we not worship and obey this "greater than Jonah" Son of Man today?

Greater than Solomon
Matthew 12:42

"The queen of the South will rise up in the judgment with this generation and condemn it, for she came from the ends of the earth to hear the wisdom of Solomon; and indeed a greater than Solomon is here."

Jesus resembles Solomon in several ways:

They are both "sons" of King David (1:1, 6).

They amazed people with their wisdom and answers to "insoluble" problems (1 Kings 3:1–28; Matthew 13:54; 22:15–46).

They spoke parables about nature and life in general (1 Kings 4:32–33; Proverbs, Song of Solomon, Ecclesiastes; Matthew 13:1–52)

They attracted seekers of wisdom from foreign lands (1 Kings 10:1–13; Matthew 15:30–32).

But Jesus is incomparably greater than Solomon. Consider:

Solomon's many wives turned his heart away from God, but Jesus remained both sexually pure and totally devoted to His Father in heaven and to His bride—the church (1 Kings 11:1–4; Ephesians 5:25–30; Hebrews 2:18; 4:15).

Solomon died, was buried, and remained in his tomb; Jesus rose victoriously from the dead and left His tomb as an empty witness to His triumph (28:1–8)

Solomon's vast wisdom came as a result of his prayer to God (1 Kings 3:6–12); Jesus Himself is the Word of God made flesh, in whom all the treasures of divine wisdom and knowledge reside eternally (John 1:1–3; Colossians 2:3). Indeed, He is the very Wisdom of whom Solomon spoke (12:42; Luke 7:35; 1 Corinthians 1:24, 30; Revelation 7:12).

Shall we turn our backs on Him, as His own people did, or shall we build our lives upon the rock of His teaching by listening to His words, believing His promises, and obeying His commands (7:24–29; 28:18–20)?

From Bad to Worse
Matthew 12:43–45

"When an unclean spirit goes out of a man, he goes through dry places, seeking rest, and finds none. Then he says, 'I will return to my house form which I came.' And when he comes, he finds it empty, swept, and put in order. Then he goes and takes with him seven other spirits more wicked than himself, and they enter and dwell there; and the last state of that man is worse than the first. So shall it be with this wicked generation."

This puzzling passage finds its proper interpretation in the light of what precedes and follows.

Jesus delivered people from possession by demons by the power of the Spirit of God, thus demonstrating that the kingdom of God had arrived on the scene. The Pharisees, however, attributed His exorcisms to Satan, thus calling good evil and showing their incurable hard-heartedness (12:22–32). They were bad trees; how could they bear good fruit (12:33–37)?

These Jewish leaders then compounded their error by demanding that Jesus produce some miraculous proof of His commission from God, which Jesus refuses to provide until He rises from the dead. Indeed, He had already given enough evidence that He was Son of God and Savior of Israel (12:38–42).

Jesus then teaches that deliverance from demons does not insure salvation. Unless devotion to Christ replaces the dominion of one evil spirit, temporary relief and reform will be swallowed up by deeper demonization and greater wickedness.

In other words, we cannot remain neutral to Christ (12:30), much less disbelieve Him (12:38–42). But even temporary faith, which brings some sort of freedom from bondage, will not protect us from the power of the devil. The parable of the sower, which follows shortly afterward, describes people who receive God's word with joy, but fall away when trouble comes, or the distractions of this world "choke the word" (13:3–9, 18–23).

Only when our nature is changed by whole-hearted faith in Christ and regeneration by His Spirit, so that we become God's children and do His will, can we be safe in God's kingdom (12:33–37; 46–50).

The King Counters His Critics

What about you? Are you relying on "self-help" programs to set you free from powerful addictions? Depending upon church attendance to guarantee salvation? Hoping that deliverance from an evil spirit will produce a fundamental change in your character? Withholding full commitment to Christ until He "proves" Himself to you? If so, every "improvement" in your life will be erased by slavery to more pernicious forces, and you will end up in lasting misery.

Now is the time to trust in Christ and follow Him fully as the only one who can "save His people from their sins" (1:21).

Outside to Speak or Inside To Listen?
Matthew 12:46–50

While He was still talking to the multitudes, behold, His mother and brothers stood outside, seeking to speak with Him.... But He answered and said..., "Who is My mother and who are My brothers?"

Notice the contrast: Jesus' immediate family stood outside, seeking to speak to Him, while His disciples were inside, listening.

This difference divides all of mankind. We are not divided primarily by blood, or language, or culture, but by our attitude towards Jesus Christ.

There are those "outside," who want to pass judgment on Christ. In this case, His family wanted to tell Him that He was working too hard.

Then there are those "inside," who want to listen to Jesus. They see Him as Teacher, Master, and Lord. They look to Him for wisdom and truth, light and life. In this case, His disciples eagerly waited upon His every word.

Those on the "outside" live according to what they think right and best for themselves. Those on the "inside" take their values from God's Word, especially the Word of God incarnate in the Man Christ Jesus.

Where are you today?

The Essence of Christianity
Matthew 12:47–50

Then one said to Him, "Look, Your mother and Your brothers are standing outside, seeking to speak to You." But He answered and said..., "Who is My mother and who are My brothers?... whoever does the will of My Father in heaven is My brother and sister and mother."

What is the Christian faith about?

Rules and regulations? No, although there are plenty of rules—called commands—which Christians must obey.

Rites and rituals? No, although Christians do engage in regular worship, both privately and together.

Reason and rationality? No, although the Christian faith is eminently reasonable and can be defended with rational arguments based upon solid evidence and true logic.

What, then, lies at the heart of Christianity? A new *relationship*:

Through faith in Jesus Christ, God's unique Son, we can become children of God the Father. Those who repent of their sins and trust fully in Christ as Savior are born again through the work of the Holy Spirit, and receive new life—the life of God.

To use another metaphor, all those who put their faith in Jesus are adopted as sons of God, with full rights to a heavenly, eternal inheritance.

As children of God, they are related to Jesus, the Son of God, as "brothers" and "sisters" and "mothers." Though He alone possesses equal status with God as the eternal Son, believers in Him also belong to this new family of God.

That means that true Christians are also related to each other as brothers and sisters.

Receiving, nurturing, and enjoying this new "family" relationship is the core of Christianity.

Who is Mary?
Matthew 12:48

But He answered and said to the one who told Him, "Who is My mother and who are My brothers?"

Christians have fallen into two errors in their views of Mary, the mother of Jesus.

By and large, Protestants have ignored her. They seem to forget that she was God's chosen vessel, through whom the Son of God was brought into this world as the God-Man, Jesus.

Mary's response to the angel Gabriel sets the standard for all who hear the word of God: "Behold the maidservant of the Lord! Let it be to me according to your word" (Luke 1:38).

On the other hand, Roman Catholic teaching about Mary goes far beyond what the Bible records.

For example, they deny that she gave birth to any children after Jesus was born, claiming that "brother" and "sister" means "cousin" in the passages which refer to Jesus' siblings. But if that were true, then "mother" should not mean that Jesus came from Mary!

In the early centuries of the Church, pagans were notorious for degenerate sexual mores. Some Christian leaders sought to counter this by stressing the value of virginity, and held up Mary as an exemplar of perpetual abstinence from sex.

Later, the Pope declared that Mary had no sin of any kind; that she herself was conceived apart from sin; and that she ascended directly to heaven. Finally, the Magisterium (teaching office) of the Roman Catholic Church has allowed that Mary be called Co-Redemptrix with Christ, and that all grace flows to us from her.

It is best to restrict ourselves to what the Bible says: Mary was Jesus' mother. Though she did not always understand Her Son and His mission, she remained loyal to Him and eventually, along with His brothers, became one of His disciples (Acts 1:14), and thus a member of His "forever family."

The Forever Family
Matthew 12:49

And He stretched out His hand toward His disciples and said, "Here are My mother and My brothers!"

Jesus called not His blood relatives, but His disciples, His true family. Why?

Those who seek to do God's will have more in common with each other than they do even with their own family of origin. Consider:

They have a common purpose in life: To know and serve God.

They have a common loyalty to their Father in heaven and to His Son, Jesus.

They have a common source of life, the Holy Spirit, who dwells in them.

They share the same experience of salvation through the forgiveness of sin, and of God's constant unmerited kindness towards them.

This life, unlike the body which they inherit from their parents, will never perish.

They share a common destiny: To live with God and His people forever.

They have a common standard of truth, the Word of God contained in the Scriptures. The Bible surpasses even family tradition and cultural norms as a source for guidance and a standard of values.

They are bound together by ties which cannot be broken, because they are united to Christ, who is the Head of this trans-national, trans-cultural body of believers.

Jesus and His disciples belong to a "forever family"—the household of God.

What Is God's Will?
Matthew 12:50

"For whoever does the will of My Father in heaven is My brother and sister and mother."

If doing God's will is the mark of the true "relative" of Jesus Christ, then what is that "will"?

Matthew's Gospel provides ample information for us to know the will of God. A quick review of the Sermon on the Mount will elucidate this concept. Doing the Father's will means obedience to His revealed commands, as recorded in the Bible (5:17–42).

More than that, fulfilling God's will involves nothing less than full conformity to the character of God, who loves the unlovely (5:48). It includes helping others (6:1–4); prayer (6:5–15); fasting (6:16–18); and seeking first His kingdom, not wealth or financial security (6:19–34).

At the end of this Gospel, Jesus commands His disciples to "make disciples of all nations" (28:18–20). Worldwide evangelism of unbelievers and edification of believers is a central part of God's will for us.

Paul tells the Thessalonian Christians that the will of God is "your sanctification, that you should abstain from sexual immorality" (1 Thessalonians 4:3).

In the next chapter, he goes even deeper: "Rejoice always, pray without ceasing, in everything give thanks; for this is the will of God in Christ Jesus for you" (1 Thessalonians 5:16–18).

A daily, diligent searching of the Scriptures will leave us in little doubt about God's will for us. Knowing is not enough, however. We need God's strength to perform what He requires.

That is why Jesus taught us to pray, "Our Father in heaven…Your will be done on earth as *it is* in heaven" (6:9–10). Amen.

Christ the King

13 The King Explains His Kingdom

"Listen Up!"
Matthew 13:3

"Behold, a sower went out to sow."

The little word, "Behold!" tells us to stop what we are doing and pay attention. At the end of this parable, Jesus emphasized the importance of what He had just said: "He who has ears to hear, let him hear!"

But why? In Jesus' time, a man going forth with seed to sow would have been a common sight. Why should we take note of such an ordinary event? Why should we hear and ponder the story Jesus has told? There are several reasons:

> This story is not mainly a tale about a farmer. Jesus later explains that the "seed" is the word of God, the message of the kingdom, the Gospel (13:19). He is talking about the truth which saves (Ephesians 1:13).

> In context, the sower is Jesus, the Preacher *par excellence*. Ever since the beginning of His ministry He has been addressing to large crowds (4:25; 5:1; 12:23) in open fields, synagogues, and private homes. It is a story about our Lord.

> By implication, the sower also represents all the followers of Jesus who will "go ... and make disciples of all nations" (28:19), preaching this gospel of the kingdom "in all the world" (24:14).

> Like Jesus Himself, all those who spread the Good News will meet with varying types of response, from incomprehension (13:19) to superficial reception (13:20–22) to real conversion (13:23). In other words, this little story is talking about everyone who heralds or hears the word of God. That's us!

> The way we listen to this parable will determine the value—what Jesus calls "fruit"—of our entire life (13:19–23). The stakes are enormous.

> Furthermore, understanding this short parable of the sower and the four soils provides the key to "all the parables" Jesus told (Mark 4:13).

> So let us ponder the parable of the sower and the soils (13:1–9, 18–23) with fresh focus.

Purpose, Priority, Power
Matthew 13:3–8

"Behold, a sower went out to sow."

From this brief story, included in three Gospels, we learn vital truths:

> The *purpose of God:* God *will* establish His kingdom on earth. Nothing will thwart His intention. (Matthew 6:10; 16:18)

> The *priority of proclamation:* The kingdom comes in this age first by preaching. Jesus proclaimed, "Repent, for the kingdom of heaven [God] is at hand" (4:17), and promised, "... this gospel of the kingdom will be preached in all the world as a witness to all the nations, and then the end will come" (24:14).

> The *presence of opposition:* The gospel message will be opposed by Satan, trouble and persecution, the cares of this world, and the deceitfulness of riches (13:19–22).

> The *proportion of productivity:* Most hearers will either misunderstand the message, or fail to produce the crops of faith-filled living (13:19–22). There are few who enter the "gate which leads to life" (7:14). "Many are called [by the public preaching of the Gospel] but few *are* chosen (22:14).

> The *power of the Word of God:* The "seed" of God's Good News will transform the lives of those who heed it, making them powerful and productive "doers" of the truth and witnesses of Christ (13:8, 23, 31–33; 5:16; 28:18–20; Acts 1:8).

> The *preciousness of the Gospel message:* Fruitfulness and futility; satisfaction and frustration; life and death—all depend upon the sharing, believing, and obeying the Word of Christ.

Friends, shall we not expend every effort, pay any price, overcome every obstacle, and discard every distraction, in order to spread abroad the word of truth, the Gospel of salvation, to the glory of our King Jesus?

The Purpose of the Parables
Matthew 13:10–11

And the disciples came and said to Him, "Why do You speak to them in parables?" He answered and said to them, "Because it has been given to you to know the mysteries of the kingdom of heaven, but to them it has not been given."

Almost everyone likes the parables of Jesus. These short stories highlight some feature of common life in His day and draw out spiritual truths valid for all time. The problem is: Why are the parables sometimes hard to understand? What, in fact, is their overall purpose in the teaching ministry of Jesus?

The answer Jesus gave to His disciples surprises us: He told parables in order to enlighten some and to leave others in the dark! "For whoever has, to him more will be given, and he will have abundance; but whoever does not have, even what he has will be taken away from him" (13:12).

As He had declared before in a prayer of praise to His Father, God hides His truth from the "wise and prudent" and unveils it to "babes" (11:25). That is, those who rely on their own reason and intuition to know God remain in the dark, while the ones who humbly confess their ignorance and ask for mercy receive light.

Here, He quotes the words of God when Isaiah was commissioned to proclaim His coming judgment and salvation to a nation that would not hear (13:14–15; Isaiah 6:9–10). However we interpret this strange passage, it is clear that those who "see" and "hear" with understanding and faith are blessed, for many have sought such revelation in vain (13:16–17). Though the Old Testament revelation was clear in some ways, those who have the unveiling of God's mysteries in Christ are recipients of a priceless gift.

Does it not therefore befit us not only to hear and heed the words of Christ, but to thank and praise God for granting us the inestimable privilege of knowing God through faith in the Gospel of His Son?

Rootless "Faith"
Matthew 13:20–21

"But he who received the seed on stony places, this is he who hears the word and immediately receives it with joy; yet he has no root in himself, but endures only for a while. For when tribulation or persecution arises because of the word, immediately he stumbles."

The parable of the sower describes not only Jesus' ministry, but that of all those who seek to share the Word of God with others.

Some hearers will receive the Christian message "with joy." Perhaps they are attracted by the idea of one true God who combines both justice and love in perfect harmony.

Maybe the portrait of Jesus as the sinless Son of God and suffering servant moves them, or the offer of eternal bliss, or the beauty of the life of early Christians. Or it may simply be the sublime moral code of the Bible that draws them to "receive" the Word.

But, sadly, they "have no root in them." The truth does not penetrate their hearts. They do not see their sin in all its awful horror, or tremble before the judgment of a holy God. They like the promises in the Bible, but do not understand that these refer primarily to spiritual blessings.

Thus, when some kind of trouble comes, they buckle. Sickness, failure, financial difficulties, unfulfilled desires—all these make them question the goodness of God, or His mighty power. Likewise, when they are rejected for being identified with Christ, they can't take it.

"This wasn't part of the original bargain!" they complain. "Why isn't God answering my prayers? I thought that faith in Him would bring happiness, health, and prosperity. God has broken His promises to me. I can't believe in Him anymore."

Of course, this response merely indicates their misunderstanding of the Gospel message and reveals their motives. They sought earthly comfort, not spiritual life. They looked for good things, not for God Himself. In other words, they never really believed in Christ.

Choked by Thorns
Matthew 13:22

"Now he who received the seed among the thorns is he who hears the word, and the cares of this world and the deceitfulness of riches choke the word, and he becomes unfruitful."

Trouble and persecution cause some professing Christians to fall away. Others fail to grow, not because of what has happened, but because of what might happen!

"The cares of this world" can be translated as "concern for this age." Those who set their hopes on this life will be filled with anxiety.

"What shall we eat? What shall we wear? Where shall we live?" They fret and worry, and spend all their time trying to ensure their safety and material security. God's Word loses its previous urgency in their lives. They neglect to read the Bible, have no time for church, and eventually drift away.

"The deceitfulness of riches" causes others to stumble. After all, money seems to promise pleasure, prestige, power, and prominence to those who get enough of it.

But what is "enough"? One very wealthy man answered that question quite simply: "Just a little bit more than I have now…" In other words, those who seek to be rich will never have "enough." In their search for more, they will be trapped by an endless pursuit of possessions.

Once you have money, you have to figure out how to save it, spend it, increase it, protect it. Your mind becomes distracted by a multitude of tasks that demand your total attention.

Instead of seeking to know and serve God, those who worship Mammon fall into a bondage that separates them from the Lord and the life and joy He offers. They will not evince love for God or for those around them, but will manifest a growing obsession with things.

Make no mistake: Anyone who says he is a Christian, but whose life revolves around a concern for this world, is a hypocrite. "You will know them by their fruits."

Fruitful Faith
Matthew 13:23

"But he who received seed on the good ground is he who hears the word and understands it, who indeed bears fruit and produces: some a hundredfold, some sixty, some thirty."

After describing three sorts of people who do not respond to the Gospel with saving faith, Jesus finally speaks of those who not only hear the Word of God, but understand it, and then go on to produce a bountiful crop.

We learn several vital lessons from the entire parable with its explanation:

> Most people who hear the Good News of Christ will not be saved. Either they will not understand, or they will receive the word with joy, but then fall away.
>
> Some, however, will receive the message with true faith, and demonstrate their trust by their changed lives.
>
> From the context, we know that bearing fruit includes perseverance under troubles and even persecution (13:21; see also 5:11–12; 10:32–39). If someone who claims to believe in Christ turns away from Him in the face of danger, then he is not yet born again.
>
> The true believer will also refuse to become embroiled in "the cares of this world and the deceitfulness of riches." Instead, he will "seek first the kingdom of God and His righteousness" (6:33). When he is tempted to "lay up ... treasures on earth" (6:19) or to "worry about tomorrow" (6:34), he will instead pray, "Your kingdom come. Your will be done ... Give us this day our daily bread." (6:10–11).

Jesus said of false prophets, "You will know them by their fruits" (7:16). Here He extends that principle to all those who profess to follow Christ: Fruitfulness, which consists in both trust and obedience, will prove the genuineness of faith.

How do we measure up to this standard? Is our faith fruitful?

The King Explains His Kingdom

Small, but Potent
Matthew 13:31, 33

"The kingdom of heaven is like a mustard seed ... The kingdom of heaven is like leaven..."

With these two parables, Jesus illustrates a central fact of God's present kingdom on earth: It seems insignificant, but possesses vast potential.

Like a tiny seed, or a little bit of yeast, God's kingdom in this age hardly appears to the untrained eye. In almost any community, only tiny proportions of people really trust in Christ and seek to follow Him.

Oh, there may be a large and prominent church building on the corner, or even a flourishing congregation of worshipers. But those whose lives really reflect the presence and power of God are small.

As a result, we see corruption and even chaos in the world. Violence, theft, lying, oppression, and moral degradation fill the news, and rightly so. Evil men rule much of the world, apparently unrestricted by God.

Meanwhile, however, a potent force quietly gathers its strength. The Spirit of God implants faith in His Word among more and more people. Around the globe, the number of believers grows daily.

At certain times and in some places, Christians—acting like salt and light in the community—exercise influence beyond their numbers, as moral standards begin to change in the general population. Indeed, some countries, and even whole cultures, have been radically improved as a result of the spread of God's Word among the masses.

Jesus predicts that someday this process will come to full fruition. Not only partially and temporarily, but fully and permanently, the entire globe will be decisively transformed by the kingdom of God.

Until that time, believers go about their daily tasks, asking God to cause His name to be glorified, His kingdom come, and His will be done, first in their own lives, and then throughout the whole earth.

The End of this Age
Matthew 13:40

"Therefore as the tares are gathered and burned in the fire, so it will be at the end of this age."

This age is coming to an end. We do not know *when* it will happen, but Jesus tells us *what* will happen:

"The Son of Man [that is, Jesus] will send out His angels, and they will gather out of His kingdom all things that offend, and those who practice lawlessness, and will cast them into the furnace of fire. There will be wailing and gnashing of teeth" (13:41–42).

In other words, judgment!

The Apostle Peter, who heard Jesus make this statement, writes about "the day of judgment and perdition [destruction] of ungodly men.... the heavens will pass away with a great noise, and the elements will melt with fervent heat; both the earth and the works that are in it will be burned up" (2 Peter 3:7, 10).

This world will someday be destroyed. All that we see—houses, cars, buildings, planes, gardens, fields, factories, forests—everything will suddenly disappear in a huge conflagration.

At the same time, those who have set their hope on this world, who have "loved" this world more than God, who have followed the "course of this world" and have allowed themselves to be "conformed to this world"—these people will be judged by God and then consigned to what Jesus calls "everlasting punishment" (25:46).

What does that say about our priorities in life?

The King Explains His Kingdom

Temporary Toleration
Matthew 13:41–43

"The Son of Man will send out His angels, and they will gather out of His kingdom all things that offend, and those who practice lawlessness, and will cast them into the furnace of fire. There will be wailing and gnashing of teeth. Then the righteous will shine forth as the sun in the kingdom of their Father. He who has ears to hear, let him hear!"

In the parable of the wheat and the weeds [tares], Jesus explains one reason why God allows the presence of wicked people in the world (13:24–30, 36–43).

As in a field of wheat, both the desired crop and the unwanted weeds grow up together (13:26). The latter are the "sons of the wicked one" (13:38)—that is, the "children" of the devil. If you think this description is too strong, remember that it comes from the lips of Jesus Himself, repeated for us in John 8:44.

Paul explains that all people are like that before God saves them, because they—we—are "sons of disobedience" and thus destined for the wrath of God (Ephesians 2:2, 3). Everyone, without exception, is in bondage to the seduction of this world, the deceptions of Satan, and the desires of our own sinful nature (Ephesians 2:1–3).

But there is another group, the "sons of the kingdom" (13:38), also called "the righteous" (13:43). They are those who, in the parable of the sower (13:18–23) hear God's word, believe it, and produce a crop of good deeds.

God allows both the wicked and the righteous to exist side by side in the "field" that is the present age. Why? Partly, it seems, because to destroy the weeds would require killing the wheat also, they are so inseparably associated at present.

At the end of the age, however, when Christ returns to judge the world and inaugurate His eternal kingdom, He will utterly eliminate all who "practice lawlessness," and consign them to unending torment, while the ones who repented, believed, and turned to Him, will "shine forth" like the sun in all its brilliance.

What can we learn from this? At the very least, lets be less agitated about the presence of evil men in this world than the presence of evil in our own hearts! Don't worry; a final reckoning and revealing is coming; may we be among the "righteous" then!

Priceless Treasure
Matthew 13:44 Part–1

"Again, the kingdom of heaven is like a treasure hidden in a field, which a man found and hid; and for joy over it he goes and sells all that he has and buys that field."

From this brief parable come several precious truths about God's kingdom, which Jesus elsewhere equates with eternal life (19:16, 23):

It is like a treasure. Untold spiritual wealth awaits those who trust in Jesus Christ. They will find in Him "all the treasures of wisdom and knowledge" (Colossians 2:3), as well as the riches of God's mercy and grace (Ephesians 2:4, 7).

It is hidden from view. Most people, blinded by the attractions of this age, do not value Christ or His kingdom. Matthew points out this fact repeatedly, even in this very chapter (13:1–23, 53–58).

It brings great joy to those who find it. The three wise men rejoiced merely to see the star leading them to the infant Jesus (2:10). How much more do those who trust in Christ experience "joy inexpressible and full of glory," even if they undergo suffering (1 Peter 1:8; 4:12–13).

Gaining eternal life through faith in Christ is worth all that we have. "Blessed *are* the poor in spirit"—if they are "rich in faith" (5:3; James 2:5)! That is why Jesus urged the rich young ruler to sell all he had, give it to the poor, and follow Him (19:21). Sadly, he refused.

Will we be like that misguided youth, or like the wise man in this parable?

Hidden Treasure
Matthew 13:44 Part–2

"Again the kingdom of heaven is like a treasure hidden if a field ... "

When we remember that "the kingdom of heaven" is another term for eternal life, and that eternal life is to know the only true God, and Jesus Christ His Son (John 17:3), we see why Jesus calls it a *hidden* treasure.

It is hidden, because you cannot easily see the coming of God's kingdom in this present age. People of Jesus' day could discern its effects—healings, liberation from demons, transforming truth taught in public, and Jesus' own spotless life.

But few could forget their previous notion that the kingdom of God would come as political liberation and deliverance from poverty and oppression. Jesus told parables to teach that this kingdom was already at work, changing individuals who would then influence society (13:31–33).

With their minds set on the things that are seen, however, most folk were blind to the presence of the kingdom. The same is true today. We seek a job, a house, a car, better health, an attractive mate, a happy marriage, pleasures of all sorts, and political freedom.

Deep inside, we really believe these things will make us happy. When God does not provide what we want, we complain, as if He had not kept His promises.

But Jesus' parables were meant to direct our attention to the hidden presence of God in our time. In fact, having Jesus, we possess "every spiritual blessing" (Ephesians 1:3). Yes, the life of the believer is "hidden with Christ in God" (Colossians 3:3).

Only the eye of faith penetrates the fog of this world to perceive the value of knowing God and joyfully forsakes all to gain a relationship with Him through faith in Christ.

The Most Precious Pearl
Matthew 13:45–46

"Again, the kingdom of heaven is like a merchant seeking beautiful pearls, who, when he had found one pearl of great price [value], went and sold all that he had and bought it."

We can see this merchant elsewhere in the New Testament.

The wise men from the East sought Jesus and, when they found Him, offered their treasures at His feet (2:11).

When Jesus called them, Andrew and Peter left their fishing nets and their father and followed Him. Matthew, the author of this Gospel, deserted his lucrative tax-gathering business at Jesus' command (4:18–20; 9:9).

Unlike her sister Martha, who was concerned with "many things," Mary chose the one thing that was needful—listening to Jesus (Luke 10:41–42). Later, she expressed her single-hearted love for Him by pouring out precious perfume (probably her dowry) upon His body (John 12:3).

The Apostle Paul gave up everything he had previously valued, considering it "rubbish," and made knowing Christ the one thing he pursued in life (Philippians 3:4–12).

Jesus warned against the worship of Mammon, the god of this world. He told His disciples to "seek first the kingdom of God and His righteousness" (6:33). He Himself sought only to do the will of His Father, even to the point of laying down His life.

Shall we follow in the steps of those who forsook many "precious" things for the one pearl of great price?

The King Explains His Kingdom

Supreme Wealth
Matthew 13:44, 46

"Again, the kingdom of heaven is like treasure... one pearl of great price..."

We must ask why the kingdom of heaven is the most valuable thing in the world and worth forsaking all else in order to obtain it.

In other words, why did the wise men travel so far to see the baby Jesus, and offer precious gifts to Him? Why did the disciples leave all and follow Him? Why did Jesus command us to seek first the kingdom of God?

Jesus Himself tells us. In the Beatitudes, He pronounces those happy who receive the kingdom, and then describes that blessedness further: They shall be comforted; inherit the earth; be filled (satisfied); obtain mercy (from God); see God; be called sons of God; receive a great reward in heaven (5:2–12).

When we sin against God and come to Him asking forgiveness, He will pardon our offenses (6:12; 9:2).

If we put His kingdom first, then our heavenly Father will also provide for us all the material things we need (6:33) When the inevitable storms of life batter us, we shall possess a firm foundation (7:24–25).

Those who enter the kingdom avoid being cast into hell, where unbelievers in "outer darkness" suffer "the furnace of fire" and "wailing and gnashing of teeth" (8:12; 13:42).

One of the most precious promises awaits those who come to Jesus, believing that He is God's chosen King: "I will give you rest" (11:28).

Perhaps best of all, we shall become members of the everlasting family of God: "whoever does the will of My Father in heaven is My brother and sister and mother" (12:50).

All this—and much more—awaits those who "seek first the kingdom of God" by "leaving all" to follow Jesus.

Only Two Kinds
Matthew 13:49–50

"So it will be at the end of the age. The angels will come forth, separate the wicked from among the just, and cast them into the furnace of fire. There will be wailing and gnashing of teeth."

In the parable of the net cast into the sea, Jesus says that it "gathered some of every kind" of fish (13:47). Yes, this world does contain all sorts of people!

We come in different colors, shapes, and sizes. Some are brilliant, others not as smart. Beautiful and plain; energetic and lethargic; athletic and clumsy; educated and uneducated—the list of contrasts goes on and on.

But, according to Jesus, at the end of the age, we shall all be divided into two kinds: wicked and just. The former will endure everlasting torment in a hell of fire (25:41). He had already said that the righteous will "shine forth as the sun in the kingdom of their Father" (13:43).

As we have seen already, Jesus does not mean that anyone is without sin or perfectly righteous. He refers, instead, to a tendency in life; an orientation towards God, oneself, and others; an inclination of the heart; a general pattern of attitudes and actions.

Disciples of Christ trust in Him, not themselves; they seek God's kingdom, not the riches of this world; they look for eternal happiness, not temporal pleasure. Knowing God's mercy, they forgive others; knowing His love, they pass it on. Hearing His word, they respond in faith and obedience. Confessing their sins, they receive daily pardon.

At the end of the age, they will enter everlasting blessedness. Everyone else will be cast into unending misery. There are only two kinds of people, and only two final destinies.

Which kind are you? If you are not sure, now is the time to forsake all and follow Christ.

The King Explains His Kingdom

Jesus the Teacher
Matthew 13:53–54

Now it came to pass, when Jesus had finished these parables, that He departed from there. When He had come to His own country, He taught them in their synagogue, so that they were astonished and said, "Where did this Man get this wisdom and these mighty works?"

From this short passage we learn a great deal about Jesus' teaching ministry.

Sometimes He taught people outside, as the earlier part of this chapter records He did by the seaside; remember that the Sermon on the Mount was given in the hill country. When speaking to such crowds, He used parables to tell them about the Kingdom of God.

At other times, He was asked to teach in the synagogues. On this occasion, Jesus read from the prophet Isaiah and applied the passage to His own life (Luke 4:16–22).

His words were extraordinary. The first groups who heard Him "were astonished at His teaching, for He taught them as one having authority" (7:28–29).

In Nazareth, the congregation commented upon the wisdom of His discourse and "marveled at the gracious words which proceeded out of His mouth (Luke 4:22). Later, police sent to arrest Him returned empty-handed, saying, "No man ever spoke like this Man!" (John 7:46).

He not only taught, but worked mighty miracles ['powers' in the original Greek].

Jesus Himself attributed this remarkable ministry to the presence and power of the Holy Spirit in His life (Matthew 12:28; Luke 4:18).

Does it not make sense for us to (1) listen to this unique Teacher and (2) ask God for the same Spirit to work in and through us?

Just an Ordinary Man?
Matthew 13:55–56

"Is this not the carpenter's son? Is not His mother called Mary? And His brothers James, Joses, Simon, and Judas? And His sisters, are they not all with us? Where did this Man *get all these things?"*

As these words from His astonished neighbors demonstrate, Jesus was an ordinary man.

He had a legal father, Joseph, and a biological mother, Mary. As a child, He was obedient to them, and He must have known their parental love. Like other children, He grew up, both physically and mentally.

But He was not an only child. After He was born, Mary gave birth to other sons and daughters. Jesus knew all about family life, and must have listened to His siblings argue with one another, for only He was without sin.

Watching His little sisters grow up, He gained insight into the feminine psyche. No wonder He could treat women with such kindness and sensitivity!

From His earliest years, He learned how to lead, for He was the oldest son. It seems that His father died before Jesus entered His ministry, so He must have acquired experience in ruling a household.

As the son of a carpenter, He learned His father's trade, so that He was known as the village carpenter (Mark 6:3). This required Him not only to make and repair wooden implements and furniture, but to run a small business.

Yes, Jesus was a man just like us. That is why He can understand all that we go through. Except that He knew no sin, He can "sympathize with our weaknesses" (Hebrews 4:15) and enter into our joys. He knows.

Why No Miracles?
Matthew 13:58

Now He did not do many mighty works there because of their unbelief.

Notice that Jesus did *some* mighty works in His hometown of Nazareth. That is why His neighbors could say, "Where did this Man get this wisdom and these might works?" when He spoke in their synagogue.

But He did not do *many* miracles there. Why? Because of their lack of faith.

They knew, and acknowledged, that Jesus had worked wonders in their midst, as we have seen. They believed that miracles could take place, and that Jesus had performed some in Nazareth.

What, then, did they not believe? See how they describe Jesus:

"The carpenter's son." The son of Mary and brother to several siblings. In other words, just an ordinary man.

Jesus was not surprised, for He said, "A prophet is not without honor except in his own country and in his own house" (13:57). The important word here is "prophet." Ever since Moses, Elijah, and

Elisha, Jews considered the ability to work wonders the mark of a true prophet.

Jesus spoke with wisdom and demonstrated the power of God by healing and delivering diseased and demonized people, but His people did not consider Him to be a prophet. In other words, they failed to recognize who He was. They did not believe in Him as God's unique messenger.

Because they did not believe in Him, Jesus would not—indeed, could not (Mark 6:5)—manifest the might of God in their midst.

The same is true today. Those who think Jesus is just an ordinary man will not experience the transforming power of His grace. They will see few, if any, miracles.

But those who trust in Him as the Prophet of God, the Word of God, the eternal Son of God, will watch manifold wonders unfold before their very eyes, and in their own hearts.

Rejected at Home
Matthew 13:57

"A prophet is not without honor except in his own country and in his own house."

Rejection happens to all of us. Sometimes people disdain us for reasons over which we have no control—our sex, race, class, intelligence, nationality.

Others do not like us because of what we do. They find our behavior offensive. Usually, they have some basis for their disfavor, though we do not want to admit that harsh fact.

Rejection hurts. We all crave attention, affection, and approval, and cringe when these are withheld from us. We feel the most severe pain when people we love despise us. Worst of all, of course, is to be disliked, or even simply misunderstood, by our own family.

Jesus had to endure that kind of suffering, too. Matthew had earlier recorded how Jesus' mother and brothers sought to distract Him from teaching the crowds (12:46–47). Not only the Jewish leaders, to whom He posed a threat, but now His own family, friends, and neighbors could not accept Him. In short, they did not believe in Him (John 7:5).

In one sense Jesus differed from us, of course. No one in Nazareth faulted His behavior, and certainly not His origin! They objected to His prophetic ministry and status.

Nevertheless, the fact remains that Jesus had to face rejection of the most precious fact of His existence—His unique relationship with God and His mission as a man.

Thus, when we have to listen to critical words, or see frowning faces, we can take immense comfort from the truth that Jesus knows.

The King Explains His Kingdom

Rejecting the Revealer
Matthew 13:57

"A prophet is not without honor except in his own country and in his own house."

By calling Himself a prophet, Jesus consciously places Himself in the long line of God's messengers who were rejected by their own people.

Jesus referred several times to the suffering and death of previous prophets: "for so they persecuted the prophets who were before you" (5:12). "You [Scribes and Pharisees] are sons of those who murdered the prophets" (23:31).

He acknowledged John the Baptist as a prophet, "and more than a prophet" (11:9) and rebuked the Jews for not honoring that great man of God (11:18).

When He was warned that Herod sought to kill Him, he replied, "it cannot be that a prophet should perish outside of Jerusalem" (Luke 13:33). Thus, while expressing His faith that He was invulnerable until His time had come, He also accurately predicted His final fate in the city of Israel's kings.

God's messengers will be persecuted! And, as Jesus clearly announced at the outset of His ministry, all who would follow Him faithfully will also suffer persecution. Why? Because they, too, proclaim the word of God to a hostile world.

But that is not the final fact, for Jesus also said, "Rejoice and be exceedingly glad [when slandered], for great *is* your reward in heaven, for so they persecuted the prophets who were before you" (5:12).

Faith and Miracles
Matthew 13:58

Now He did not do many mighty works there because of their unbelief.

The Gospels record many miracles wrought by Jesus. In almost every case, Jesus responded to someone's request for help. In other words, He rewarded faith.

He also explicitly stated the necessity of faith for all who want some benefit from God:

"Ask, and it will be given you" (7:7).

"Go your way; and as you have believed, *so* let it be done for you." (8:13).

"Be of good cheer, daughter; your faith has made you well" (9:22).

"Do you believe that I am able to do this?" ... "According to your faith let it be to you." (9:28, 29).

"All things *are* possible to him who believes" (Mark 9:23).

On more than one occasion, He rebuked His disciples for their "little faith" (16:8). When they asked why they had not been able to cast out a certain demon, He explained, "Because of your unbelief; for assuredly, I say to you, if you have faith as a mustard seed, you will say to this mountain, 'Move from here to there,' and it will move; and nothing will be impossible for you" (17:20).

We must balance these statements with others which teach that God only answers prayers that are according to His will; that believing in Jesus solely for the sake of miracles is not enough; that we must seek Christ and His kingdom, not signs and wonders; that all who follow Christ must trace the steps of His suffering; and that even Satan and his messengers can work miracles.

Nevertheless, the fact remains: Jesus promised that "these signs will follow those who believe" (Mark 16:17). Christians in China have experienced God's wonder-working power. Is unbelief keeping mighty works from "following" us?

14 The King Cares for His People

Multiple Mistakes
Matthew 14:3–4

For Herod had laid hold of John and bound him, and put him *in prison for the sake of Herodias, his brother Philip's wife, because John had said to him, "It is not lawful for you to have her."*

Just as one lie leads to another, so one sin begets others.

Herod had taken his brother Philip's wife Herodias from him. When John the Baptist rebuked Herod for that wicked deed, the angry king threw the brave prophet into a dungeon.

But the king was not the only person in the palace seething with resentment against John. Herodias, who had cooperated with Herod's adultery, hated John for his prophetic rebuke. She sought a way to destroy this man whom both the people and the king admired so much.

On Herod's birthday, his step-daughter Salome danced before the assembled guests. We must assume that her dancing was lewd and lust-inciting, for the evil king responded with a promise to give her anything she wanted, up to half his kingdom.

He quickly regretted this foolish oath, for his wife prompted Salome to demand the head of John the Baptist on a platter. Herod could have renounced his rash promise, but did not possess the courage to do so in front of all his friends.

Thus, the greatest prophet in the history of Israel was sacrificed on the altar of lust, adultery, hatred, and pride. Perhaps if Herod had not cast longing eyes on his brother's wife, none of this would have happened.

"When desire [lust] has conceived, it gives birth to sin; and sin, when it is full-grown, brings forth death" (James 1:15).

Impossible Task?
Matthew 14:16

But Jesus said to them, "They do not need to go away. You give them something to eat."

Crowds had followed Jesus into the wilderness to hear His teaching and receive His healing touch. As the day waned, His disciples urged the Lord to disperse the multitude so that they could go to nearby towns and buy food.

But Jesus would have none of that. "You give them something to eat," He commanded.

But they protested, "We have here only five loves and two fish."

Jesus had given them an impossible task! Surely, He must know how little food they had on hand. How could He expect them to feed such a large number of people?

Of course He knew! And of course He did not think they could complete this assignment—apart from Him!

"Bring them [the loaves and fish] here to Me," He instructed. Then He worked a miracle so stunning that all four Gospel accounts record it in detail. Drawing upon His divine power, Jesus multiplied this meager meal so that five thousand men, plus their families, ate to satisfaction.

Likewise with us. Our Lord often imposes "impossible" tasks upon us. He assigns jobs which we cannot do. He issues commands which we cannot obey. He lays burdens upon us which we cannot carry—apart from Him!

Why? Not because He is cruel, but because He is kind. He intends to demonstrate His mighty power and His immense pity upon us and those around us. When we offer to Him our tiny strength and paltry resources, He magnifies and multiplies what we have, enabling us to "feed" multitudes of "hungry" people.

All we have to do is trust Him.

The King Cares for His People

Who Comes First?
Matthew 14:13–14

When Jesus heard it [i.e., the death of John the Baptist] He departed from there by boat to a deserted place by Himself. But when the multitudes heard it, they followed Him on foot from the cities. And when Jesus went out He saw a great multitude; and He was moved with compassion for them, and healed their sick.

As soon as He heard that His cousin and forerunner had been beheaded by Herod, Jesus sought refuge in the wilderness. He wanted to be alone for a while.

Perhaps He sought time to ponder the career of the brave prophet. The execution of John would also remind Jesus of the inevitable fate of all faithful spokesmen of God. With opposition from the Pharisees growing, He could foresee that His own early death was certain.

His plan for a personal retreat with His disciples was frustrated, however, by the eagerness of the crowds. They chased Him on foot to the other side of the lake and sought His healing touch. We know from other sources that they also desired to hear His heavenly teaching.

Jesus faced a choice: Would He disperse the crowd, insisting on His own longing for rest and His right to a bit of privacy? After all, He had worked tirelessly on their behalf for quite a while already. Did He not deserve some respite, a little vacation, especially while He grieved the loss of John?

Or would He put aside His own desires, abandon His own agenda, forget His own needs, and answer the call of the crowds? For most of us, the dilemma would have been acute.

But for the one who "did not come to be served, but to serve, and to give His life a ransom for many" (20:28), the outcome was certain: "He was moved with compassion for them, and healed their sick."

Not only so, but at the end of a long and tiring day, He insisted that this demanding assembly of needy people be invited to dinner, despite the lack of food!

No wonder we adore Him!

Christ the King

Looking Upward
Matthew 14:19–20

And He took the five loaves and the two fish, and looking up to heaven, He blessed and broke and gave the loaves to the disciples; and the disciples gave to the multitudes. So they all ate and were filled...

The disciples looked down—at the crowd, and at the paltry amount of food in their hands. Jesus looked up to God.

Later that evening, when the disciples saw Jesus walking on the water, Peter believed Jesus enough to obey His command to join Him on the waves. But then Peter looked at the wind and the waves, and began to sink (14:29–30).

Confronted with a man unable to hear or speak, Jesus looked up to God in heaven and healed him (Mark 7:34).

It all depends on where we look. If we focus on our material needs, we shall be consumed with worry. If we look at the birds of the air and the flowers of the field, and remember how God cares for them, we shall be filled with faith and peace.

If we fix our eyes on what can be seen, we shall lose heart, for our "outward man is perishing," but if we look to what is unseen, we shall be encouraged, for "the inward *man* is being renewed day by day," because this "light affliction, which is but for a moment, is working for us a far more exceeding *and* eternal weight of glory"

(2 Corinthians 4:16–17).

Jesus refused to be confined to what He could see with His eyes. Instead, He directed His attention to His invisible heavenly Father. Trusting in God, He worked mighty miracles.

As we run the race that is set before us, let us, likewise, be constantly "looking unto Jesus, the author and finisher of *our* faith" (Hebrews 12:2).

The King Cares for His People

God Provides
Matthew 14:20–21

So they all ate and were filled, and they took up twelve baskets full of the fragments that remained. Now those who had eaten were about five thousand men, besides women and children.

Through faith in God, and by His own divine power, Jesus fed a huge crowd by multiplying a few loaves and fish. This miracle stunned His disciples so much that all four Gospels record it. John tells us that the crowd immediately moved to make Jesus their king.

Jesus had told His followers not to worry about food and drink, but to trust their Father to provide (6:25–34). We are to pray for our daily bread (6:11).

We must also work with our hands, as a number of His parables indirectly teach (13:1–9, 24–30, 31–33, 47–48; 20:1–14; 21:33–34). Indeed, severe punishments await those who refuse to work (25:14–30; see also 2 Thessalonians 3:6–12).

Nevertheless, when all is said and done, we need not worry, for God will provide for His people. Unless, for some extraordinary purposes, He wills that we suffer hardship and hunger (2 Corinthians 11:27; Hebrews 11:37–38), we can count on Him to give us what we need each day.

Even when the situation seems impossible, we may be confident of His power to supply our needs. This crowd in the desert had no way of getting enough to eat, but Jesus served enough food to satisfy them all.

Thus, under all circumstances, we can say with David, "The LORD *is* my Shepherd; I shall not want" (Psalm 23:1).

Where Is Jesus?
Matthew 14:23–24

And when He had sent the multitudes away, He went up on the mountain by Himself to pray. Now when evening came, He was alone there. But the boat was now in the middle of the sea, tossed by the waves, for the wind was contrary.

After feeding five thousand men, plus women and children, Jesus dismissed the crowd, for they were about to make Him king. He also sent His disciples off by boat, to get them away from the popular political movement.

In the middle of the night, the little boat was in the middle of the sea, making little headway because of contrary winds.

Imagine the questions in the minds of the disciples:

Why did Jesus refuse to ride the enthusiasm of the multitude into Jerusalem and overthrow a corrupt government? Why did He make them return to the other side of the lake without their Master? Why was everything going wrong for them? Where was Jesus? In their time of need, what was He doing? Didn't He care about them?

As readers, we know the answer: Jesus was alone on the mountain, praying. No doubt He knew of their doubts and troubles. Certainly He could feel the direction of the wind, and (as man) perhaps even see their little struggling craft. In a while He would walk out upon the waters, still the storm, and propel their vessel to its destination (John 6:21).

For now, however, He was engaged in something far more important, and much more useful to His world-centered disciples: Prayer for them.

Are we not like those frustrated, frightened fishermen? Obsessed with the wind and the waves, stuck in our own little boat, forgetful of ways in which God has provided for us. Self-centered, focused on this world, forgetting God—we need Jesus' prayers!

Praise God that our Savior "always lives to make intercession for [us]" (Hebrews 7:25) and is even now at the Father's right hand doing just that! (Romans 8:34)

The King Cares for His People

Who is Jesus?
Matthew 14:25–27

"Now in the fourth watch of the night Jesus went to them, walking on the sea. And when the disciples saw Him walking on the sea, they were troubled, saying, "It is a ghost!" And they cried out for fear. But immediately Jesus spoke to them, saying, "Be of good cheer! It is I; do not be afraid."

His disciples had just seen Jesus feed 5,000 men and their families with only five loaves of bread and two fish. Before that, He had healed countless incurable people with a word or a touch, and had cast out demons, demonstrating His power over illness and evil spirits.

But they were still not prepared for what they saw—a man walking on water! Great prophets in ancient days had performed wonders, but even Moses had had to part the Red Sea to pass to the other side on dry land.

Limited by their inexperience and only a dim understanding of their Master, they could only assume that a ghost was approaching them, so they responded with a cry of terror.

Jesus calmed their hearts with two commands surrounding a momentous truth. "Cheer up! Don't be afraid!" Why? "It is I!"

In the Greek, "It is I" is literally, "I am," the two-word phrase which God had used to name Himself to Moses at the burning bush.

Thus, when the water-walking Man identified Himself as "I am," He revealed His full divinity. Jesus was—and is—none other than God, Yahweh, come in the flesh.

No wonder He could heal the sick and deliver the demonized! For Him, multiplying loaves and fish presented no difficulty, for the entire universe had been created through Him (John 1:3), and owes its continued existence and order to His powerful word (Colossians 1:17; Hebrews 1:3).

Is there anything He cannot do for us now? With Him at our side—indeed, dwelling within us—why should any true believers be afraid?

Faith and Doubt
Matthew 14:28–31

And Peter answered Him and said, "Lord, if it is You, command me to come to You on the water." So He said, "Come." And when Peter had come down out of the boat, he walked on the water to go to Jesus. But when he saw that the wind was boisterous, he was afraid; and beginning to sink he cried out, saying, "Lord, save me!" And immediately Jesus stretched out His hand and caught him, and said to him, "O you of little faith, why did you doubt?"

At first, Peter's faith was strong enough to send him out of the boat and into the roaring sea, walking on the rowdy waves towards Jesus. Imagine the exhilaration he must have felt!

But then he shifted his attention away from Christ to the raging wind. Immediately, fear gripped him and he desperately called out for help.

Notice that he still had faith in Jesus' power to save him from drowning. But he had lost faith in the Lord's ability to empower him to continue treading upon the water.

So much is he like us! Though we believe that Jesus can do wonders *for* us, we do not fully trust Him to work *in and through* us. We fix our gaze upon our weakness and upon our surroundings rather than upon the one who commands the wind and the waves. We look at the creation rather than the Creator, and what we can do rather than what He has done.

How much better for us to keep our eyes on Jesus! Daily looking into His Word, the Bible; trusting in Him to fulfill His promises; relying on Him for strength to do His will in our lives.

He will probably not order us to walk on water. But He has told us to love God with all our heart, soul, mind, and strength; to love our neighbor—even our hateful enemy—as ourselves; to seek first God's kingdom and not to worry about material things; to rejoice even in persecutions for His sake.

Shall we trust Him to give what He commands?

Worship Him!
Matthew 14:33, 35–36

Then those who were in the boat came and worshiped Him, saying, "Truly You are the Son of God." ... And when the men of that place recognized Him, they sent out into all that surrounding region, brought to Him all who were sick, and begged Him that they might only touch the hem of His garment.

When we realize who Jesus is, then our first reaction should be wonder, awe, and praise.

Seeing Him walk on water, rescue Peter from drowning, and calm the raging wind and waves, the disciples in the boat fell at Jesus' feet in adoration, wonder, and praise, saying, "Truly You are the Son of God."

They were following the example of the Magi when they came to the manger in Bethlehem: "they saw the young Child with Mary His mother, and fell down and worshiped Him. And when they had opened their treasures, they presented gifts to Him" (2:11).

Having begun his Gospel with the adoration of the Wise Men, Matthew ends it with two similar scenes:

The women who had seen the empty tomb rushed to tell the disciples. On the way, "... Jesus met them, saying, 'Rejoice!' So the came and held Him by the feet and worshiped Him" (28:9).

Some time later, the eleven disciples want to Galilee, to the mountain where Jesus told them to meet Him. "When they saw Him, they worshiped Him" (28:17).

John likewise brackets the beginning and end of his account of Jesus' life and works. Nathaniel responded to Jesus' supernatural knowledge with the cry, "Rabbi, You are the Son of God! You are the King of Israel!" (John 1:49). After his doubts had been dispelled by seeing the risen Jesus, Thomas exclaimed, "My Lord and my God!" (John 20:28).

As the divine Son of God, equal with the Father in dignity, power, and glory, Jesus deserves our adoration, praise, and worship. "Let all the angels of God worship Him," writes the author of the Letter to the Hebrews, quoting the Old Testament (Hebrews 1:6; Psalm 97:7).

If those sinless, glorious heavenly beings are called upon to worship their Lord, how much more should sinful men and women praise the one who has redeemed us by His own blood!

Healing Touch
Matthew 14:35–36

And when the men of that place recognized Him, they sent out into all that surrounding region, brought to Him all who were sick, and begged Him that they might only touch the hem of His garment. And as many as touched it *were made perfectly well.*

These verses conclude a chapter in Matthew's Gospel replete with stunning demonstrations of the power of Jesus.

First, the Lord fed five thousand men, plus women and children, simply by multiplying five loaves of bread and two fish (14:13–21). Then He walked on the surface of a stormy sea; enabled Peter to do the same; delivered him from drowning when his faith failed; and stilled the winds and the waves merely by getting into the boat (14:22–32).

Now we read that all those who merely touched the hem of Jesus' robe were made instantly well (14:36).

The question is, How do we access this mighty power? How can we "touch" Jesus in order to be made whole?

First, we must hear about Him. People came to Christ for healing after being summoned by their friends and neighbors. This points to the necessity of broad-scale *evangelism*.

Next, we see that those who invited the sick engaged in fervent petition to Jesus for their friends. We are enabled to "touch" Jesus as others intercede for us. That points to our duty to *pray* for those around us.

Finally, we must actually reach out and "touch" Jesus ourselves. The evangelism and prayer of others will not suffice; to access His power, we need to extend the hand of *faith*.

In the *Gospel of Matthew*, Jesus repeatedly commends the faith of those who sought Him for help (8:10; 9:2, 22, 29; 15:28). Likewise, He criticizes the "little faith" of His doubting disciples (6:30; 8:26; 16:8; 17:20).

To encourage us to trust fully in His goodness and greatness, He promises that if we have faith even as tiny as a mustard seed, we can "move mountains" (17:20; 21:21).

If we want Jesus to make us well, either physically or spiritually, He requires that we place our trust in Him. Such trust comes only as we receive the Word of God, where we find ample proof of the power of Christ to save.

15 The King Expands His Territory

"Honor Your Father and Mother"
Matthew 15:3

He answered and said to them, "Why do you also transgress the commandment of God because of your tradition?"

The Pharisees and scribes had criticized Jesus' disciples for violating tradition by not washing their hands before eating. Jesus' reply constitutes a counter-charge: They were breaking the law of God in their zeal to honor the tradition of their elders.

What law did they transgress? "Honor your father and mother"! In other words, they honored the customs of their ancestors, but dishonored their own parents, and taught others to do so also, thus violating a clear command of God.

In particular, Jesus shows how these lovers of ancient tradition deprived parents of their children's financial help. By allowing their disciples to claim that what they owed their parents was dedicated to religious purposes, they diverted funds from the needy to the greedy.

How about us? The command to honor our father and mother still stands. What excuses do we find to disobey God's will?

Perhaps we think they are foolish, so we look down on them. Maybe we remember their offenses towards us, and withhold forgiveness from them. Sometimes children even fail to give elderly parents necessary help and support. More often, we are too busy to spend quality time with them.

One very common "tradition" in America enables even Christians to dishonor their parents: Since the time of Freud, counselors have encouraged people to blame their father and mother for their emotional troubles. Under the guise of understanding ourselves and seeking inner healing, we all too easily criticize our parents before others.

How much better it would be to "confess" the sins of our parents to God alone, asking Him to forgive them for the ways they have hurt us, and seeking His comfort and consolation.

In other words, how much better it is to honor the clear commandment of God, even if it runs counter to what everyone else is doing, and transgresses the current "tradition."

Heart Worship
Matthew 15:8

"These people draw near to Me with their mouth, and honor Me with their lips, but their heart is far from Me."

Responding to the criticism of His disciples by the Pharisees, Jesus rebukes them for their hypocrisy by quoting God's words through the prophet Isaiah. Their devotion to the traditions of their elders masks disobedience to God's clear commands. That, in turn, reveals an inner alienation from God.

Outwardly, they seem like sincere worshipers, but their hearts wander far from the Lord.

Always, God desires our hearts. "You shall love the LORD your God with all your heart..." Jesus reminded the Jews, quoting the Old Testament (22:37; Deuteronomy 6:5).

"Blessed *are* the pure in heart, for they shall see God" (5:8). "Whoever looks at a woman to lust for her has already committed adultery with her in his heart" (5:28). "Do not lay up for yourselves treasures on earth, ... For where your treasure is, there will your heart be also" (6:19, 21).

But who can approach God with a spotless heart? Only those who have purified their hearts by obeying the truth (1 Peter 1:22), whose hearts have been "purified [cleansed] ... by faith" (Acts 15:9).

Inner transformation, likewise, comes to us by the work of the Holy Spirit, who gives us a new heart as we trust in Christ (Hebrews 8:8–10).

May God give us grace to avoid the empty worship of the Pharisees and to "worship the Father in spirit [i.e., by the Holy Spirit] and truth; for the Father is seeking such to worship Him" (John 4:23).

Deep Dirt
Matthew 15:18–19

"But those things which proceed out of the mouth come from the heart, and they defile a man. For out of the heart proceed evil thoughts, murders, adulteries, fornications, thefts, false witness, blasphemies."

Contrary to the Pharisees, who worried about ritual defilement resulting from contaminated food entering the mouth, Jesus cared more about real damage caused by uttering foul words.

Even more, He located the source of our moral uncleanness deep within us, in the heart—our motives, desires, thoughts, intentions, and emotions.

From the depths of our personality proceed an unruly throng of wicked attitudes and actions. "Evil thoughts" lead to evil works and words, so He mentions them first.

Then Jesus refers to four of the Ten Commandments, mentioning sexual sins twice. "Blasphemies" could include malicious or defaming words against either God or other men, and bring us back to the defilement caused by what comes out of our mouth.

Who can even glance at this list without shame? "Who can say, 'I have made my heart clean, I am pure from my sin'?" (Proverbs 20:9) Indeed, "The heart *is* deceitful above all *things*, and desperately wicked" (Jeremiah 17:9).

Our only recourse is to cry out with David, "Create in me a clean heart, O God" (Psalm 51:10).

Faith that Conquers
Matthew 15:28

Then Jesus answered and said to her, "O woman, great is your faith! Let it be to you as you desire." And her daughter was healed from that very hour.

What did this Gentile woman do to elicit Jesus' praise?

First of all, despite His attempts to remain hidden in her village, she found Him out (Mark 7:24).

Then, she came to Him, crying out, "Have mercy on me, O Lord, Son of David! My daughter is severely demon-possessed" (15:22). Notice how she views Jesus: He is Lord, and rightful Son of David. What a contrast to the Pharisees and other Jewish leaders!

She trusted in His goodness, that He would be willing to liberate her daughter, and in His greatness, that He would be able.

When Jesus replied that He was sent primarily to serve God's people, the Jews, she approached even more closely "and worshiped Him, saying, 'Lord, help me!'" (15:25) She refused to believe that He would not grant her request. Indeed, rather than being put off by His apparent indifference towards her, she worshiped Him.

But Jesus tested her one more time by reminding her that she was a Gentile, and thus not entitled to the same treatment God had promised the people of Israel.

She admitted that point, and did not try to dispute with Him, but held on to her trust in His inherent generosity towards all who came to Him for help: "Yes, Lord, yet even the little dogs eat the crumbs which fall from their masters' table" (15:27).

This combination of humility and desperate boldness demonstrated that she possessed true faith in Christ, and gained her daughter's deliverance and healing.

Oh, to be like this unnamed woman!

Tests of Faith
Matthew 15:23–24, 26

But He answered her not a word.... But He answered and said, "I was not sent except to the lost sheep of the house of Israel."... But He answered and said, "It is not good to take the children's bread and throw it *to the little dogs."*

Three times Jesus either ignored or deflected this desperate woman's cry for help. Why?

Did He not care for her poor daughter, who was afflicted by a demon? Of course he did! We have seen His compassion at work all throughout the Gospel story up to this point (8:16–17; 9:36). Perhaps, then, He refused to help a non-Jew? But a Roman centurion had gained his request of Jesus (8:5–13).

From His final commendation of her faith we know His purpose in putting her off. Clearly, He intended to test her and to allow her trust in Him to shine all the more brightly.

In addition, He was teaching His disciples that the Gospel was for Gentiles as well.

So it is with us. God allows us to endure various trials in order to test and to prove the true value of our faith in Him (1 Peter 1:7). He sends us through the fire and the water in order to produce patience, which leads to a more rounded and complete trust (James 1:3–4).

So then, we can rejoice even amidst trouble, "knowing that tribulation produces perseverance; and perseverance, [proven] character; and [proven] character, hope" (Romans 5:3–4).

And this hope will not be disappointed, for "the love of God has been poured out in our hearts by the Holy Spirit who was given to us" (Romans 5:5).

Man with a Mission
Matthew 15:24

But He answered and said, "I was not sent except to the lost sheep of the house of Israel."

Though He meant mostly to test the faith of the woman from Canaan, Jesus' statement highlights His sense of mission.

> He was *sent* by God. Knowing that He came from God to do the Father's will, Jesus sought always to obey. Though fully equal with God, He did nothing on His own initiative, but always at His Father's command. (John 5:19–20, 23, 30; Philippians 2:6–8)
>
> He came to save "*sheep*." As the Good Shepherd, Jesus would lay down His life for the sheep whom God had given Him (John 10:11). The Son of David would, like that great shepherd-king, do all He could to protect and provide for His flock.
>
> He came to save *lost* sheep. "All we like sheep have gone astray; we have turned, every one, to his own way" (Isaiah 53:6). He came to "save that which was lost" (18:11). Lost, because they had gone astray and had no one to gather them back into the fold (9:36). Lost, because they had wandered off the path and would perish unless someone came to help (18:12–14).
>
> He came to save the lost sheep of *the house of Israel*. During His earthly ministry, Jesus focused on the Jews, the chosen people of God. That is why He instructed His disciples to go only to "the lost sheep of the house of Israel" (10:6). He could not do everything all at once, so He observed the priorities of God: First Israel, then the Gentiles (28:19). His eventual healing of this woman's daughter, like the earlier healing of a centurion, showed that He intended to save all "His people"—including Gentiles—"from their sins" (1:21).

From this rich sentence we could harvest many sorts of fruit, but let us note, at least, that (1) Jesus cares for the weak, the wandering, the wounded, the lost. (2) He was a man with a clear sense of mission, a mission which He accomplished (John 17:4, 12). (3) He intends for us to follow in His steps (4:19; 8:22; 9:9; 16:24).

The Great Physician
Matthew 15:30–31

Then great multitudes came to Him, having with them the *lame, blind, mute, maimed [crippled], and many others; and they laid them down at Jesus' feet, and He healed them. So the multitude marveled ... and they glorified the God of Israel.*

For the fourth time in his Gospel, Matthew gives a summary statement of Jesus' healing ministry. But this one is different, for Jesus has entered into Gentile territory. Having left the area near the seacoast, He heads inland and goes up onto a mountain, perhaps to have some time alone with His disciples. Once again, however, He cannot remain hidden, and crowds come, bearing their sick for Him to heal.

We see His greatness first, in that He did not refuse them, though it seems that He wanted solitude, and had perhaps gone away from Jewish regions in order to escape the crowds.

Then we notice that He is meeting the needs of Gentiles, which no Rabbi would do. Though He was sent primarily to Jews, His love and compassion reached far beyond the borders of Israel to the entire world (Matthew 28:19–20). Perhaps that was His real reason for this "excursion" into Gentile territory: He was going to give a preview of the great move of the Gospel into the nations.

He healed multitudes, not just a few isolated sick people. Furthermore, the list of maladies indicates that His power extended to every sort of illness. Nothing could resist the life-giving energy of His touch or His word. In each case, He restored people to total health, so that they could function normally.

These poor Gentiles, who had exercised such faith in Him, were not disappointed. Nor were they dense—they knew that Jesus was a Jew and that He derived His creative ability from God Himself. Perhaps He had also given them some instruction, for they rendered glory, not to their own "gods," but to the God of Israel.

For a variety of reasons, Jesus does not always answer prayers for total and immediate healing today, though miracles do sometimes still take place. That should not cause us to doubt either His pity or His power, however. In whatever way He thinks best, He will demonstrate His deity in our bodies, if only we come to Him in faith (see 2 Corinthians 12:9; Philippians 1:20).

Christ the Compassionate
Matthew 15:32

Now Jesus called His disciples to Himself and said, "I have compassion on the multitude, because they have now continued with Me three days and have nothing to eat. And I do not want to send them away hungry, lest they faint on the way."

Notice the compassion of Christ. He cares. He knows their condition, that they have run out of food because they have sought His presence and His power.

See the kindness which makes Him unwilling to dismiss the crowd, because He knows they will collapse from hunger before they can find any food to replenish their strength. He knows their limits.

Since Jesus is "the express image of [the Father's] person (Hebrews 1:3), to see Him is to see the Father (John 14:9). In the compassion of Jesus, therefore, we discern the heart of the God who sent Him.

The God who made us with bodies "knows our frame; He remembers that we *are* dust," and He "pities those who fear Him" "as a father pities *his* children" (Psalm 103:13–14).

He knows what we need before we ask (6:8), and He cares.

Thus, we are not to imagine that He has no regard for our material needs. Though He may lead us into a wilderness to test us, as He did the ancient Israelites, that does not mean that His heart is hard towards our physical limits.

When Yahweh spoke to Moses from the burning bush, He revealed both His full awareness of the misery of His people's bondage in Egypt, but also His determination to deliver them (Exodus 3:7–8). He had "seen [their] ... oppression ... and ... heard their cry," and was going to rescue them.

Why? Because "God is love" (1 John 4:8). And that love was demonstrated most vividly in the life, and especially the death, of His Son, the compassionate Christ.

Grumbling or Gratitude?
Matthew 15:36

And He took the seven loaves and the fish and gave thanks ...

Faced with a crowd of four thousand men, plus their families, and having only a few fish and loaves of bread with which to feed them, Jesus did the unexpected.

He gave thanks.

He could have complained about several things—the lack of peace and quiet; the constant demands on His time and energy; the obvious unbelief of His disciples, though they had seen Him feed an even larger crowd; not to mention the paucity of His resources.

Indeed, His ancestors had consistently complained, even after God had marvelously delivered them from slavery in Egypt. "... you have brought us out into this wilderness to kill this whole assembly with hunger!" they shouted at Moses (Exodus 16:3).

Given daily manna from heaven, they next grumbled about the lack of water, then about the absence of meat in their diet, then about the sameness of each day's food, with no spices and vegetables to add interest. Nothing could satisfy them.

They are not the only grumblers, however. Paul describes all of us when he writes, "although they knew God [from the created order], they did not glorify *Him* as God, nor were thankful..." (Romans 1:21).

Ingratitude invites—even demands—the wrath of God, for it denies Him the glory, honor, trust, praise, and thanks which rightly belong to Him (Romans 1:18, 32). Furthermore, it eats like a cancer in our souls, giving birth to all sorts of wickedness and vice (Romans 1:21–32).

But Jesus, the embodiment of true Israel, set a contrary example: Surrounded by a hungry multitude in the wilderness and holding a paltry meal in His hands, He gave thanks.

As we follow in His steps, let us remember to be "giving thanks always for all things to God the Father in the name of our Lord Jesus Christ" (Ephesians 5:20).

A Table in the Wilderness
Matthew 15:32–37

"I have compassion on the multitude, because they have now continued with Me three days and have nothing to eat."... So they all ate and were filled...

The Lord had instructed His followers not to "worry about your life, what you will eat..." (6:25). Instead, they are to "seek first the Kingdom of God and His righteousness," knowing that "all these things shall be added to you" (6:33).

But notice the condition: We are to "seek first the kingdom of God and His righteousness."

In other words, to be fed by the Father through Jesus, we must, like this multitude, follow Him into the wilderness and continue there with Him.

> We must follow Him into the wilderness of *self-denial*: "If anyone desires to come after Me, let him deny himself, and take up his cross, and follow Me" (16:24). The Lord will not long feed the habits of self-indulgence. Let the crowd pursue pleasure; we are to seek to die to self.

> Nor will our holy Father support a life of sin. We must trace His footsteps into the wilderness of *righteousness*: "But seek first ...His righteousness" (6:33).

> We must continue with Him in the wilderness of solitary *prayer*: "What! Could you not watch with Me one hour? Watch and pray, lest you enter into temptation" (26:40–41).

> Shall we not also go with Him into the wilderness of *fasting*? "Then Jesus was led up by the Spirit into the wilderness... and when He had fasted forty days and forty nights, afterward He was hungry" (4:1–2).

In a word, the promise of provision applies to those who are willing to "follow in His steps" by offering their lives as a "living sacrifice," even unto death (1 Peter 2:21; Romans 12:1; Revelation 12:11).

Don't Worry!
Matthew 15:30, 37

... And He healed them. ... So they all ate and were filled...

Those who were brought to Jesus with incurable illness received healing. The crowd that followed Him into the wilderness was fed by the Lord.

Jesus had told His disciples, "do not worry about your life..." (6:25). Now He shows them—once again—why they need not fret about material things.

God will take care of His people!

All they have to do is "seek first the kingdom of God and His righteousness" by following Jesus, and they will have all they really need.

In other words, the Father will not let those who seek Him lack any good thing (Psalm 34:10). If we faithfully put Him first and remember to pray, "Give us this day our daily bread" (6:11), "all these things"—food, clothing, shelter—"shall be added to" us (6:33).

That is why Paul could write, "Be anxious for nothing, but in everything, by prayer and supplication, with thanksgiving, let your requests be made known to God" (Philippians 4:6).

And that is why he could add this unconditional promise, "And the peace of God, which surpasses all understanding, will guard your hearts and minds through Christ Jesus" (Philippians 4:7).

Helping Others
Matthew 15:30, 36

Then great multitudes came to Him, having with them the *lame, blind, mute, maimed, and many others; and they laid them down at Jesus' feet... And He took the seven loaves and the fish and gave thanks, broke* them *and gave* them *to His disciples; and the disciples* gave *to the multitude.*

God uses people to help other people.

In the first case, we have friends and relatives bringing their loved ones to Jesus for healing. In the second, the disciples distribute food directly to the seated crowd.

Of course, Jesus could have healed people without having them brought to Him, and He could have fed the multitude without the disciples' participation.

But God's ordinary way of blessing His people involves bringing others into the process.

In this way, He accomplishes many purposes. He allows us to work with Him—a great privilege. As we learn to discern the needs of those around us, we develop compassion and unselfishness, which reflect the character of God.

We were made to love, for we were created in the image of God, who is love (1 John 4:7). As we fulfill our destiny by serving our neighbors, we grow into that likeness to our God which He intends us to enjoy (Romans 8:29; Ephesians 4:13, 24; 1 John 3:2).

Why use the word "enjoy"? Because "It is more blessed to give than to receive"(Acts 20:35). To live only for ourselves is to consign ourselves to a walking death. True joy flows only from love, as Jesus pointed out long ago (John 15:10–12; see also Galatians 5:22).

What a privilege—to be fellow workers with God! (1 Corinthians 3:9)

Priorities
Matthew 15:30, 32

Then great multitudes came to Him... And [He] said, "I have compassion on the multitude, because they have now continued with Me three days..."

Great confusion surrounds the question of the role of Christians in meeting the enormous physical needs in this world. Should we try to fill every hungry mouth and cure every painful disease?

Jesus' example and teaching provide clear guidelines.

For one thing, He did not heal all those in Palestine who were afflicted with illness. Nor did He invite everyone in Galilee to dinner, or open a soup kitchen for the poor and hungry.

He healed those who came—or were brought—to Him in faith. He fed those who had left home to pursue Him into the wilderness to receive blessings and teaching from the Master.

In other words, He concentrated upon those who believed in Him and followed Him.

Likewise, in the parable of the sheep and the goats at the end of His ministry (25:31–46), He did not say that our final destiny would hang upon whether we fed all the hungry in this world, or gave drink to all who thirst, or took in all strangers, clothed all the naked, or visited all the prisoners.

No. He said very clearly—twice—that "Inasmuch as you did it to one of the least of these My brethren, you did it to Me."

In other words, we shall be judged on the basis of our faith in Christ, demonstrated by our love for other believers. "For whoever does the will of My Father in heaven is My brother and sister and mother" (12:50).

And what is His will? "And this is His commandment: that we should believe on the name of His Son Jesus Christ and love one another, as He gave us commandment" (1 John 3:23).

Paul put it this way: "Therefore, as we have opportunity, let us do good to all, especially to those who are of the household of faith" (Galatians 6:10). We start with family, and then reach out.

Christ the King

16 The King Calls Us to Faith

Sinful Sign-seeking
Matthew 16:4 Part–1

"A wicked and adulterous generation seeks after a sign, and no sign shall be given to it except the sign of the prophet Jonah." And He left them and departed.

The religious leaders of the day sought constantly to trip Jesus into doing or saying something for which they could accuse them. This time they asked for a "sign from heaven" to authenticate His ministry of teaching (16:1).

Consider the brazen audacity of this request! The Lord had already provided multiple proofs of His authority, as Matthew's readers would know from just the previous two chapters. In response to great need, Jesus had fed five thousand men and their families (14:13–21) and healed crowds of sick people, eliciting spontaneous praise from the grateful multitudes (14:34–36; 15:29–31). Then He had satisfied the hunger of another four thousand families by multiplying seven loaves of bread and two small fish (15:32–38).

No wonder Jesus had called them "blind leaders of the blind" (15:14)! Despite abundant evidence, they simply would not accept Jesus as a legitimate teacher sent from God, much less the promised Messiah.

After pointing out that they were adept at foretelling the weather by observing the color of the sky, Jesus rebukes the Pharisees and Sadducees for not being able to discern "the signs of the times" (16:2–3). Blinded as they were by their own prejudice and unbelief, they could not see that the healing and feeding miracles done by Jesus marked Him as God's Son and the Savior of His people.

Before we judge them too quickly, should we not examine our own hearts? How often do we base our "faith" in Christ upon tangible, visible "signs" that conform to our ideas of "proof"? It is so easy to ignore the evidence of God's power and love that surround us in daily life, and the record of the Scriptures, and look for something else upon which to base our trust in God and in His Son Jesus.

Even religious people like these Pharisees and Sadducees can be so focused on the material world that they cannot perceive the work of God among them.

That is why we need to pray for God to open the eyes of our hearts, giving us "the spirit of wisdom and revelation" enabling us to know Him (Ephesians 1:17). Only in His light do we see the light of the glory of God in the face of Christ Jesus (Psalm 36:9; 2 Corinthians 4:6).

The Sign of Jonah
Matthew 16:4 Part–2

"A wicked and adulterous generation seeks after a sign, and no sign shall be given to it except the sign of the prophet Jonah." And He left them and departed.

Like all Old Testaments prophets, Jonah prefigures Christ.

> He came from the region which would later be called Galilee, thus refuting the ignorance of the Jewish leaders who asserted, "No prophet has arisen out of Galilee" (Joshua 19:13; 2 Kings 14:25; John 7:52).

> He announced a coming judgment, as Jesus would do (5:22, 29; 7:23, 27; 8:12; 10:15, 26, 28; etc.)

> He offered himself up to death as a sacrifice in order to save many others (Jonah 1:12–15; Matthew 20:28).

> He was sent to minister not only to Jews (2 Kings 14:25), but also to Gentiles (Assyrians), though much less willingly than Jesus (8:5–13; 14:32–38).

> Most pertinently to this saying of Jesus, after going into the depths of the sea for three days—symbolic of death—he "rose again" when God caused the great fish to spew him out onto dry land—symbolizing the resurrection of Jesus (12:40).

> Significantly, after this "resurrection," his preaching to the Gentiles brought salvation from the wrath of God (Jonah 3:1–10), foreshadowing the worldwide proclamation of the Gospel of repentance and faith for the forgiveness of sins (24:14; 26:13; 28:19; Luke 24:47; Acts 11:18).

> So, what does this have to do with us in the 21st century? Many things, but at least we should remember that not only the Jewish

leaders, but also the residents of several entire villages in Galilee, and indeed most of the nation, refused to heed the words of Jesus, the "greater than Jonah" (12:41; Romans 9:31; 10:16).

As in that day, when Jesus "left them and departed," so it will be for those who persist in unbelief. The time for salvation through faith will pass away, and give place to eternal judgment, especially for "religious" people who refuse to accept God's anointed Savior (13:40–42; 23:33; 25:1–13, 31).

"Behold, now *is* the accepted time; behold, now *is* the day of salvation" (2 Corinthians 6:2). Should Jesus' followers not be imploring our neighbors to "be reconciled to God" (2 Corinthians 5:20)?

Unnecessary Doubt
Matthew 16:8–10

"O you of little faith, why do you reason among yourselves because you have brought no bread? Do you not yet understand, or remember the five loaves of the five thousand and how many baskets you took up? Nor the seven loaves of the four thousand and how many large baskets you took up?"

Jesus had warned His disciples to "beware of the leaven [yeast] of the Pharisees" (16:6, 11). They thought it was because they had forgotten to bring bread with them into the boat, but He referred to the "teaching" of the Pharisees and the Sadducees.

What was their teaching? They had just asked him—again—for a "sign from heaven" that would prove His authority to teach (16:1). Since He had for the second time just miraculously fed a large crowd, their demand clearly stemmed from unbelief.

Jesus' disciples also seemed to be in danger of worrying about their lack of bread. What is the link between them and the Jewish leaders? Both seemed to forget the mighty miracles Jesus had just performed. At least, they both failed to draw the proper conclusions.

The Pharisees and Sadducees failed to believe that Jesus was the Son of God. The disciples seemed in danger of doubting that Jesus would provide for them in a breadless boat, even though He had fed the multitudes on the shore.

In other words, the religious leaders did not believe in Jesus' person; the disciples did not trust in His provision.

How about us? With so much evidence for Jesus' miracles, including His mighty resurrection, do we still doubt either His deity or His devotion to the care of His people?

A Portrait of His Person
Matthew 16:13–20

Jesus ... asked His disciples, saying, "Who do men say that I, the Son of Man, am?"

From this conversation with His disciples, we learn seven marvelous truths about our Lord:

He is the *Son of Man*, truly human like us, but also divine, like the Son of Man prophesied in Daniel 7:13–14.

He is the *Prophet* foretold by Moses (Deuteronomy 18:15), as even the people knew in a limited way: "Some *say* John the Baptist, some Elijah, and others Jeremiah or one of the prophets."

He is *"the Christ,"* the Anointed One promised by the Old Testament, as Peter boldly confessed. He thus fulfills the Old Testament "types" of prophet, priest, and king, uniquely endowed by God to complete His saving work.

He is *"the Son of the living God,"* a title stressing His unique relationship with God, even His sharing of God's divine nature (see John 10:30, 36; Philippians 2:6–11).

He is the builder of the church: "on this rock I will build My church," which is founded on the truth believed and conveyed by the Apostles, and which grows up in union with the Him (Ephesians 2:20–21).

He is the *Lord of life and of death*, who grants "the keys of the kingdom" to His apostles and to church leaders to pronounce forgiveness for all who repent and believe, and doom to all who persist in stubborn unbelief and rebellion.

And in all of this He is *Jesus*, whose name means "Yahweh [is] salvation," for He has come "to save His people from their sins" (1:21).

Surely such a one deserves our wholehearted worship and service!

Divine Necessity?
Matthew 16:21 Part–1

From that time, Jesus began to show to His disciples that He must go to Jerusalem, and suffer many things from the elders and chief priests and scribes, and be killed...

"He *must* ... suffer ... and be killed."

Why was it *necessary* for Jesus to suffer and die? Was He not the Son of God, entirely without the guilt of sin and thus not liable to the penalty of death? Did He not possess all authority to teach, to heal, to cast out demons, to still the wind and the waves, and even to forgive sins—which only God possesses the right to do (5:29; 8:3, 13, 15, 16, 26; 9:6)?

Who—or what—could compel Jesus to do anything, much less to suffer death at the hands of sinful men? No wonder His disciples, for whom Peter soon spoke in protest, could not accept this saying. It was just too improbable, even impossible!

But Jesus insists that He is under some sort of obligation. There was some divine necessity for the Son of God to endure rejection, torture, and even death. That means, of course, that this compulsion came from God Himself. But how could God be "forced" to allow His only Son to endure the shame of the Cross?

Not just because He, like all other prophets, must inevitably be rejected and killed, usually in Jerusalem (5:12; 13:57; 21:11). Nor because, as prophet, Jesus had offended the religious leaders of His day, who determined to eliminate Him (23:27; 12:14).

Clearly, only in this way could Jesus "save His people from their sins" (1:21). He must "fulfill all righteousness" (3:15). For all the types and final purpose of the law *to be* fulfilled, (5:17–18), the Christ had to be offered up as a sacrificial lamb (5:17–18; Exodus 12; Leviticus 16). The prophetic scriptures spoke of a coming Servant of God who would bear the sins of the people (Isaiah 53).

The cup of God's wrath which we deserve had to be drunk by His chosen substitute (Psalm 75:8; Isaiah 51:17, 22; Jeremiah 25:15; 49:12; Ezekiel 23:33; Matthew 26:39–44, 54; John 18:11).

In other words, "it pleased the LORD to bruise Him" (Isaiah 53:10). The "necessity" dwelt in the heart of the Father and the submissive obedience of the Son, who loved us and willingly gave Himself for us

(Galatians 2:20; Ephesians 5:2). Our gracious God was compelled to secure our salvation from sins by the sacrifice of Christ by the depth of His love for us.

The holiness and justice of God required a sacrifice; the love and mercy of God provided the sinless God-Man, Jesus Christ. This was the divine "necessity."

Required Resurrection
Matthew 16:21 Part–2

From that time Jesus began to show to His disciples that He must ... suffer ... and be killed, and be raised the third day.

The resurrection of Jesus Christ on the third day had to take place! "He *must* ... be raised." No less than His suffering and death, the stupendous victory of Jesus over the grave was a divine necessity. But why?

Jesus had to come out of the tomb on the third day because, as God's prophet, He had foretold this reversal of death. Not only here, or on the two other occasions when Jesus warned His disciples of impending events (17:22–23; 20:18–19), but twice when He declared to the Jewish leaders that He would give them no other sign of His authority than that of the prophet Jonah (12:39–40; 16:4). As Jonah had been in the belly of the great fish three days, so the Son of Man would be [only] three days in the depths of the earth.

Unless Jesus was to rise from the dead before the general resurrection in which most Jews believed, many of His promises make no sense, such as His guarantee that those who confess their faith in Him before men will be acknowledged by Him before God (10:32). He will "reward each according to his works" (16:27), granting them eternal life and a share in His rule when He "sits on His throne of glory" (19:28–29; 25:34, 46).

Likewise, His numerous warnings of final judgment are based on the certainty of His resurrection (7:21–23; 13:41–42; 25:31–46). Furthermore, how could He speak of His "coming" again from heaven if He did not intend first to "go" to heaven by rising from the dead (24:27, 30, 39, 44; 25:13, 19, 31; 26:64)?

The King Calls Us to Faith

As the Son of David, and yet greater than David, He is heir to the promises of a heavenly throne made to Israel's king (22:43–45). As Peter would later explain, the prophetic Psalms that spoke of the King's victory over death must point to Jesus (Acts 2:25–32).

What "Gospel of the kingdom" could be preached to all the nations if the main subject of that message was to lie rotting in a grave? (24:14; 26:13; 28:19). Only if "all authority in heaven and earth" had been given to the risen Christ could He send His ambassadors to proclaim "repentance and remission of sins ... in His name to all nations" (Luke 24:47).

Indeed, the resurrection of Jesus shortly after His death forms an essential element of the *Gospel of Matthew* from the very beginning: Jesus is not only fully human, but was "conceived ... of the Holy Spirit" (1:20). He is "Immanuel ... God with us," and God cannot be held by the chains of death (1:23). He came to save His people from their sins—the penalty, power, and finally the presence of our inborn iniquity—which He could only accomplish by a sacrificial death and a triumphant resurrection (1:21).

In short, the resurrection of Jesus was grounded in God's eternal will for us.

Christ the King

From Death to Life
Matthew 16:24–25

"If anyone desires to come after Me, let him deny himself, and take up his cross, and follow Me. For whoever desires to save his life will lose it, but whoever loses his life for My sake will find it."

Jesus had just told His disciples that He "must go to Jerusalem, and suffer many things…, and be killed, and be raised on the third day" (16:21). Now He summons others to take the same road to eternal life.

If we desire to go after Jesus, then we must take three "steps":

Deny self. We must renounce our own earthly desires and give up our personal ambitions. Say "no!" to sin. Resist temptation. "Put to death the [evil] deeds of the body" (Romans 8:13). "Put to death your members which are on the earth: fornication, uncleanness, passion, evil desire, and covetousness, which is idolatry" (Colossians 3:5).

Take up our own cross. First century Jews knew what that meant. A long, lonely path carrying one part of the cross, then horrible pain while the Roman soldiers nailed the criminal to it, followed by hours, perhaps days, of excruciating agony in the hot sun, while jeering crowds gawked at the dying man. Countless Christians suffer brutal torture at this moment just because of their faith. Others must endure the scorn, rejection, and even hatred of colleagues, neighbors, and even friends and family.

Follow Jesus. Walk in His steps. He left the glories of heaven to become a man; He emptied Himself of divine honor for a while in order to live like a servant. Wandering from place to place, He had no bed to call His own. At the end He possessed nothing but a seamless robe.

But after the Cross, what? Resurrection, elevation to the right hand of the Father, glory, honor, and unending joy.

Those who follow Jesus to the death will find themselves enjoying everlasting life and love with Him. Surely that is worth the cost!

17 The King's Glory and Suffering

"Hear Him!"
Matthew 17:1–8

While he [Peter] was still speaking, behold, a bright cloud overshadowed them; and suddenly a voice came out of the cloud, saying, "This is My beloved Son, in whom I am well pleased. Hear Him!"

Jesus had taken Peter, James, and John up to a high mountain, where "... He was transfigured [transformed] before them. His face shone like the sun, and His clothes became as white as the light."

As the three disciples watched, two others, Moses and Elijah, appeared with Jesus, talking with Him about His upcoming death and resurrection in Jerusalem (Luke 9:31). Peter, not knowing what else to say, suggested they build three huts, one for each of the great men. That is when the cloud and the voice silenced him and sent all of them to their knees in awe and fear.

What does all this mean? The transformation of Jesus' appearance partly fulfills His prediction that "some standing here ... shall not taste death till they see the Son of Man coming in His kingdom" (16:28). The brightness of His clothes and face point towards the glorious appearance of the Risen Christ that stunned Paul on his way to arrest Christians in Damascus (Acts 9:3–9) and felled John on the island of Patmos (Revelation 1:12–17).

Moses had seen the reflection of God's glory on Mount Sinai, and all Israel gazed upon the shining cloud of God's presence for forty years in the wilderness. Elijah had witnessed the power of God on Mount Carmel, when the idols were defeated in a dramatic showdown. Then he fled in fear of the queen to Moses' mount in the wilderness, where he, too, heard God's voice.

The voice of God the Father recalls the prophecies of Isaiah about the Servant of God who would later suffer for His people (Isaiah 42, 53). But it does more: The Lord directly identifies Jesus as His unique Son, greater than all the prophets, including Moses and Elijah.

The conclusion: From now on, God's people must listen to Jesus, the last and greatest Prophet, the one predicted by Moses (Deuteronomy 18:15), and more than a prophet, for He is also Priest and King, indeed, the very Son of God.

Listen to Him!

Mountain-moving Faith
Matthew 17:20 Part–1

"Assuredly, I say to you, if you have faith as a mustard seed, you will say to this mountain, 'Move from here to there,' and it will move; and nothing will be impossible to you."

Coming down from the mountain where He had been transformed before the wondering eyes of three of His disciples, Jesus finds a discouraging situation. The nine followers who had remained below had not been able to deliver a demon-possessed boy.

Jesus expressed His frustration with their failure in strong words: "O faithless and perverse generation, how long shall I be with you? How long shall I bear with you?"

After healing the boy, Jesus explained why His disciples could not cast out the demon—"because of your unbelief"—and then promised that even tiny faith, if sincere, could move mountains.

From this short account, we learn that:

> Failure to believe in God's power and pity is a moral failure. Otherwise, why would Jesus have rebuked them so sharply? He had given them ample evidence of His divine power and of His love; He had commissioned them to heal the sick and cast out demons. Why had they not been able to trust Him this time also?

> Even a little faith can work wonders. All we have to do is rely fully on God's power, revealed to us in the words and works of Jesus. Simple confidence in God's promises will do, for—as Mary had discovered—nothing is impossible with God (Luke 1:37). The Jesus who had performed countless miracles, and after rose from the dead, is with us also (28:20).

Faith must be expressed. We must "say to this mountain, 'Move'"! As Jesus further explained, "This kind does not go out except by prayer and fasting."

True faith does not forget the suffering of Christ. Jesus had told them once, and would repeat, that He must soon suffer and die, and that His followers must be willing to walk in His steps. Fasting reminds us of our weakness apart from Him and of our sin, which made His death necessary. This keeps us from trusting in our own faith rather than in Him.

The Power of Prayer
Matthew 17:20 Part–2

"...if you have faith as a mustard seed, you will say to this mountain, 'Move from here to there,' and it will move; and nothing will be impossible for you."

Just what things are possible to those who ask with faith?

This passage tells us that believing prayer can cast out demons.

In earlier narratives in Matthew, faith brought cleansing to a leper (8:2–3); healing to the servant of a Roman centurion (8:8–13); full health and deliverance to all who came to Jesus (8:16); new life to Jairus' daughter (9:18, 25); relief from a chronic hemorrhage (9:20–22); sight to two blind men (9:27–30).

Peter walked briefly on the roiling waves (14:28–31), and a Gentile woman obtained release for her demon-possessed daughter (15:22, 28).

The Apostles continued this sort of ministry after Jesus' ascension, as we witness repeatedly in the Book of Acts. Surely, they remembered Jesus' repeated promises, such as: "If you can believe, all things are possible to him who believes" (Mark 9:23). "And whatever things you ask in prayer, believing, you will receive" (21:22). "If you ask anything in My name, I will do *it*" (John 14:14).

We need that same confidence. That is why Paul prayed that the Christians in Ephesus would know "what *is* the exceeding greatness of His power toward us who believe, according to the working of His mighty power which He worked in Christ when He raised Him from the dead and seated *Him* at His right hand in the heavenly places" (Ephesians 1:19–20).

Of course, we must ask in His name—according to the truths He has revealed; trusting in His merit alone; willing to follow His example of service, submission, and suffering; utterly committed to obeying all that He has commanded (28:20). God will not grant requests made only "to spend ... on [our] pleasures" (James 4:3).

Nevertheless, the promise stands: If we fully trust in Christ, our prayers can be used by God to remove from our paths all that would keep us from doing God's will, even "mountains"!

Unanswered Prayer?
Matthew 17:20 Part–3

" ... if you have faith ... nothing will be impossible for you."
Really, Jesus?

Why, then, do so many prayers seem to fall back from heavens of bronze? Why does God remain silent while millions cry out in anguish? So much suffering, so little relief, even for believers!

With aching hearts, children watch their aged parents waste away. Agonized mothers beg God to heal their incurably ill offspring. Prisoners endure years of sleepless nights, brutal beatings, biting handcuffs, and endless interrogation. How many millions pass their days afflicted with disease, hunger, and racking pain?

"Blessed *are* those who mourn, for they shall be comforted.... Blessed are you when they revile and persecute you .... Rejoice and be exceedingly glad, for great *is* your reward in heaven" (5:4, 11–12).

"Concerning this thing [Paul's thorn in the flesh] I pleaded with the Lord three times that it might depart from me. And He said to me, 'My grace is sufficient for you, for My strength is made perfect in weakness'" (2 Corinthians 12:8–9).

"In the world you will have tribulation [trouble, pain]; but be of good cheer, I have overcome the world" (John 16:33).

The King's Glory and Suffering

"... Jesus began to show His disciples that He must go to Jerusalem, and suffer many things ... and be killed" (16:21). "If anyone desires to come after Me, let him deny himself, and take up his cross, and follow Me" (16:24).

"He began to be sorrowful and deeply distressed. Then He said to them, 'My soul is exceedingly sorrowful, even to death...' He went a little farther, and fell on His face, and prayed, saying 'O My Father, if it is possible, let this cup pass from Me; nevertheless, not as I will, but as You *will*.' ... Again, a second time, ... 'Your will be done.' ... and prayed the third time, saying the same words" (26:37–44).

"... if we ask anything according to His will, He hears us" (1 John 5:14).

The Limits of Prayer
Matthew 17:19–20 Part–4

Then the disciples came to Jesus privately and said, "Why could we not cast it out?" So Jesus said to them, "Because of your unbelief; for assuredly, I say to you, if you have faith as a mustard seed, you will say to this mountain, 'Move from here to there,' and it will move; and nothing will be impossible for you."

Jesus promises unlimited power in prayer for those who believe—but within certain limits! Not every prayer will be answered as or when we wish. Paul begged three times for his thorn to be removed; Jesus requested thrice that, if possible, He would not have to drink the cup of God's wrath. Both petitions were denied, as have been countless "legitimate" requests since then.

Is Jesus' promise meaningless, then? Should we just lamely say, "If it is Your will," each time we pray, with no expectation that God will grant what we desire? No!

Faith will "move mountains," and "nothing will be impossible" for those who believe, if we are praying according to His revealed will.

The disciples had been commanded to cast out demons as part of their commission from Jesus (10:8). For some reason, when they encountered this particular evil spirit in the young boy, their faith failed them. Had they only believed, they could have delivered the lad.

Likewise, we have been given clear commands from God. If we trust in Christ alone for our salvation, and rely on His Spirit alone for our sanctification (growth in holiness), then whenever we ask God for strength to do His will, He will give it to us.

"... love your enemies, bless those who curse you, do good to those who hate you, and pray for those who spitefully use you and persecute you" (5:44).

"But seek first the kingdom of God and His righteousness" (6:33).

"Go therefore and make disciples of all the nations" (28:19).

"Rejoice always, pray without ceasing, in everything give thanks; for this is the will of God" (1 Thessalonians 5:16–18).

Divine Fisherman
Matthew 17:25–27

"What do you think, Simon? From whom do the kings of the earth take customs or taxes, from their sons or from strangers?" Peter said to Him, "From strangers." Jesus said to him, "Then the sons are free. Nevertheless, lest we offend them, go to the sea, cast in a hook, and take the fish that comes up first. And when you have opened its mouth, you will find a piece of money; take that and give it to them for Me and you."

This rather strange story illustrates a number of vital truths:

> As Son of God, Jesus did not have to pay the Temple tax required of every Jew. Peter had seen Jesus transformed and enveloped in a bright and glorious cloud, and he had heard the voice of the Father, "This is My beloved Son, in whom I am well pleased" (17:2, 5). He had observed Jesus heal a boy by casting out a demon who would not obey the disciples (17:14–18). He knew that he would truly find a coin in the mouth of the next fish.

> As a man, Jesus obeyed all the laws of His time. He attended all the required feasts in Jerusalem, offered all the necessary sacrifices, and commanded His followers to do the same.

The King's Glory and Suffering

As unique Son of Man and as the anointed Servant of God, He combined both the divine glory prophesied by Daniel (Daniel 7:13–14) and the necessity to suffer predicted by Isaiah (Isaiah 53). Indeed, He had Himself just said, "The Son of Man is about to be betrayed …, and they will kill Him" (17:22–23).

Thus, He submitted, not only to the Temple tax, but also to the unjust religious and political rulers of His day when they wrongly arrested, tried, convicted, and crucified Him.

As the God-Man, He identified Himself with those He came to save: He supplied Peter with one coin to pay for both of them. Later, He rebuked Paul for persecuting believers by asking, "why are you persecuting Me?" (Acts 9:4). Disciples of Jesus, therefore, are "called…[to] follow His steps" in submission, even if it means suffering (1 Peter 2:13–25) a lesson Peter both lived and taught after Jesus had ascended.

Christ the King

18 Greatness in the Kingdom

Ambition and Envy
Matthew 18:1–3

At that time the disciples came to Jesus, saying, "Who then is greatest in the kingdom of heaven?"

Jesus had taken with Him only Peter, James, and John up to the mountain where He was transfigured (17:1–9). In the passage just before this one, Jesus directs Peter to catch a fish with a coin in its mouth to pay the Temple tax for both of them.

Earlier, Jesus had told Peter that He would build His church upon the rock of that disciple's faith (16:18).

Apparently moved by ambition and envy, the other disciples ask, "Who, then, is greatest in the kingdom of heaven?" Is it Peter, Lord? Or James, or John? If so, why? Why not one of us? Because we could not cast out that demon (17:14–21)?

Clearly, they had missed the significance of the recent displays of Jesus' *majesty*: His glorious appearance on the mountain. The words of the Father, "This is My beloved Son, in whom I am well pleased. Hear Him!" Instantly curing a boy whom they could not help. Predicting His resurrection from the dead. Miraculously finding a coin in the mouth of a fish.

So, also, they had missed His *meekness*: Two predictions that He must "suffer many things ... and be killed." His submission to the Temple tax, though He was the divine Son of the Father, the very dwelling place of God on earth.

Did they not understand that only *Jesus* is greatest in the Kingdom? And that He had shown the way to greatness by humbling Himself, even unto certain death?

Whenever we take our eyes off Jesus—His transcendent majesty and His messianic meekness—we are blinded by ambition and envy. We seek to get, not to give; to rule, not to serve. Immediately, our friends become enemies, or at least obstacles, to our own lofty goals and driving desires.

"Let this mind [attitude] be in you which was also in Christ Jesus, who, being in the form of God ... humbled Himself and became obedient to *the point of* death, even the death of the cross" (Philippians 2:5–8).

True Greatness
Matthew 18: 3–4

"Assuredly, I say to you, unless you are converted and become as little children, you will by no means enter the kingdom of heaven. Therefore whoever humbles himself as this little child is the greatest in the kingdom of heaven."

By placing a little child in their midst, Jesus provided an object lesson on humility. The disciples sought prominence, privilege, and power: Greatness. Little did they know how evil was their ambition! How warped their value system, how misplaced their priorities!

They must "be converted"—changed, turned—from this preoccupation with self-advancement, and become like little children. Not that little ones are without sin, but that, as Jesus explains, they are relatively humble.

A child knows his relative position in the family. Aware of his youth and weakness, he understands that he can trust his parents, and must obey them. Rarely does he presume to be "great" in the household! Usually, he does what he is told.

Could the disciples not remember that their Master, though equal with God, had humbled Himself to be born as a little child? Obedient to His parents, Jesus grew up to do all that His heavenly Father commanded.

As He had told them twice in recent days, Jesus the unique Son of God was destined to die a horrible death at the hand of sinners. He would obey His Father's will, like a little child.

In so doing, He would then be "highly exalted" to the right hand of the Father, and given "the name that is above every name, that at the name of Jesus every knee should bow ... and *that* every tongue should confess that Jesus Christ *is* Lord, to the glory of God the Father"(Philippians 2:9–11).

Shall we not both worship and imitate the one who is "greatest in the kingdom of heaven"?

The Way Up is Down
Matthew 18:4

"Therefore whoever humbles himself as this little child is the greatest in the kingdom of heaven."

How can we humble ourselves? By renouncing and relinquishing some things we hold dear, such as:

"Royalty": Jesus was Prince of heaven, the Son of the Great King. Yet He "emptied Himself" of His privileges, "taking the form of a bondservant, *and* coming in the likeness of men" (Philippians 2:7). So must we divest ourselves of all the rights and privileges of rank and status, real or imagined.

Self-rule: Jesus could command armies of angels, but He "became obedient to *the point of* death, even the death of the cross" (Philippians 2:8). He sought not His own will, but the will of God. Obedience to His Father dominated His life.

Selfishness: He "did not come to be served, but to serve, and to give His life a ransom for many" (20:28). He lived for others. He "loved us and [gave] Himself for us, an offering and a sacrifice to God" (Ephesians 5:2).

Righteousness: God "made Him who knew no sin *to be* sin for us..." (2 Corinthians 5:21). On the Cross He suffered the truly horrible rejection of His Father, who punished Jesus for our sins, "the just for the unjust" (1 Peter 3:18). Away with all boasting, supposed merit, illusions of goodness on our part! No more self-justification, self-defense, self-righteousness! Others know that we have sin; if we say otherwise, we deceive only ourselves (1 John 1:8).

Restless discontent and grumbling: "Therefore humble yourselves under the mighty hand of God, that He may exalt you in due time" (1 Peter 5:6). "Therefore be patient, brethren, until the coming of the Lord" (James 5:7). "Shall we indeed accept good from God, and shall we not accept adversity?" (Job 2:10). "... in everything give thanks" (1 Thessalonians 5:18).

"... nevertheless, not as I will, but as You *will*" (26:39).

"Therefore God has highly exalted Him" (Philippians 2:9).

Connected to Christ
Matthew 18:5 Part–1

"Whoever receives one little child like this in My name receives Me."

By "little child," Jesus means "believer." We can say this because He has used little children as the pattern for humble repentance, the requirement for entering the kingdom of God (18:3). He defines "these little ones" as those "who believe in Me" (18:6). And He says "in My name," meaning that He refers to spiritual things.

So, to "receive" a believer is to receive Jesus Christ Himself. Why? Because all true followers of Jesus are connected to Him by their:

Character: Like Jesus, they have humbled themselves, trusting and obeying God the Father (18:3).

Conduct: They "hunger and thirst for righteousness" (5:6); show mercy (5:7); seek to make peace (5:9); love their enemies (5:44); and "seek first the kingdom of God and His righteousness" (6:33).

Concern: Like their Master, they care for other believers, the "little ones" of whom He spoke, and for whom He died.

Cross: They have denied themselves, taken up their cross, and walked in His steps (16:24). They suffer persecution for righteousness and for His sake (5:10–12).

Communion: they "abide" in Him by hearing His words and prayer (John 15:7); Christ lives in them (Galatians 2:20); they are "in Christ" by grace through faith (Ephesians 1:1, 3, 4, 7, 11, etc.).

Thus, to receive, accept, and care for another Christian is to accept Christ Himself!

"Inasmuch as you did *it* to one of the least of these My brethren [believers], you did *it* to Me" (25:40).

The Importance of "Little" Things
Matthew 18:5 Part–2

"Whoever receives one little child like this in My name receives Me."

Unlike His disciples, who were obsessed with "greatness," Jesus valued "little things."

To receive a believer ("little child") is to receive Christ (18:5).

To cause a "little one" (believer) to sin is ruinous (18:6).

To indulge even a "little" temptation is to risk hell (18:8–9).

To despise one of these "little ones" means to ignore their special place in God's eyes (18:10).

To allow even one "sheep" to go astray is to defy God's will (18:14).

To ignore the correction of one brother is to face expulsion from the church (18:15–17).

Even a little group of Christians enjoys the presence of God (18:20).

Not to forgive the "little" debt that someone who has offended us owes is to bring down the wrath of God for the huge debt we owe Him (18:21–35).

To those who are "faithful over a few things," God will entrust "many things" (25:23).

Maybe we should take our eyes off of what seem to be "big" things and concentrate on the "little" things that matter so much to Jesus and to God!

"He is despised and rejected by men … He was despised, and we did not esteem Him" (Isaiah 53:3).

"Therefore God also has highly exalted Him" (Philippians 2:9).

My Brother's Keeper?
Matthew 18:6

"Whoever causes one of these little ones who believe in Me to sin, it would be better for him if a millstone were hung around his neck, and he were drowned in the depth of the sea."

After he had killed his brother Abel, Cain was given an opportunity by God to confess his crime. "Then the LORD said to Cain, 'Where *is* Abel your brother?' He said, 'I do not know. *Am* I my brother's keeper?'" (Genesis 4:9)

Jesus answers with a resounding "Yes!" We are to love our neighbor as we love ourselves (22:39). Positively, we are to seek his good; negatively, we are to avoid doing anything to harm him, especially spiritually.

Paul wrote, "Let each of us please *his* neighbor for *his* good, leading to edification" (Romans 15:2). In other words, "Let no one seek his own, but each one the other's *well-being*" (1 Corinthians 10:24).

In the early church, that meant not eating food offered to idols in the presence of one who thought that was sinful and might be tempted to do what he considered to be wrong.

But the general principle applies today: We should speak and do only what will build up others in faith, hope, and love. Anything else is forbidden to us. That is, if our words or actions will tempt others to sin, we must refrain, even if it costs us.

For women, that might mean refusing to wear something that is in style, but would tempt men to lust. For men, it might mean controlling their speech and their hands in order to protect a woman's heart and her moral purity.

Before we participate in any action, we need to ask, "How will this help others know and serve God better?" Our goal is not simply to please people, but to further their love for God.

Otherwise, as accomplices to their disobedience, we shall pay a very heavy penalty. Cain was wrong.

Greatness in the Kingdom

The Seriousness of Sin
Matthew 18:8–9

"If your hand or foot causes you to sin, cut it off and cast it from you. It is better for you to enter into life lame or maimed, rather than have two hands or two feet, to be cast into the everlasting fire. And if your eye causes you to sin, pluck it out and cast it from you. It is better for you to enter into life with one eye, rather than having two eyes, to be case into hell fire."

Using exaggeration for effect, Jesus urges upon His disciples the seriousness of sin. His point: Any earthly loss is worth avoiding eternal punishment.

He had already warned His followers against adultery with similar language (5:27–30). Now He points out the importance of accepting other believers and the danger of pride.

Passion and pride lie at the root of almost all sin, and must be resisted at the source. Anything that tempts us must go: Any practice, person, possession, place, pleasure, position—anything that would hinder us from obeying God—must be utterly avoided and rejected.

Otherwise, we risk eternal agony. Jesus does not mince words about the penalty of sin: "Everlasting fire"; "hell" (referring to a garbage dump that continuously smoldered outside the gates of Jerusalem); "destruction" (7:13); "outer darkness," where there is "weeping and gnashing of teeth" (8:12; 25:30); "the furnace of fire," where there is "wailing and gnashing of teeth" (13:42); "everlasting punishment" (25:46).

Jesus came to "save His people from their sins" (1:21). For that purpose, He determined to "give His life a ransom for many" (20:28). To pay for our sin, He had to "suffer many things ... and be killed" by crucifixion (16:21; 26:2). No one can imagine the horror He felt when He drank to the full the "cup" of God's righteous wrath against sinful humanity (26:39; 27:46).

Those who trust in Jesus receive forgiveness of sins (1 John 1:9). The evidence of their faith consists largely in their hatred and rejection of the sin which made His death necessary. True faith leads to everlasting life (25:46).

But persistent partnership with evil brings eternal death. The stakes could not be higher. Which shall we choose?

Guardian Angels
Matthew 18:10

"Take heed that you do not despise one of these little ones, for I say to you that in heaven their angels always see the face of My Father who is in heaven."

Who are these angels? The Greek word means "messenger," and they often perform that vital function.

An "angel of the Lord" appeared to Joseph to command him to take Mary as his wife, announcing to him also that her child was the savior whom God had sent to deliver His people form their sins (1:20–23).

After the birth of Christ, he was warned by an angel to go to Egypt to escape King Herod's wrath (2:13), and when that wicked king had died, an angel told Joseph to take his little family back into Israel (2:19–20).

Angels ministered to Jesus after His victory over Satan's temptations in the wilderness (4:11). Had He wished, Jesus could have summoned armies of angels to defend Him against the soldiers sent to arrest Him (26:53).

We learn from Jesus that angels will accompany Him when He returns with the glory of God at the end of time, after He has first sent them out to gather in His elect and to expel all who persist in rebellion (13:39, 41, 49; 16:27).

Unlike most pictures purporting to portray angels, they resemble men, not women or children ("little cherubs"!) and have no wings. They often appear in shining glory, like mighty warriors, sending those who see them to their knees in awe and adoration (Luke 24:4, 5). Unlike men, however, they have no sex life (22:30).

In summary, angels are "ministering spirits sent forth to minister for those who will inherit salvation" (Hebrews 1:14). Does that mean that each believer has an individual "guardian angel" who follows him around and protects him from all harm?

Perhaps Jesus simply wants to emphasize the care and concern that God has for every person who follows Christ, a care which leads Him to send angels to our assistance whenever we need it. The bottom line: We are on His mind day and night!

The Way to Joy
Matthew 18:12 Part–1

"What do you think? If a man has a hundred sheep, and one of them goes astray, does he not leave the ninety-nine and go to the mountains to seek the one that is straying?"

Jesus here describes not only a good and faithful shepherd but also Himself.

He left the multitudes of angels (about whom He has just spoken), who had not gone astray, to come to this earth "to save that which was lost" (18:11).

He could have enjoyed the "comforts" of heaven, with His Father and with the company of beautiful, brilliant, and blessed angels. But no! His Father does not will that any of the elect shall perish. The Son always does what His Father wants.

Father and Son agreed, from all eternity, to save millions of the fallen sons and daughters of Adam and Eve, lest they perish eternally in hell.

So, like the shepherd who goes into the mountainous territory, with all its dangers from lions, serpents, and bears, Jesus came to this fallen earth to seek and to rescue the "lost sheep of the house of Israel," and then, through His disciples "all the nations" (10:6; 15:24; 24:14; 28:19).

But the way will be long, and hard, and lead eventually to His death on a cross. Having withstood Satan in the wilderness (4:1–11), He will face him again and again, until finally the ancient enemy's power is broken decisively by the Cross and the empty tomb (Ephesians 1:1:20–21; Colossians 2:15; 1 Peter 3:22).

And why? What motivates the eternal Son of God to become a man so that He might save sinful men and women?

His own joy! "And if he should find it, assuredly, I say to you, he rejoices more over that *sheep* than over the ninety-nine that did not go astray" (18:13). "Who for the joy that was set before Him endured the cross, despising the shame, and has sat down at the right hand of the throne of God" (Hebrews 12:2).

And shall we not seek the same joy in the same way?

Lost Sheep
Matthew 18:12 Part–2

"What do you think? If a man has a hundred sheep, and one of them goes astray, does he not leave the ninety-nine and go to the mountains to seek the one that is straying?"

God's people are compared to sheep, because:

> We are *little*. Compared to our spiritual enemies—Satan, the world, and our own sinful desires—we are small and weak. Nor do we measure up to our own expectations for ourselves; we constantly fall short of our goals. We are powerless to restrain our pride and our passions, and we cannot reform ourselves.

> We are *lost*, for we have wandered off the path. Separated from God's flock, we are alone, isolated, and vulnerable. We thought we knew where we were going, but now we do not know where we are or how to return to the right road. The way that seemed right to us has turned out to be wrong. The night falls, darkness surrounds us, and we cannot see they way home.

> We are *lost*, also, in the sense that we are perishing. Our ignorance, folly, and rebellion have woven a web from which we cannot extricate ourselves. Enemies close in to attack and devour us—additions, anxiety, alienation, even despair. We may be surrounded by other people, but we feel alone, for they cannot help us. Worst of all, God seems very far away.

But "the Son of Man has come to save that which was lost" (18:11)! Jesus, the Good Shepherd, has brought light and life into this dark and deadly vale of tears. Obedient to His Father's will, He has laid down His life for His sheep. There is hope!

Our sins can be forgiven; our bondage broken; our wounds healed; our grief assuaged. Light dispels the darkness; liberty loosens our tongue; love floods our heart; life conquers death.

All we have to do is to admit that we are "lost sheep" and return to the "Shepherd and Overseer of [our] souls"—Jesus, who is "the way, the truth, and the life" (1 Peter 2:25; John 14:6).

Greatness in the Kingdom

The Seeking Shepherd
Matthew 18:12–14

"If a man has a hundred sheep, and one of them goes astray, does he not leave the ninety-nine and go to the mountains to seek the one that is straying? And if he should find it, assuredly, I say to you, he rejoices more over that sheep *than over the ninety-nine that did not go astray. Even so it is not the will of your Father who is in heaven that one of these little ones should perish."*

Jesus had begun by warning, "Take heed that you do not despise one of these little ones" (18:10). Now He explains why: Like a careful and caring shepherd, God values each one of His people.

Remember that the disciples had started this by arguing about who was greatest in the kingdom (18:1). Jesus continues to challenge their mindset: What men consider "great" or important usually conflicts with God's evaluation.

Earlier, the Lord had taught them that even "little" people are significant in God's eyes. Now He reminds them of the preciousness of every individual believer.

Every man, woman, and child bears the image of God, who created us. Moreover, the soul of each individual believer has been purchased with the blood of Jesus, the Good Shepherd who laid down His life for the sheep. His Father attaches infinite worth to every single Christian. Can we do any less?

In an age which measures "greatness" by numbers—"more is better"—Jesus' words come as a sharp rebuke. We want many to come to know Christ, but they must come one-by-one, and we must attend to each one separately. If even one professing Christian leaves our fellowship, no effort should be spared to recover that erring "sheep."

Otherwise, how can we claim to know the mind of Christ? In describing the seeking shepherd who goes out to find the wandering sheep, He reveals to us His own heart.

What a comfort should this be to us when we wander! He will not let us go. When He brings us back, often by afflicting us with severe discipline, His joy resounds in the heavens.

God's Will
Matthew 18:14

"Even so it is not the will of your Father who is in heaven that one of these little ones should perish."

God does not want even one believer to perish because of sin. For that reason, He sent His Son to seek and "to save that which was lost" (18:11; Luke 9:56). Jesus came to "save His people from their sins" (1:21) and was willing to pay any price, including death under the wrath of God, to achieve that purpose.

In the Garden of Gethsemane, He struggled with the horror of impending doom at the hand of a righteous God, for He was innocent. Each time He asked to be delivered from this death, however, He added, "nevertheless, not as I will, but as You *will*" (26:39).

Jesus accepted the will of His Father as His own. The Good Shepherd laid down His life for the sheep whom God had given to Him (John 10:11, 15, 29).

He wants us to do the same. "Follow Me," He said to His first disciples, and the same command comes to us today. If we pray, "Your will be done," as Jesus taught us (6:10), then we must, like our Master, commit ourselves to accomplish the revealed will of the Father.

Otherwise, we may questions whether we belong to Him. "Not everyone who says to Me, 'Lord, Lord,' shall enter the kingdom of heaven, but he who does the will of My Father in heaven" (7:21).

Unless our lives are devoted to seeking and saving those who are lost, and to assisting believers to know and serve God better, then we may question our relationship to Christ.

How can we claim to be followers of Christ if ambition, greed, comfort, pleasure, and other idols rule in our hearts? Those who live only for the things of this world; who place their own desires first; who neglect the eternal welfare of others—such people bear so little resemblance to Christ that we may doubt whether they belong to Him at all.

On the other hand, "He who wins souls *is* wise" (Proverbs 11:30). The people who seek above all to help others know and serve God can be called wise, because they have aligned their will with God's.

Controlling Conflict
Matthew 18:15 Part-1

"Moreover, if your brother sins against you, go and tell his fault between you and him alone."

With this one sentence, Jesus offers us the key to controlling almost all private conflicts with other Christians.

Notice: The person is a "brother"—a fellow Christian. This person has "sinned"—he has done something which clearly violates God's revealed will. He has sinned "against you"—this is a private matter, which concerns him and me.

What am I to do when that happens? Tell my friends? Pour out my troubles to all who will hear? Seek out a counselor? Gossip? No! I am to go to that person alone, in private.

"But he won't listen to me!" How do you know? Have you tried? Do you really think so little of that person, and so much of yourself, that you are convinced he will not hear a just complaint, if it is offered in a humble spirit?

"But it will hurt our relationship if I go to him directly." Your relationship with him is already damaged, for he has sinned and you are upset.

"But he will dislike me and even hurt me!" How do you know? Furthermore, he has already shown disregard for you by sinning, so you have little to lose. Unless, of course, you are wrong!

"But I don't know what to say!" That is an excuse. Just say, "Brother (or sister), when you did that, I felt bad. Can we talk about it?" God will guide the conversation.

"But I'll lose my temper!" First follow Jesus' advice about the speck and the plank (7:1–4), and Paul's in Ephesians 4:26–32. But go! It is better to risk getting a little angry than to nurture resentment in your heart.

Regaining a Brother
Matthew 18:15 Part–2

"Moreover if your brother sins against you, go and tell him his fault between you and him alone. If he hears you, you have gained your brother."

Jesus continues His instructions—which for Christians are commands—for how to deal with conflict.

First, we must go privately to the one who has sinned against us. Simply, calmly, and humbly—for we are sinners ourselves—we should inform him that his activity has hurt us and that we think it was wrong.

Our attitude should be marked by an awareness that our brother, though perhaps wrong, is important to God. To tempt him to sin by treating him poorly is to place our own souls in danger (18:6–9). To despise him is to trample underfoot the blood of Christ, who died for him, and to disdain the love which God has for him (18:10–14).

The purpose of our visit is to inform him of the offense we think he has committed, and seek reconciliation. It is not to judge, condemn, or punish, for which we have no right.

Perhaps, after we have said how we felt when he hurt us, we can just ask for an explanation. Maybe there is something we do not understand. In fact, misunderstanding lies at the root of many conflicts.

In any case, we go to say how we feel about what happened. "I was upset when you did that," is enough, though we might add, "And I don't understand why you did it. Could you please tell me?"

Such a meek and mild approach will disarm many potential enemies and restore our relationship. We might even discover something we have done wrong, and thus draw closer to God through repentance and renewed trust in God's grace!

For, as Jesus says, if our brother "hears" us, we have "gained" (or regained) our formerly close relationship. That is, if he accepts our complaint as legitimate, expresses some sorrow about how we feel, and admits his fault, then we can once again enjoy his fellowship in Christ.

Isn't that worth the trouble, and far better than gaining an enemy?

The Next Step
Matthew 18:16

"But if he will not hear, take with you one or two more, that 'by the mouth of two or three witnesses every word may be established.'"

But what if our brother spurns our approach? Sometimes people simply will not admit that they have done anything wrong. Even worse, it is not uncommon for people to answer our complaint with a counter-charge.

If his criticism is just (and that may well be the case, since we are all sinful), we should humbly admit our fault, without justifying ourselves. A simple, "You're right about that. I'm sorry," will be sufficient, as long as it is sincere and not immediately followed by a re-stating of our grievance!

Nevertheless, if we do not think the other person has been willing to listen, and are still upset, we can take the next step.

Without telling anyone else, we can ask one or two people to go with us to seek reconciliation with a brother. It is vital that we not tell them ahead of time what we think the other person has done wrong. Not only would that prejudice them, but it would make our brother suspicious of them.

No, we are just trying to get one or two others to witness our second attempt to talk to our brother. That way, someone else will be present when we try again. Explain it to your brother thus:

"Our conflict still bothers me. I would like to discuss it again with you, and have invited this person (these people) to be here as we talk. They don't know anything about what I am going to say."

Very few conflicts can survive this second attempt, for two reasons: Your brother will have to listen to you, and may even try to understand. And you will have to listen to him with understanding. With two silent witnesses standing by, you will make every effort to be kind and gentle with each other, and that may suffice to resolve the problem.

You are not asking the others to mediate at this point, but just to be there. Afterward, they can testify to what was said, either for or against you or your brother.

Church Discipline
Matthew 18:17

"And if he refuses to hear them, tell it to the church. But if he refuses even to hear the church, let him be to you like a heathen and a tax collector."

After going privately to the brother who has sinned against us, if he refuses to listen to us we are to take two or three others with us as witnesses of our second attempt.

If they agree with us, and he refuses to accept their evaluation of the matter, then we may take the matter to the church. Here, the "church" probably means, first, the elders of the congregation, who represent the church.

If the elders—and later, the entire congregation—agree with us and conclude that the brother has sinned, and he refuses to accept their judgment, then he must be treated like a non-believer. At that point, we are not to have fellowship with such a person, nor is anyone else in the church.

The purpose of this process is to "gain a brother," to restore friendship and communion, to heal the breach caused by his offense and our reaction. Jesus has another goal in mind, too: That the church maintain its reputation (and His) by expelling anyone who persists in unrepentant sin.

Indeed, one of the main reasons people criticize Christianity lies in the failure of the church to discipline its members. Only as we follow the guidelines Jesus gave us will we preserve some sort of a reputation for goodness and godliness for God's people.

But remember that we cannot just lightly pass judgment on a fellow Christian, or gossip about his faults to others, or refuse to talk to him directly about his supposed transgression of God's will as revealed in the Bible.

No! We must follow, step-by-step, the process our Lord has outlined so clearly. In this way, almost all conflicts between Christians would soon be resolved.

Binding and Loosing
Matthew 18:18–20

"Assuredly, I say to you, whatever you bind on earth will be bound in heaven, and whatever you loose on earth will be loosed in heaven."

Since this verse has spawned so much misunderstanding, we must first say what it does *not* mean.

Jesus does not here give unqualified authority to any one person in a church organization (such as the Pope or a priest) to grant special indulgences, dispensations or pardon for sins against God.

Martin Luther's objections against such claims still stand: Only God can forgive sins, and He does so on the basis of the sacrifice of Christ on the Cross, not because money has been paid, or a Mass said, or prayers offered, or a priest makes a pronouncement.

On the other hand, nor does it refer to the common practice of "binding" Satan in prayer, particularly binding some demon or evil spirit who is supposed to have special power over a person or place. Jesus is talking about church discipline, not about evil spirits and how to deal with them.

Furthermore, Satan was already "bound" when Jesus inaugurated His ministry. The Lord has overcome the "strong man," whom He "saw fall like lightning from heaven," and whose power He thoroughly broke at Calvary and the empty tomb (Luke 11:14–22; 10:17–20; John 12:31; Colossians 2:14–15).

Rather, the "binding" and "loosing" are limited to the authority of the church, speaking through its leaders (plural!), and only after a very careful process of investigation and entreaty, to pronounce that a member may not be allowed into fellowship for a while.

That is, if a professing believer sins against another believer, and refuses to admit his fault or repent of his offense, the church leaders may require that he be treated like a non-believer, at least for a while.

In doing so, they are merely reflecting the revealed will of God, who will ratify their actions. That is because the church leaders have found that a member has violated a clear command of God as contained in the Bible, and not some minor church regulation.

The Power of Prayer
Matthew 18:19–20

"Again I say to you that if two of you agree on earth concerning anything that they ask, it will be done for them by My Father in heaven. For where two or three are gathered together in My name, I am there in the midst of them."

Jesus had just taught that a decision by the church to expel a member who did not repent would reflect God's will. Now He seems to broaden the promise: Whatever even a small group of believers ask for in prayer will be granted.

We must note the conditions which surround this guarantee.

They must gather in Jesus' name. In the Bible, the "name" of a person, and especially the name of God, represented far more than a mere identifying title.

The "name" stands for the person himself. Thus, Jesus instructed His disciples to pray to God the Father, "Hallowed be Your name" (6:9).

After His resurrection, Jesus commissioned them to baptize new believers "in the name of the Father, and of the Son, and of the Holy Spirit, teaching them to observe all things that I have commanded you" (28:19–20). His own name, Jesus, foretold that He would "save His people from their sins" (1:21).

Thus, to gather in the name of Jesus is to trust Him as God's Son and our Savior. That implies that we are sinners in need of God's grace, so our prayers will reflect humility, repentance, and an awareness that we deserve nothing.

Further, those who gather in His name confess Jesus as absolute Lord and master of their lives. Committed to obey all His commands, they will ask for nothing that contradicts the revealed will of God.

As followers of Christ, they will gladly suffer persecution for His sake (5:11); they will seek to love their enemies (5:43–48); their primary passion will be for God's glory, His kingdom, and His rule on earth (6:9–10, 33). Above all, they will not join those who "Practice lawlessness" while professing to serve Christ (7:21–23).

Christian Unity
Matthew 18:19

"Again I say to you that if two of you agree on earth concerning anything that they ask, it will be done for them by My Father in heaven."

God delights in Christian unity. In fact, He requires it.

"Behold, how good and how pleasant *it is* for brethren to dwell together in unity!... For there the LORD commanded the blessing—life forevermore" (Psalm 133:1, 3).

In His last prayer on earth for His disciples, Jesus asked "that they may all be one, as You, Father, *are* in Me, and I in You; that they also may be one in Us, that they world may believe that You sent Me" (John 17:21).

The Apostle Paul taught that believers are one body in Christ (Romans 12:5), but he also urged us to manifest that essential unity in our attitudes and actions: "fulfill my joy by being like-minded, having the same love, *being* of one accord, of one mind" (Philippians 2:2).

Peter, writing to Christians facing persecution, urged them to be "of one mind, having compassion for one another" (1 Peter 3:8). Immediately before that exhortation, he had warned husbands to live with their wives "with understanding, giving honor to the wife ... that your prayers may not be hindered" (1 Peter 3:7).

Towards the end of his long life, the Apostle John repeated Jesus' promise about prayer: "And whatever we ask we receive from Him," but he added the reason why, "because we keep His commandments" (1 John 3:22).

And what are the commandments? "... that we believe on the Name of His Son Jesus Christ and love one another" (1 John 3:23).

Those who believe in Jesus gather in His name; those who love another will agree about what they ask in prayer. They thus fulfill the requirements Jesus laid down for effective prayer.

In other words, holding a common faith in the bond of love enables even two believers to pray with confidence that God will grant their request.

Ultimate Intimacy
Matthew 18:20

"For where two or three are gathered together in My name, I am there in the midst of them."

There is much depth and mystery here, but at least we can say that the relationship of Christ with Christians is profoundly intimate.

Notice, they are *in Him*. They gather in His name. As we have seen, that means that they share a common trust in Him, a united love for Him, a fervent desire to do His will, a commitment to follow His example.

To be "in" Christ means to enjoy spiritual union and communion with Him. Comparing Himself to a vine, Jesus told His disciples, "Abide in Me" (John 15:4). Paul describes the Christians in Thessalonica as "the church of the Thessalonians in God the Father and the Lord Jesus Christ" (1 Thessalonians 1:1).

"In" Christ we are blessed with spiritual blessings; chosen by God to be His adopted sons, with total access to His presence; accepted by the Father; redeemed through the blood of Jesus; united into one body with other believers; granted a share of His inheritance; given the Spirit; raised up from spiritual death and given new life" (Ephesians 1:3, 4, 6, 7, 10, 13; 2:5).

As Christians draw closer to Christ individually by faith, they grow up in Him, and into His likeness. Speaking the truth to one another in love, they are built up as a body in union with Him as their head (Ephesians 4:1–3, 15–16).

Thus, when believers come together to hear the Word of God and to pray, they are not just entering a room, or joining a group of people. Their faith in Christ and love for each other transform that meeting into a holy conference with Christ Himself.

Does that not mean that we should see each encounter with another believer as an encounter also with the risen Lord?

Believers gathering in the name of Jesus are not only in Him; He is "in the midst of them" (18:20). "Abide in Me, and I in you," He commanded (John 15:4).

Though His body now resides in heaven, His Spirit dwells in the hearts of all who trust Him, and in the midst of even the smallest group of Christians assembled in His name. As He promised after His resurrection, He will be with them *"even* to the end of the age" (Matthew 28:20).

God will answer the prayers of two or three sincere, loving believers because Jesus is in their midst. The Father always grants the requests of His Son. When He looks at the small band of Christians, He sees His Son among them, and treats them as if their prayers were those of Christ.

"And whatever you ask in My name, that I will do, that the Father may be glorified in the Son" (John 14:13).

But notice the condition: "He who has My commandments and keeps them, it is he who loves Me. And he who loves Me will be loved by My Father, and I will love him and manifest Myself to him.... If anyone loves Me, he will keep My word; and My Father will love him, and We will come to him and make our home with him" (by the Spirit) (John 14:21, 23). The command? "... love one another" (John 15:12).

In other words, if we "agree," with faith and love, our corporate prayers will be answered.

Oh, for eyes to see this priceless presence of Christ!

Forgiveness Unlimited
Matthew 18:21–22

Then Peter came to Him and said, "Lord, how often shall my brother sin against me, and I forgive him? Up to seven times?" Jesus said to him, "I do not say to you, up to seven times, but up to seventy times seven."

Perhaps the hardest thing to do in life is to forgive someone who repeatedly offends you. It is much easier to pardon, or even overlook, an occasional slap in the face, but to forgive someone who has time and again hurt you seems unreasonable.

Until, that is, the force of the parable which Jesus immediately told Peter has gripped us.

One servant owed his king the equivalent of millions of dollars, and was about to be thrown into debtors' prison, along with his whole family, but the monarch was moved by his pleas for pity, and the entire debt was canceled.

That same servant then went out and found one of his fellow servants who owed him three month's wages, but could not pay, and who begged him to have patience until he could clear the debt. But this ungrateful wretch threw his fellow servant into prison until the amount would be fully remitted.

When the other servants found out and reported this dastardly deed to the sovereign, the king said, "You wicked servant! I forgave you all that debt because you begged me. Should you not also have had compassion on your fellow servant, just as I had pity on you?" (18:32–33) He then handed him over, not to prison, but to torturers, to extract the last penny.

Jesus concludes: "So My heavenly Father also will do to you if each of you, from his heart, does not forgive his brother his trespasses" (18:35).

Here is the point: The wicked servant saw the speck in his fellow servant's eye, but not the plank in his own eye (7:3). So it is with us when we refuse to forgive those who have offended us. We have forgotten the Lord's Prayer, "forgive us out debts, as we forgive our debtors" (6:12), and the Lord's explanation, "For if you forgive men their trespasses, your heavenly Father will also forgive you. But if you do not forgive men their trespasses, neither will your Father forgive your trespasses" (6:14–15).

The logic is simple: We will reflect to others our sense of God's grace (Ephesians 4:32–5:1; Colossians 3:13). Failure to forgive multiple offenses demonstrates a deeper failure to remember God's manifold grace towards us, and calls into question the very nature of our relationship to God as loving Father.

Maybe we should focus more on what we owe God, rather than on what others owe us!

19 The King on Family and Health

Male and Female
Matthew 19:4 Part–1

"Have you not read that He who made them *at the beginning 'made them male and female'...?"*

Jesus' answer to a question from the Pharisees about divorce teaches (directly or indirectly) several vital truths.

The first is that Jesus believed the first few chapters of Genesis. He is quoting Genesis 1:27 as if it were a straight narrative of fact. To deny the historical accuracy of the creation account is to call Jesus a liar, or an ignorant fool.

The second is that God created mankind. We are not the product of evolutionary development; the apes are not our ancestors. Darwin's theory never possessed adequate scientific evidence to prove that all of life developed from the "simple" to the "complex," but recent discoveries have shown that his major thesis was wrong.[*]

But the focus of Jesus' words lies elsewhere: "He made them male and female."

Mankind consists of two sexes, two types, two fundamental expressions: male and female. We are one in our humanity, but significantly different. Man and woman together express the image of God; separately, we reflect only part of His nature and being (Genesis 1:26–27).

Momentous consequences flow from this simple truth. For example:

Despite our fallen nature, we still, as male and female, bear the image of God. At the least, that requires us to respect the other sex. We are not to denigrate one another. Nor are we to manipulate and use the other sex.

More than that, we can find in each gender the imprint of God Himself. Particularly in our differences, we see various facets of the immeasurable riches of God's person. No wonder people in love break out in songs of worship! They are responding to the traces of divinity in the beloved.

---

[*] See Denton's *Evolution: A Theory in Crisis*; Behe's *Darwin's Black Box*; Johnson's *Darwin on Trial*; and Strobel's *The Case for a Creator* for more information.

Equal and Different
Matthew 19:4 Part–2

"Have you not read that He who made them at the beginning 'made them male and female.'...?"

Jesus affirms the statement by Moses that God made man "male and female," which follows the affirmation that He made them "in His *own* image" (Genesis 1:26–27).

Taken together, these two sentences teach us a great deal about men and women.

As created in the image of God, they are fully equal in God's sight. Intellectually and morally, they both reflect that nature of God. Men and women possess the same worth, and deserve the same respect.

Men and women who believe in Christ have another fundamental unity: They are "one in Christ Jesus" (Galatians 3:28). Bought with the same blood, they are equally redeemed, justified, and accepted by God. They are, as Peter says, "heirs together of the grace of life" (1 Peter 3:7). Both receive equal access to the Father through faith in Christ, and both are endowed with spiritual gifts from God.

On the other hand, as male and female, they possess deep differences.

The most obvious of these is their anatomy. Men beget children; women conceive, carry, bear, and nurse them. To some degree, biology *is* destiny, for these roles (and privileges!) cannot be exchanged.

Mostly as a reflection of this radical distinction, men and women think, respond, communicate, and feel in different ways. In general—and there are many exceptions—women tend to be more relational, and men more goal-oriented. To build relationships, women tend to talk more than men, who tend to focus on work.

Women tend to be a bit more tender-hearted than men, a fact that even the Hebrew word for compassion reflects: It refers to the womb of a mother. Men tend to think more abstractly, women more concretely. And so on.

We can either deny and denigrate these differences, or rejoice in them, but we cannot eradicate them. They come from God!

Called to Lead
Matthew 19:4 Part–3

"... He who made them *at the beginning made them male and female."*

Just as Father and Son, though entirely equal, fulfill different roles in creation and redemption, so men and women have different functions on earth.

Jesus was fully equal with God the Father in eternity, power, and deity but, as Son, He submitted Himself to become a man in order to save us from our sins. Throughout His life on earth, He always sought and performed His Father's will. In the Divine economy, the Father leads and the Son follows.

Likewise, men are to lead, in the family and in the church. Of course, leaders must follow the example of Jesus, who came "to serve, and to give His live a ransom for many" (Mark 10:45).

Husbands, for example, are to love their wives "as Christ loved the church, and gave Himself for her" (Ephesians 5:25). Elders must "Shepherd the flock of God" not "as being lords..., but being examples" (1 Peter 5:2, 3).

There is never any excuse for harsh, demanding, or abusive exercise of authority.

As the Son of God submitted Himself to the Father, so women are to submit to their husbands in the home and to men in the church. In keeping with this principle, Jesus chose only men as His apostles, and the Apostles gave instructions for male leadership in each congregation (1 Corinthians 14:34–38; 1 Timothy 2:8–3:13; Titus 1:5–9; 2:5; 1 Peter 3:1–7).

Just as the submission of Christ does not imply His inferiority to the Father, so the submission of women to husbands and to elders in the church does not deny their equal worth before God. It is merely a matter of roles, relationships, and responsibilities.

This (admittedly hierarchical) order in the home and in the church does not derive from cultural norms, as many claim. Rather, it flows from the very nature of God Himself, from the nature of men and women as He has created us, and from the facts of the Fall.

(1 Corinthians 11:3–9; 1 Timothy 2:13–14).

Two Become One
Matthew 19:6

"So then, they are no longer two but one flesh."

Jesus draws this conclusion from Genesis 2:24, "Therefore a man shall leave his father and mother and be joined to his wife, and they shall become one flesh."

In other words, marriage joins a man and a woman in a union so close that the Bible calls them "one flesh."

Notice how this description of marriage rules out polygamy and homosexual relationships. The one-flesh union can take place only between one man and one woman.

Notice, also, that this union can occur only after we leave father and mother. Though we continue to respect them and honor them, and our affection for them never dies, marriage creates a new and even deeper bond.

Further, the one-flesh union requires an intentional cleaving, or clinging, to each other. Marital intimacy cannot be built on multiple loyalties and manifold commitments. We must concentrate our longings for intimacy on our spouse, and seek consciously to develop a growing closeness with that one person.

In other words, though man and wife become "one flesh" as soon as they are married, they must preserve and nurture that relationship by constant "clinging"—companionship, commitment, and closeness in mind, body, and spirit.

Indeed, it is just because marriage surpasses all other bonds, even that between parent and child, in its potential for personal communion, that "a man shall leave his father and mother." What else could impel us to distance ourselves from those who gave us life and everything else we know?

Paul expresses this oneness by the beautiful image of the human body. The husband is the head, the wife his beloved body. Just as we nurture and tenderly care for our own bodies, so should a man nourish and cherish his wife (Ephesians 5:22–33).

How strong is the connection between man and wife? "He who loves his wife loves himself" (Ephesians 5:28). In other words, they are "one flesh."

Defeating Divorce Part–1
Matthew 19:1–9

"So then, they are no longer two but one flesh. Therefore what God has joined together, let not man separate."

Answering the question, "Is it lawful for a man to divorce his wife for *just* any reason?" Jesus replies, simply, "No!"

He gives several reasons for this prohibition:

> Man and wife are "one flesh." Marriage creates a union so close that the two are now considered as one. The Apostle Paul says, "he who loves his wife loves himself" (Ephesians 5:28).
>
> God has joined them together. Though they may have married under parental pressure or the power of passion, yet the result is God's doing. No human may sever this divinely-created union.
>
> Their unity reflects the very nature of God for, as Jesus has just reminded them, He "made them" in His own image as "male and female" (19:4; Genesis 1:26, 27). To destroy this union is to deface the image of God.
>
> Though Jesus does not say so here, we know from the Old Testament that God compared His relationship with Israel to a marriage. The Lord had bound Himself to His people in a covenant of love, and saw Himself as their husband. Divorce destroys this comparison.
>
> Likewise, Jesus refers to Himself as the bridegroom of His people, and the rest of the New Testament compares His union with all believers to an indissoluble marriage (9:15; 25:1; John 3:29; Romans 7:4; Ephesians 5:22–33).

Since marriage mirrors the relationship between Christ and His church, any breach of this covenant makes it that much harder to bear witness to God's grace to us.

Defeating Divorce Part–2
Matthew 19:6

"So then, they are no longer two but one flesh. Therefore what God has joined together, let not man separate."

Jesus' teaching on divorce contrasted sharply with the views of the Pharisees. Though not always speaking with one voice on this subject, they agreed that a man could divorce his wife for sufficient cause.

They appealed to a passage in the Law of Moses which assumed that divorce would take place and regulated its practice (Deuteronomy 24:1–4). Jesus did not accept their view—that Moses had actually approved of divorce, much less that he had "commanded" it—but blamed the need for that law upon "the hardness of your hearts" (19:8).

In the Bible, "hardness of heart" almost always implies a state of obstinate rebellion against God, a condition that leads to eternal destruction. His use of this phrase demonstrates what Jesus thought of the spiritual condition of those who initiated divorce.

It is because people cannot love their enemies as God has loved us (5:43–48), and cannot forgive as the Father has forgiven us, even up to "seventy times seven" (6:12; 18:22), that they choose to break their marriage vows.

In the passage just before this one, Jesus had told a parable about forgiveness, concluding with a solemn warning of awful punishment for those who fail to show mercy: "So My heavenly Father also will do to you if each of you, from his heart, does not forgive his brother his trespasses" (18:34–35).

The Pharisees were convinced that they were right and others were wrong. Is that not that what people who resort to divorce also believe?

Have they not forgotten Jesus' teaching, "Judge not, that you be not judged" (7:1)?

How can those who withhold mercy have confidence that God will be merciful to them? How can those who seek to break the covenant of marriage—a covenant which mirrors God's faithfulness to all who trust in Him—count on God's promise of forgiveness?

Defeating Divorce Part–3
Matthew 19:6

"So then, they are no longer two but one flesh. Therefore what God has joined together, let not man separate."

Jesus' teaching on marriage and divorce agrees with the words of Malachi, the last writing prophet in the Old Testament.

> Because the LORD has been witness
> Between you and the wife of your youth,
> With whom you have dealt treacherously;
> Yet she is your companion and your wife by covenant.
> But did He not make *them* one,
> Having a remnant of the Spirit?
> And why one?
> He seeks godly offspring.
> Therefore take heed to your spirit,
> And let none deal treacherously with the wife of his youth.
> For the LORD God of Israel says
> That He hates divorce…
>
> Malachi 2:14–16

Through His prophet, God tells us that He "hates divorce," and why.

Divorce amounts to betrayal and treachery, for a young woman entrusts herself to a man in the expectation that he will love, cherish, and care for her as long as they both live.

Divorce breaks faith with the closest companion a man can have. From his early years, this woman has lived with him, slept with him, worked with him, hoped and dreamed with him. How can he cast her off (usually for someone younger and prettier)?

Divorce breaks a solemn covenant, one which mirrors the promise God has made to be faithful to His people. How can a man who breaks the marriage covenant presume upon the promises of God's covenant?

God made man and wife one, as He is one. They are not to separate.

God intends that unity to bring children into the world. And not just children, but "a godly offspring." Parents have the solemn responsibility to teach—by word and example—their children about the love of God (Deuteronomy 6:7; Ephesians 6:4). But how can children believe in a promise-keeping God if their parents do not keep their marriage promises?

Defeating Divorce Part–4
Matthew 19:9

"And I say to you, whoever divorces his wife, except for sexual immorality [fornication], and marries another, commits adultery; and whoever marries her who is divorced commits adultery."

Jesus here repeats what He taught in the Sermon on the Mount (5:32). What does He mean? Christians have debated this since the time of the Reformation, but the unanimous (except for one minor church leader) position until 1500 was:

Christians should not divorce each other, and those who have been divorced should not remarry.

The only exception is for "fornication." Since Matthew's Gospel always carefully distinguishes between the words "adultery" and "fornication" [sexual immorality], Jesus cannot be referring to infidelity after marriage [adultery]. What, then, does "fornication" signify?

There are have several explanations, but the best one seems to "sexual relations before marriage with someone other than your spouse." Remember how Joseph wanted to divorce Mary when he discovered that she was expecting a baby? They were engaged, and he thought she had been unfaithful to him. He could have put her away—"divorced" her—but he obeyed the command of the angel to marry her instead.

Thus, if, after engagement, you discover that your intended spouse had has sexual relations with someone else, you may break the engagement and marry another person. Or—to "loosen" the exception further—if, after marriage, you discover that your mate was unfaithful to you before the marriage, you make seek a divorce.

But then the person who was unfaithful may not marry. It seems that the "innocent" person may marry again, but this whole matter is so bound up with Jewish customs at the time that we should probably follow the versions given us by Mark and Luke, who wrote for non-Jews:

"Whoever divorces his wife and marries another commits adultery; and whoever marries her who is divorced from *her* husband commits adultery" (Luke 16:18; Mark 10:11–12; Romans 7:1–3; 1 Corinthians 7:10–11, 39; Malachi 2:16).

Single for God
Matthew 19:12 Part–1

"There are eunuchs who were born thus from their mother's womb, and there are eunuchs who were made eunuchs by men, and there are eunuchs who have made themselves eunuchs for the kingdom of heaven's sake."

Hearing Jesus' prohibition of divorce and remarriage after divorce, His disciples concluded, "It is better not to marry." Jesus agreed, but taught that "All cannot accept this saying [i.e., remain single and celibate], but only *those* to whom it has been given [by God]."

Some men have—in effect—emasculated themselves by deciding to remain single and celibate "for the kingdom of God." He does not mean that men should castrate themselves, as some early Christians believed.

No! He refers to a conscious decision to forgo the pleasures of marriage, and sexual relations that are possible within marriage, in order to serve God with a single mind.

Jesus Himself was such a man. For the sake of His mission, which He knew would be short, and because He would later become the Bridegroom of the Church, He did not marry. Paul, likewise, remained single. As a Pharisee, he had probably been married, but then divorced by his unbelieving Jewish wife.

Possibly out of his own experience, Paul wrote, "But I want you to be without care [concern, trouble]. He who is unmarried cares for the things of the Lord—how he may please the Lord. But he who is married cares about the things of the world—how he may please *his* wife" (1 Corinthians 7:32–33).

Nowhere does the Bible even hint that the married life is an inferior choice. Indeed, some of the most beautiful teaching in Scripture deals with the union of man and wife (Ephesians 5:22–34; Song of Solomon).

But the fact is that a single person is free to concentrate fully upon pleasing God. Those who sacrifice sex and marriage for the Lord's service will be richly rewarded. They will avoid some trouble. They will understand both Jesus and His great apostle better. They will be free to spend more time in the Word and in prayer; to teach and to counsel others; and to follow wherever Christ shall lead.

Subduing Sex
Matthew 19:12 Part–2

"... and there are eunuchs who have made themselves eunuchs for the kingdom of heaven's sake."

There are at least three possible attitudes towards sex: Some consider it a great evil, and do all they can to avoid it or suppress it. Others consider it a great—perhaps the greatest—pleasure, and do all they can to indulge it. Both of those approaches fail to reflect the teaching of the Bible.

God created man and woman in His own image, and blessed both them and their sexuality (Genesis 1:26–28). That is why the Letter to the Hebrews says, "Marriage *is* honorable among all, and the [marriage] bed undefiled" (Hebrews 13:4).

But sex is not the greatest good, for the body will pass away, with all of its pleasures (22:30; 1 Corinthians 6:13). And God intends for sexual activity to take place only within the marriage of one man and one woman. That is why the Bible warns, "fornicators and adulterers God will judge" (Hebrews 13:4).

Like all bodily functions, sex can be used to glorify God or to gratify our own sinful cravings. As a gift from God, it must be used according to His guidelines, lest we suffer great loss.

Jesus gave us one of those guidelines when He said, "seek first the kingdom of God and His righteousness, and all these things [bodily needs] will be added to you" (6:33).

Those who, for the sake of the kingdom of God, decide not to marry, are not denying their sexuality, but subduing it. Likewise for those who remain pure before marriage, and those who remain faithful within marriage. In a sense, they also have "made themselves eunuchs for the sake of the kingdom."

God wants our wholehearted devotion and total submission. He requires single-minded service from His people (22:37). That is why we must subdue our bodies, which are the temple of the Holy Spirit. "You were bought with a price; therefore glorify God in your body" (1 Corinthians 6:20).

How did Paul handle his single estate? "I discipline my body and bring it into subjection" (1 Corinthians 9:27). Why? "For the gospel's sake" (1 Corinthians 9:23). That is, for the kingdom.

The Value of Children
Matthew 19:13–15

But Jesus said, "Let the little children come to Me, and do not forbid them; for of such is the kingdom of heaven."

Some people had brought their children to Jesus for prayer, and had been rebuked by His disciples. Jesus' response highlights the immense worth of children in His eyes.

Why are children so important to Jesus?

They issue from marriage, the sanctity, permanence, and exclusive bond of which Jesus had just uttered a ringing affirmation (19:3–10). They reflect the union of their parents, the promise of the future, and the life of God.

They also naturally possess an attitude central to the kingdom of heaven (God): humility.

Not long before, Jesus had silenced His disciples' selfish quest for supremacy by saying, "... unless you are converted and become as little children, you will by no means enter the kingdom of heaven. Therefore whoever humbles himself as this little child is the greatest in the kingdom of heaven" (18:3–4).

- Little children do not pretend to be strong, or capable, or knowledgeable; they know they are weak.
- Children trust their parents to take care of them.
- They believe what their parents say (true or false!). Aware of their dependence upon their parents, they ask for what they need without hesitation.
- They love to be with their father and mother.

This is not to say that children are without sin; or that this story is meant to teach the propriety of infant baptism (Jesus did not baptize them; He blessed them).

But Jesus' statement challenges our notions of a person's worth. It is not based on power, or position, or possessions. Furthermore, He points us to an essential quality of all true followers of Christ—humble reliance upon God the Father.

In other words, "Blessed *are* the poor in spirit, for theirs is the kingdom of heaven" (5:3).

Who is Good?
Matthew 19:16–17 Part–1

Now behold, one came and said to Him, "Good Teacher, what good thing shall I do that I may have eternal life?" So He said to him, "Why do you call Me good? No one is good but One, that is, God."

This young man strikes us as very attractive, at least at first.

We know that he is young (19:22); certainly in this passage we see his youthful zeal and ardor to do what is right.

Luke tells us also that he is a ruler (Luke 18:18), perhaps in the local, or even the national, governing council. Perhaps this authority came from his own talent and intelligence; perhaps he inherited a high position.

Most likely, however, his power flowed from his great wealth, for Matthew says "he had great possessions." As a former tax-collector, Matthew should know!

Notice also that he admires Jesus, calling Him not only Rabbi—Teacher—but "Good Teacher." Unlike most of the leaders of Israel, he acknowledged Jesus' wisdom and virtue, and sought to learn from Him.

He also had a firm grasp on the most important thing: gaining eternal life. While others in his situation may have been content with power, prestige, and possessions, he knew that these were not enough. They will all perish. We must have eternal life.

Remarkably, however, Jesus rebukes him. He does not accept the title, "Good Teacher." We cannot believe that Jesus considered Himself anything but good. To what, then, does He object?

It seems that the Lord saw into this young man's heart and discerned that he had no concept of absolute goodness. He thought that a mere mortal could be really good. Jesus, knowing that He was being classed with other men, insisted that "No one *is* good but One, *that is*, God."

Clearly, this man did not see the vast gulf between God's perfect holiness and the paltry performance of all mere men. Do we?

Was Jesus a Good Teacher?
Matthew 19:16–17 Part–2

Now behold, one came and said to Him, "Good Teacher, what good thing shall I do that I may have eternal life?" So He said to him, "Why do you call Me good? No one is good but One, that is, God."

At first, this rich young ruler seems respectful to Jesus. He calls Him "Good Teacher" and asks what he must do in order to have eternal life.

Jesus' rebuke alerts us to fundamental flaws in his attitude, however. We have seen that he did not understand the infinite gulf of distance between God's absolute righteousness and the very imperfect conduct of all mere men.

There is more, however. Something is wrong with the way he looks at Jesus. Was Jesus a teacher? Yes! Was He a good teacher? Yes—the best ever! He was good; He taught what is good; He taught well.

But He is not *just* a teacher. Others saw this clearly. The leper worshiped Him and called Him, "Lord" (8:2), as did a would-be follower (8:21), and the disciples when their boat was about to be swamped in the storm (8:25). A demon called Him Son of God (8:29).

Two blind men addressed Him as Son of David (9:27), believing He could restore their sight. The Gentile woman who sought His help for her demon-possessed child cried out, "Lord, help me!" (15:25), as did a father with an afflicted son (17:15). Peter declared Him to be "the Christ, the Son of the living God" (16:16).

This confident, successful man was blind to the moral grandeur of Jesus. He came for information, not transformation, much less salvation. To him, Jesus was just another distinguished religious teacher.

Jesus would have none of his shallow admiration. Very brusquely, He rejected the title, "Good Teacher," and turned this man's attention to the blinding purity of God. Only as he saw his sin could he understand the real goodness and greatness of Jesus.

The same is true for us.

Was Jesus Good?
Matthew 19:16–17 Part–3

"Why do you call Me good? No one is good but One, that is, God."

Not only did the rich young ruler fail to see that Jesus was much more than a teacher, he also failed to understand that if He was only a teacher, He was not good!

The Pharisees had clearer vision.

When Jesus compared Himself to Moses by issuing ethical commands from a mountain (5:1–7:27); countered their teaching with His own authoritative utterances (7:29); declared a paralytic's sins forgiven (9:2); allowed His disciples to break the Pharisees' Sabbath rules (12:1–8); cast out demons with a mere word (12:22–24); received praise from the crowds as He entered Jerusalem (21:16); and told parables directed at their hypocrisy (21:33–45)—when He did all this and more, they drew a simple conclusion: This man is a liar, deceiver, pretender, and blasphemer! He deserves death.

Their rage knew no bounds when they heard His answer to the demand of the High Priest, "Tell us if You are the Christ, the Son of God!" "*It is as* you said. Nevertheless, I say to you, hereafter you will see the Son of Man sitting at the right hand of the Power [God] and coming on the clouds of heaven" (26:63–64).

In a sense, they were right. Unless Jesus was the Son of God, the Messiah sent by God to "save His people from their sins" (1:21), the Lord from heaven, even Immanuel, God with us (1:23)—unless He spoke the truth about Himself, in other words—then He is not a good teacher, but a very bad one.

Jesus will not save those who regard Him merely as a good teacher, for they do not seek salvation from Him. He will answer this man's question, but not until He has challenged his fundamental misunderstanding of the "good teacher" whose instruction he has sought.

What about us? Are we trying to have Jesus as only a "good teacher" in our lives? If so, we shall end up thinking that He is neither good, nor a good teacher. The loss will be ours, not His.

God's Mirror
Matthew 19:16–19

"Good Teacher, what good thing shall I do that I may have eternal life?"... "... if you want to enter into life, keep the commandments." He said to Him, "Which ones?" Jesus said, "'You shall to murder,' 'You shall not commit adultery,' 'You shall not steal,' 'You shall not bear false witness,' 'Honor your father and your mother,' and 'You shall love your neighbor as yourself.'"

Brushing aside the mass of rules and regulations which the Pharisees had added to God's Law, Jesus repeats five of the last six commandments from the Ten Commandments, and adds the summary statement from Leviticus 19:18.

He had already implicitly referred to the first four commands, which call us to worship and serve God alone. Now He turns the spotlight on our duty to others.

Jesus' response to the rich young ruler's sincere, but naïve, question put a moral mirror in front of his conscience. In doing so, He reflected Old Testament teaching. If anyone could fully obey all these requirements from God, he would indeed have eternal life (Leviticus 18:5).

But, as Paul pointed out, no one is "justified ... by the works of the law"—that is, by performing all the duties which God commands (Galatians 2:16). What, then, was the real purpose for the moral law which God revealed?

Paul writes of his own experience, "... I would not have known sin except through the law" (Romans 7:7). God meant for these ethical mandates to expose our sinful heart, so that we would repent and turn to Christ for salvation (Galatians 3:19–24).

Likewise, Jesus' recitation of the Old Testament was intended to help the young man to see that he could not do any "good thing" that would bring him eternal life. He would not only have to understand that Jesus was more than a "good teacher," but also that he was a "bad student"!

What about us? If we have not actually committed murder or adultery, have we also fully loved others as ourselves? And have we been pure in heart (5:8, 21–22, 28)? Looking into the mirror of God's moral law, what do we see?

The Main Obstacle
Matthew 19:20–22

The young man said to Him, "All these things I have kept from my youth. What do I still lack?" Jesus said to him, "if you want to be perfect, go, sell what you have and give to the poor, and you will have treasure in heaven; and come, follow Me."

With stunning spiritual blindness, the young man imagined that he had fully observed all of God's commandments, including, "Love your neighbor as yourself." At that point, Jesus had to abandon His gentle approach and strike at the heart. He knew precisely what idol held sway in the man's soul, and spoke the word that exposed his root sin.

"Sell what you have and give to the poor ... and come, follow Me."

Such counsel would not have surprised Jesus' disciples. After all, Peter and Andrew, James and John, had left all to follow Jesus (4:18–22). At the beginning of His ministry, Jesus had pronounced blessing upon those who "hunger and thirst for righteousness" (5:6); had taught them pray for their "daily bread" (6:11); and had warned, "You cannot serve God and mammon" (6:24).

Instead of storing up wealth on earth, they were told to "lay up for yourselves treasures in heaven," where nothing can rob, or reduce the value of, such investments (6:19–20). Not only would single-minded service of God bring peace of mind and eternal reward (6:33), but it would liberate the heart from inner conflict (6:21–24).

Jesus demanded total commitment from would-be followers (8:18–22) and required that His disciples take up their cross and follow Him (16:24–27). In the parables of the hidden treasure and the pearl of great price, Jesus stressed the surpassing worth of the Kingdom of heaven (13:44–46).

So, His challenge to this rich youth was nothing new. Like many others, then and now, he allowed possessions to hold first place in his affections. Perhaps they represented security, or status, or success, or satisfaction. In any case, his devotion to things had clouded his mind so that he could not see his fundamental sins of unbelief and selfishness.

That is why he thought he could just do a "good thing" and have eternal life. He did not understand the radical nature of his sin, or the unique holiness of God or his desperate need for a Savior.

What is keeping us from recognizing our sin and the true reason Jesus came—not just to teach us to do good, but to deliver us from being bad?

The Peril of Possessions
Matthew 19:23–24

"Assuredly, I say to you that it is hard for a rich man to enter the kingdom of heaven. And again I say to you, it is easier for a camel to go through the eye of a needle than for a rich man to enter the kingdom of God."

In Jesus' day, many saw wealth as a sign of God's blessing. Even today, people do all they can to acquire possessions—a big house, new car, profitable portfolio, and ample retirement fund.

But Jesus issues a stern warning to those who are rich: Wealth can keep us out of the kingdom of God.

We must first ask, Who are the rich? Surely not I! I barely have enough to get by, especially when you consider all my expenses and future obligations.

In the Bible, the rich are those with more than enough, unlike the poor, who do not have enough. The "rich" have options. They are not locked in a struggle just for food, clothing, and shelter. They can enjoy fancy meals, stylish clothing, and spacious, comfortable homes—not to mention new cars, entertainment systems, and all the latest technological gadgets.

Why does all this "stuff" hinder people from receiving eternal life?

Because "where you treasure is, there your heart will be also" (6:21). Instead of loving God with all our heart (22:37), we set our affections on what we own, or want to acquire.

With our eyes set on catalogs, advertisements, stock quotations, and all the goods on display in the mall, we cannot see clearly (6:22–23).

Lacking a single focus, we swerve from the service of God. Instead, we put our time, energy, and attention on Mammon—the god of wealth (6:24). We neglect God, ignore His claim on our lives, and follow the lead of our own greed.

Even worse, like this rich young ruler, those with more than enough easily become proud, relying on their possessions rather than upon God (1 Timothy 6:17). Focused on themselves, they neglect the needs of the poor (1 Timothy 6:18) and fail to love their neighbor as themselves (22:39).

Anything is Possible Part–1
Matthew 19:26

"With men this is impossible, but with God all things are possible."

Jesus had warned, "it is easier for a camel to go through the eye of a needle than for a rich man to enter the kingdom of God." The disciples responded with amazement, "Who then can be saved?" for they had thought that wealth indicated God's blessing and favor.

Jesus' reply gets to the heart of the matter. Yes, it is impossible for men to save themselves. But God can do anything.

From the opening sentence of the Bible, God's omnipotence shines forth. "In the beginning God created the heavens and the earth" (Genesis 1:1). Upon that fundamental fact of history, the Scriptures erect a magnificent edifice of marvelous miracles.

Long past the age of childbearing, Sarah conceived a son by her aged husband Abraham. When she first heard the promise that she would have a son within a year, she laughed in disbelief, but God said, "Is anything too hard for the LORD [Yahweh]" (Genesis 18:14).

Trapped between the Red Sea and the chariots of Pharaoh, the children of Israel cried out in terror, only to witness the stupendous power of God, who parted the waters, led them through on dry land, and swamped their enemies in the returning waters (Exodus 14).

That was only the beginning. For forty years God fed them in the wilderness with manna, bread from heaven. Afterward, Joshua led them across the Jordan River, whose flood-tide waters were stopped by the command of God (Joshua 3).

Obeying God's strange command to march around Jericho once daily without a sound for six days, then seven times on the seventh day, ending with a trumpet call and a mighty shout, they thrilled to see the high walls crumble to the ground (Joshua 6).

Gideon had won a great victory over impossible odds with a tiny band of courageous soldiers (Judges 7). Surrounded as it was by a vast Assyrian army, Jerusalem had been delivered (2 Kings 18–19).

Truly, nothing is impossible for God!

Anything is Possible Part–2
Matthew 19:26

"With men this is impossible, but with God all things are possible."

Jesus' disciples were no strangers to His power. They had watched, amazed, as the lame were made whole, the blind received sight, lepers were cleansed, even the dead were raised to life.

Merely by touching the hem of His robe, a woman with an incurable hemorrhage found healing (9:20–22). A mute man's mouth was opened, once Jesus had expelled a demon from him (9:32–33).

Their Master had walked on the water and calmed the wind and the storm (14:24–33). Twice had He fed thousands of people by producing plenty of food out of a paltry supply (14:13–21; 15:32–39).

Before their very eyes, Jesus had been transfigured, so that His face shone like the sun and His garments glowed with a brilliant whiteness. With their own ears they heard the words of God, "This is My beloved Son" (17:2–5).

Nevertheless, they could not believe that people could renounce worldly wealth for the invisible riches of the coming kingdom. They had seen enough malice directed towards Jesus to know the grip of envy, pride, and hatred.

Even their own hearts told them that sin would not easily be overcome. Despite Jesus' own example of humility, they were still jockeying for position and prominence in the coming kingdom.

Jesus' word prohibiting divorce and remarriage left them disheartened about marriage itself, because they could not see how a man could live with a woman he no longer loved.

From one standpoint, their doubt makes sense: They had not yet seen Jesus risen from the dead and ascended into heaven, nor had they received the Holy Spirit. But we live on the other side of the empty tomb and of Pentecost. Shall we not trust that with God, all things are possible?

Anything is Possible Part–3
Matthew 19:26

"With men this is impossible, but with God all things are possible."

Even though they had seen Him work countless miracles, the disciples balked at the idea that men could save themselves from sin. And well they might. They knew the grip of unbelief and disobedience in their own lives, and saw all too clearly how their countrymen worshiped the things of this world.

Jesus acknowledged the truth of their assertion—"With men this is impossible"—but re-directed their attention. No, sinners cannot free themselves from their bondage to pride and passion, but God can. Indeed, Jesus came for that very purpose, to "save His people from their sins" (1:21).

If they had only considered their own experience, they would have conceded that Jesus had utterly changed them from being fishers of fish to "fishers of men" (4:18–22). Matthew himself, formerly a greedy tax collector, left all to follow the Master (9:9).

By liberating those possessed by demons, Jesus had demonstrated His superior moral power and authority (8:28–34). Proud rulers had bowed to Him in humble supplication (9:18); even a Roman centurion had begged for help (8:5).

But, in one sense, they were right. No one can change the human heart to seek after righteousness—except God. As Paul would write later, we are all "dead in trespasses and sins" until God gives us new life in Christ (Ephesians 2:1, 5).

Not until Pentecost, when the Holy Spirit was poured out upon them, did the Apostles know the transforming power of God in the deepest recesses of the soul (Acts 2:1–4; 1:15–18). After that, they lost all fear; forgot their personal ambitions; and boldly testified to Christ as Lord and Savior.

Under the impulse of the Spirit, the first believers followed the example of Jesus and His followers by freely sharing their possessions with each other (Acts 2:44–45; 4:34–37). What the rich young ruler had been unable to do—God's Spirit performed in the lives of those who trusted in Christ.

With God, anything is possible!

A Good Investment
Matthew 19:29

"Everyone who has left houses or brothers or sisters or father or mother or wife or children or lands, for My name's sake, shall receive a hundredfold, and inherit eternal life."

The rich young ruler had refused to sell all his possessions, give to the poor, and follow Jesus. Peter, on the other hand, pointed out how he and the other disciples had "left all" to follow Him.

Now Jesus issues a guarantee: If anyone forsakes all that he holds dear in this world, he will gain more than he gave up, both in this life and in the world to come.

But what does our Lord mean?

Should all Christians immediately sell everything, distribute the proceeds to the poor, abandon their families, and go wandering around the countryside as itinerant evangelists?

Such a conviction created the monasteries and bands of preaching friars in the Middle Ages. Renouncing all ties to family, fields, and finances, thousands of dedicated believers joined special societies—monastic orders—in the belief that they were treading a higher way of holiness.

On the other hand, Paul ordered the rich not get rid of all their wealth, but to be "rich in good works" (1 Timothy 6:18). He also commanded children to take care of their widowed mothers (1 Timothy 5:4, 8). Elsewhere, we are told to "do good and to share" (Hebrews 13:16).

Furthermore, how could Jesus, who upheld the union of man and wife and forbade divorce (19:6), have meant for His disciples to forsake their wives and children?

The question centers on the word "leave." Though it can mean radical physical separation, it could also refer to an inner renunciation.

Here, Jesus probably has two purposes: 1. To encourage all who have lost everything for the sake of following Him and 2. To challenge all believers to place everything precious on the altar in total dedication to His service.

Christ the King

20 Servants of the Servant King

Genuine Greatness
Matthew 20:26–28

"Yet it shall not be so among you; but whoever desires to become great among you, let him be your servant. And whoever desires to be first among you, let him be your slave—just as the son of Man did not come to be served, but to serve, and to give His life a ransom for many."

The rich young ruler had position, power, and great possessions, and would not give them up. The disciples had forsaken all their possessions to follow Jesus (19:27), but they wanted to trade their humble, powerless position for a place of great prominence in the coming kingdom of Christ (20:20–21, 24).

What a contrast to Jesus! He had just told them, for the third time, that He would be betrayed, condemned, delivered up to the Gentiles, mocked, scourged, and crucified (20:18–19). How could His disciples immediately argue over who would sit next to Him on His throne of glory?

Jesus rebukes them in several ways: First, He warned that they would "drink the cup" of suffering and "be baptized" with the agony of persecution, just as He would be (20:23). Then He frankly tells them that only the Father has the authority to assign rank in the kingdom. After a description of the way earthly rulers exercise authority, Jesus finally points the way to true greatness.

Citing His own supreme example, He draws a map to real prominence in God's kingdom: If you want to be great, become a servant. If you desire preeminence, become a slave.

Give up your rights; your ambitions; your pleasures. Renounce your own agenda; repudiate your own desires; reject your own goals.

Instead, seek to serve. Look out for others' interests, not yours. Live for others, not yourself. Seek their welfare more than your own (see Romans 15:2–3; Ephesians 5:21–6:9; Philippians 2:1–9; 1 John 3:16).

Jesus came to "save His people form their sins," including—and especially—selfishness, pride, and personal ambition (1:21). As we repent, trust in Him, and follow in His steps, we find both true freedom and genuine greatness.

Service, Sacrifice, and Supremacy
Matthew 20:27–28

"And whoever desires to be first among you, let him be your slave—just as the Son of Man did not come to be served, but to serve, and to give His life a ransom for many."

Having shown the way to greatness, Jesus now points out the path to preeminence.

Slaves have no rights. Without question or hesitation, they must do as they are told. Totally possessed by their master, they live for his pleasure and purpose alone.

In God's kingdom, preeminence belongs to the one who thinks not of himself but of others, who lives for others and gives all for their welfare.

Their prime example is Jesus Christ. Notice:

> His original glory. He was the eternal "Son of Man" of Daniel's glorious vision (Daniel 7:13–14). To Him alone belongs an eternal kingdom and glory befitting a Person of equal worth with the Father (Philippians 2:5–6, 10–11).

> His historical humiliation. He "came"—that is, He descended to earth to take on human flesh and blood, to become like us in every way, except without sin (Hebrews 2:14, 17; 4:15). "And the Word became flesh and dwelt among us" (John 1:14).

> His selfless service. He came "not to be served, but to serve." Healing, teaching, feeding, delivering from demons, Jesus met the felt needs of the crowds who thronged about Him.

> His sacrificial death. "... and to give His life a ransom for many." In conscious fulfillment of the Suffering Servant prophecy of Isaiah 53, Jesus submitted to horrible and unjust treatment in order to "save His people from their sins" (1:21). He died for us, "the just for the unjust" (1 Peter 3:18), having borne "our sins in His own body on the tree [cross]" (1 Peter 2:24).

Would you be a leader at home, church, work, or in society? Follow Jesus, the suffering servant of God.

Persevering Prayer
Matthew 20:29–34

And behold, two blind men sitting by the road, when they heard that Jesus was passing by, cried out, saying, "Have mercy on us, O Lord, Son of David!" Then the multitude warned them that they should be quiet; but they cried out all the more, saying, "Have mercy on us, O Lord, Son of David."

These two men must have heard that Jesus had healed a pair of blind men some time before (9:27–31). Perhaps they also knew of the prophecy about the days of the coming Messiah:

> Then the eyes of the blind shall be opened,
> And the ears of the deaf shall be unstopped.
> Then the lame shall leap like a deer,
> And the tongue of the dumb sing.
>
> Isaiah 35:5–6

Would not the one who had given sight to the blind, hearing to the deaf, leaping to the lame, and songs to the mute, also open their eyes?

But the crowds found their cries annoying, and sought to silence them. Such is the perversity of the human heart, even of some who claim to follow Jesus, that they hinder others from being blessed.

No matter. The two suppliants would not be denied. All the louder they pleaded for mercy.

Unlike many, they put their faith in the Messiah, not in men. Despite the opposition of those around Jesus, they focused on what they knew about Him: Son of David, Lord, the one who could and would heal.

Surely they knew of God's promise to send a descendant of David to rule over His people (Ezekiel 37: 21–25). Though they may not have realized that Jesus is also God, they approached Him humbly, addressing Him as Lord. No one could dampen their faith.

Unlike the two disciples who had grasped at power and glory for themselves, all these men wanted was to see. And unlike the rich young ruler, they knew He was more than a teacher. Maybe that is why, after Jesus granted their request, they "followed Him."

May we also persevere, not only in prayer, but also in our pursuit of Christ.

Christ the King

21 The King Enters His Capital

Meekness and Majesty Part–1
Matthew 21:1–11

All this was done that it might be fulfilled which was spoken by the prophet, saying: "Tell the daughter of Zion, 'Behold, your King is coming to you, lowly, and sitting on a donkey, a colt, the foal of a donkey."

When Jesus rode into Jerusalem on a little donkey, He displayed both meekness and majesty. Matthew's Gospel had already given indications of each of these aspects of His divine-human person.

In meekness Jesus was born to a young Jewish girl. Even the place of His birth indicated His lowly position as a member of God's people, for His parents were in Jerusalem at the command of the Roman Emperor.

After living as a refugee in Egypt with Joseph and Mary, Jesus returned to Israel, where He grew up as an ordinary boy. Coming to the waters of the Jordan, He had to persuade His cousin John to baptize Him in order "to fulfill all righteousness" (3:15).

Forty days in the desert without food left Him weak and vulnerable to Satan's temptations. In the days of His ministry, that normal human frailty showed up repeatedly, as when He fell asleep, exhausted, in a storm-tossed boat.

Day after day, He endured rejection from His own people, especially the leaders of the nation, who accused Him of blasphemy, gluttony, drunkenness, and demon-possession.

Finally, in accordance with His own specific predictions, He submitted to arrest, interrogation, unjust accusation, beatings, mockery, and the horrors of the Cross.

So, we may imagine His thoughts as He sat astride that donkey between lines of cheering people on the way into Jerusalem. In this city, where so many prophets had died, He would "give His life a ransom for many" (20:28). Here He would fulfill His purpose to serve, not to be served, to give, not to receive.

Had He been just an ordinary man, this humility and patience under trial would be awesomely unique. The wonder of it magnifies many times when seen through the lens of His majesty.

Meekness and Majesty Part–2
Matthew 21:2–3

"Go into the village opposite you, and immediately you will find a donkey tied, and a colt with her. Loose them and bring them to Me. And if anyone says anything to you, you shall say, 'The Lord has need of them,' and immediately he will send them."

Yes, Jesus rode into Jerusalem on a lowly donkey, and He entered the city knowing He would leave its walls within a few short days carrying His cross to Calvary.

But even the manner of His entry manifested His divine majesty, though veiled in human flesh.

He displayed His authority by directing His disciples to secure a mount for Him.

He demonstrated His omniscience by predicting what they would find.

His sovereign rule of the world enabled Him to possess the animal and her colt for His royal use.

His consciousness of destiny allowed Him to accept worship and adoration as He rode over cloaks covering the road.

The one who had just given sight to two blind men, and—as we know from John's Gospel—raised Lazarus from the dead, proceeded into the City of David knowing that He was David's long-promised Heir and God's beloved Son.

In a word, Jesus was "Lord," as He called Himself, instructing His disciples to say, "The Lord has need of them." Such an explanation compelled the owner of the animals to present them for Jesus' use.

In one sense, of course, the Lord has no "need" of anything, least of all our imperfect service.

But if He chooses to "have need" of our frail bodies, shall we not give ourselves wholly to Him, like lowly donkeys to be ridden by our Majestic Master?

Majestic Meekness Part–3
Matthew 21:3–11

"Behold, your King is coming to you, lowly, and sitting on a donkey, a colt, the foal of a donkey."

On His final journey to Jerusalem, Jesus enters the city in a magnificent display of both His royal majesty and His matchless meekness.

We see His *majesty* in the way He commands His disciples to bring a donkey and her colt to Him to ride. He may have arranged for this ahead of time, perhaps even with a payment. But His instructions demonstrate His absolute ownership of the entire world, "And if anyone says anything to you, you shall say, 'The Lord has need of them,' and immediately he will send them" (21:3). As King, Jesus can requisition anything He needs. His use of the title "Lord" for Himself is consistent with earlier indications that He assumed His identity with Yahweh of the Old Testament (see 7:21–23, for example).

As He rode into the city, the crowd—stirred by the resurrection of Lazarus form the dead (John 12:17–18)—hailed Him as "Son of David," implying that the long-awaited Deliverer had come to be their victorious king (2 Samuel 7:12–16; Psalm 89:3–4). They welcomed Him like a conquering hero, openly acknowledging what the Wise Men had somehow known (2:2), and what His birth in Bethlehem indicated (2:6).

At the same time, however, we must contemplate the extraordinary *meekness* of Christ amidst the joy of the multitudes.

Instead of mounting a war stallion and leading His followers in armed revolution, He announced His peaceful intentions by sitting upon a lowly donkey, as the prophet Zechariah had predicted centuries before (Zechariah 9:9). That same prophet had spoken of a Shepherd who would be struck (Zechariah 13:7) and a firstborn, somehow identified with Yahweh Himself, who would be pierced (Zechariah 12:10).

On Palm Sunday, as we now call it, Jesus rode into the city, not to rebel against the Romans, but to redeem sinful rebels against God; not to subjugate His enemies, but to serve the purposes of God by suffering.

He knew that He had been born to "save His people from their sins" (1:21), and He had taught that the meek "shall inherit the earth" (5:5). The day would come for Him to return in glory to judge the earth (7:21–23; 13:40–43; 25:1–46; 26:64) and to rule with a "rod of iron" (19:28; 22:42–45; Psalm 2:6–9).

For now, however, He was bound to fulfill His own predictions of suffering (16:21; 17:12, 22–23; 20:18–19) as a "ransom for many" (20:28). Eminent greatness and supremacy would come, but only after humble service unto death, even death on a cross (20:26–28; Philippians 2:5–11). The same sequence applies to us (16:24–25).

The Temple of the Lord
Matthew 21:12

Then Jesus went into the temple of God and drove out all those who bought and sold in the temple, and overturned the tables of the money changers and the seats of those who sold doves.

Jesus' action demonstrated both His passion for worship and His zeal for the salvation of all nations.

When Solomon dedicated his magnificent temple, he asked the Lord to hear the prayer of the Gentiles who would come there to worship, so that "all peoples of the earth may know Your name and fear You" (1 Kings 8:41–43).

Driving out all the merchants and the animals they bought and sold, Jesus quoted Isaiah's prophecy that God's temple would be a "house of prayer for all nations" (Isaiah 56:7; Mark 11:17).

We know that this action took place in the Court of the Gentiles, the only part of the Temple accessible to non-Jews. Jesus would not tolerate commerce in the area where "all nations" were meant to call upon the name of God, such was His passion for purity.

All true Christians are now the temple of the living God, indwelt by the Holy Spirit of God (1 Corinthians 3:9, 16; 6:15; Ephesians 2:21–22). As individuals and as a group, we are meant to worship Him with a pure heart, and to help others—the "nations"—worship the Lord.

Have we allowed ourselves to be used for some other purpose? Like the merchants of ancient times, have we given ourselves over to the pursuit of personal profit rather than the pure worship of God? Even worse, have we hindered others from approaching God because of our selfishness?

If so, are we ready to face the Lord, who "will suddenly come to His temple" and purify His people "like a refiner's fire" (Malachi 3:1, 2)?

Passion for Prayer
Matthew 21:13

And He said to them, "It is written, 'My house shall be called a house of prayer,' but you have made it a 'den of thieves.'"

When He drove out the merchants from the Temple, Jesus not only displayed His passion for purity, but also His passion for prayer.

He prayed at His baptism by John (Luke 3:21). He preceded His public ministry with forty days of sustained prayer and fasting (4:1–2). As soon as He had gathered His first disciples, He taught them how to pray (6:9–13).

With strong promises, He urged His followers to "Ask, and it will be given to you; seek, and you will find; knock, and it will b opened to you" (7:7).

It seems that He especially wanted to commend corporate prayer, for He said, "Again I say to you that if two of you agree on earth concerning anything that they ask, it will be done for them by My Father in heaven" (18:19).

Repeatedly, He granted the requests of those who came to Him for help and healing. Indeed, after He had uttered the words quoted above, He healed the blind and the lame who came to Him.

Regardless of whether they verbally implored His assistance, their very coming constituted a silent prayer.

Prayer includes praise—or ought to! Jesus clearly delighted in the praise of the children who cried out, "Hosanna to the Son of David!" He checked the complaints of the Jewish leaders by quoting the words of Psalm 8:2 "Out of the mouth of babes and nursing infants You have ordained strength."

The very next day, He re-stated His promise to the disciples: "And whatever things you ask in prayer, believing, you will receive" (21:22).

Jesus lived what He taught. As He faced the supreme trial of His life, He went into the garden to pray, "O My Father, if it is possible, let this cup pass from Me; nevertheless, not as I will, but as You *will*" (26:39). God heard His prayers, and enabled Jesus to fulfill His destiny.

Such was Jesus' passion for prayer. Shall we not do likewise?

Moving Mountains
Matthew 21:21–22

So Jesus answered and said to them, "Assuredly I say to you, if you have faith and do not doubt, you will not only do what was done to the fig tree, but also if you say to this mountain, 'Be removed and be cast into the sea,' it will be done. And whatever things you ask in prayer, believing, you will receive."

Jesus had just caused a fig tree to wither up and die, merely by speaking a word to it (21:18–19). To His astounded disciples, He then made the above amazing promise.

Of course, we must be careful to note the other passages of the Bible about prayer, lest we take this promise out of context.

We must pray secretly, not to be seen by others (6:5–6). Our prayers should include the major petitions contained in the Lord's Prayer (6:9–13), with God's glory, will, and kingdom taking priority. Since we are forgiven sinners, we must pray with a heart of forgiveness towards others (6:14–15). And we need to pray with others of like mind (18:19–20).

Sometimes, one request will suffice. Often, however, only persistent, earnest entreaties will be heard (7:7; 15:21–28). As followers of Jesus, we shall, of course, approach God with the same submission that found utterance in the Garden of Gethsemane, "Not as I will, but as You *will*" (26:39).

That means, of course, that we may not expect God to grant requests that are meant only for our own pleasures (James 4:3). No, we are to seek only what pleases God and equips us to imitate Christ on earth.

Nevertheless, with all these conditions, the promise remains: If we believe that God can move mountains through our prayers, we can ask Him to do so. The question is, Do we have faith?

What "mountain" hinders you from glorifying God? Is it doubt, or fear, or lack of love? Does some cherished idol still have a place in your heart? Do you lack strength, or wisdom, or resources to obey His commands and spread His word among the nations?

Ask in faith, and He will level all obstacles on your way to the cross and the crown that will follow!

The Authority Question
Matthew 21:23

Now when He came into the temple, the chief priests and the elders of the people confronted Him as He was teaching, and said, "By what authority are You doing these things? And who gave You this authority?"

Though we know from other passages that their motives were bad, the Jewish leaders did ask a good question: By what authority did Jesus teach, heal, and banish merchants from the temple?

Indeed, each one of us must answer the same question: Who is Jesus, and what authority does He possess?

Early in His career, Jesus demonstrated authority over diseases by healing people, and over demons by casting them out with a simple command (4:23–24; 8:16). The evil spirits recognized Him, and called Him "Son of God" (8:29).

The people, also, perceived that He was different from the teachers of the Jewish Bible, for He "taught them as one having authority" (7:29).

How could they do otherwise, when He uttered such words as, "whoever hears these sayings of Mine, and does them, I will liken him to a wise man who built his house on the rock" (7:24)?

As part of His mission to mobilize a band of followers to expand His work, Jesus called twelve disciples and "gave them power *over* unclean spirits ... and to heal all kinds of sickness" (10:1).

A sense of supreme authority emanated from Jesus from the beginning of His ministry, when He summoned four fishermen to forsake all and become His disciples: "Follow Me" (4:19, 21).

After His resurrection, Jesus flatly stated, "All authority has been given to Me in heaven and on earth. Go and make disciples of all the nations, baptizing them in the name of the Father and of the Son and of the Holy Spirit, teaching them to observe all things that I have commanded you; and lo, I am with you always *even* to the end of the age" (28:18–20).

There is no doubt about Jesus' claim to absolute authority; His exercise of authority and power; and the submission of many followers to His total lordship.

Christ the King

Required Course
Matthew 21:24–25 Part–1

But Jesus answered and said to them, "I also will ask you one thing, which if you tell Me, I likewise will tell you by what authority I do these things: The baptism of John—where was if from? From heaven or from men?"

Jesus countered one question with another. To the demand from the Jewish religious and political leaders that He state by what authority He conducted His ministry (21:23), He responded with a prior requirement: They must first declare their stance on the ministry of John the Baptist.

Not only was this a wise move politically, but it reflected God's way of working with us. If they said that John was acting solely on his own, then the people would reject them, for he was acknowledged to be a prophet.

On the other hand, any admission that John's call to repentance issued from God Himself would expose their own refusal to obey. That was their "political" dilemma.

Deeper still was the theological challenge. In brief, Jesus would not satisfy their quest for more knowledge of Him, because they had not absorbed and obeyed the revelation already granted to them.

In general, if we do not believe, or act upon, what light God has already bestowed upon us, we cannot expect to receive further insight about Him and His way.

In particular, John had spoken of Jesus as the coming savior and judge. Men must repent in order to prepare for the coming of the Lord. But the Jewish leaders had not repented of their sins, for they considered themselves righteous already.

Thus, they could not hear or heed the message of Jesus, nor could they bow before His divine authority.

We stand in a similar position. Unless we repent of our sins daily, we cannot hope to grow in our knowledge of Him or advance in our pilgrimage as His disciples.

The King Enters His Capital

Asking Questions
Matthew 21:24–25 Part–2

"I also will ask you one thing, which if you tell Me, I likewise will tell you by what authority I do these things: The baptism of John—where was if from? From heaven or from men?"

Jesus asked these questions not to obtain information which He lacked, but to reveal the hard hearts of His enemies. You will often find Jesus using this method to expose the thoughts and intentions of the people around Him, and to challenge them to reflection, repentance, and faith.

"You are the salt of the earth, but if the salt loses its flavor, how shall it be seasoned?" (5:13)

"So why do you worry…?" (6:28)

"Why do you look at the speck in your brother's eye, but do not consider the plank in your own eye?" (7:3)

"Why are you fearful, O you of little faith?" (8:26)

[Speaking of John the Baptist] "What did you go out into the wilderness to see? A reed shaken by the wind?" (11:7)

[To those who charged Him with violating the Sabbath] "What man is there among you who has one sheep, and if it falls into a pit on the Sabbath, will not lay hold of it and lift *it* out?" (12:11)

[When criticized for breaking Jewish traditions] "Why do you also transgress the commandment of God because of your tradition?" (15:3)

"Who do men say that I, the Son of Man, am?… But who do you say that I am?" (16:13, 15)

"For what profit is it to a man if he gains the whole world, and loses his own soul?" (16:26)

[To those who came with a request] "What do you wish?" (20:21)

Perhaps we should follow His example in this also.

Challenging Questions
Matthew 21:24–25 Part-3

"I also will ask you one thing, which if you tell Me, I likewise will tell you by what authority I do these things: The baptism of John—where was it from? From heaven or from men?"

Critics of Christianity often pose difficult questions. These deserve good, solid, responsible answers.

But sometimes it might be good to follow Jesus' example and pose a few questions of our own. A few possible examples:

What is your philosophy of life?

Where does it come from?

How do you know that your point of view is right?

What do you think the meaning of life is?

How do you deal with frustration?

How do you deal with rejection?

How do you deal with your anger?

How do you deal with guilt—real guilt, not just guilty feelings?

What do you think happens after death?

Are you prepared to face death?

Are you happy?

Would you like to be really happy?

Can you tell me what you think the Bible says about happiness?

Would you like for me to tell you what the Bible (or Jesus) says about happiness?

Responding with a Questions
Matthew 21:24–25 Part–4

"I also will ask you one thing, which if you tell Me, I likewise will tell you by what authority I do these things: The baptism of John—where was if from? From heaven or from men?"

Sometimes challenging statements need to be countered with challenging questions, such as:

"There is no God!" Really? How do you know?

"Science has proven that God does not exist?" That's interesting. When was the experiment done? In what journal was it reported?

"Evolution shows that God does not exist." Do you mean macro-evolution or micro-evolution? If micro-evolution (the fact that change takes place within species), that has nothing to do with creation.

"All of life developed from the simple to the complex." Have you read Michael Behe's *Darwin's Black Box*, which shows that even the smallest units of life are "irreducibly complex" and could not have developed from anything "simpler"?

"I mean that all of life comes from time and chance." Have you seen what the mathematicians and statisticians have said about that? Have you read William Dembski's *Intelligent Design*?

"There is just too much evidence for Evolution!" Really? Have you read *Evolution: A Theory in Crisis*, by Michael Denton (an atheist), who shows that there is virtually no evidence for macro-evolution? Or *Icons of Evolution*, by Jonathan Wells, who demonstrates that the ten most commonly cited examples of Evolution are either frauds or false? Or *Darwin on Trial*, by Philip Johnson, who proves that the case for Evolution is so weak as to be unsupportable?

"The Bible contradicts the assured results of science." Which "assured results" did you have in mind? Are you aware that the "assured results" of science change every few years?

"Genesis is filled with unscientific myths and legends." Would you please name two for me? By the way, have you read *Faith, Form, & Time*, by Kurt Patrick Wise, who holds a PhD. in paleontology from Harvard? It's a careful study of Genesis in the light of modern science, and finds no contradiction between the two.

My Critic, My Friend
Matthew 21:33–41

"And the vinedressers took his servant, beat one, killed one, and stoned another."

In the parable of the wicked tenants, Jesus described the sorry history of Israel. Almost every time God sent them a prophet to rebuke them for their sins and warn them of impending judgment unless they repented, they rejected God's messenger.

Remember how they treated Moses, Micaiah, and Jeremiah. John the Baptist lost his head because he told King Herod he should not have taken his brother's wife for himself. Now Jesus was about to be killed because He declared to them that their deeds were evil (John 7:7).

When Jesus asks the Jewish leaders what the owner of the vineyard will do to the tenants who rejected his servants, they said, "He will destroy those wicked men miserably, and lease *his* vineyard to other vinedressers" (21:41).

Our Lord replied, "Therefore I say to you, the kingdom of God will be taken from you and given to a nation bearing the fruits of it," and pronounced a crushing judgment upon them (21:43).

What about us? Have we, too, rejected God's messengers? Perhaps we have ignored the parts of the Bible we do not like. Worse yet, maybe we have simply not accepted it as God's Word.

In another way we show contempt for God's messengers: When others point out our flaws, we usually defend ourselves, and often denounce them as well. Just like the ancient Hebrews, we refuse to listen to criticism, no matter how just it might be.

By not humbly receiving negative comments about our person or our performance, we show ourselves to be spiritual cousins to the Pharisees, who counted themselves righteous, criticized others, and condemned the only sinless Man who ever lived.

My critic is my friend, for he speaks for God. Even when he exaggerates or lacks kindness, he at least alerts me to how I am perceived by others. Shall I continue to declare myself perfectly innocent, or shall I admit my faults and failings, and cast myself upon the mercy of God? The stakes are very high.

22 The King Confounds His Enemies

Wedding Invitation
Matthew 22:2–3 Part–1

"The kingdom of heaven is like a certain king who arranged a marriage for his son, and sent out his servants to call those who were invited to the wedding; and they were not willing to come."

Almost everyone loves a wedding. The bride and her maids are dazzlingly beautiful, the groom and his friends splendidly handsome. For a few minutes, the world stops to watch a wonder.

Love displaces lust; giving replaces greed; service supplants selfishness. Most of all, fickleness gives way to faithfulness.

How much more a royal wedding! What can match the majesty and glory of the joining of the son of the king with his bride? Who would not covet an invitation to such an event?

Alas, in this parable Jesus paints a sad portrait. The king has called his people to the marriage feast of his son, the prince. But the people do not want to come. So, His Majesty dispatches messengers to issue another invitation, but they are ignored—people are too busy. Some of these heralds even suffer violence at the hands of this wicked mob.

Before we react with indignation, let us ponder Jesus' point: The Jews of His day, like their rebellious ancestors, had despised both John the Baptist and now their own Messiah. Though some had merely turned away to their own private pursuits, others—the leaders—resorted to violence against God's chosen servants.

How about us? Surely, we would not kill a preacher of righteousness!

But do we go our own way, ignoring the gracious invitation of our God to the wedding banquet of His Son? Busyness may lack malicious intent, but the effects are the same: We scorn the generosity of our heavenly King and miss out on a great party. More than that, we fail to hear the gentle wooing of Jesus, who came to earth to get a bride for Himself. Who is the bride? Those who honor the invitation to the wedding!

To reject, or even to ignore, this summons—remember, it comes from God the King—is to deprive ourselves not only of a marvelous meal but of a matchless marriage.

Matchless Marriage
Matthew 22:2–3 Part–2

"The kingdom of heaven is like a certain king who arranged a marriage for his son, and sent out his servants to call those who were invited to the wedding..."

Jesus' parable describes in story form what God has done: He has arranged a wedding to His Son for all who will trust in Jesus.

In the Old Testament, God called Himself the husband to His people Israel. The New Testament clarifies that relationship by identifying Jesus as the Son of God and as the Bridegroom. Those who believe and follow Christ are together the bride, the church.

Already in Matthew's Gospel, Jesus has called Himself the bridegroom (9:15). In addition to this parable, He tells a similar one in chapter 25. Paul writes that Christ is the Head of the Church, His body (Ephesians 5:22–32). In the last book of the Bible, we read that the "new Jerusalem" will come down out of heaven like "a bride adorned for her husband," who is Christ Himself (Revelation 21:2).

What a matchless wedding this will be! Consider what God promises to give those who unite to His Son in faith:

Everlasting security: He will never leave us nor forsake us (Hebrews 13:5).

Constant care: He "nourishes and cherishes" his body (Ephesians 5:29).

Sacrificial love: "Christ also loved the church and gave Himself for her" (Ephesians 5:25).

Unconditional acceptance: "that He might sanctify and cleanse her..." (Ephesians 5:26)—meaning that He will take us as we are, so that He might make us make us what He is, holy and blameless.

Safety and salvation: "Christ is head of the church; and He is Savior of the body" (Ephesians 5:23).

Unimaginable intimacy: "For we are members of His body" (Ephesians 5:30).

Christ and Caesar
Matthew 22:15–22

"Render [pay] therefore to Caesar the things that are Caesar's, and to God the things that are God's."

Seeking to ensnare Jesus with a trick question, the Pharisees and Herodians conspired to catch Him in a statement that would lead to His immediate arrest.

For these two groups to cooperate was an indication of their desperation and of their hatred for Jesus, for they were old enemies. Herod's followers supported this non-Jewish tyrant, who was a Roman puppet. The Pharisees represented the revolutionary patriots, who wanted above all to expel the hated Romans.

But they agreed that Jesus posed a threat to both their agendas, for He spoke of another kingdom, greater than any earthly power, and the masses hailed Him as King.

After some smooth words of flattery, they sprung their trap: "Is it lawful to pay taxes to Caesar, or not?" If Jesus said, "Yes," the people would abandon Him. A "No" answer would bring down the wrath of Rome and lead to a speedy death.

In His infinite wisdom, Jesus escaped their trap by re-defining the matter entirely. Forcing them to admit that the coins with which taxes would be paid had on it the picture and name of Caesar, He responded with the famous words quoted above.

He thus taught them, and us, that: (1) The rulers of this world, no matter how wicked, deserve our respect, taxes, and obedience. (2) On the other hand, there is another Ruler—God—who deserves our ultimate loyalty.

Rebels and revolutionaries loathe the first part of that truth, and despots hate the second.

Jesus Himself lived by what He taught, for He later meekly submitted to an unjust arrest, unfair trial, and undeserved death at the hands of wicked rulers. His disciples followed in His steps. Shall we?

Christ the King

Double Ignorance
Matthew 22:23–33

Jesus answered and said to them, "You are mistaken, not knowing the Scriptures nor the power of God."

The Sadducees had tried to trap Jesus with a question about the resurrection, in which they did not believe. Nor did they accept the possibility of miracles or the existence of angels.

In other words, they were skeptics, rationalists, trusting in only what their own limited experience and reason—based on certain assumptions—would support.

Like our own modern intelligentsia, they considered themselves progressive, scientific, up-to-date. This apparently "reasonable" attitude won them favor with the political rulers, though not with the masses.

Jesus, before responding to their trick question, exposes the root problem: Their double ignorance.

They did not know the Scriptures, which in their day was the Hebrew Bible, what we call the Old Testament. Although they probably would have read it—after all, they were part of the priestly class—they clearly had not pondered its meaning. Otherwise, they would have known that even the writings of Moses, which they acknowledged to be from God, assume the reality of the resurrection of the dead.

Even worse, they did know "know" the power of God. Their silly question reflected deep disbelief in the Creator's ability to bring the dead to life.

Though they had read the history of God's deliverance of His people from Egypt, they did not see how the One who had parted the Red Sea could break the bonds of death and usher in a new sort of life far different from the one we now know.

How about us? Do we really know the Bible? And if we have read it, do we "know"—that is, really believe—the immense might of our God?

Marriage in Heaven?
Matthew 22:30

"For in the resurrection they neither marry nor are given in marriage, but are like angels of God in heaven."

With their limited concept of God's power, the Sadducees could only imagine that if there were life after death—which they did not believe—it would have to be just like what we know here on earth.

Jesus both affirms the reality of the next life and illuminates its character.

Those whom God raises up to eternal life with Himself will possess new and glorious bodies. As Paul later wrote, Jesus "will transform our lowly body that it may be conformed to His glorious body, according to the working by which He is able even to subdue all things to Himself" (Philippians 3:21).

The body "is sown [dies] a natural body, it is raised a spiritual body" (1 Corinthians 15:44).

In this new state, there will be no sexuality as we know it now. We shall not lose our identity as men and women, but neither shall we experience the difference as we do today.

This means that marriage is temporary. Perhaps that is why Paul had earlier counseled, "even those who have wives should be as though they had none, those who weep as thought they did not weep, those who rejoice as though they did not rejoice ... For the form of this world is passing away" (1 Corinthians 7:29–31).

Think of the implications! Both the joys and sorrows of marriage belong only to this transitory life. Marriage—or the lack of it—is not fundamental to our existence.

What a difference this truth should make to married and single alike! Regardless of our current situation, we can find deep delight in Christ, who alone is our life (Colossians 3:4).

Our Only Hope
Matthew 22:31–32

"But concerning the resurrection of the dead, have you not read what was spoken to you by God, saying, 'I am the God of Abraham, the God of Isaac, and the God of Jacob'? God is not the God of the dead, but of the living."

With these words Jesus not only silenced the Sadducees, who did not believe in angels, spirits, or the resurrection from the dead, but also guaranteed for His followers a future filled with hope.

The God who called, guided, protected, and loved Abraham, Isaac, and Jacob cannot die. He said, "I will be your God," and He will be ours, too, forever and ever (Psalm 48:14). The great "I AM" who revealed Himself to Moses cannot die, nor can His mercies ever fail; they are new every morning, and rest eternally upon those who trust in Him (Exodus 3:14–15; Lamentations 3:22–23; Psalm 103:17).

For that reason, those who trust in Him, though their bodies die, will "live" forever. If God is "alive" to them, then they are in some sense already "alive" to Him. Jesus' profound insight into this truth fueled His conviction that God will raise the Old Testament saints and all true believers at the last day.

Everywhere in the Gospel of Matthew, Jesus is portrayed as promising a bright future for His disciples. They will inherit the kingdom of heaven (5:3, 10). Their grief will be assuaged by His comfort (5:4), surely when they see Him face to face (5:8). Even if they are persecuted unto death, their reward for perseverance and for the good works they have done will be great in heaven (5:11–12; 16:27; 24:34–40). They will join Abraham, Isaac, and Jacob in the kingdom of heaven (8:11) as they all "shine forth as the sun" (13:43).

On the other hand, a terrible fate awaits those who fail to repent, believe, and follow Christ. Their resurrected bodies will be "cast into hell," the region of "outer darkness," where there will be "weeping and gnashing of teeth" (5:30; 8:12; 13:42) as they suffer "everlasting punishment" (25:46). Thus, we should "not fear those who kill the body but cannot kill the soul. But rather fear Him who is able to destroy both soul and body in hell" (10:28).

The Apostles held firmly to the same hope, the return of Christ, "who will transform our lowly body that it may be conformed to the His glorious body" (Philippians 3:21; see also Romans 8:23). The ancient patriarchs and saints persevered in faith and obedience because they "waited for the city which has foundations, whose builder and maker *is* God" (Hebrews 11:10) Struggling on their earthly way, subject to all the frustrations of this life, they "confessed that they were strangers and pilgrims on the earth" who desired "a better, that is, a heavenly *country*" (Hebrews 11:13, 16).

May we, like them, place our hopes not on health, wealth, or worldly "happiness," but "upon the grace that is to be brought to [us] at the revelation of Jesus Christ" (1 Peter 1:13).

The Main Thing in Life Part–1
Matthew 22:37–38

Jesus said to him, "'You shall love the LORD your God with all your heart, with all your soul, and with all your mind.' This is the *first and great commandment."*

From their careful study of the Old Testament, the Pharisees had counted more than 600 commandments. Then they debated among themselves about which of these deserved the most emphasis.

Like the Sadducees, however, they hoped to entangle Jesus with a question forcing Him to take a stand that would alienate Him from one party or another by choosing one commandment over another as most important (22:34–36).

Jesus' answer displayed both His profound understanding of the Word of God and His divine wisdom.

Quoting the word of Moses in Deuteronomy (6:5; 10:12; 30:6), He cut through the details of the current debate and concentrated on the core of our duty towards God: Wholehearted, single-minded love.

God deserves our total devotion and affection for several reasons:

> He made us. We belong to Him. He is our Owner and Master. If a dog displays loyalty and affection for his master, how much more should we to our God?

> He gives us all that we have. Food, shelter, air, water; daily life; family, friends, work; possessions and pleasures—all these descend from our generous God.

He has made Himself known to us. Unlike pagan "gods" who cannot speak, our Lord has revealed His nature, works, and will to us through the prophets, the apostles, and supremely through His own Son Jesus. He has sent His Son to die for our sins, so that we may have fellowship with Him forever. He could have destroyed us forever in hell, but in His love He delivered us from His own righteous wrath.

The Main Thing in Life Part–2
Matthew 22:37

"You shall love the LORD your God with all your heart, with all your soul, and with all your mind."

Is God unjust to require of us total and complete dedication and affection? Of course not! In addition to the reasons given previously, consider also that:

He has wooed us like an ardent lover. He first chose Israel from among nations more numerous and mighty than they, and set His love upon them as His special people. Then He rescued them from slavery in Egypt. Thus, when Moses told them to "love the LORD your God with all your heart, with all your soul, and with all your strength," he was not commanding something unreasonable (Deuteronomy 6:5). Then, after manifesting His ways and will to Israel for more than 2,000 years, He sent His own son to deliver them and all who trust in Him from bondage to sin, death, and the devil. Now not only descendants of Abraham, but also all non-Jews who believe in Christ belong to this "chosen generation ... royal priesthood ... holy nation ... [God's] own special people (1 Peter 2:9).

He bears with us, despite our manifold faults and failings. He "*is* merciful and gracious, slow to anger, and abounding in mercy.... He has not dealt with us according to our sins" (Psalms 103:8, 10). "If we confess our sins, He is faithful and just to forgive *our* sins" because of Jesus, who is the "propitiation for our sins" (1 John 1:9; 2:2).

He alone satisfies the weary soul, and replenishes the sorrowful soul (Jeremiah 31:25). No one else truly understands or fully cares, and no one else can bind up our broken hearts or fill us with unshakeable joy and peace.

Surely He is worth our entire affection and adoration!

The Second Thing
Matthew 22:39–40

"And the second is like it: 'You shall love your neighbor as yourself.' On these two commandments hang all the Law and the Prophets."

Our first and foremost duty—and delight—is to love God with all our heart, soul, mind, and strength.

The second most important task in life is to love our neighbors as we love ourselves.

Who is my neighbor? The person next to me at any time, whether physically or mentally, as in the news media.

By using the word "neighbor" the Scripture alerts us to the priorities of love. We begin with those closest to us, such as our family, and then move outwards in our care and concern.

If I am walking down a crowded street, my "neighbors" are those around me. At home, my neighbors are my spouse, or parents, or children, or siblings. The starving child on the evening news is also a "neighbor," though a more distant one.

For Christians, "neighbors" include members of their church, as well as believers around the world.

The nearer neighbors have a greater claim upon me. Thus, I must first fulfill my duty to my wife, then to my children, then to others outside our little family, beginning with my parents and brothers and sisters.

Near neighbors require more of our time, energy, and resources. We must not neglect them in order to help others. On the other hand, we cannot limit our kindness to our immediate family and friends.

At the very least, we can pray for all those in trouble. A phone call, a letter, a brief visit, or a gift may be all we can afford, but these can convey affection and care.

The principal point is clear: Make love our aim.

A Sure Guide to Love
Matthew 22:39

"'You shall love your neighbor as yourself.'"

But how do I love my neighbor?

Jesus, quoting Moses, provides practical advice: Do for others what you would want them to do for you (see also 7:12).

Do you want to be treated with respect? Show respect for others.

Do you want someone to listen to you? Listen long and hard to others.

Do you want others' prayers? Pray for them.

Are you looking for practical help? Reach out and offer assistance.

Do you feel lonely? Give someone a call or a visit.

In the home, do you expect others to honor your personal preferences? Do the same for them.

At work, do you look for quality and excellence? Set the standard by your own performance.

If you help someone, do you look for some sign of gratitude? Say "Thank you" often.

Would you like your spouse to be more attractive? Attend to your own appearance and behavior.

The rule works the other way, too, as Confucius noted long ago: Don't do to others what you don't want them to do to you.

If you do not like criticism, be sparing in your criticism of others. If messiness bothers you, be neat. If you do not want people to interrupt you when you talk, then be quiet while they speak. If you do not want people to talk about you behind your back, avoid gossip.

The bottom line: Treat others as you want to be treated.

The Heart of the Matter
Matthew 22:37–40

"'You shall love the LORD your God with all your heart, with all your soul, and with all your mind.' This is the first and great commandment. And the second is like it: 'You shall love your neighbor as yourself.' On these two commands hang all the Law and the prophets."

Wholehearted love for God and our neighbor stands at the center of the Old Testament ("the Law and the Prophets").

This first command reflects the supreme excellence and worth of God. How can we not adore the one who created the cosmos, upholds the universe, and provides for and protects His people?

The focus on love reflects the very core of God's being: "God is love" (1 John 4:8). These two commands, separately and together, also expose the corruption of the human heart. Who has, even for a full hour, fulfilled either of these mandates?

Truly did David exclaim, "in Your sight no one living is righteous" (Psalm 143:2).

Thankfully, this summary of God's requirements for us points toward His gracious provision of forgiveness.

First, the entire sacrificial system enabled unholy men to approach a holy God.

Then, with increasing clarity, the Prophets and writers announce a coming Savior. Isaiah's portrait of the Suffering Servant assumes that no one can satisfy God's just demands, and that He must punish sin according to His law (Isaiah 53).

But Isaiah goes further, for he speaks of one who was "wounded for our transgressions ... bruised for our iniquities ... And the LORD has laid on Him the iniquity of us all" (53:5–6). In short, Jesus' masterful summary of the essence of ethics directs our attention to Himself, who would soon "save His people from their sins" (1:21).

Whose Son is Jesus?
Matthew 22:41–45

While the Pharisees were gathered together, Jesus asked them, saying, "What do you think about the Christ? Whose Son is He?" They said to Him, "The Son of David." He said to them, "How then does David in the Spirit call Him 'Lord,' saying: 'The LORD said to my Lord, "Sit at My right hand, till I make Your enemies Your footstool."'? If David then calls Him 'Lord,' how is He his Son?"

After confounding all the attempts of the Jewish leaders to trap Him with trick questions, Jesus goes on the offensive. Quoting Psalm 110:1, He highlights their ignorance both of the Bible and of His own nature.

Like other Jews, these leaders looked for a descendant of the great king David to come and expel the Romans, bringing political liberation.

As His birth in Bethlehem shows, Jesus did stand in David's line. That is why He accepted the praises of the people who welcomed Him into Jerusalem with cries of "Hosanna to the Son of David!" (21:9)

But His birth from a virgin, mighty works, matchless teaching, and sinless character proved that He was more than a son of David. He was also Son of God.

David himself, inspired by the Holy Spirit, foresaw the coming of one whom he, though supreme in Israel, should call "Lord," and to whom God would give ultimate authority.

Jesus' question did not deny His descent from David. He aimed, rather, to illuminate the ignorance of the teachers of the Bible who did not realize that the Christ—the Anointed One of God—would be more than a mere man.

In this way, He indirectly answered their previous question, "By what authority are You doing these things? And who gave You this authority?" (21:23) He acted with the authority of the eternal Son of God. He still does.

The King Confounds His Enemies

Who's In Charge?
Matthew 22:44

"'The LORD said to my Lord, "Sit at My right hand, till I make Your enemies Your footstool."'"

Guided by Jesus' own interpretation later writers of the New Testament applied these words of David in Psalm 110 to the risen Christ (see Acts 2:30, 34–35; Hebrews 1:13).

In his letter to the Ephesians, Paul says that God "put all *things* under His feet, and gave Him *to be* head over all *things* to the church" (Ephesians 1:22). Jesus rules the world! He manages all things for the sake of His church, which is His body.

Nothing happens to you or to me that does not pass through the permission of Christ as risen Lord and King of the universe. All the events of history, including the wars, famines, and suffering of our own time, somehow serve to advance the kingdom of Christ.

"Therefore God also has highly exalted Him and given Him the name which is above every name [that is, "Lord"], that at the name of Jesus every knee should bow, of those in heaven, and of those on earth, and of those under the earth, and *that* every tongue should confess that Jesus Christ *is* Lord, to the glory of God the Father" (Philippians 2:9–11).

Actually, even during His lifetime Jesus demonstrated His absolute authority. What else do we deduct from His healings, casting out of demons, quieting the storm, multiplying loaves and fishes to feed the crowds? Who else could forgive sins and issue commands?

Do we acknowledge Him as Lord of our own lives? If so, do we observe His teachings, including the Last Command (28:18–20)?

Do we trust Him with all that we are, and have, and ever hope to be? "Come to Me, all *you* who labor and are heavy laden, and I will give you rest" (11:28).

Christ the King

23 The King Exposes Hypocrites

Stern Warnings
Matthew 23:1–36

"But he who is greatest among you shall be your servant. And whoever exalts himself will be humbled [put down, abased], and he who humbles himself will be exalted [lifted up, honored]."

Jesus deserves not only our adoration and affection, but also our careful attention. In this passage, He issues stern warnings, first to His disciples and then to His critics.

He tells His disciples to beware of the example of the religious teachers of the day, the scribes and the Pharisees. Though some of their instruction derived from the law given through Moses, much of it was false and misleading (23:16–23).

Equally bad is their example, for "they say, and do not do" (23:3). That is, they are hypocrites who do not live according to their own professed standards (23:25–28).

Moreover, "all their works they do to be seen by men" (23:5). Whatever good deeds they perform issue not from a heart of love for God or others, but from a lust for praise and honor from other men (23:13–14).

From Jesus' explicit words to His followers, it would seem that the fundamental flaw in the religious leaders of His day consisted in pride. They sought prominence, praise, and power. Not content with the clear words of Moses, they added their own subtle interpretations and equivocations, with the result that they, not God's Word, became the arbiters of righteousness.

As forcefully as possible, Jesus warned these blind leaders of the blind that they would fall into the same pit (23:19, 24, 26), for the judgment of God upon all hypocrisy, pride, and false teaching would come swiftly and terribly upon them, as He then detailed in the following two chapters of Matthew's Gospel (24 and 25).

What about us? Are we not also tempted to exalt ourselves, to deny our words by our lives, and to neglect the clear teaching of the Bible in favor of our own ideas? Which of us is not guilty of such sins?

Does not pride lurk in our bosom, drive our actions, and express itself in our attitude towards God's revelation?

Rather than standing in judgment upon the scribes and Pharisees, we need to ask God to forgive us for being too much like them, and pray for humility, love for God, and faithfulness to His written revelation.

Hypocrisy
Matthew 23:3

"... they say, and do not do."

In this chapter, Jesus denounces the teachers of the Scriptures, most of whom belonged to the sect of the Pharisees.

Though He condemns them for several faults, their greatest crime was hypocrisy. Listen to His words:

"For you devour widows' houses, and for a pretense make long prayers" (23:14). While seeming to be pious, they preyed on poor widows' property.

"For you cleanse the outside of the cup and dish, but inside they are full of extortion and self-indulgence. Blind Pharisee, first cleanse the inside of the cup and dish, that the outside of them may be clean also." (23:25–26). They were scrupulous about ceremonial purity, but paid no attention to the impurity of their hearts.

"For you are like whitewashed tombs which indeed appear beautiful outwardly, but inside are full of dead *men's* bones and all cleanness. Even so you also outwardly appear righteous to men, but inside you are full of hypocrisy and lawlessness" (23:27–28).

These biting words should pierce to the heart of every person on earth.

How often do we seem better than we are? How much do we judge others by standards which we ourselves fail to meet?

No wonder people do not want to accept our criticism! We are so blinded by the beam in our own eye that we cannot see clearly to remove the splinter in our neighbor's eye (7:1–5).

The Christian church would stand much higher in the eyes of the world if only its members lived more consistent lives, beginning in our own homes.

The Way to Ruin
Matthew 23:12

"And whoever exalts himself will be humbled, and he who humbles himself will be exalted."

We see this principle worked out in history time after time.

The men of Babel thought they would build a tower reaching up to heaven, but God confounded their communication and dispersed them around the world.

Pharaoh, trusting in his might, resisted the command of God to liberate the Hebrew slaves, and suffered the devastation of his country, the death of his son, and the defeat of his army.

God prophesied the fall of Babylon in these words: "I will halt the arrogance of the proud, and lay low the haughtiness of the terrible" (Isaiah 13:11).

Isaiah later expands this warning to all in authority: "It shall come to pass in that day [the day of judgment] *that* the LORD will punish on high the host of exalted ones, and on the earth the kings of the earth" (Isaiah 24:21).

The self-righteous Pharisees of Jesus' day saw their hopes for freedom from the Romans utterly crushed when Jerusalem suffered destruction in A.D. 70, and their name has become a symbol of picky, pompous pride ever since.

We exalt ourselves when we insist that we are right, and others wrong, when we speak without listening, or use our power to silence or crush those under our authority (including our children).

Even more dangerous is the person who refuses to bow before Almighty God in humble repentance and childlike faith.

If we ignore His righteous laws, despise His gracious promises, refuse His generous gifts; if we insist on going our own way, relying on our own strength, and trusting in our own wisdom—then we, too, face inevitable humiliation and ruin.

Jesus the Prophet
Matthew 23:13

"But woe to you, scribes and Pharisees, hypocrites!"

These words encapsulate Jesus' stinging rebuke to the religious leaders of His day. In this entire chapter, He exposes their sin and pronounces a terrible doom upon them for their self-righteous hypocrisy.

Before looking at some of His specific charges against them, let us consider what we can learn about Jesus from this unique section of the Gospels.

Here we see Jesus' *bravery*. He knew that they had plotted to kill Him, and that His time for a terrible death was near. With more pleasing words, or by withdrawing to Galilee, He could have avoided the horror of crucifixion and all the related suffering, but He boldly attacks those who presumed to teach people the Law of God, knowing their murderous response.

Note also His *knowledge* of their teaching and their conduct. Far from ignorant of the culture in which He lived, Jesus displays an exact understanding of the current intellectual and religious climate. As He had throughout His ministry, Jesus points out to His hearers specific errors and inconsistencies of the prevailing elite, warning the people against them in clear detail.

In almost every sentence, we perceive Jesus' *mastery of logic, argument, and rhetoric*. He shows the fallacies of the Pharisees' reasoning and subjects them to the most eloquent derision and denunciation, not to mention biting humor: "Blind guides, who strain out a gnat and swallow a camel!" (23:24)

In addition to His understanding of their words and deeds, Jesus saw into the depths of their hearts, and discerned their motives. In this way, He demonstrates yet again His *deity*, for God alone knows the heart. "... inside they are full of extortion and self-indulgence" (23:25).

Has anyone ever spoken like this Man?

The King Exposes Hypocrites

Inside Out
Matthew 23:25–26

"Woe to you, scribes and Pharisees, hypocrites! For you cleanse the outside of the cup and dish, but inside they are full of extortion and self-indulgence. Blind Pharisee, first cleanse the inside of the cup and dish, that the outside of them may be clean also."

All of Matthew 23 is taken up with Jesus' fierce denunciation of the teachers of the Bible in His day. The main charge which He brings against them is hypocrisy: "they say, and do not do" (23:3).

Here we see the heart of the problem: These men focused on externals more than internals. They concentrated upon actions rather than attitudes, behavior more than belief, hand more than heart.

The result? They outwardly appeared righteous, but inwardly were "full of hypocrisy and lawlessness" (23:28).

Beginning with the Beatitudes, Jesus stressed the priority of the inner man: "Blessed *are* the poor in spirit,… those who mourn [over sin],… who hunger and thirst for righteousness,… the merciful,… the pure in heart" (5:3–8).

He knew that "the thought is the father of the deed," for He denounced resentment as the root of murder, lust as the source of adultery (5:21–22, 27–28).

He urged inward, rather than outward, devotion (6:1–18), and a life of seeking God rather than the things of this visible world (6:19–34). Above all, He powerfully exposed and condemned self-righteousness, which leads to critical attitudes and actions (7:1–5).

In short, He showed that we must be changed from the inside out. Just doing what seems good to others will not please God. We must love the Lord our God with all our heart, and soul, and mind (22:37).

But how? "Repent, and believe in the Gospel" (Mark 1:15). All day, every day, day after day.

Hard Words
Matthew 23:33 Part–1

"Serpents, brood [offspring] of vipers! How can you escape the condemnation of hell?"

When he saw the self-righteous, hypocritical Jewish leaders coming to hear him preach, John the Baptist had said, "Brood of vipers! Who warned you to flee from the wrath come?" (3:7)

Jesus used similar language towards them after they accused Him of expelling demons by the power of Satan: "Brood of vipers! How can you, being evil, speak good things? For out of the abundance of the heart the mouth speaks" (12:34).

When these same leaders taunted Him with the accusation that He had been born in sin, Jesus replied, "You are of *your* father the devil" (John 8:44), to which they responded, "... You are a Samaritan and have a demon" (John 8:48).

What is going on here? Wasn't Jesus supposed to come and "save His people from their sins" (1:21)? Did He not issue the invitation for the weary to come to Him for rest? Of course!

But He also pronounced blessing only upon the "poor in spirit,... those who mourn [for sin],... the meek,... the merciful, the pure in heart..." (5:3–8).

The proud, critical, complacent, self-righteous; the hypocrites who outwardly seem good but are inwardly defiled—these receive nothing but woe and condemnation.

Why? Because "whoever exalts himself will be humbled" (23:12). The one who sees only the speck in another's eye, but not the beam in his own, does not feel the need for God's mercy. Thus, he does not repent of his sin and beg for forgiveness.

Such a person cannot be saved, for he does not humbly receive the Savior.

Coming Condemnation
Matthew 23:33 Part–2

"Serpents, brood [offspring] of vipers! How can you escape the condemnation of hell?"

Many believe Jesus to be the embodiment of God's love and bringer of peace, which is true.

But people often forget that He also warned of impending judgment.

From the beginning, He warned, "Repent, for the kingdom of heaven is at hand" (4:17). As the descendant of David and the Son of God, Jesus was the promised King who would come to "Break [the nations] with a rod of iron" (Psalm 2:9; Revelation 2:27).

Denouncing resentment as the moral equivalent of murder, Jesus warned of "hell fire" (5:22). To those who contemplated sexual sin, He said, "If your right eye causes you to sin, pluck it out and cast *it* from you; for it is more profitable for you that one of your members perish than for your whole body to be cast into hell" (5:29).

A Roman centurion demonstrated faith in Jesus, leading Him to pronounce doom on Jews who did not believe in Him: "But the sons of the kingdom will be cast out into outer darkness. There will be weeping and gnashing of teeth" (8:12; see also 13:42; 24:51; 25:30).

When He commissioned His followers to embark on a preaching mission, He re-directed their anxiety: "do not fear those who kill the body but cannot kill the soul. But rather fear Him who is able to destroy both soul and body in hell" (10:28).

Cities who would not receive Him were told that their punishment would be even worse than the destruction which came upon Sodom (11:23–24).

Yes, Jesus came to "save His people from their sins" by dying for them on the Cross. But only those who repent and trust in Him belong to "His people." What about you?

The Sending Word
Matthew 23:34–35

"Therefore, indeed, I send you prophets, wise men, and scribes; some of them you will kill and crucify, and some of them you will scourge in your synagogues and persecute from city to city, that on you may come all the righteous blood shed on the earth..."

Notice the remarkable language of Jesus here. "I send you prophets..." This man from Galilee speaks as if all the Old Testament prophets had come at His command, though He had not yet been born.

How could this be? With these words, Jesus identifies Himself as closely as possible with God, who commissioned prophets, wise men, and students of the Scriptures, to instruct His people in the truth.

How this aids our understanding of the entire Bible! The Old Testament speaks about Jesus (Luke 24:24–27) because its writers were sent by Him. Long before His birth as a man, the Son of God appointed men to reveal the truth of God to His people, the Hebrews.

As the living, eternal Word of God (John 1:1–3), He inspired His chosen servants to communicate God's words.

Isaiah's thrilling vision gives us the clearest demonstration of this pre-incarnate ministry of Jesus. At the beginning of his work as a prophet, he "saw the Lord" (Isaiah 6:1). But God the Father is invisible. No one has, or can, see Him (John 1:18).

Who, then, appeared to Isaiah? The Son of God, who is the Word of God, who became the God-man Jesus. As the apostle John wrote, Isaiah "saw His glory and spoke of Him" (John 12:41).

Jesus announces here that He will send more messengers—the Apostles—who will be handled as brutally as were the prophets before them.

How do we treat these representatives of Christ?

Perfect Patience
Matthew 23:34–38

"Therefore, indeed, I send you prophets, wise men, and scribes: some of them you will kill and crucify, and some of them you will scourge in your synagogues and persecute from city to city, that on you may come all the righteous blood shed on the earth.... O Jerusalem, Jerusalem, the one who kills the prophets and stones those who are sent to her! How often I wanted to gather your children together, as a hen gathers her chicks under her *wings, but you were not willing! See! Your house is left to you desolate..."*

Jesus' diatribe against the Jewish leaders discloses the perfect patience of God. The divine patience is:

Persistent: He kept sending messengers to the stubbornly-rebellious Hebrew people.

Proactive: Some people are passively patient, waiting to see what will happen. Yahweh took the initiative by speaking to them through spokesman *before* their troubles befell them.

Prophetic: Rather than mildly keeping silent, or ignoring the sins of the Jews, God specifically exposed their transgressions and warned them of impending judgment.

Pitiful: Full of pity and compassion, the Lord urged His people to turn from their wicked ways to avoid destruction. Jesus even compares Himself to a mother hen eager to care for her endangered chicks.

Punitive: In the end, however, the patience of God ran out. By the time Jesus denounced them, the Jewish leaders had resolutely refused to heed all warnings. That left them without excuse, and doubly guilty. They had not only defied God, but spurned His patience. A terrible fate hung over their proud heads.

How do we respond to the patience of God?

The Compassionate Christ
Matthew 23:37–39

"O Jerusalem, Jerusalem, the one who kills the prophets and stones those who are sent to her! How often I wanted to gather your children together, as a hen gathers her chicks under her wings, but you were not willing!"

Jesus concludes His scorching denunciation of the scribes and Pharisees with a revelation of His tender heart towards those who would soon dispatch Him to the Cross.

He bears no illusions about the hard and wicked hearts of His enemies. For centuries, the custodians of God's truth had "murdered the prophets" (23:31), with the full consent of the citizens of Jerusalem, a city which habitually "kills the prophets, and stones those who are sent to her."

Nor does the Lord fail to pronounce a terrible judgment upon these rebellious people, in words that echo the prophets of old: "See! Your house is left to you desolate" (23:38; Isaiah 5:9; 6:11; Jeremiah 12:11; 33:10; Ezekiel 26:19; Micah 7:13; Zephaniah 1:13; 3:6; Haggai 1:9; Zechariah 7:14).

The populace, imitated by their children, had greeted Jesus when He entered the city a few days before with the words of Psalm 118, "Hosanna...! 'Blessed is He who comes in the name of the LORD!'" (21:9). Jesus had noted the irony of that acclamation when, quoting the same psalm, He described Himself as "the stone which the builders rejected" (21:42). He knew that the fickle crowd would soon follow their leaders in a demand that He be crucified (27:22).

With a solemn warning, Jesus announces that they will not see Him again until they can greet Him with sincerity (23:39), and leaves the Temple for good.

That is why His lament for Jerusalem strikes us so powerfully. Despite their terrible hatred of Him and all the previous messengers of God, Jesus yearns for their return to the only Savior and Protector, and bewails their stubborn refusal to accept God's love.

For it is *God* whom they have spurned! In the Old Testament, Yahweh says that He had sent messengers to His people that they might avoid impending judgment (Jeremiah 7:1–7). Now we learn that the Sender

The King Exposes Hypocrites

was the eternal Word of God, now incarnate as Jesus of Nazareth, the last Prophet whom they would refuse to heed, to their awful loss.

The Sender has become the Sent One. Unwilling to see His erring flock perish eternally, and impelled by unfathomable love, He has come to take upon Himself the punishment of faithless Judah. Jesus departs from the Temple, not in anger, but in a sorrow no man can penetrate, determined to "save His people from their sins" (1:21).

What matchless mercy! What divine devotion! What conquering compassion! "O come, let us adore Him!"

Christ the King

24 The King Predicts His Return

Invisible Instability
Matthew 24:1–2

Then Jesus went out and departed from the temple, and His disciples came up to show Him the buildings of the temple. And Jesus said to them, "Do you not see all these things? Assuredly, I say to you, not one stone shall be left here upon another, that shall not be thrown down."

Jesus' departure was more than physical. As God's chosen prophet, priest, and king for Israel, Jesus had been rejected. He had just warned them of God's impending judgment. Now He withdraws His gracious presence, leaving them exposed to God's righteous wrath.

But His disciples did not understand. Apparently deaf to what He had just said, they pointed out to Him the huge blocks of stone at the base of the temple area. Like many thousands of other pilgrims, they were overwhelmed with the grandeur, beauty, and apparent stability of this huge structure.

They failed to see that the entire edifice would come toppling down within their lifetime. Indeed, the city itself would be destroyed by Roman armies, in fulfillment of Jesus' warning.

How could that happen? Sin had defiled the city and the sanctuary of God. Outwardly, the structure seemed indestructible. Inwardly, like the Jewish leaders and people, it was doomed to destruction.

This had happened before, when Solomon's magnificent temple had been completely leveled by the Babylonian armies because of Israel's idolatry and rebellion. Then, as in Jesus' time, the Jews thought it could not happen, but it did.

The same fate will befall any "proud tower" built by men. What we consider indestructible will fall under God's judgment. No matter how mighty, no nation can withstand the righteous wrath of the Lord.

When that occurs, will we be surprised, or ready?

Beware of Deceivers
Matthew 24:4–5

"Take heed that no one deceives you. For many will come in My name, saying, 'I am the Christ,' and will deceive many."

His disciples asked Jesus when the temple would be destroyed, and what signs would precede His coming and the end of the age. In His reply, Jesus did not reveal the timing of these momentous events. Instead, He urged them to be careful, lest they be deceived by imposters.

You only have to examine church history, and especially the record of the past one hundred years, to see that we need this warning. Indeed, many false "christs" have arisen, and millions have been misled.

Some of these fakes have sought political power. Claiming to restore peace, prosperity, and pride to a broken and discouraged people, they concentrate all authority in their own hands. Then they silence and suppress any form of criticism or opposition. Inevitably, they exterminate thousands—and sometimes millions—of their own people, all in the name of national salvation.

Other false messiahs seek religious supremacy. Almost always, they claim special revelation from God, as well as a unique relationship with Him. Not content to transmit the teachings of the Bible, they propagate new doctrines.

Usually, these counterfeit "christs" denounce all other teachers as heretics. Only they possess a pure understanding of the truth. The keys of the kingdom of God rest in their hands alone.

Like their political counterparts, they cannot tolerate disagreement or discussion; dialogue about dogma is forbidden.

Jesus' warning applies to us as much as it did to His disciples: Be careful! Do not be deceived!

The King Predicts His Return

The Beginning of Sorrows
Matthew 24:6–8

"And you will hear of wars of rumors of wars. See that you are not troubled; for all these things must come to pass, but the end is not yet. For nation will rise against nation, and kingdom against kingdom. And there will be famines, pestilences, and earthquakes in various places. All these are the beginning of sorrows."

Before Jesus returns, increasing pain and sorrow will convulse the world. If we heed His prophecy:

Though we strive for peace, we shall not be surprised when war breaks out.

We shall ask for our daily bread, but not marvel at widespread hunger.

We shall pray for good health for ourselves and others, but not be caught off guard by pandemic diseases.

We shall entreat God to protect us, but not think it strange when the earth trembles or the heavens blast us with wind and rain.

These disasters are not, as some allege, proofs that our God is absent, or impotent, or indifferent to our suffering. Instead, they testify to the prophetic prescience of Jesus, display the power and righteous anger of God, and point towards the return of the Risen Christ to judge and renew the world.

Thus, we must beware of those who promise perfect peace, prosperity, and protection in this life. Despite their apparent good will, such men conceal a lust for absolute power and an arrogance that defies God.

Instead, Christians will regard all these plagues as indications that our Lord will come back for His people at the appointed time, to deliver us from the wrath to come and usher in an eternity of harmony and happiness.

Hard Times Coming
Matthew 24:9–13

"Then they will deliver you up to tribulation and kill you, and you will be hated by all nations for My name's sake. And then many will be offended, will betray one another, and will hate one another. Then many false prophets will rise up and deceive many. And because lawlessness will abound, the love of many will grow cold. But he who endures to the end shall be saved."

Jesus predicted that wars, famines, earthquakes, and plagues would beset the world with increasing frequency as the end of history nears. Now He warns that the church itself will pass through intense suffering, which will come in various forms and have various effects:

"They"—those who hate the Gospel of Christ—will deliver believers up to trouble, leading often to death. They will bring all the powers of society and state to bear upon the church, seeking to eliminate Christianity. Believers will find themselves facing death for the sake of their faith in Christ. Indeed, people will hate them. This enmity will come not from their wicked deeds, though they will be accused of various crimes, but simply for their belief in Jesus as the only Savior.

External stress will produce internal strain: Many church members will stumble and fall because of this persecution. Under extreme pressure, they will even betray Christians. Indeed, hatred will pollute the formerly pure streams of love within the fellowship.

To make matters worse, within the church many will arise who claim to know and speak God's word, but they will be imposters, false prophets. The majority of church attenders, who perhaps have not fed themselves on God's Word, will believe these fraudulent "prophets" and be deceived.

As they see utter lawlessness overwhelming society, many will become disgusted, cynical, and bitter. They will lose hope, which is a major prerequisite for love, and their hearts will be hardened and cold.

But, while "many" will fall away, a few will remain faithful. They will trust in God, hold fast to His word, refuse to follow false teachers, love their enemies, and suffer death rather than deny their Lord. These—and only these—will be saved. May we be among their number!

The King Predicts His Return

The Gospel of the Kingdom Part–1
Matthew 24:14

"And this gospel of the kingdom will be preached in all the world as a witness to the nations, and then the end will come."

With these words, Jesus gives us the one unmistakable sign of the imminence of His return. Wars, famines, earthquakes, and plagues—these will continue, intensify, and increase in frequency, but who knows their limit? We can, however, measure when the gospel of the kingdom has been preached in all the world as a testimony to the nations.

Let us examine this key statement of our Lord closely, therefore, that we may both understand its meaning, and apply its teaching to our lives.

"This gospel of the kingdom will be preached." Not any other so-called "gospel," but *this* one.

In his day, Paul had to confront the "gospel" of works righteousness. He firmly opposed this error, insisting that justification comes by faith alone (Galatians 1:6–7; 2:7, 14–17). Indeed, he castigated all those who brought another message and pronounced a curse upon them.

We face similar challenges to the gospel today. For example, some preach political liberation as the essence of the Christian message, ignoring our fundamental spiritual need and the essentially future nature of our hope in Christ.

Others put physical healing at the center of their teaching. Drawing upon a few verses, usually interpreted out of context, they claim that everyone who has faith will be healed.

It is true that Christians still bring wellness to people through prayer, as well as through medicine, but we must await His return before we receive the glorified body that will no longer be subjected to pain, suffering, and death (Romans 8:17–25; 1 Corinthians 15:42–43; Philippians 3:21).

Jesus *did* make the lame to walk, the blind to see, the deaf to hear, and the mute to speak. He healed all kinds of illnesses and diseases. Furthermore, He commanded His disciples to do the same. Gifts of healing have been placed in the Body of Christ for that purpose. But this is not the core of the gospel we are to preach.

Still others—again quoting one or two verses—proclaim inner healing as the essence of the Good News. True, God does restore our souls

(Psalm 23:3) and comfort the downcast (2 Corinthians 1:3–5). To find such inner peace, however, we must repent of our sins, forgive those who have offended us, and place our trust and hope fully in God alone. Jesus came primarily to heal those who acknowledged that they were "sick" with sin (1:21; 9:2–8).

The Gospel of the Kingdom Part–2
Matthew 24:14

"And this gospel of the kingdom will be preached in all the world as a witness to all the nations, and then the end will come."

What, then, is "this gospel [good news] of the kingdom"?

God is king. He rules from heaven with absolute authority (6:9, 10, 13).

God is holy and just. He must, and will judge all who fail to honor, worship, and obey Him (7:23; 10:28).

God has sent His Son Jesus to "save His people from their sins" by dying on the Cross for their redemption (1:21; 20:28).

God's kingdom came to earth in a new way when His Son began His ministry. "The kingdom of heaven is at hand" (4:17; 12:28).

We must, therefore, *"Repent*, for the kingdom of heaven is at hand" (4:17).

The kingdom grows by the *spread of the Word* of God (13:1–23).

Those who *receive the Word and bring forth fruits* of righteousness and obedience will enter the kingdom (7:24; 13:23).

"Blessed *are* the *poor in spirit*, for theirs is the kingdom of heaven.... Blessed *are* those who are *persecuted* for righteousness' sake, for theirs is the kingdom of heaven" (5:3, 10).

Those who do and teach righteousness, while remaining humble like little children, will be *great in the kingdom* (5:19; 18:3–4).

The kingdom of God will come in all its fullness when Christ the King returns in glory to reward all His faithful followers and to punish all those who rejected Him (5:12; 11:21–24; 12:41–42; 13:41–43; 19:28; 24:45–51; 25:1–46).

The King Predicts His Return

No Pain, No Gain
Matthew 24:29–30

"Immediately after the tribulation of those days ... the sign of the Son of Man will appear in heaven, and then all the tribes of the earth will mourn, and they will see the Son of Man coming on the clouds of heaven with power and great glory."

After the gospel has been preached to all the peoples of the world, and the church has gone through a long period of trouble, culminating in the Great Tribulation, the Lord will return.

Other theories of the Second Coming have become quite popular, but they will not stand careful scrutiny. According to Jesus, He will come back only *after* His people have passed through intense suffering.

Until then, we must be prepared to suffer.

Jesus Himself taught this truth clearly on many occasions:

"Blessed *are* those who are persecuted for righteousness' sake ... Blessed are you when they revile and persecute you, and say all kinds of evil against you falsely for My sake" (5:10–11).

"And you will be hated by all for My name's sake. But he who endures to the end will be saved" (10:22).

"And he who does not take his cross and follow after Me is not worthy of Me" (10:38).

"In the world you will have tribulation [trouble, affliction]; but be of good cheer, I have overcome the world" (John 16:33).

Likewise, Paul warned that "to you it has been granted on behalf of Christ, not only to believe in Him, but also suffer for His sake" (Philippians 1:29; see also 1 Peter 4:12–19).

May God give us grace to endure to the end!

The King is Coming!
Matthew 24:30

"Then the sign of the Son of Man will appear in heaven, and then all the tribes of the earth will mourn, and they will see the Son of Man coming on the clouds of heaven with power and great glory."

While on earth, the Son of Man—Jesus' favorite title for Himself—had no place to lay His head (8:20). Unlike most in authority, He came not to be served, but to serve, and to give His life as a ransom for many (20:28).

Constantly spoken against by those who hated Him (11:19; 12:32), He was finally betrayed by one of His disciples, just as He had predicted (17:22).

But Jesus also predicted that He would one day return with kingly power "in the glory of His Father with His angels, and then He will reward each according to his works" (16:27).

Now, only a few days before His death, Jesus again solemnly prophecies His return. Drawing upon the ancient words of Daniel, He warns that the Son of Man will come "on the clouds of heaven with power and great glory" (24:30; see Daniel 7:13, 14).

Then, the saying of Zechariah the prophet will also be explained and expanded: "All the tribes of the earth will mourn" because "they will look on Me whom they pierced" (Zechariah 12:10–12).

They will be filled with regret and remorse, because they ignored, despised, and rejected the Person of whom the Gospel of the kingdom spoke as it was preached in all the earth (24:14).

It will be too late then to repent. There will be no more forgiveness for sinners, for they had refused to believe in the Savior. The door to the wedding banquet has been shut. They would not trust in the lowly Son of Man; now they must tremble before the Lord of heaven and earth, who will judge each one according to his works.

Will you mourn, or rejoice, to see the returning Son?

The Great Gathering
Matthew 24:31

"And He will send His angels with a great sound of a trumpet, and they will gather together His elect from the four winds, from one end of heaven to the other."

Jesus has told His disciples what will happen after His death and resurrection.

First, the destruction of the Temple in Jerusalem because the Jews would not receive Jesus their Savior, the Son of God.

Then, an age—which has turned out to be two thousand years already—of suffering for all mankind: Wars, earthquakes, famines, plagues. During this time, true followers of Jesus will also meet with hostility, hatred, and relentless persecution.

Many imposters will arise, claiming to be the Christ, but we are to ignore them as we await the return of our Lord.

Meanwhile, the gospel of the Kingdom will be preached in all the earth as a witness to the nations. When that task has been completed, "the end will come" (24:14).

The Son of Man will descend from heaven on clouds of glory, while the angel sounds the trumpet declaring the end of this age and the beginning of the new creation.

From every corner of the world, and from Paradise itself, both the living and the dead will be assembled. All those who have trusted in Christ—the chosen ones—will be gathered together for an endless reunion.

God's eternal purpose to "gather together in one all things in Christ" will be accomplished (Ephesians 1:10). Believers from "every tribe and tongue and people and nation" will join together in endless praise of the Lamb of God who came "to save His people from their sins" (Revelation 5:9; Matthew 1:21).

Will you be present at that great gathering?

Are You Ready?
Matthew 24:42, 44

"Watch therefore, for you do not know what hour your Lord is coming.... Therefore you also be ready, for the Son of Man is coming at an hour you do not expect."

Jesus ends His discourse on the end times with several parables and warnings. He wants His people to be ready for His return.

"As the days of Noah *were*, so also will the coming of the Son of Man be" (24:37). Right before the disastrous Flood, people were "eating and drinking, marrying and giving in marriage" (24:38). Suddenly, the great deluge swept them away.

Noah had preached to them for one hundred years, but they had not repented. When the waters overwhelmed them, it was too late (24:38–39).

The Lord tells us that He will come back when we do not expect Him. Men and women will be busy at work when Jesus returns to judge the world (24:40–41).

Like a thief in the night, Jesus will come unannounced (24:43).

How can we prepare? The parables that follow tell us.

By fulfilling our duties, like a faithful steward who manages his master's household well (24:45–51).

By constant readiness, like members of a wedding party who are fully prepared to receive the Bridegroom, even in the middle of the night (25:1–13).

By wisely using the resources He has given us (25:14–30).

By acts of kindness done to other believers, for Christ is present in them (25:31–46).

Are we ready for His return?

The King Predicts His Return

Two Actions, Two Outcomes
Matthew 24:45

"Who then is a faithful and wise servant, whom his master made ruler over his household, to give them food in due season?"

Jesus drives home the urgency of the warning to prepare for His return with this parable of two servants.

One was "faithful and wise." Faithful, because he followed his master's orders to provide for the members of the house.

Wise, because "Blessed *is* that servant ... Assuredly, I say to you that he [the returning master] will make him ruler over all his goods" (24:46–47).

The man who is serves Christ and those around him will reap a rich reward.

"But if that evil servant says in his heart, 'My master is delaying his coming,' and begins to beat *his* fellow servants and to eat and drink with the drunkards, the master of that servant will come on a day when he is not looking for *him* and at an hour what he is not aware of, and will cut him in two and appoint him his portion with the hypocrites. There shall be weeping and gnashing of teeth" (24:48–51).

Disregard for the Master; destructive treatment of others; and dissolute self-indulgence will reap a bitter harvest of everlasting punishment and pain.

Choices matter. As we are now, so shall we be then, when Christ returns to judge the living and the dead.

"Therefore you also be ready, for the Son of Man is coming at an hour you do not expect" (24:44).

Christ the King

25 The King Calls Us to Watch

Before It's Too Late
Matthew 25:1–13

"Then the kingdom of heaven shall be likened to ten virgins [maidens] who took their lamps and went out to meet the bridegroom. Now five of them were wise, and five were foolish."

With another parable, Jesus again warns His disciples to be ready for His return.

In those days, the groom would come with his bride, perhaps in the middle of the night, to enjoy a party with their friends. The men would be with him, and the women would wait until they heard his joyful shout of invitation.

The wise maidens had made preparations. They had oil for their lamps, or torches. The foolish ones had lamps, but no oil for them to burn brightly.

Thus, when the bridegroom came, only half of the maidens were ready to enter with him into the wedding feast. The others were shut out.

Jesus is our heavenly Bridegroom. One day, perhaps very soon, He will come back and gather all His people together for an endless wedding banquet. Are we ready?

These ten women represent those who have only a formal association with Christianity—"lamps"—but not an inner experience of Christ—"oil"—and those who have both. Some may have prayed some prayer of accepting Jesus, but they do not have the Holy Spirit. They have not been born again.

Thus, at His coming, Jesus will say, "I do not know you" (25:12). In other words, He does not have a personal relationship with them.

The point of this parable? Now is the time to get ready for the return of Christ! And how? By true repentance and faith, as well as a life that shows we know Him. Do not delay—get right with God now, or it may soon be too late.

Christ the King

From Little to Much
Matthew 25:14–30

"For the kingdom of heaven is like a man traveling to a far country, who called his own servants and delivered his goods to them. And to one he gave five talents, to another two, and to another one, to each according to his own ability..."

With yet another parable, Jesus teaches His followers how to prepare for His imminent return.

To each of three servants the master gave a different amount of money—one, two, or five talents. At today's prices, one talent of silver would be worth at least $6,400. The servants to whom the master had given two and five talents invested them and doubled their money.

Upon his return, the master commended each servant who had made good use of the money: "Well *done*, good and faithful servant; you were faithful over a few things; I will make you a ruler over many things. Enter into the joy of your lord" (25:21).

The other servant, however, had taken his one talent of silver and buried it in the ground. His reason? He did not trust in his master's goodness and kindness, even though he had been given money to use.

To him, the master replied, "You wicked and lazy servant ... So take the talent from him, and give *it* to him who has ten talents.... And cast the unprofitable servant into the outer darkness. There will be weeping and gnashing of teeth" (25:26–30).

What "talents"—abilities, time, resources—has God given you? Are you using them well, to increase your Master's honor and advance His kingdom? Or are you wasting your life away?

When the Lord returns, it will be too late to start being profitable servants.

The stakes are high. "Use it or lose it"—eternally.

The Great Divide
Matthew 25:31–33

"When the Son of Man comes in His glory, and all the holy angels with Him, then He will sit on the throne of His glory. All the nations will be gathered before Him, and He will separate them one from another, as a shepherd divides his sheep from the goats. And He will set the sheep on His right hand, but the goats on the left."

Jesus says that a great day of judgment is coming. At that time, He will return with great glory and power, and everyone in the world will be assigned to one of two groups: "sheep" and "goats."

The sheep will be honored—put on the Lord's right hand; and the goats rejected—put on His left hand (the custom in those days).

Then each will be given a judgment: To the sheep, Christ will say, "Come, you blessed of My Father, inherit the kingdom prepared for you from the foundation of the world" (25:34). That is, they will "go ... into eternal life" (25:46).

The goats, on the other hand, will hear these awful words, "Depart from Me, you cursed, into the everlasting fire prepared for the devil and his angels" (25:41). "Everlasting punishment" will be their doom (25:46).

This judgment will be final; there will be no appeal. Notice, also, that there is no middle ground, no "Purgatory," as Roman Catholics teach. Either life or death, blessing or curse, reward or punishment.

And the decision will have eternal consequences. Everlasting life for those who are blessed, and endless punishment for the cursed ones, with no annihilation of the soul to terminate their torment.

Are we living in the light of this truth? Do we bend every effort to prepare for the judgment day of the Lord? Or are we letting lesser concerns—like fame, fortune, fun, and family pressures—distract us from the most important question: Which side will I be on?

Christ the King

Who is Jesus?
Matthew 25:40

"And the King will answer and say to them, 'Assuredly, I say to you, inasmuch as you did it to one of the least of these My brethren, you did it to Me.'"

In this remarkable passage, Jesus reveals two truths about Himself.

> He is divine. "When the Son of Man comes in His glory, and all the holy angels with Him, then He will sit on the throne of His glory.... Then the King will say to those on His right hand, 'Come you blessed of My Father, inherit the kingdom prepared for you...'" (25:31–34). He is the Son of Man spoken of by Daniel (Daniel 7:13–14), to whom is given an everlasting kingdom. Thus, He is King—commander of the angelic armies of God, ruler of the nations, judge of the world. He is the eternal Son of God, equal in power, wisdom, and glory to the Father, while being subject to the Father's will as loyal Son.

> He is fully human. How else could He call His followers "brothers"? Born of the virgin Mary, descended from Adam, Abraham, and David, He is truly man, just like us (except without sin). Matthew's Gospel presents Jesus as baby in a cradle, and then in danger of His life (2:1–15); as a young child (2:19–20); as a grown man capable of hunger (4:2). He walked on this earth, teaching and healing, until His enemies had Him killed.

Because He is both God and man, Jesus could represent both parties on the Cross, absorbing in Himself the wrath of God on our behalf.

And because He is both God and man, Jesus has the right to judge all of us according to a simple standard: How did we treat His followers?

Is Jesus Your Brother?
Matthew 25:40

"... inasmuch as you did it to one of the least of these My brethren [brothers], you did it to Me."

If we are to be judged according to how well we treated Jesus' "brothers," then the question is, Who are these brothers?

The Lord Himself answered this question early in His ministry: "whoever does the will of My Father in heaven is My brother and sister and mother" (12:50).

This statement marks a clear division among all mankind. Only those who do God's will are considered members of Jesus' family.

The next question becomes, What is God's will? Matthew's entire Gospel contains the answer, as does the rest of the New Testament, indeed, the whole Bible.

The Apostle John gets to the core of the matter with this brief statement: "this is His commandment: that we should believe on the name of His Son Jesus Christ and love one another, just as He gave commandment" (1 John 3:23).

In other words, those who trust in Jesus Christ as Lord and Savior, and who express their faith by love for other Christians, do the will of God the Father, and are thus "brother and sister and mother" to Jesus.

But that leads us to ask, What does "love one another" mean? This parable of Jesus tells us:

When fellow Christians are in need, we must seek to supply what they lack. Feed the hungry, give drink to the thirsty, welcome the stranger, clothe the naked, visit the sick and imprisoned.

"By this we know love, because He laid down His life for us. And we also ought to lay down *our* lives for the brethren. But whoever has this world's goods, and sees his brother in need, and shuts up his heart from him, how does the love of God abide in him?" (1 John 3:16–17).

Limited Liability
Matthew 25:40

"Assuredly, I say to you, inasmuch as you did it *to one of the least of these My brethren, you did* it *to Me."*

Our obligation to other Christians is clear: We should treat them as we would Jesus Himself. As He laid down His life for us, so we should be willing to sacrifice ourselves for other followers of Christ.

But what about our obligation to non-believers? Must the Church of Christ feed *all* who are hungry, clothe *all* the naked, heal *all* the sick? Many would say so, and much money and effort has been expended on such endeavors.

Notice Jesus' words however: "Unto one of the least of these *My brethren*"—that is, His followers, as we have seen.

Contrary to popular belief, Christians are neither to see all people on earth as the "brothers" of Jesus, nor are they required to meet all their physical needs!

We must observe the priorities set forth in the Bible: First help our "family" in Christ, then those outside the family. As Paul said, "as we have opportunity, let us do good to all, especially to those who are of the household of faith" (Galatians 6:10).

Even Jesus observed this principle: He fed only those who had followed Him into the wilderness to hear His teaching and receive healing (14:13–21; 15:32–39).

Perhaps we can put it this way: The organized church must care for its needy members (Acts 4:34–35; 6:1; 1 Timothy 5:3–16). Individual believers, however, are to act as light and salt in the world, and each of us is to love our neighbor as ourselves.

Yes, we must all do what we can to make this world a better place, but we must start at "home"!

26 The King's Departure

Hatred in High Places
Matthew 26:1–5

... He said to His disciples, "You know that after two days is the Passover, and the Son of Man will be delivered up to be crucified." Then the chief priests, the scribes, and the elders of the people assembled at the palace of the high priest, who was called Caiaphas, and plotted to take Jesus by trickery and kill Him.

The entire Jewish establishment conspired to do away with Jesus. Why?

From a human standpoint, we can understand their hostility.

In all His teachings, He called for a degree of holiness and righteousness that "exceeds *the righteousness* of the scribes and the Pharisees," in order to enter the kingdom of God (5:20).

By healing and doing good on the holy day, He failed to observe the Sabbath as their man-made traditions required. Thus, they considered Him a lawbreaker.

But He returned the accusation, denouncing them for hypocrisy, self-righteousness, and greed, and pronouncing woe upon them because of the impending judgment of God (23).

Not even their beloved Temple escaped His prophetic words, for He predicted that it would be utterly destroyed when God poured out His wrath upon a rebellious people (24:2).

He defied all their expectations of a coming savior by riding humbly into Jerusalem, refusing to lead a rebellion against the hated Romans, and claiming to be the Son of Man spoken of by Daniel (24:30).

His entire life challenged their pretensions, their power, their prestige, and their position. No wonder they hated Him! Should we be surprised when Christians encounter the same hostility in high places around the world today? After all, "A disciple is not above *his* teacher, nor a servant above his master" (10:24).

Why This Waste?
Matthew 26:6–9

And when Jesus was in Bethany at the house of Simon the leper, a woman came to Him having an alabaster flask of very costly fragrant oil, and she poured it on His head as He sat at the table. But when His disciples saw it, they were indignant, saying, "Why this waste? For this fragrant oil might have been sold for much and given to the poor."

We know from John's Gospel that this woman was Mary, the sister of Martha and of Lazarus, whom Jesus had just raised from the dead (John 12:1–3; 11:1–45). She and Martha were apparently serving the meal in Simon's house.

The Gospel of Mark tells us that the perfume was worth a year's wages (Mark 14:3–9). The alabaster jar, which was broken to release its contents, would also have been very costly (Mark 14:3). Perhaps Mary was pouring out the major part of her dowry upon Jesus' head and feet (see John 12:3).

The entire action breathes a spirit of deep devotion, lavish love, extravagant affection. Not content with anointing Jesus' head, she anoints His feet as well (John 12:3). Having sat at Jesus' feet to listen to His teaching (Luke 10:39), and fallen at His feet to lament His absence when her brother died (John 11:32), Mary now lingers at His feet to wipe them with her long tresses—a woman's glory (1 Corinthians 11:15).

Why this "waste"? What prompted this worship? Mary had surely heard Jesus teach many times, and learned from others what He said. His words brought life and light and love into her hungry heart.

"Blessed *are* the poor in spirit, for theirs is the kingdom of heaven" (5:3).

"Lay up for yourselves treasures in heaven … seek first the kingdom of God and His righteousness" (6:20, 33).

"Come to Me, all *you* who labor and are heavy laden, and I will give you rest" (11:28).

"The Son of Man is about to be betrayed into the hands of men, and they will kill Him, and the third day He will be raised up" (17:22–23).

"The Son of Man did not come to be served, but to serve, and to give His life a ransom for many" (20:28).

Having heard about His many miracles, and seen Him bring her own brother out of the tomb, Mary knew who Jesus was; what He could do; and what He was about to suffer. Her smitten heart simply had to offer to Him all she had. Shall we do any less?

Lasting Fame
Matthew 26:10–13

"Assuredly, I say to you, wherever this gospel is preached in the whole world, what this woman has done will also be told as a memorial to her."

What did Mary give to Jesus? And what did she receive in return?

She gave Jesus her *attention*. While others were busy—maybe too busy—Mary found time to sit at Jesus' feet and drink in His heavenly doctrine (Luke 10:38–42). Jesus' comment that she had anointed Him for His burial reveals the hidden chambers of Mary's heart, where words of the Lord's impending death were reverberating (26:12). Clearly, her mind was focused on Christ, and not upon this world.

She exhausted her *assets*. As we have seen, the value of the perfume and of the alabaster jar exceeded a year's income, and may have represented her hope for marriage, since without a dowry a woman could not expect to be chosen as a wife. Thus,

She offered to Him all of her *aspirations*. It may have seemed to her that the death of Jesus would mean the end of all hope, so she seized this moment to proffer to Him her hopes and dreams, her deepest longings and strongest fears, in one last act of worship.

She poured upon His body all of her *affection*. It is as if she saw Jesus as her true Husband, upon whom she lavished her love. True devotion yearns to give, to serve, to express tender care, no matter what the cost.

What, then, did Mary receive?

From mean-spirited men, nothing but scorn and rebuke, and even a complaint to Christ, just as her sister Martha had complained (Luke 10:40).

But from Jesus, the strongest possible affirmation: "she has done a good work for Me.… Assuredly, I say to you, wherever this gospel is preached in the whole world, what this woman has done will also be told as a memorial to her" (26:10, 13).

This stunning announcement resonates with many chords of precious truth. Among them:

There is a "gospel"—good news—that Jesus wants all nations to hear, and He will fulfill His own purpose (24:14; see also 28:18–20; Mark 16:15). That "good news" centers on the death, burial, and resurrection of Jesus Christ for the forgiveness of our sins (1:21; 20:28; Luke 24:46–47). Indeed, for two millennia the story has been relayed, from one generation to another, of how this woman offered all she had to Him who "for our sakes became poor, that [we] through His poverty might become rich (2 Corinthians 8:9).

May the one who thus honored Mary receive our heartfelt praise, now and forever!

Who is Judas?
Matthew 26:14–16

Then one of the twelve, called Judas Iscariot, went to the chief priests and said, "What are you willing to give me if I deliver Him to you?" And they counted out to him thirty pieces of silver. So from that time he sought opportunity to betray Him.

Judas, the arch-betrayer, was one of the twelve disciples whom Jesus had chosen to be apostles during His earthly ministry (10:1–4). Along with the others, he preached the message of the kingdom of God, performed miraculous healings, and cast out demons in the name of Jesus (10:7–8).

Trusted by the others, who were entirely unsuspecting, he was given charge of their common purse, out of which he distributed money for the poor. He also took dedicated funds for himself, for he was a thief (John 12:6).

Money seemed to have dominated his thoughts, for he was the spokesman and apparent ringleader for the disciples who rebuked Mary for her "extravagant" worship of the Lord (John 12:4–5; Matthew 26:8–9). Right after Jesus' rebuke for such misplaced priorities, Judas went out to betray his Master (26:10–16).

So who was he, really?

Outwardly, he seemed to be a model disciple of Christ, for he belonged to the chosen company of the apostles and behaved well enough to maintain the trust of the others. He clearly possessed some sort of faith, or he would not have been able to work miracles. From his preaching of the kingdom message, we know also that he had a clear understanding of at least the rudiments of truth.

The King's Departure

On the other hand, from his attitude towards Mary, and his selling of Jesus, we realize that his eye was not good. He wanted to lay up for himself treasures on earth by purloining funds from the offerings given to support Christ and His team. He was not seeking first the kingdom of God and His righteousness (6:19, 23, 33).

We now see that this wretched thief was a devoted worshiper of Mammon, not of God. With divided heart, he was loyal to his idol and despised Jesus. We may put the matter starkly and say that he loved Mammon and hated God and his Anointed One (6:24).

Judas will be able to say on the last day, "Lord, Lord, have [I] not prophesied in Your name, cast out demons in Your name, and done many wonders in Your name?" (7:22; see also Hebrews 6:4–6)

Like countless others who have appeared to be devout believers, however, he will hear those terrible words, "I never knew you [that is, He never had an intimate relationship with him]; depart from Me, you who practice lawlessness!" (7:23) He never really belonged to Christ's people; that is why he went out from them (1 John 2:19). What a warning to us!

Communion with Christ and Each Other
Matthew 26:26–29

"Take, eat; this is My body." Then He took the cup, and gave thanks, and gave it to them, saying, "Drink from it, all of you. For this is My blood of the new covenant, which is shed for many for the remission of sins."

Just before He faces His ultimate trial, Jesus shares one last Passover meal with His disciples, at the end of which He inaugurates what we now call the Lord's Supper (or Communion, or the Eucharist).

This meal resembles the Jewish Passover, even as it announces and represents a new era in God's dealing with His people.

The blood of the lamb sprinkled over the door of each Israelite home finds its fulfillment in the blood of Christ which was shed on the Cross.

The death of a lamb foreshadows the self-sacrifice of Jesus, the Lamb of God who alone can take away the sins of the world. Notice: There is no lamb mentioned in any accounts of the last Supper, though there almost certainly had to be one; are the Gospel writers trying to shine a beam of light upon the final Lamb?

Deliverance from bondage to Pharaoh points towards release from slavery to the penalty, power, and finally the presence of sin.

Eating the Passover with family looks to the creation of a new family born again through faith in Christ to become children of God.

Formation of Israel as the people of God heralds the creation of the new people from every race and nation who belong to God through faith in Christ.

Remembering the mighty deliverance by God from Egypt will be replaced by a memorial to the redemption from sin which was accomplished by Christ.

Instead of a fellowship based on the blood of one's parents, there will be a far deeper communion in the Holy Spirit, bought with the blood of Christ.

The Mosaic Covenant, which featured laws that could not transform the soul, is displaced by the New Covenant, in which God's laws are written on our hearts by the Spirit.

How about you? Do you trust in Jesus as the only one who can save you from your sins? If you partake of the Lord's Supper at church, do you remember with gratitude the mighty salvation which He has wrought for you, with faith and thanksgiving?

The King's Departure

Over-Confidence
Matthew 26:31–35

Then Jesus said to them, "All of you will be made to stumble because of Me this night..." Peter answered and said to Him, "Even if all are made to stumble because of You, I will never be made to stumble." Jesus said to him, "Assuredly, I say to you that this night ... you will deny Me three times."

This passage relates the *prediction* of Jesus and the *presumption* of Peter.

Jesus predicted five upcoming events: (1) As their Shepherd, He would be "struck"—that is, captured and killed—as prophesied in the Old Testament. (2) As His sheep, they would all be scattered—that is, they would desert Him in fear. (3) He would rise again from the dead. (4) After His resurrection, He would go before them to Galilee, their common home. (5) In addition to being "scattered," Peter would actually deny Jesus three times that very night.

In the face of these clear prophecies, and despite all that he had seen and heard in the previous three years, Peter boldly disagreed with Jesus. "Even if I have to die with You, I will not deny You!" (26:35) The other disciples joined in this protestation of loyalty.

Aside from being a gross insult to the wisdom and authority of their master, this rejection of His predictions demonstrated ignorance of themselves.

Clearly, they did not know the strength of the temptation that would soon come upon them. Nor did they perceive their own inner weakness. They were especially blind to their fear of death, and how that would lead them to run away and leave Jesus to face danger alone.

We must be careful not to commit the same mistake. None of us is immune to temptation. As Paul warned, "let him who thinks he stands take heed lest he fall" (1 Corinthians 10:12).

Prevailing Prayer
Matthew 26:36–46

"Watch and pray, lest you enter into temptation. The spirit indeed is willing, but the flesh is weak.... O My Father, if this cup cannot pass away from Me unless I drink it, Your will be done."

As events proceed inexorably towards their *denouement* on Calvary, Jesus seeks both solitude with God and support from His closest companions. He finds the former, but fails to receive the latter.

Peter, James, and John, who had been with Jesus on the Mount of Transfiguration, fell asleep in the Garden of Gethsemane, despite repeated wake-up calls from someone who longed for fellowship in the supreme trial of His life.

He had offered them the cup of blessing in the Upper Room, but the price was high: His own blood (26:28), referred to in His prayer as the "cup" from which He shrank in horror, for this was the cup of God's wrath against sinners (Psalm 75:8; Isaiah 51:17; Jeremiah 25:15; Ezekiel 23:33; Zechariah 12:2; Revelation 14:10).

James and John had glibly said they were willing to partake of this bitter potion when they sought preferential treatment (20:22), but now they are too selfish even to pray with the one who alone possessed the right to take upon Himself the punishment due for the sins of the world. Peter had promised even to die for Jesus, as had they all, but when it came to living for Him as intercessors, it was too much (26:33, 35). So much for good intentions. As Jesus said, "The spirit indeed *is* willing, but the flesh *is* weak" (26:41).

Thanks be to God! Deliverance from ourselves, Satan's power, and the righteous wrath of God does not depend upon men, but fell up the mighty shoulders of the Son of God, Jesus, who as the Son of Mary renewed the combat His ancient forebears had lost in Eden. His flesh, too, was weak, but His spirit cried out to God. After confirming that He must indeed die in order to "save His people from their sins" (1:21), Jesus pledges Himself again to God's redemptive purpose: "Your will be done."

The letter to the Hebrews tells us that He "offered up prayers and supplications, with vehement cries and tears to Him who was able to save Him from death, and was heard because of His godly fear" (Hebrews 5:7).

His righteous innocence recoiling from the prospect of being considered a criminal, His natural aversion to death and His utter grief

The King's Departure

at the coming separation from His Father produced a piercing agony, so that "... His sweat became like great drops of blood" (Luke 22:44), but still He persevered: "Your will be done."

His disciples were still asleep when He returned from this hour of wrestling in prayer, but the battle had been won. Our Champion had gained for us what our first parents had lost in paradise. A Man had determined to obey God at any cost. O come! Let us adore Him.

Betrayal!
Matthew 26:48–49

Now His betrayer had given them a sign, saying, "Whomever I kiss, He is the One; seize Him." Immediately he went up to Jesus and said, "Greetings, Rabbi!" and kissed Him.

Have you ever been betrayed?

Has your best friend failed you? Has your spouse left you for someone else, or just for personal fulfillment? Maybe your parents have neglected you, abandoned you, or allowed you to be sacrificed on the altar of their own convenience, pleasure, or passion.

When we break a promise, that is betrayal. Those who reveal secrets are traitors, as are those who do not keep commitments. Being friendly to a person while speaking ill of him to others counts, too.

Divorce is the ultimate betrayal, as is any form of physical abuse.

So, most of us have either suffered betrayal, or have been guilty of it ourselves. In any case, Jesus knows!

He had chosen Judas as one of the select few. They had eaten, traveled, served, and worshiped together. John's Gospel tells us that Judas was entrusted with the common purse for all the disciples.

And yet this man conspired with the Jewish leaders who wanted to capture and kill his teacher. To make matters worse, the hypocrite arranged to identify Jesus in the darkness with a friendly greeting.

As he approached the Lord, the traitor said, "Greetings, Rabbi [Teacher]," and then gave Him the kiss that was customary in those days. How he had sunk to the depths of wickedness, malice, and perfidy!

But notice Jesus' response: "Friend, why have you come?" (26:50) Was there any man like Him?

Our Way, or God's?
Matthew 26:52–54

"Put your sword in its place, for all who take the sword will perish by the sword. Or do you think that I cannot now pray to My Father, and He will provide Me with more than twelve legions of angels? How then could the Scriptures be fulfilled, that it must happen thus?"

A large crowd of Temple guards had come to arrest Jesus. As they seized Him, Peter drew a sword and sliced off the ear of the High Priest's servant, thinking to defend his teacher.

But Jesus rebuked him. The Lord gave three reasons why His disciples should not resist His capture:

Those who take part in armed revolution run the risk of a violent death.

Jesus can take care of Himself, for a simple request to the Father would unleash the power of angelic armies in His defense.

As He had repeatedly taught, the Messiah was destined to die at the hands of evil men, in order to fulfill God's promises of salvation from sin for His followers (1:21; 16:21; 17:22–23; 20:18–19; 26:24).

Though scholars differ about whether Jesus' words about taking up the sword apply to national defense or to the defense of the helpless, we can be sure that:

Violent revolution is wrong. All the more so is any armed attempt to resist religious persecution.

When we are attacked, either physically or verbally, let us cry out to God in prayer for deliverance, just as the Psalmist did.

God's purpose for our lives includes persecution and suffering for the sake of Jesus' name. When it comes, let us submit humbly to His will, like our Lord, who taught us to rejoice at that time (5:11–12). Peter later learned this lesson well (1 Peter 2:13–14; 4:12–19).

Self-Defense
Matthew 26:55–56

In that hour Jesus said to the multitudes, "Have you come out, as against a robber, with swords and clubs to take Me? I sat daily with you, teaching in the temple, and you did not seize Me. But all this was done that the Scriptures of the prophets might be fulfilled."

After rebuking Peter for trying to defend Him by force, Jesus turns His penetrating words upon the mob which had seized Him.

First, He asks a rhetorical question: Has this armed force come to arrest a revolutionary (the probable meaning of "robber")?

He thus exposes the silliness of their actions. A real rebel would have armed his followers and led them in violent revolt, whereas Jesus had aborted the single feeble effort to free Him.

Then, He states the obvious: During the previous week of public teaching, the authorities had not made a move against Him. Clearly, He had broken no law, and offered no legitimate grounds for arrest.

Finally, He ridicules their presumption, by repeating what He had just said to Peter: These wicked cowards were only instruments in the hand of Almighty God, whose sovereign purpose prompted their servile act.

God had decreed from all eternity that His Son must die for sinners. He would be betrayed, arrested, unjustly tried, mocked, beaten, scourged, and finally pierced through—all for our iniquities.

As the angel had told Joseph, this child of Mary came to "save His people from their sins." To do so, He must bear the penalty we deserve, including both public shame and punishment, as well as divine wrath.

With these simple words alone, Jesus defended Himself. The disciples saw that their cause was lost, and fled in terror. The soldiers carried out their orders. And our salvation was guaranteed.

Responding to Accusations
Matthew 26:59, 62–63a

Now the chief priests, the elders, and all the counsel sought false testimony against Jesus to put Him to death ... And the high priest arose and said to Him, "Do You answer nothing? What is it these men testify against You?" But Jesus kept silent.

Knowing that Jesus had committed no crime, but hating Him and lusting for His death, the Jewish leaders hired false accusers to attack Him.

The problem was, their witnesses could not agree. Finally, however, two of them asserted that Jesus said He would destroy the temple and then rebuild it.

They entirely misunderstood, or willfully misquoted, His words, perhaps because they had been spoken at least two years before. Nevertheless, their accusations met the legal requirement—there must be two in a capital trial—and were enough to convict Jesus.

Faced thus with death unless He could disprove their charges, Jesus remained silent. Indeed, He had kept quiet during the entire proceeding, even though He could easily have refuted the accusations.

How brave He was! How filled with dignity, inner strength, faith in His Father, commitment to His mission! And how wise and prudent, for He well knew that nothing He said would be accepted, for these men sought His death by any means.

What about us? How do we respond to unjustified criticism? Do we not usually try to explain ourselves, or defend ourselves, or even to attack the person criticizing us?

Sometimes, of course, that is necessary, either to protect ourselves from legal damage, or to promote the truth.

But usually, in a private setting, and sometimes even in public, we should just keep quiet, knowing that Jesus understands. And He is with us!

Jesus' Identity and Destiny
Matthew 26:63–64

And the high priest answered and said to Him, "I put You under oath by the living God: Tell us if You are the Christ, the Son of God!" Jesus said to him, "It is as you said. Nevertheless, I say to you, hereafter you will see the Son of Man at the right of the Power, and coming on the clouds of heaven."

Although He had kept silent when falsely accused, Jesus spoke clearly when commanded to speak the truth. From this exchange, we learn a great deal about Him:

> He is the Christ, the one chosen and anointed by God with the Holy Spirit, sent into the world to "save His people from their sins" (1:21).

> He is the Son of God. In those days, only the Roman emperor could claim that title, so Jesus faced certain death with His response. But He had to admit reality. From all eternity, He has been God's uniquely beloved Son, equal in substance, power and dignity with the Father, though always willing to do His will.

> He is the Son of Man prophesied by Daniel (Daniel 7:13–14). Fully man, yet also divine, He was entitled to an everlasting kingdom over all the earth.

> After His death, resurrection, and ascension, He would sit at the right hand of the Father ["the Power"], where He is now. All things in heaven and earth have been made subject to Him (Ephesians 1:20–22).

> One day, He will return "with the clouds of heaven." These clouds remind us of the shining pillar of glory that manifested God's guiding presence in the wilderness (Exodus 13:21–23; Daniel 7:13).

> At this second coming, Jesus will judge the living and the dead (7:21–23; 25:31–46).

Will you be ready?

Humiliation
Matthew 26:65–68

"He has spoken blasphemy!" ... "He is deserving of death." Then they spat in His face and beat Him; and others struck Him *with the palms of their hands, saying, "Prophesy to us, Christ! Who is the one who struck You?"*

Having been falsely accused, Jesus now suffers abuse at the hands of the Jewish leaders. What should have been a dignified court of elders has disintegrated into an unruly mob, inflamed with hatred and cruelty. These supposed spiritual and political rulers of God's people show themselves to be thugs and brutes, nothing more.

First, they reject His honest assertion that He is the Christ and that they will see Him come in glory. These words they term blasphemy—an impious, profane offense against God. Little did they know how wrong they were!

Then they began to spit upon Him, surely a contemptuous act in any culture, expressing their total scorn for a Man who was infinitely superior to all of them.

Some beat Him, inflicting not just pain but humiliation. Luke tells us that others blindfolded Him. Then they hit Him and mockingly asked, "Prophesy! Who is the one who struck You?" (Luke 22:64) Jesus knew all things, but in His humanity allowed Himself to be treated as if He had to rely on His eyes to gather information.

How total His submission! How utterly undeserved was this mockery and scorn! How bravely He bore it all, with such immense self-control and dignity! He could have vaporized them with a single breath of His holy wrath, but He patiently endured it all for our sake.

As Peter, who was watching from afar, later wrote, "when He was reviled, [He] did not revile in return; when He suffered, He did not threaten, but committed *Himself* to Him who judges righteously" (1 Peter 2:23).

And all in order to "save His people from their sins" (1:21).

Learning from Peter
Matthew 26:69-75

And Peter remembered the word of Jesus who had said to him, "Before the rooster crows, you will deny Me three times." So he went out and wept bitterly.

What a contrast between Peter and his Master!

When Peter and the others ran away, Jesus walked forward to meet His betrayer and the thugs he brought to arrest Him (26:46–56; John 18:4–8).

While Peter denied even knowing Christ, Jesus confessed that He was the Son of God, fully cognizant of the consequences (26:63–64).

Humanly speaking, what led to these starkly opposite responses?

The most significant, of course, is that Jesus had the Spirit of God and Peter did not. The Lord's victory in the wilderness, like His triumphs during His arrest, trial, and sufferings, came from the anointing with the Spirit which was given Him at His baptism (3:16).

Peter, on the other hand, did not receive the Spirit until the Day of Pentecost, as Jesus had promised (Luke 24:49; Acts 1:5, 8; 2:4, 38). On that day, he and the other apostles received repentance unto life; they fully trusted in Christ; they received the Spirit; they were born again; they were "saved" (3:11; Acts 10:43–45, 47; 11:14–18; John 3:3, 5; see also Romans 8:9–10). We should note that after Pentecost Peter never again denied his Lord, but boldly proclaimed the Gospel of Christ to those who had killed Jesus (Acts 2:14–40; 3:11–26; 4:1–31).

Still, we can learn from Peter's failure on the night when Jesus was betrayed.

Jesus overcame temptation in the wilderness by quoting the Word of God, upon which he had clearly meditated at length (4:3–10). Peter obviously had failed to ponder the warnings Jesus had given him that he would betray Christ three times (26:34).

Faced with a terrible temptation, Jesus prayed. Peter slept when he should have been begging for strength to overcome Satan's wiles (26:39–45; 6:13).

Rather than following Jesus closely, as John did, he followed "at a distance" (26:58; John 18:15–16). He placed himself in the midst of

God's enemies, forgetting his spiritual weakness and vulnerability (26:41), and perhaps trusting in his own ability to defend himself, as he had tried to protect Jesus in the Garden (26:51).

Years later, obviously having learned his lessons, he wrote, "Be sober, be vigilant; because your adversary the devil walks about like a roaring lion, seeking whom he may devour. Resist him, steadfast in the faith, knowing that the same sufferings are experienced by your brotherhood in the world" (1 Peter 5:8–9).

27 The Suffering King

Deadly Mammon
Matthew 27:3–10

Then Judas, His betrayer, seeing that He had been condemned, was remorseful and brought back the thirty pieces of silver to the chief priests and elders, saying, "I have sinned by betraying innocent blood." And they said, "What is that to us? You see to it!" Then he threw down the pieces of silver in the temple and departed, and went and hanged himself.

Clearly, Judas had been in love with this present world for a long time (2 Timothy 4:10; 1 John 2:15). Having stolen money regularly from the common purse which had been entrusted to him, he has sold Jesus for the price of a slave (John 12:6; Exodus 21:32). Now that Jesus has been condemned, he is filled with remorse, for he knows that an innocent man has been betrayed by him and condemned by the Jewish leaders.

The money they paid is like fire in his hand; he must get rid of it; but they will not take it from him. Their scruples about accepting "blood money" for Temple purposes highlight their hypocrisy, and lead them to use it to purchase a field for burying aliens to the promises of Israel (27:6–10).

Matthew sees here the fulfillment of ancient prophecies (Jeremiah 19 and Zechariah 11) that expose the judgment of God which was going to fall upon the wicked rulers of Israel in previous times. Those events foreshadowed the rejection by the Jews of their true Shepherd and King, Jesus, and presaged the horrible fate that would befall Jerusalem when the Romans destroyed it in A.D. 70 (23:35; 24:1–21). At that time, the entire region became a "field of blood."

Thus, both Judas and the authorities in Jerusalem put the love of this world—possessions, power, prestige—above the love of God and of His people. In direct contrast to Jesus, who gave Himself as a ransom for many (20:28), they paid and received money to destroy the Messiah and save themselves.

How about us? In what ways have we loved this present world more than God and His kingdom? What have we paid, or received, to betray our Master? Which of our actions show that we are "enemies of the cross of Christ" (Philippians 3:18)?

Perhaps we have been obsessed with laying up treasures on this earth, rather than seeking first the kingdom of God (6:19–21, 33). On the final day, what will it profit us to have gained this whole world, if we lose our very soul (16:25–26)? It is not worth much to "find life" in this age and then to lose it for all eternity (10:39).

If pleasure, or popularity, or position turn us from following Christ, then we shall hear those awful words, "I never knew you" on the last day (7:23).

Equally futile will be bitter remorse without genuine repentance (Judas), or a hard heart that disclaims all responsibility for what we have done (the priests and elders). Only true turning from sin and faith in Christ will deliver us from deadly Mammon.

Injustice!
Matthew 27:11–26

When Pilate saw that he could not prevail at all, but rather that *a tumult [uproar, riot] was rising, he took water and washed* his *hands before the multitude, saying, "I am innocent of the blood of this just Person. You see* to it.*"*

Everything about the trial of Jesus reeks of injustice.

Not only was He illegally tried and condemned by the midnight assembly of Jewish leaders, but even the famous Roman law broke down in the face of rank wickedness and fear.

First, the accusation, that Jesus said He was king of the Jews, was misleading. Our Lord never made that claim, though He did accept acclamation as "Son of David," which implied some sort of kingship.

But He certainly did not intend to lead an armed revolt against Rome, as the Jewish leaders insinuated. "My kingdom is not of this world," He told Pilate (John 18:36).

The Suffering King

In the face of Jesus' silence before His accusers, Pilate sought to release this obviously innocent man. His own investigation, as well as His wife's warning, had convinced him that Jesus was not guilty, so Pilate sought to release Him.

He was prepared to execute a notorious revolutionary, Barabbas, but the crowd, spurred on by their rulers, called for Jesus' death instead.

"Why, what evil has He done?" Pilate replied.

"Let Him be crucified!" they shouted back (27:23).

So this Roman magistrate, who held the power of life and death and who had earlier shown no scruples about offending his Jewish subjects, caved in to the mob's demands. He freed a murderer and crucified an innocent man. Injustice!

Yes, but this was all done according to the "determined purpose and foreknowledge of God" (Acts 2:23).

Mocking the King
Matthew 27:27–31

When they had twisted a crown of thorns, they put it on His head, and a reed in His right hand. And they bowed the knee before Him and mocked Him, saying, "Hail, King of the Jews!"

From the opening of his Gospel to its conclusion, Matthew takes pains to display Jesus as King. In the first verse, He is called "son of David," to whom God had said, "your house and your kingdom shall be established before you. Your throne shall be established forever" (2 Samuel 7:16), and "son of Abraham," to whom God promised, "kings shall come from you" (Genesis 17:6).

Jesus began His ministry by preaching, "Repent, for the kingdom of heaven is at hand" (4:17), and proclaimed that the kingdom of heaven would be conferred upon the poor in spirit and those who are persecuted for righteousness' sake (5:3, 10). He taught with the authority of a king (7:29), cast out evil spirits with a royal command (8:32), and subdued the winds and the waves with a simple word (8:26).

Calling Himself Son of Man, He invoked the ancient prophecies of Daniel, to whom it was revealed that "all peoples, nations, and languages" would "serve Him. His dominion *is* an everlasting dominion" (Daniel 7:14).

Over the centuries, Israel had rejected God as King in order to establish their own human rulers, and had consistently refused to submit to their only real Sovereign. As a consequence, they had come under the harsh rule of foreign potentates, such as the Assyrians, Babylonians, and now the Romans.

Roman legionnaires now feign obeisance to Jesus as the King of the Jews. Stripping Him, clothing Him in the scarlet robe of commanders, pressing a thorny crown into His skull, placing a reed into His hands as a substitute scepter, kneeling before Him in false humility, and greeting Him as they would Caesar, followed by spitting and buffeting, they mean to heap scorn and shame upon Him.

Little do they know that future Roman Emperors would declare Jesus to be their King. Their play-acting foretells the day when "every knee shall bow ... and ... every tongue should confess that Jesus Christ *is* Lord" (Philippians 2:10–11). Quite unaware that they are already fulfilling the prophecies in Daniel, as well as Micah (Micah 5:2, 4) and Isaiah (Isaiah 9:6–7; 11:1–10), they imagine that because Jesus came the first time "lowly, and sitting on a donkey," He will not return "sitting at the right hand of the Power, and coming on the clouds of heaven (21:5; 26:64).

Lest we be too critical of these pagans, however, let us remember that we, too, mock the King of Kings whenever we fail to obey His teaching; to submit respectfully to those in authority over us; to exercise authority with gentleness; or to trust in Him alone to save us. How prone we are to put our hope in false messiahs, and to scorn our only Savior!

The Suffering King

Carrying the Cross
Matthew 27:32

Now as they came out, they found a man of Cyrene, Simon by name. Him they compelled to bear His cross.

Matthew had already recorded Jesus' solemn words, "And he who does not take his cross and follow after Me is not worthy of Me" (10:38). "If anyone desires to come after Me, let him deny himself, and take up his cross, and follow Me" (16:24).

Now he records the story of the first man who—albeit unwillingly—carried the cross of Christ, following in His steps. Though Jesus, as a carpenter, was surely strong enough to bear His own cross, this event reveals just how brutal were the beatings He had already endured, and what carrying the cross entails for His disciples.

Indeed, Jesus and His apostles tell us clearly that to deny oneself, take up the cross, and follow Him means to:

> Determine to suffer in the flesh as Jesus did, living no longer "for the lusts of men, but for the will of God" (1 Peter 4:1–2).

> Be "persecuted for righteousness' sake" (5:10). Speaking out boldly against sin, refusing to participate in popular depravity, and taking abuse for it (10:1; 1 Peter 4:3–4).

> Rejoice when men "revile and persecute you, and say all kinds of evil against you falsely for My sake" (5:11; 1 Peter 4:13, 16).

> Bravely proclaim the Gospel of salvation through repentance from sin and faith in Christ alone, despite threats, pain, and even death (10:7, 27, 32; Acts 3:11–26; 4:5–20, 23–31).

> Risk the loss of the approval of family members in order to follow Christ faithfully (10:21–22, 34–37; 16:24–26; 19:29–30).

> Give up wealth, houses, and financial security to imitate the one who, though rich, yet for our sakes became poor (8:19–20; 19:23–29; 2 Corinthians 8:9).

> Put to death the evil deeds of the body by the power of the indwelling Holy Spirit (5:29–30; Romans 8:13; Galatians 5:24; 1 Peter 2:11).

> Exercise self-discipline in all things in order to be useful to God (1 Corinthians 9:1–27).

> May God give us grace to do!

Salvation through Suffering
Matthew 27:33–44

"You who destroy the temple and build it in three days, save Yourself! If You are the Son of God, come down from the cross." Likewise the chief priests also, mocking with the scribes and elders, said, "He saved others; Himself He cannot save. If He is the King of Israel, let Him now come down from the cross and we will believe in Him. He trusted in God; let Him deliver Him now if He will have Him; for He said, 'I am the Son of God.'"

Perhaps even more than the agony of crucifixion, the mocking scorn of the people and their religious leaders broke the heart of our Savior (Psalm 69:9, 20).

Jesus had refused the narcotic offered Him to lessen the pain (27:34), and was now enduring the slow, agonizing torture of the Cross, His hands and feet pierced; the weight of His body supported by transfixed palms and perhaps a small block of wood for His feet; stripped and exposed to the reproach of passersby—He must have been a miserable spectacle.

A crucified king? How could it be? Everything about this scene is a parody of royalty.

The monarch has no splendid robes. Instead of a palace guard, He is watched by foreign soldiers. The title over His head, "This is Jesus, the King of the Jews" (27:37), was written as a sardonic insult by a Roman governor to the corrupt Jewish officials.

In place of loyal citizens, He is taunted by a crowd that derides Him for His failure to save Himself. Instead of admiring courtiers, He looks down upon the horrid glee of self-righteous religious leaders who have finally caught their prey. They allude to Scriptures to "prove" that His plight demonstrates that His kingship is a fraud.

And all because He would not save Himself from physical pain and death. They simply could not understand His mission, "To save His people from their sins" (1:21). Oblivious to the prophecies and types of a Suffering Savior, they pour contempt on His self-sacrifice, even as their ridicule fulfills the Psalm that most fully describes His total agony (Psalm 22:8; see also Isaiah 53 and Psalm 69).

The Suffering King

They had seen Him save the sick from illness. What they could not see was the real meaning of Jesus' healing miracles—to point to deliverance from sin and death. Nor could they understand that the Son of Man "must go to Jerusalem, and suffer many things from the elders and chief priests and scribes, and be killed" (16:21; 17:22–23; 20:18–19). Obsessed with earthly power and privilege, they could not imagine that the Son of Man had come to earth "to serve, and to give His life a ransom for many" (20:28).

What about us? Do we also suspend faith in Christ upon His deliverance of us from earthly pain and trouble? Are we not prone to say, "If you take me down from this 'cross' I'll believe in You?" Have we also forgotten that salvation comes only through suffering (16:24–25; Acts 14:22; Romans 8:17; Philippians 1:29; 1 Peter 1:6–9)?

Dedication and Desperation
Matthew 27:55–66

And many women who followed Jesus from Galilee, ministering to Him, were there looking on from afar...

All hope is gone. The Lord is dead, deserted by friends and enemies alike. All their high hopes lie dashed at the foot of the Cross, where a pool of blood mixed with water bears silent witness to what seems to be the end.

These devoted women had followed Jesus from Galilee to Jerusalem, supplying His needs and those of His disciples. They had seen and heard much to excite thrilling expectations that He would bring in the kingdom of God before their very eyes.

But now they are gazing upon the twisted body of a broken, lifeless man hanging limply upon the cruel cross, callously guarded by veterans of Roman conquests. Suddenly two men appear, Joseph of Arimathea and Nicodemus, carrying heavy spices. Richly dressed and moving confidently, they take the body of Jesus down from the Cross, having obtained Pilate's permission to bury Him.

Lovingly they wrap Him in linen cloths, mixing the perfumes in to hide the inevitable stench of decay. Perhaps with help from their servants, these two hitherto secret followers of Christ carry the corpse to Joseph's own tomb, which lay in a nearby garden, and place it on a shelf inside, rolling a heavy stone over the entrance. Then they return to their luxurious homes, their act of devotion completed.

But the women stay behind. Their love will not allow them to leave Jesus, even when everyone else has gone. Mary Magdalene had been freed by Jesus from seven demons. Salome was the mother of James and John, the "Sons of Thunder" (Mark 3:17), and another Mary was the mother of James the Less (Mark 15:40). Jesus' own mother Mary, who had watched the final agony, had been taken home by John, the Beloved Disciple. Hour after hour they sat, keeping guard in their own way, weeping for sure, but unwilling to part from the one they loved more than life itself, till at last darkness compelled them to go.

The next day, a group of frantic men take counsel, seeking a way to prevent Jesus' disciples from stealing His body and thus give credence to His prediction that He would rise again on the third day (16:21; 17:23; 20:19; 26:61). They had followed closely His teachings, even if they did not believe them. With Pilate's permission, they place their own guard at the entrance of the tomb, not out of dedication and love, but desperation and malice. While the women are gathering more spices to anoint the body of Christ, they and their lackeys are engaged in a fruitless effort to preserve their power and position.

Friend, to which group do you belong? Are you so grateful for what Christ has done for you, and so attached to Him, that you will not forsake Him, even when all seems lost? Or do you stand with those who know about Him but do not know Him, and who look upon Him with indifference, if not hatred?

28 The King's Commission

Who Moved the Stone?
Matthew 28:5-6

But the angel answered and said to the women, "Do not be afraid, for I know that you seek Jesus who was crucified. He is not here; for He is risen, as He said. Come see the place where the Lord lay."

On the third day after the death of Jesus, women who loved Him went to the tomb to anoint His body with embalming spices. To their amazement, the heavy stone blocking the entrance had been rolled away.

Two rich friends of Jesus had procured His body from the Roman governor Pilate and had placed it in a new tomb. After a heavy stone had been rolled into place, the sealed sepulcher was guarded by soldiers.

Could Jesus have moved the stone from the inside? No! For one thing, many had seen Him die. Even if, as some falsely claim, He had only fainted, there was no way that this man, weakened by beatings and the torture of the Cross, could have made his escape.

Did the disciples of Christ move the stone? They were all so frightened that they had run away from Him in the garden where He was arrested. Later, Jesus found them huddled behind locked doors, afraid of the Jews. How could this cowardly group overcome armed guards, steal the body, and then boldly proclaim that He had risen from the dead?

Certainly, the Jews had no reason to unseal the tomb and remove Jesus' corpse. Even if they had, once the disciples began to say Jesus had risen, they could simply bring out the body as contrary evidence.

The only possibility is that, as Matthew records, God, through a mighty angel, rolled away the rock that blocked entrance to the tomb. He did that, not to release Jesus, who had already risen, but to allow the women to see for themselves the empty tomb, and know that Jesus had truly risen from the dead.

He can do the same for you today!

Jesus and the Resurrection Part–1
Matthew 28:5–6

"You seek Jesus who was crucified. He is not here; for He is risen, as He said."

Christians believe in a crucified, risen Savior.

Jesus came to "save His people from their sins" (1:21). After a spotless life filled with good deeds, matchless teaching, and marvelous miracles, He was unjustly put to death like a criminal.

But God raised Him up, demonstrating that Jesus truly is the Son of God, "Immanuel ... God with us" (1:23) and vindicating Him as righteous and holy (Acts 3:14).

The empty tomb also proclaims that Jesus' death on the Cross satisfied the holy wrath of God against our sins and opened the way to heaven for all believers.

He had predicted His death and resurrection many times (12:39–41; 17:23), so we can believe that Jesus will come "on the clouds of heaven with power and great glory. And He will send His angels with a great sound of a trumpet, and they will gather together His elect from the four winds, from one end of heaven to the other" (24:31).

We can also trust His promise that He will "sit on the throne of His glory. All the nations will be gathered before Him," and He will judge them according to how they have treated His people (25:31–46).

Even now, we should accept His assertion that "all authority has been given to Me in heaven and on earth" (28:18).

Because He is the risen Lord, we must obey His command to "Go therefore and make disciples of all the nations, baptizing them in the name of the Father and of the Son and of the Holy Spirit, teaching them to observe all things that I have commanded you" (28:19–20).

Above all, we believe His promise: "I am with you always, *even* to the end of the age" (28:20).

Jesus and the Resurrection Part–2
Matthew 28:6

"He is not here; for He is risen, as He said."

Just as Jesus' resurrection vindicates His death; verifies His identity; and validates His promises to return, so the empty tomb explains much of what He said and did.

As crucified and risen Lord and Savior, He could turn cowardly fishermen into "fishers of men" (4:19).

Since He Himself has passed through death to life, we can believe that "the meek ... shall inherit the earth.... The pure in heart ... shall see God" (5:5, 8).

Only a death-conquering Christ could say to those who are reviled, persecuted, and slandered for His sake, "Rejoice and be exceedingly glad, for great *is* your reward in heaven" (5:11–12).

Had He not known that He would overcome the bonds of mortality, how could Jesus have commanded us to "lay up ... treasures in heaven" (6:20)?

Would a man whose career would be utterly terminated in a stone-cold tomb be able to say, "All things have been delivered to Me by My Father, and no one knows the Son except the Father. Nor does anyone know the Father except the Son, and *the one* to whom the Son wills to reveal *Him*" (11:27)?

If He had not risen from the grave, how could we now respond to His invitation, "Come to Me all *you* who labor and are heavy laden, and I will give you rest" (11:28)?

Or these words: "where two or three are gathered together in My name, I am there in the midst of them" (18:20). "With God all things are possible" (19:26).

Jesus' teaching flowed from His certainty that He would transcend death and ascend to heaven. Because He was right, we can believe His every word!

Jesus and the Resurrection Part–3
Matthew 28:7

"Tell His disciples that He is risen from the dead..."

Jesus' resurrection not only makes sense out of many of His *words*, but clarifies many of His *works*. Because the empty tomb vindicates His divine origin and nature, it sheds light on His many miracles.

Throughout His ministry, He went about doing good, and constantly healed "all kinds of sickness and all kinds of disease among the people" (4:23).

Likewise, we see how even the unruly winds and the waves obeyed His command to be quiet (8:23–27).

As soon as demons saw Him, they fell down at His feet, begging for mercy, for they knew that He was the "Son of God" with power to torment them (8:29).

His resurrection declares Jesus to be fully divine, the Son of Man prophesied by Daniel, so that He did indeed have "power on earth to forgive sins" (9:6).

On more than one occasion, He demonstrated death-destroying power by raising others from the dead (9:23–26). For such a Man, granting sight to the blind and speech to a mute would have been simple (9:27–33).

In the light of the resurrection, should we be surprised that Jesus fed five thousand people with only a few loaves and fish, and then four thousand in the same way? (14:13–21; 15:32–39).

With His power as the Son of God, Jesus could walk on the sea, and even enable Peter to do the same (14:22–33). Such might flowed from Him that a simple touch from the sick brought full recovery (14:34–36).

As God's creative Word made flesh, and as the appointed Judge, Jesus could say a word and cause a fig tree to wither up and die (21:18–19).

What an immense privilege to know Him as the one who came "to save His people from their sins" (1:21).

The King's Commission

Who's in Charge? Part–1
Matthew 28:18

"All authority has been given to Me in heaven and on earth."

During His brief ministry on earth, Jesus demonstrated His unique authority in various ways:

> He defied the authority of Satan, resisting his temptations and asserting the superior authority of the Word of God (4:1–11).
>
> He claimed authority over men by calling disciples to leave all and follow Him (4:19; 8:22; 9:9).
>
> He showed authority over illness by healing all sorts of sickness (4:23).
>
> He commanded evil spirits to obey His word and release their captives (4:24; 8:28–34).
>
> He stilled the wind and the waves with a simple command (8:23–27).
>
> He taught with such authority that the crowds marveled (5:21–48; 7:28–29).
>
> He extended His authority by sending and empowering disciples to replicate His teachings and miracles (10:1–42).
>
> He defied current tradition by claiming to be Lord even of the Sabbath (12:8).
>
> He broke the power of death by raising people to life (9:18–26).
>
> He reversed the effects of the curse upon this fallen world by restoring sight to the blind and speech to the mute (9:27–34).
>
> He astonished religious leaders by asserting the right to forgive sins (9:1–8).

Will we bow before His absolute authority today?

Who's in Charge? Part–2
Matthew 28:18

"All authority has been given to Me in heaven and on earth."

Jesus demonstrated His comprehensive authority on earth in various ways, as we have seen.

Because He is Lord, He also possesses all authority in heaven. Note:

> This authority was given to Him. Though eternal like the Father, and fully equal as God, yet the Son of God holds His authority as a gift from His Father, the fount of all power and right.
>
> In some sense, His resurrection ushered Jesus into a new relationship with the universe. One earth, He was the Son of God in weakness; now He is shown to be the "Son of God with power" (Romans 1:4).
>
> Because of His incarnation and death, God has "highly exalted Him and given Him the name which is above every name, that at the name of Jesus every knee should bow, of those in heaven, and of those on earth ... *that* every tongue should confess that Jesus Christ *is* Lord, to the glory of God the Father" (Philippians 2:9–11).
>
> As risen Lord, Jesus sits now at the right hand of the Father, "far above all principality and power and might and dominion, and every name that is named, not only in this age but also in that which is to come" (Ephesians 1:20–22). "All *things*" have been put "under His feet," and He is "head over all *things*" for the sake of the church (Ephesians 1:22–23).

The implications of this fact are vast and stunning.

He rules the universe for the sake of His people. Since we are "in Him," we share His authority over evil spirits and, relying on His strength, we can withstand all the wiles of the evil one. No good deed will be impossible for those who trust in Him!

The Church's Constitution
Matthew 28:18–20 Part–1

"All authority has been given to Me in heaven and on earth. Go therefore and make disciples of all nations, baptizing them in the name of the Father, and of the Son, and of the Holy Spirit, teaching them to observe all things that I have commanded you; and lo, I am with you always, even *to the end of the age."*

After declaring His absolute sovereignty over the entire universe, Jesus issues His last commandment to the gathered disciples. This "Great Commission" contains the core of all we need to know about the church's nature and mission on this earth.

While some debate whether evangelism should hold first priority, or whether we should first concentrate upon building up our own congregation through worship, fellowship, and teaching, Jesus' final words resolve this question quite clearly and comprehensively.

"Go": We are a pilgrim people, on the move, in the world but not of it, composed of believers from "all nations."

"Make disciples": By bringing people to faith and incorporating them into the Body of Christ ("baptizing"), and by building them up with correct doctrine that emphasizes obedience ("teaching"), we fulfill the Lord's mandate.

At all times—every day up until the end of the age—we enjoy the presence of our risen Lord and Savior, the ruler of the universe.

By His authority, we summon others to believe and obey, and by His powerful presence, we are enabled to follow in His steps, until we all assemble in the eternal kingdom.

On the Move
Matthew 28:18–20 Part–2

"All authority has been given to Me in heaven and on earth. Go therefore and make disciples of all the nations, baptizing them in the name of the Father, and of the Son, and of the Holy Spirit, teaching them to observe all things that I have commanded you; and lo, I am with you always, even *to the end of the age."*

According to the grammar of the original Greek, Jesus' final command was "to make disciples of all the nations."

Three participles amplify what He meant.

First, we are to "Go." Actually, this participle should be rendered, "as you go." That is to say, we should be a mobile people.

Most Christians remain rooted to this earth. Houses, jobs, family ties, and local loyalties bind us to our present location.

Recently, massive migrations have altered the picture somewhat. Millions are leaving rural areas and congregating in cities, some of them huge metropolises. Usually, financial factors impel such moves.

Even urban residents change locations regularly these days, often moving from one city to another to find, or keep, a job.

But have we really "gone" at the leading of Jesus? Or are we merely laying up treasures on earth? Is it because we "seek first the kingdom of God and His righteousness" (6:33) that we uproot ourselves?

All too often, though we may change our mailing address, we have retained our basic attachment to this present age, one that will soon be incinerated.

When Jesus said, "As you go," He referred to an entirely different mindset: A pilgrim mentality that stretches forward to disciple all the nations.

The King's Commission

Going with Him
Matthew 28:18–20 Part-3

"All authority has been given to Me in heaven and on earth. Go therefore and make disciples of all the nations, baptizing them in the name of the Father, and of the Son, and of the Holy Spirit, teaching them to observe all things that I have commanded you; and lo, I am with you always, even *to the end of the age."*

"As you go, make disciples of all the nations."

Notice that Jesus *assumes* we shall be on the move.

And why not? After all, He had called the first disciples by saying, "Follow Me" (4:19).

Jesus Himself set the pattern for our "going."

First, He left His heavenly home to become a man like us. He made Himself of no reputation, taking the form of a bondservant, *and* coming in the likeness of men" (Philippians 2:7). Though He was the eternal Son of God, He became Jesus of Nazareth, Immanuel, "God with us" (1:23).

Even in the womb, Jesus was "on the go," as Mary traveled with Joseph from Galilee to Bethlehem in Judea (2:1; Luke 2:1–7).

Shortly after His birth, the baby boy was taken by His parents to Egypt to escape the murderous fear of King Herod (2:13–14). Then the little family moved back to Galilee (2:22–23). All this travel took place in fulfillment of prophecy, and set the tone for the rest of His life.

Most of Jesus' ministry consisted of constant travel throughout Palestine—Galilee, Samaria, Judea, even neighboring Gentile lands.

All the while, He could say that "the Son of Man has nowhere to lay His head" (8:20). And shall we seek to be permanent settlers on this earth?

What is a Disciple?
Matthew 28:18–20 Part–4

"Go therefore and make disciples of all the nations…"

But what is a disciple? From Jesus' own teaching, we see what He meant by this term.

A disciple will "repent, and believe in the Gospel," knowing that "the kingdom of God is at hand" (4:17; Mark 1:15).

A disciple will leave all else to obey Jesus' call: "Follow Me, and I will make you fishers of men" (4:19–20).

A disciple of Jesus will be poor in spirit; mournful over sin; meek; hungry and thirsty for righteousness; merciful; pure in heart [that is, seeking only one thing, to know God]; committed to making peace between enemies (5:1–9).

A true disciple will be so different that he will be persecuted for righteousness' sake and for the name of Christ, looking to a heavenly reward (5:10–13).

A disciple will be like salt and light in this stale, corrupt, and dark world. His good works will be done in such a way that others will praise the Father in heaven (5:13–16).

A disciple of Jesus will make war on anger and lust; keep his marriage vows; speak the truth; go "the second mile" in serving others; and even love his enemies as God has loved him (5:21–48).

A follower of our Lord will give generously; pray without ceasing; fast in secret. That is because he does not lay up treasures on this earth, but in heaven. He seeks to serve God alone, not money and what it can buy (6:1–24).

A disciple of Jesus will not worry about tomorrow, but "seek first the kingdom of God and His righteousness" (6:25–34).

Disciples are Different
Matthew 28:19

"Go therefore and make disciples..."

A follower of Jesus will seek in every way to imitate His master's total holiness (5–6).

But a Christian (for they are the disciples of Christ) will not be proud, haughty, or self-righteous.

When he sees a fault in another, a disciple will not arrogantly seek to correct that person. Instead, he will ask God to show him the "plank" in his own eye. He will pray for the Lord to forgive him and change him.

He will also ask God to forgive and transform the other. Finally, if the Lord leads, he will speak gently to his brother about the flaw. In all this process, he will merely be doing what he would have others do to him (7:1–12).

A disciple of Jesus will take the initiative to resolve conflict. If he knows his brother has something against him, he will go quickly to seek to set things straight (5:23–24).

On the other hand, if his brother offends him, he will speak a word of gentle rebuke in private (18:15).

A disciple will seek to enter the kingdom of God by the only way possible: a narrow gate of absolute dedication and surrender. He will build the house of his life upon the rock of Jesus' words and ways (7:13–14, 24–27).

He will seek to love God with his whole being, and his neighbor as himself (22:37–39), regardless of the cost. That is, he will "take his cross and follow" Christ daily (10:38), relying entirely on the strength of the Holy Spirit (Acts 1:8; Romans 8:4, 12–13; Galatians 5:22–25).

Are you a disciple of Jesus Christ?

Making Disciples Part–1
Matthew 28:19–20

"Go therefore and make disciples…"

Having described the disciples of whom Jesus spoke, that is, the *product* we desire, let us now examine the *process* by which they are made.

We turn for this to the example of Jesus Himself. How did He "make disciples" while on earth?

He began with preparation. First, He fully identified with the people He came to disciple. The eternal Son of God became a man like us when he was born to the virgin Mary (1:18).

He deepened this connection by submitting to the baptism of John, thereby joining Himself to us not just in His human nature, but in His association with sinners (3:13–15).

At His baptism, Jesus received the all-important assurance that He was the Son of God, in whom the Father fully delighted (3:17).

During His first thirty years, He must have studied, pondered, and memorized the Scriptures, for the rest of His life displayed an intimate and profound understanding of the Word of God (see 4:4–10).

He did not see the body as evil; after all He created all things. But Jesus subdued His body with forty days of fasting in the desert (4:2).

Before preaching to others, Jesus first learned to obey God in all things. He extinguished all the fiery missiles of Satan in His wilderness trials (4:1–10).

After all this preparation, Jesus finally commenced His public ministry as a disciple-maker. And how did He begin? By calling all men to "repent, for the kingdom of heaven is at hand" (4:17).

Making Disciples Part–2
Matthew 28:19

"Go therefore and make disciples…"

Jesus made His general summons to a repentant, God-centered life more personal by calling individual men: "Follow Me," He said (4:19).

From their response (they left everything), and from His teachings elsewhere, we know that Jesus was calling them to a life of total commitment.

For Christ, discipleship meant forsaking all other loyalties; renouncing all position and possessions; and giving oneself totally to the kingdom of God (6:19–34; 8:18–22; 9:9–10; 16:24–25; 19:21).

After gathering His followers, Jesus demonstrated before them His compassion for the masses of sick, demon-possessed, and wayward people (4:22–25; 8:1–17; 9:35–36).

But demonstration was not enough. Jesus instructed His disciples constantly.

He taught them what a true disciple looked like in the Beatitudes (5:1–12); God's moral will for them (5:13–48); how to be pious without being pretentious (6:1–18); and the necessity of a single-minded trust in God (6:25–34).

He showed them how to deal with difficult people (7:1–12); resolve conflicts (5:23–26; 18:15–20); recognize false prophets and professions of faith (7:15–23; 23:1–39); and build their lives on a lasting foundation (7:13–27).

His curriculum included teaching on evangelism and the resulting persecution (10:1–42); the kingdom of God (13:1–52); marriage and family (19:1–15); and the end times (24:1–25:46).

How does our life and teaching compare with that of Jesus?

Making Disciples Part–3
Matthew 28:19

"Go therefore and make disciples..."

In all His instruction, Jesus was both practical and demanding. He insisted upon the highest standards of commitment and consecration and did not fail to live what He taught.

From His forty-day fast in the wilderness, He walked before His men in self-denying, loving service, even unto death.

He showed them how to heal, and how to teach (4:23–7:29).

He taught them how to pray (6:9–15; 7:7–11), and modeled a life of constant intercession and praise (11:25–26; 14:19; 15:36; 26:36–46; Mark 1:35; Luke 11:1–4).

He called them to forsake all, even family (10:37), to serve God, and he demonstrated such commitment before them (12:46–50).

He warned of rejection (5:10–12; 10:16–39), and did not falter when His own people sought to kill Him (13:53–58; Luke 4:16–30).

He demanded total holiness of life and purpose (5:21–37; 6:19–34), and lived without sin Himself (26:59–60; 27:18–19; 23–24; Hebrews 4:15).

He urged them to have faith in God to work the "impossible" (8:26; 9:22, 29; 15:28; 17:20; 21:20–22), and did miracles before them with that same sort of faith (8:23–27; 9:18–25; 14:13–33; 21:18–19).

He told them to love sacrificially, and even to love their enemies (5:43–48), and showed this throughout His life, but supremely on the Cross, where He both paid the penalty for our sins and asked God to forgive those who had crucified Him (27:46; Luke 23:34).

"Show and tell": That is how Jesus made disciples!

The King's Commission

All the Nations
Matthew 28:19

"Go therefore and make disciples of all the nations..."

Matthew probably wrote his Gospel for Jewish Christians, but its universal scope is apparent.

When the angel announced that Jesus would "save His people from their sins" (1:21), he was not limiting "His people" to the Jews.

We see this in the genealogy of our Lord. Jesus' ancestors included Rahab of Jericho, Ruth the Moabitess, and Bathsheba, the wife of a Hittite.

As an infant, He was worshiped by wise men from the East (2:1–12). Crowds came to Him from both Jewish lands and from Gentile territories (4:25).

Despite His focus on the Jews, Jesus gladly healed the servant of a Roman centurion (8:5–13), then cast out an army of demons from a Gergesene on the other side of the Jordan River (8:28–34).

After testing her with apparent rejection, Jesus rewarded the persistent faith of a Gentile woman who begged for her daughter's deliverance from demons (15:21–28). He had already fed five thousand Jews; now He gave food to four thousand non-Israelites (15:32–39).

The Lord repeatedly challenged the prevailing view that limited the grace of God to descendants of Abraham, pronounced judgment on His countrymen for rejecting Him, and announced salvation to people of all nations (8:10–12; 11:20–24; 12:41–42, 48–50; 21:28–22:14; 23:1–39; 25:31–46).

He also predicted a world-wide mission: "This gospel of the kingdom will be preached in all the world as a witness to all the nations, and then the end will come" (24:14).

We are heirs of that sweeping promise! We are also privileged to participate in its fulfillment, as we make disciples of "all the nations."

Bring Them In!
Matthew 28:19

"...baptizing them in the name of the Father, and of the Son, and of the Holy Spirit..."

"Making disciples" includes two basic activities, the first of which is evangelism, namely, helping people come to faith, bringing them in.

"Baptizing" people assumes that we have proclaimed to them the Good News of God's saving work in Jesus Christ, His Son.

Before they can be baptized, they need to know who God is and what He has done for us in Christ. They must see that there is only one God, Maker of heaven and earth, a being who is completely holy and just, and who requires us to be the same.

Then, they must see that we are not good enough to approach God. In fact, our sins have made a separation between us and God, so that we are, in Paul's words, "children of wrath" (Ephesians 2:3).

But God in His mercy has sent His eternal Son, the Word through whom He created the universe, to become a man, Jesus. From the beginning, this unique person was "Immanuel ... God with us" (1:23).

Truly man and truly God, He came to "save His people from their sins" (1:21), chiefly by dying in our place on the Cross as a ransom and then rising again on the third day (16:21; 17:22; 20:18–19, 28).

If we trust in Him alone as our Savior, then we can become children of God the Father and receive the Holy Spirit (John 7:37–39; Acts 2:38; Romans 8:9–17; Galatians 3:2, 14, 26; 4:4–7; etc.).

All those who receive this message with sincere repentance and faith may be baptized (Acts 8:32–37; 10:38–48; 11:15–18; Colossians 2:12; 1 Peter 3:21).

This sort of evangelism should be the first priority of every Christian and every church. Is it yours?

The King's Commission

Build Them Up!
Matthew 28:20

"...teaching them to observe all things that I have commanded you..."

To make disciples, we must teach. Indeed, the word "disciple" originally meant "student." Of course, in the time of Jesus, a "student" or "disciple" was more than a mere listener, as we have seen, but he was at least that—someone who learned a body of material from a teacher.

So, Christian disciple-makers cannot dispense with instruction. Two points must be noticed here:

First, we need to instruct believers in all that Jesus has commanded. When we review the contents of Matthew's Gospel, we realize that Jesus commanded a great deal. Though some of His teaching falls into the category of "doctrine," including predictions of the future (see chapters 13 and 24–25, for example), much of it can be termed "ethics"; that is, Jesus told His followers not only what to *believe*, but how to *obey*.

We think here of the Sermon on the Mount (5–7). Those who consider themselves disciples of Christ should memorize this great sermon and pass it on to newer adherents to the Lord, for its principles are binding.

On the other hand, Jesus' commission to the apostles before they went off on their first preaching tour (10:5–42) contains some words that applied only to those men at that time, such as the command not to go to the Gentiles, but only to "the lost sheep of the house of Israel" (10:5–6). Obviously, that injunction has been superseded by the Great Commission which we are now pondering. Most of the Lord's directions to them apply directly even to us now, however, such as His warnings of rejection and even persecution (10:16–26); admonition not to fear those who can only kill the body (10:28–31); and a clear requirement that the true disciple of Christ must "take his cross and follow after" the Lord (10:38).

Throughout the Gospel, we are told by the Lord Christ how to handle conflicts in the church (18:15–35); why divorce and remarriage are wrong (19:1–10); how to attain "greatness" in the kingdom of God

(20:20–28); and what are the greatest commandments of all (22:34–40). As we have seen, Jesus' powerful indictment of the scribes and the Pharisees exposes our tendencies towards pride, hypocrisy, and deviation from God's Word (23:1–36).

Even the prophetic passages remind us that we must be ready at all times for the return of Christ (24:42, 44; 25:13), and of the necessity of using what God has given us (25:14–30), and the imperative of loving our brothers and sisters in Christ when they are in need (25:31–46).

The second thing to note is that all this teaching is meant to lead to obedience; Christian "students" are to "observe" all that Jesus commands. We must keep His commands, heed His warnings, follow His instructions. We are to be not just hearers, but doers of the Word (James 1:22).

Constant Companion
Matthew 28:20

"And lo, I am with you always, even to the end of the age."

After commanding His disciples to make disciples of all nations, Jesus comforts them with the promise of His abiding presence.

So, Matthew's Gospel ends as it had begun, with "Immanuel ... God with us" (1:23).

Let us think further, *Who* is "with us"?

He is "the Son of David, the son of Abraham" (1:1). Fully human in every way (except sin), He can both understand and sympathize with our weaknesses and temptations (Hebrews 4:15).

A refugee almost from birth (2:13–23), He lived in this world of instability and change. He grew up in a normal household; obeyed His parents; held a job as a carpenter; and then embarked on a career as a traveling teacher and healer.

He knew hunger and thirst; weariness, toil, and danger; rejection and slander; betrayal and abandonment; torture and death (4:1–2; 8:23–24; 12:24; 13:55–58; 20:18–19; 21:23; 26:1–5; 26:40, 47–56, 57–75; 27:1–50).

The King's Commission

Thus, Jesus knows our situation. He has "been there, done that."

But He is also the one who healed the sick; forgave sinners; raised the dead; stilled the wind and the waves; fed multitudes with scanty resources. His compassion led Him to give His life as a ransom for many. He knows, and He cares (8:1–17; Mark 10:45).

He not only knows and cares, but, having risen from the dead, He commands the entire universe (28:18).

This Jesus is with us now, in His words and by His Spirit. He knows, He cares, He commands—for us!

Challenging Conditions
Matthew 28:18–20

"And lo, I am with you…"

Jesus promised His perpetual presence, but only to those who follow Him.

He did not offer to be with those who "lay up treasures on earth," serving Mammon instead of God (6:19–24).

Nor to those who avoid the narrow gate and the difficult way, or those who build their lives on the sands of this world's lies instead of upon the rock of His words (7:13–14, 24–27).

Those who fear the death of the body more than the destruction of the soul will not enjoy His companionship, especially on the last day (10:28, 33).

If we allow "the cares of this world and the deceitfulness of riches" to choke His words, we shall look for His smile in vain, not only now but on the last day (13:22).

Indeed, if we put anything, even our family or life itself, ahead of our loyalty to Christ, then we shall walk alone all our days (10:37–39).

He only guaranteed that He would be with those who fulfilled the conditions. And what are these?

"Go therefore and make disciples of all the nations" (28:19). As someone has said, "There is no 'Lo!' without a 'Go!'"

Christ the King

Unless we move out of our comfort zone and into the battlefield, denying self that others might have life eternal, we shall not experience the abiding balm of His love.

If our lives are fully committed to the Great Commission, we shall never be lonely, for the Great Commander will be at our side. More than that, He will dwell in our hearts.

Coming Consummation
Matthew 28:20

"And lo, I am with you always, even to the end of the age."

Jesus' last words foretell a coming consummation, a conclusion to this entire age.

At that time, the poor in spirit will possess the kingdom; those who now mourn will finally be comforted; the meek shall inherit the earth; those who hunger and thirst for righteousness will be satisfied at last; the merciful shall obtain mercy; the pure in heart shall see God; those who are persecuted for the sake of righteousness will receive the kingdom of heaven; and the ones whom the world ridicules, slanders, and kills will receive a great reward (5:3–12).

Those who have laid up "treasures in heaven" will enjoy their wealth forever (6:19–21).

Those who have entered by the narrow gate, and traveled the difficult way, will receive everlasting life (7:13–14).

Many "will come from east and west, and sit down with Abraham, Isaac, and Jacob in the kingdom of heaven," enjoying a never-ending wedding feast with Christ (8:11; 22:1–10; 25:1–10).

Those who acknowledged Christ as Lord in the face of death will be acknowledged by Him before the Father (10:32), and those who have dared to lose their lives for His sake will find them forever (10:39; 16:25).

"Then the righteous will shine forth as the sun in the kingdom of their Father" at the time of the last and greatest harvest (13:43).

"When the Son of Man sits on the throne of His glory," those who have left all for His name's sake "shall receive a hundredfold, and inherit eternal life" (19:28–29).

Constant Companion
Matthew 28:20

"And lo, I am with you always..."

As risen Lord, Jesus is with us "all the days," for that is what the original Greek says. He is with you:

When you leave all to follow Him (4:20, 22).

When your family members are sick (8:14–15).

When the winds and the waves threaten to capsize your little boat (8:23–27).

When your friends revile you for following Him (9:9–13).

When all hope seems to be lost, but you hold onto your faith in Him (9:18–26).

When you are utterly exhausted (11:28).

When there are too many guests and too little food (14:13–21; 15:32–39).

In the middle of the night, when your once-strong faith fails you (14:22–33).

On the mount of illumination and in the vale of humiliation (17:1–21).

When the fickle crowd shouts, "Hosanna!" and when they cry, "Crucify!" (21:9; 27:22).

When false friends plan to betray you, and true friends rashly promise to stand by you (26:14–15, 33–35).

When your closest companions desert you in your hour of greatest need (26:36–46, 56).

At all times, without exception, Jesus is with you!

Awesome Judgment
Matthew 28:20

"...even to the end of the age."

Not only will Jesus reward those who have faithfully followed Him, but He will punish those who have refused His summons to obey.

"Repent, for the kingdom of heaven is at hand" (3:2) were His opening words at the beginning of His ministry. For the next several years, He strongly warned people of the impending doom upon those who failed to repent.

Even if they have performed miracles in Jesus' name and preached God's Word, those who practice lawlessness will be banished from the presence of the Lord (7:21–23).

If we fail to build our house on the foundation of His words, it will collapse in the coming storm of God's fury (7:24–27).

He spoke of "outer darkness" (8:12; 22:13; 25:30) and a fiery "hell" often, for those guilty of anger and abusive language (5:22); lust and adultery (5:27–30); rejecting the Messiah (8:12); leading others into sin (18:6–9); lawlessness (13:41); rejecting God's prophets (23:33–35); and even hypocrisy and false teaching (23:15).

Unrepentant sinners will suffer death of the soul along with the body (10:28). Those who waste their time and resources will be thrown into "outer darkness," where there will be "weeping and gnashing of teeth" (25:30), along with inconsolable wailing (13:42, 50).

And, contrary to what some are saying, this torment will be everlasting, unending, eternal, just as will be the heavenly happiness of the faithful (25:46).

This judgment will fall suddenly upon the whole earth (24:36–44). Will you be ready?

Now is the time to trust in the Lord Jesus, the King and Savior of the nations, for grace, mercy, and peace with God; such faith will bring everlasting life (John 3:16; Romans 5:1–21).

The Author

G. Wright Doyle received a B.A. with Honors in Latin from the University of North Carolina at Chapel Hill in 1966; a B.D. (M.Div.) with Honors from the Virginia Theological Seminary in 1969; and a PhD. in Classics from the University of North Carolina in 1975, with a dissertation on St. Augustine. He studied Mandarin Chinese at the Taipei Language Institute in Taiwan (1976–1978, 1980–1981).

Since 1989, the Doyles have lived in Charlottesville, Virginia, where Wright is Director of China Institute (chinainst.org), a ministry founded in 1989, and of Global China Center, which began operating in 2004 (globalchinacenter.org). He advises China ministry groups; he and his wife Dori also serve as advisers to the Chinese Christian Fellowship at the University of Virginia. A frequent preacher in Chinese churches, he has been asked to address Chinese groups in England, North America, and Taiwan.

Wright served as Associate Professor of Greek and New Testament at the China Evangelical Seminary, Taipei (1980 to 1988). Since 2004, he has taught courses in New Testament and Systematic Theology for China Evangelical Seminary in Taiwan and in North America, China Reformed Theological Seminary in Taipei, the Chinese program of Reformed Theological Seminary, Washington, D.C., and Central Taiwan Theological Seminary. He has lectured and presented papers at universities in the United States, England, Taiwan, and the People's Republic of China.

Wright is the author of *Jesus: The Complete Man; The Lord's Healing Words; Carl Henry: Theologian for All Seasons;* and *China: Ancient Culture, Modern Society* (with Dr. Peter Xiaoming Yu).

Wright supervised the translation by his students of Gingrich and Danker's *Greek-English Lexicon of the Greek New Testament* into Chinese; edited an abridgment of the Chinese edition of Carl Henry's *God, Revelation, & Authority*; and composed seven other volumes which have been translated into Chinese.

Wright is the General Editor of the *Biographical Dictionary of Chinese Christianity* (bdcconline.net) and, with Dr. Carol Lee Hamrin, co-editor of Wipf & Stock's *Studies in Chinese Christianity*.

The Doyles have one married daughter.

www.ingramcontent.com/pod-product-compliance
Lightning Source LLC
Chambersburg PA
CBHW022057150426
43195CB00008B/166